VIZ GRAPHIC NOVEL

SILENT MÖBIUS ™

VOL. 6

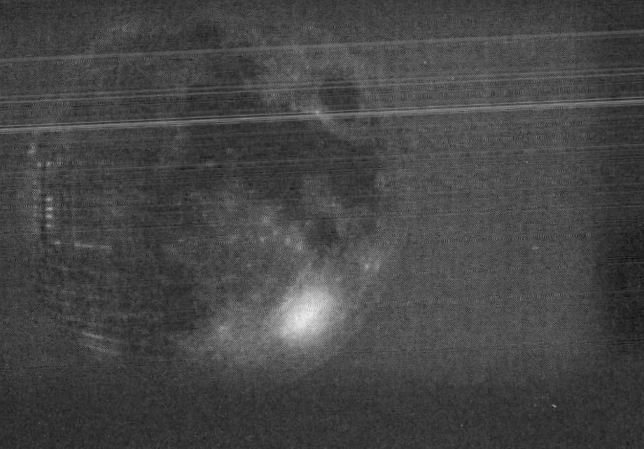

STORY AND ART BY KIA ASAMIYA

1999 A.D.

On a visit to Japan for work on a shadowy project, the hermetic magician Gigelf Liqueur becomes involved in a disaster. A gate is opened to another world—the world of Nemesis, home of evil entities known as Lucifer Hawks who visited our Earth in ancient times. Soon afterward, Gigelf Liqueur is never seen again.

2023 A.D.

Tokyo has become a mega-city, but sightings of the mysterious and murderous Lucifer Hawks are on the rise. In response, Rally Cheyenne forms a special police group known as the A.M.P.—Attacked Mystification Police Department. With the help of officers Lebia Maverick, Nami Yamigumo, and Kiddy Phenil, the A.M.P. handles "Third Attraction" cases—cases involving the invaders. For Rally Cheyenne, the matter is personal: for she is the child of a Lucifer Hawk and a human mother, and her sister, Rosa, willingly vanished long ago into her father's dark world.

2026 A.D.

Two new members join the A.M.P.: Yuki Saiko, an inexperienced psychic, and Katsumi Liqueur, who is blessed or cursed with her father's magical powers. Finding herself a target because of her gifts, Katsumi gradually learns more about her father's legacy. To the Lucifer Hawks, she is a living "key" between Nemesis and Earth, and an important part of their plans.

2028 A.D.

Mana Isozaki, a friend of Rally Cheyenne's, becomes the A.M.P.'s new acting commander. They need the extra manpower, because their enemies' strength is increasing...

MEET THE A.M.P.

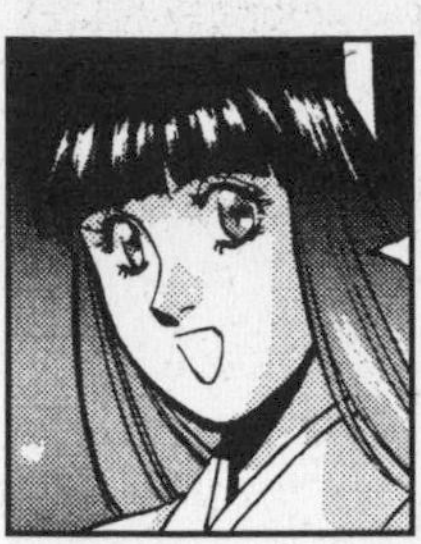

NAMI YAMIGUMO
IDENTITY: Priestess

Heir to the House of Yamigumo and inheritor of its divine Ki-Rin dagger, Nami was put in the care of Rally Cheyenne at the age of 15 to develop her powers. A Shinto priestess, she can call upon many kinds of shamanic magic.

KATSUMI LIQUEUR
IDENTITY: Sorcerer

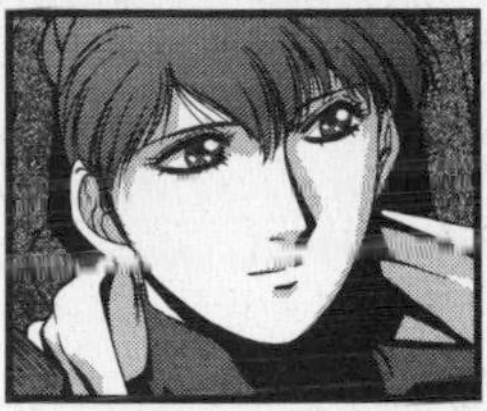

Katsumi is the daughter of the great magician Gigelf Liqueur, who was responsible for bringing the Lucifer Hawks to Earth. Her mother was a talented wizard as well. Her boyfriend, Robert DeVice, is an ordinary police officer. In combat, Katsumi wields the living weapon called Grospoliner, King of Swords.

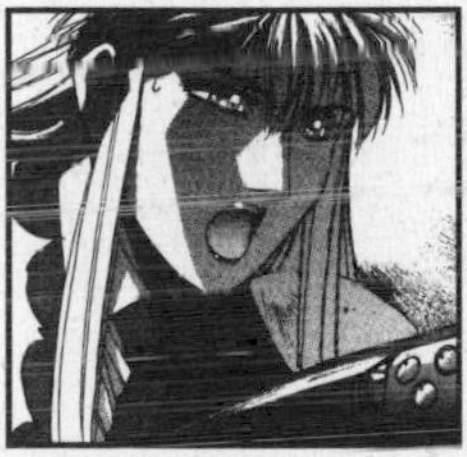

LEBIA MAVERICK
IDENTITY: Visionaire

Lebia Maverick specializes in computer operations; cybernetic systems in her body allow her to mentally enter 'computer logic space.' Her data bank is stored in an orbital satellite, giving her a memory capacity 3000 times that of an ordinary visionaire and far beyond a normal human being's.

RALLY CHEYENNE
IDENTITY: Superintendent

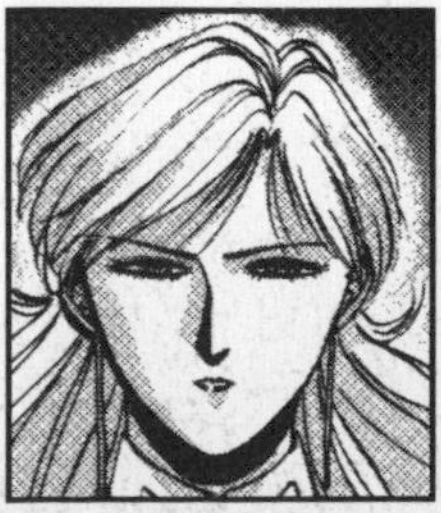

The product of crossbreeding between a Lucifer Hawk and a human woman, Rally used her powers to turn the A.M.P. into the human race's strongest defense. She acts as the A.M.P.'s liason to the government, leaving day-to-day operations to her hand-picked replacement, Mana Isozaki.

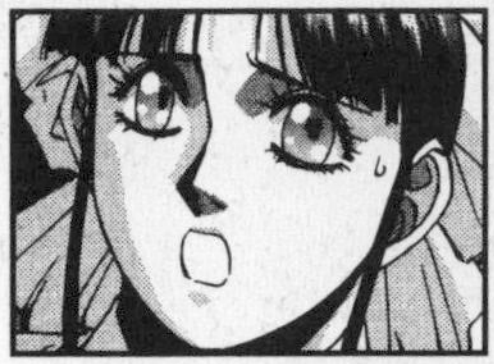

YUKI SAIKO
IDENTITY: Psychic

The youngest member of the A.M.P., Yuki was raised in a secret project to develop ESPer weapons. She has rejected the violent, telekinetic aspect of her training, and relies mostly on her intuition and precognitive abilities.

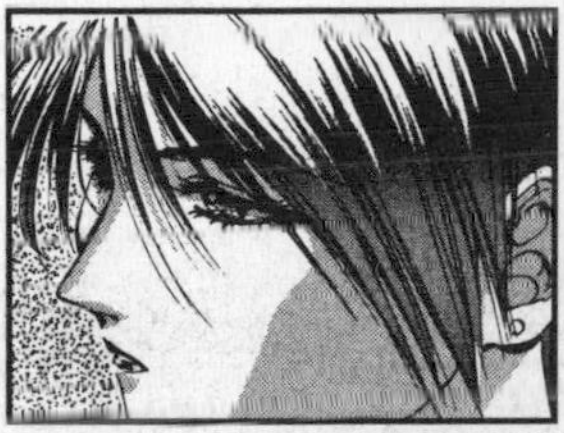

MANA ISOZAKI
IDENTITY: Commander

The most recent and mysterious addition to the A.M.P., she is second in rank only to Rally Cheyenne. A stern, highly capable officer, she uses a form of magic derived from Indian Buddhism.

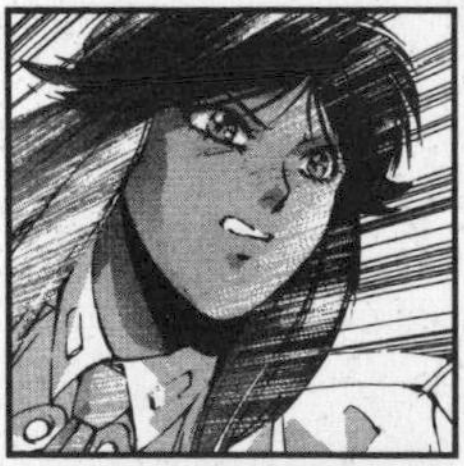

KIDDY PHENIL
IDENTITY: Cyborg

In 2023, detective Kiddy Phenil was nearly killed in combat by a megadyne (cyborg). She was saved by a combat-graft which replaced 70% of her body with bionic parts, giving her super-strength, but making her into what she hated most.

This volume contains the monthly comics
SILENT MÖBIUS: CATASTROPHE #1
through #6 in their entirety.

STORY AND ART BY KIA ASAMIYA

**ENGLISH ADAPTATION BY
FRED BURKE & AKIKO YAGI**

Touch-Up Art & Lettering/Dan Nakrosis
Cover Design/Hidemi Sahara
Graphics & Layout/Sean Lee
Editor/Jason Thompson

Managing Editor/Annette Roman
Editor-in-Chief/Hyoe Narita
Publisher/Seiji Horibuchi
Director of Marketing/Dallas Middaugh
Assistant Sales Manager/Denya S. Jur
Assistant Marketing Manager/
Jaime Starling

Printed in Canada

Published by Viz Communications, Inc.
P.O. Box 77010 ▪ San Francisco, CA
94107

10 9 8 7 6 5 4 3 2 1
First printing, April 2001

Vizit our web sites at **www.viz.com,
www.pulp-mag.com,
www.animerica-mag.com**, and
www.j-pop.com!

CONTENTS

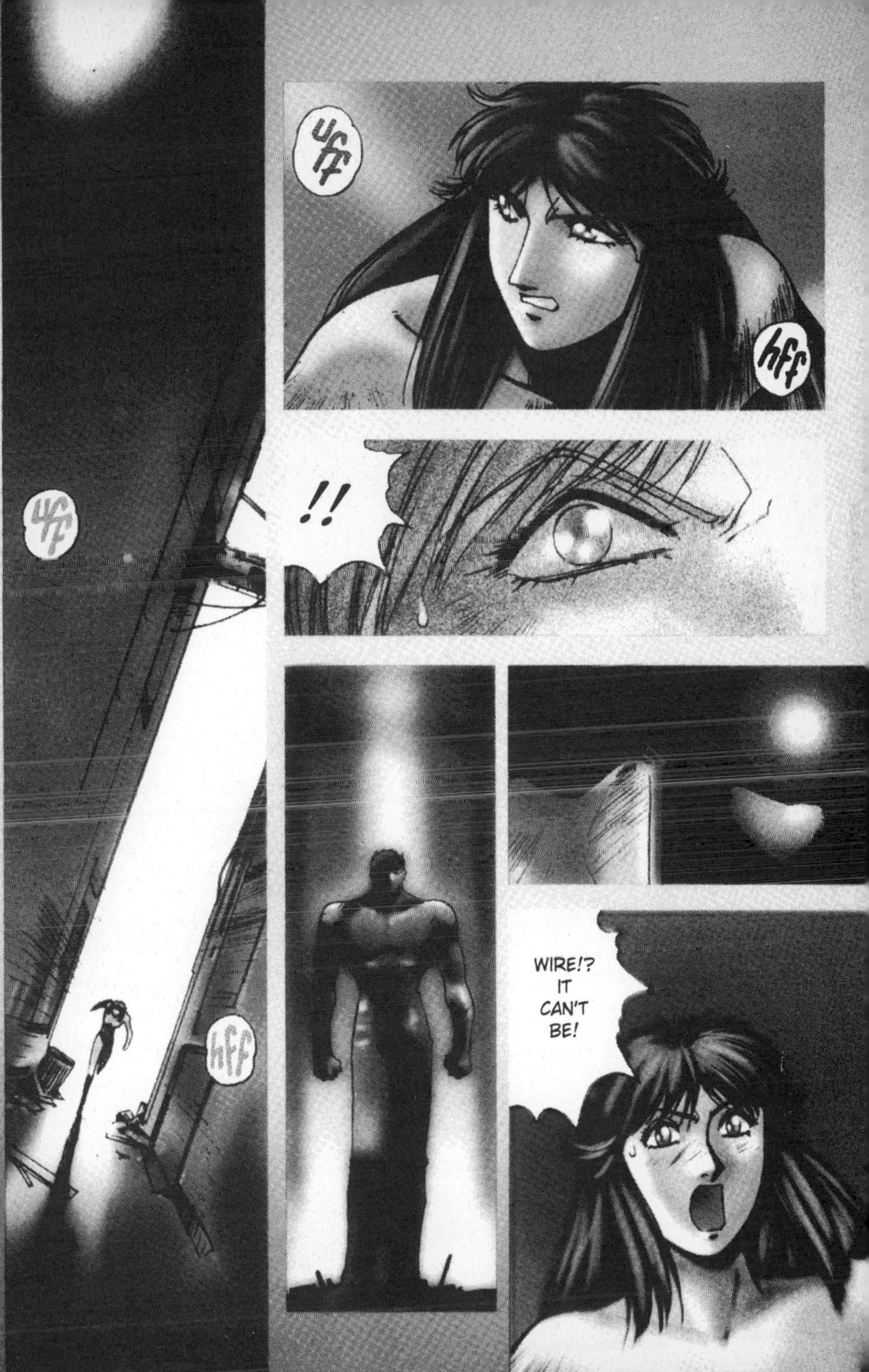
uff
hff
uff
hff
!!
WIRE!? IT CAN'T BE!

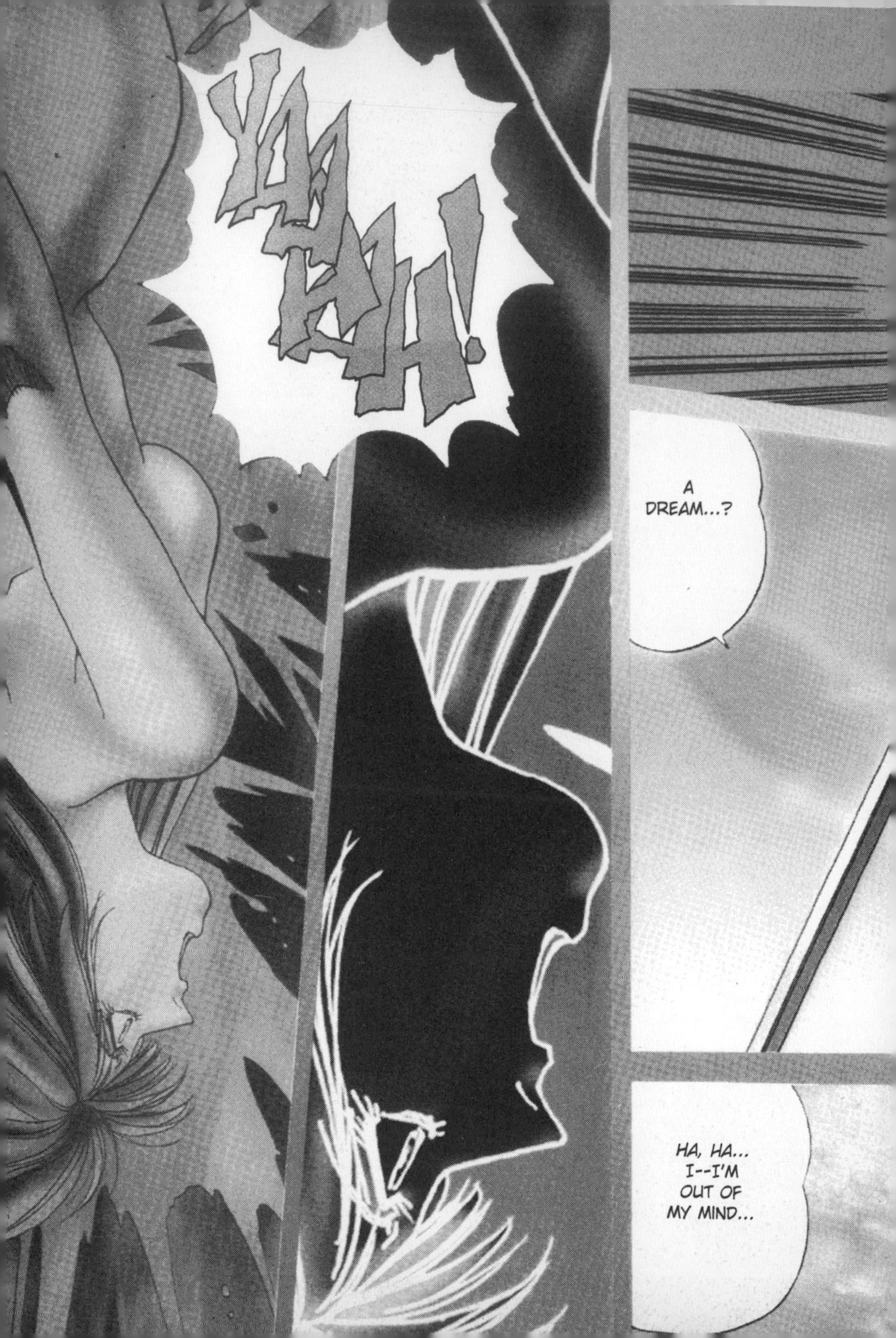
YAAAAH!
A DREAM...?
HA, HA... I--I'M OUT OF MY MIND...

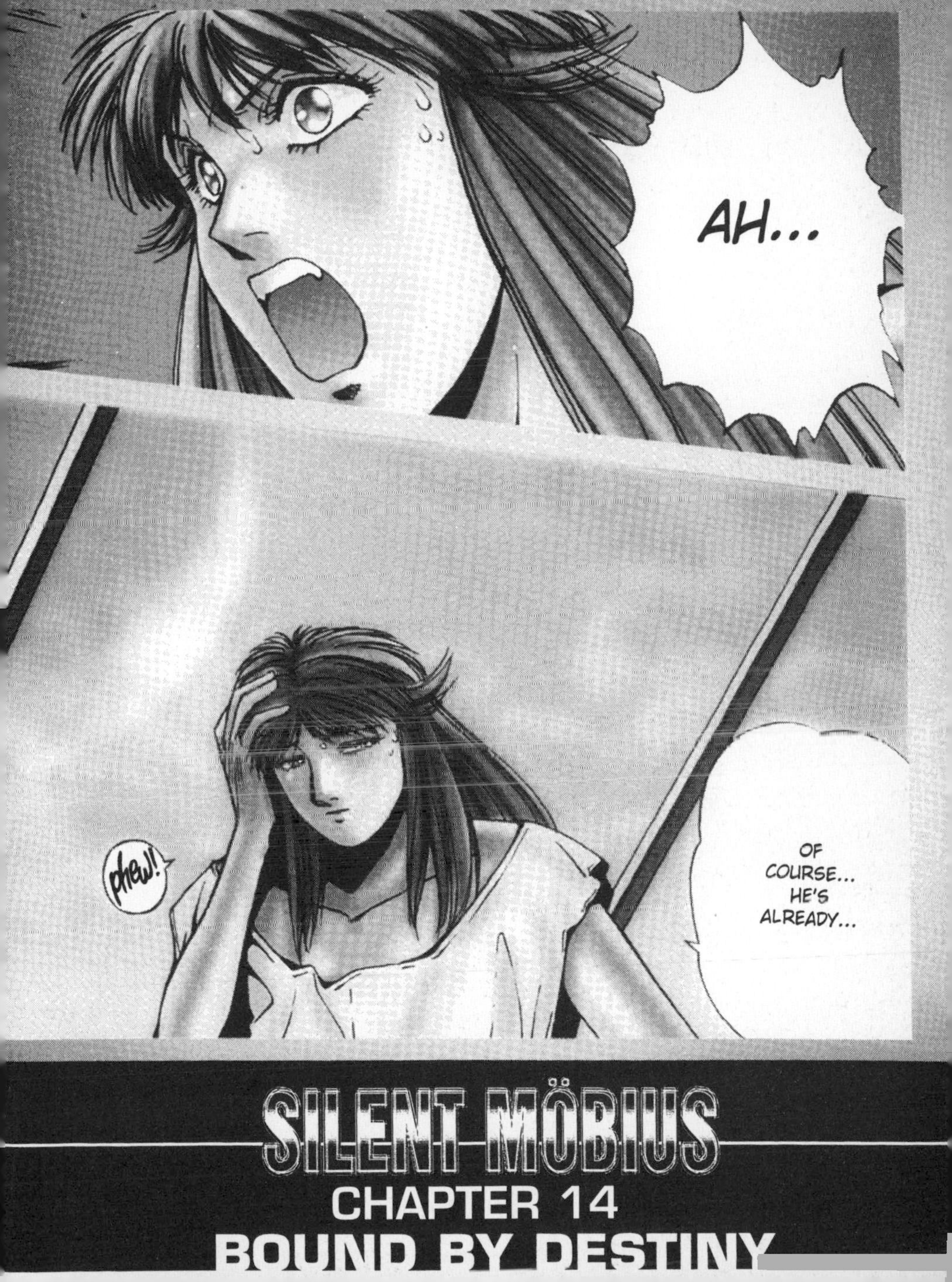
AH...
phew!
OF COURSE... HE'S ALREADY...

SILENT MÖBIUS

CHAPTER 14

BOUND BY DESTINY

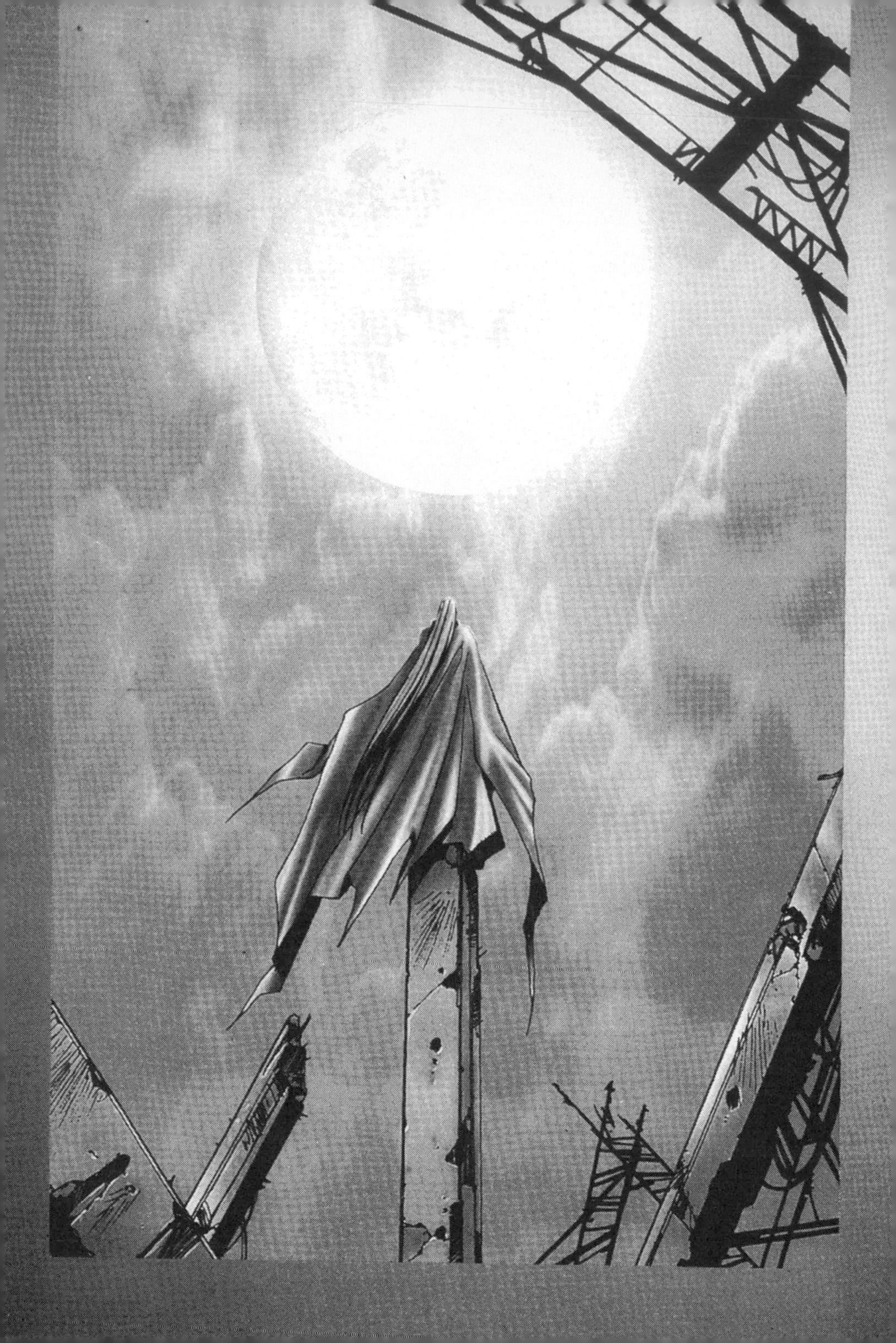

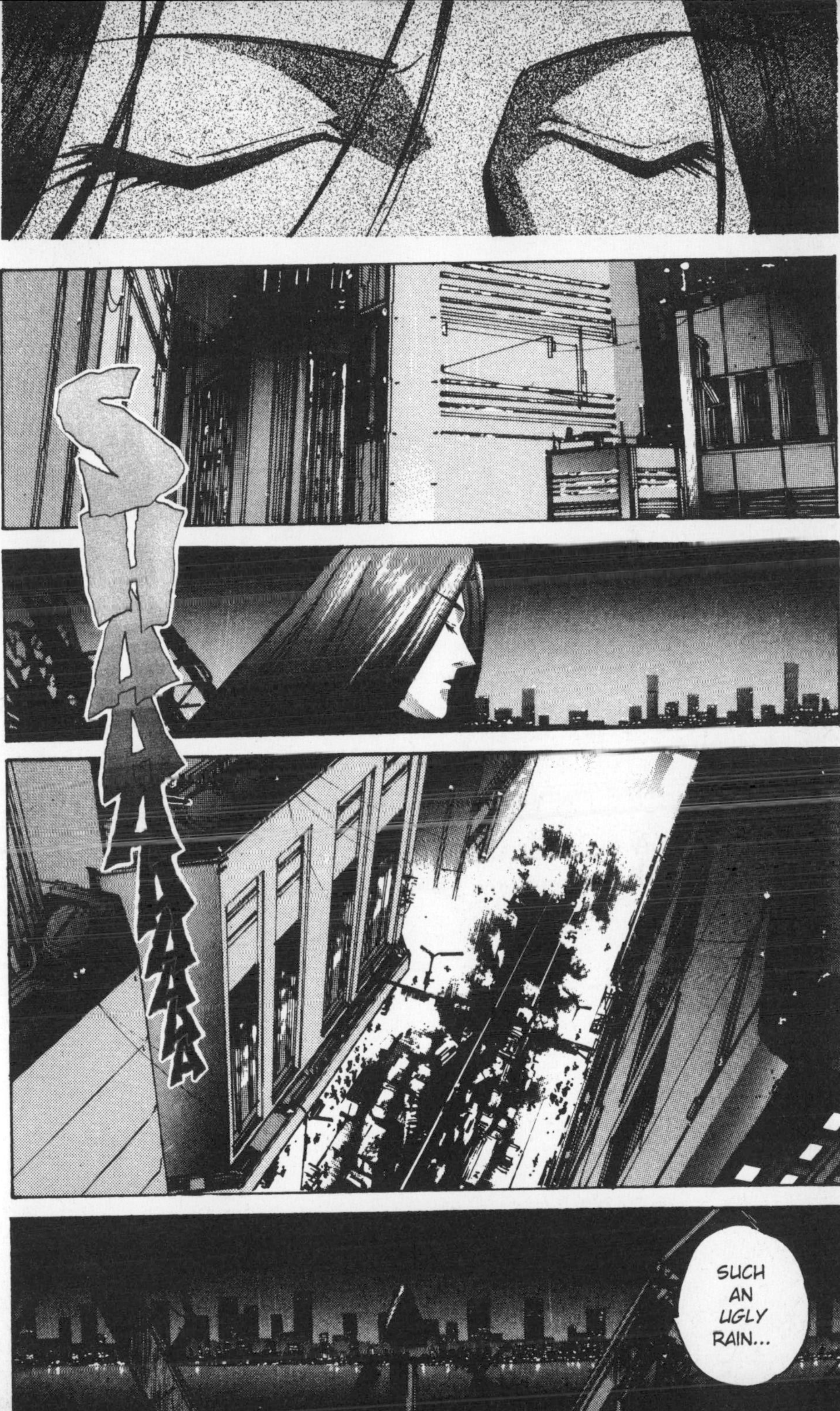
SHAAAAAAAA
SUCH AN UGLY RAIN...

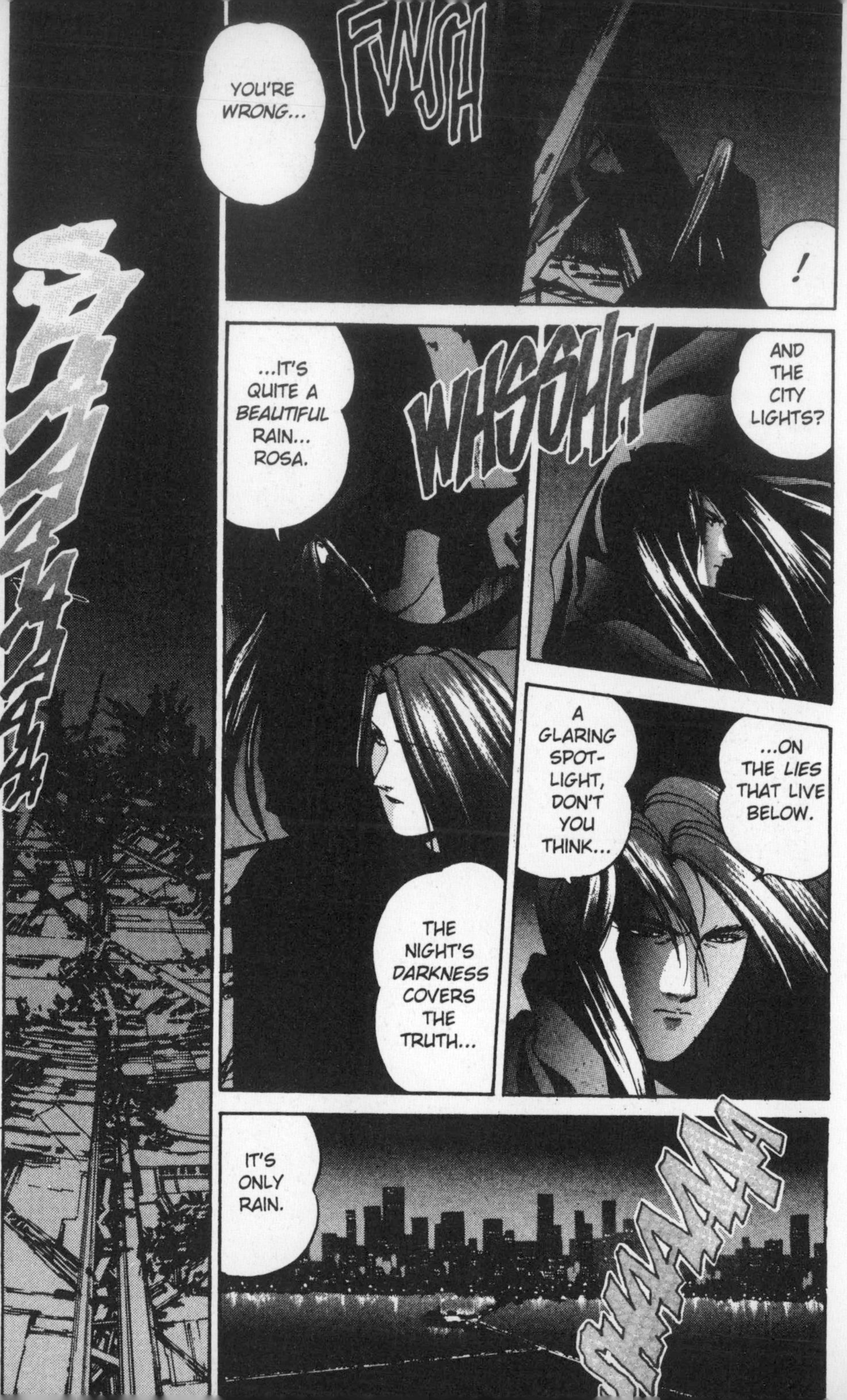
YOU'RE WRONG...
FWSH
!
...IT'S QUITE A BEAUTIFUL RAIN... ROSA.
WHSSHH
THE NIGHT'S DARKNESS COVERS THE TRUTH...
AND THE CITY LIGHTS?
A GLARING SPOT-LIGHT, DON'T YOU THINK...
...ON THE LIES THAT LIVE BELOW.
IT'S ONLY RAIN.

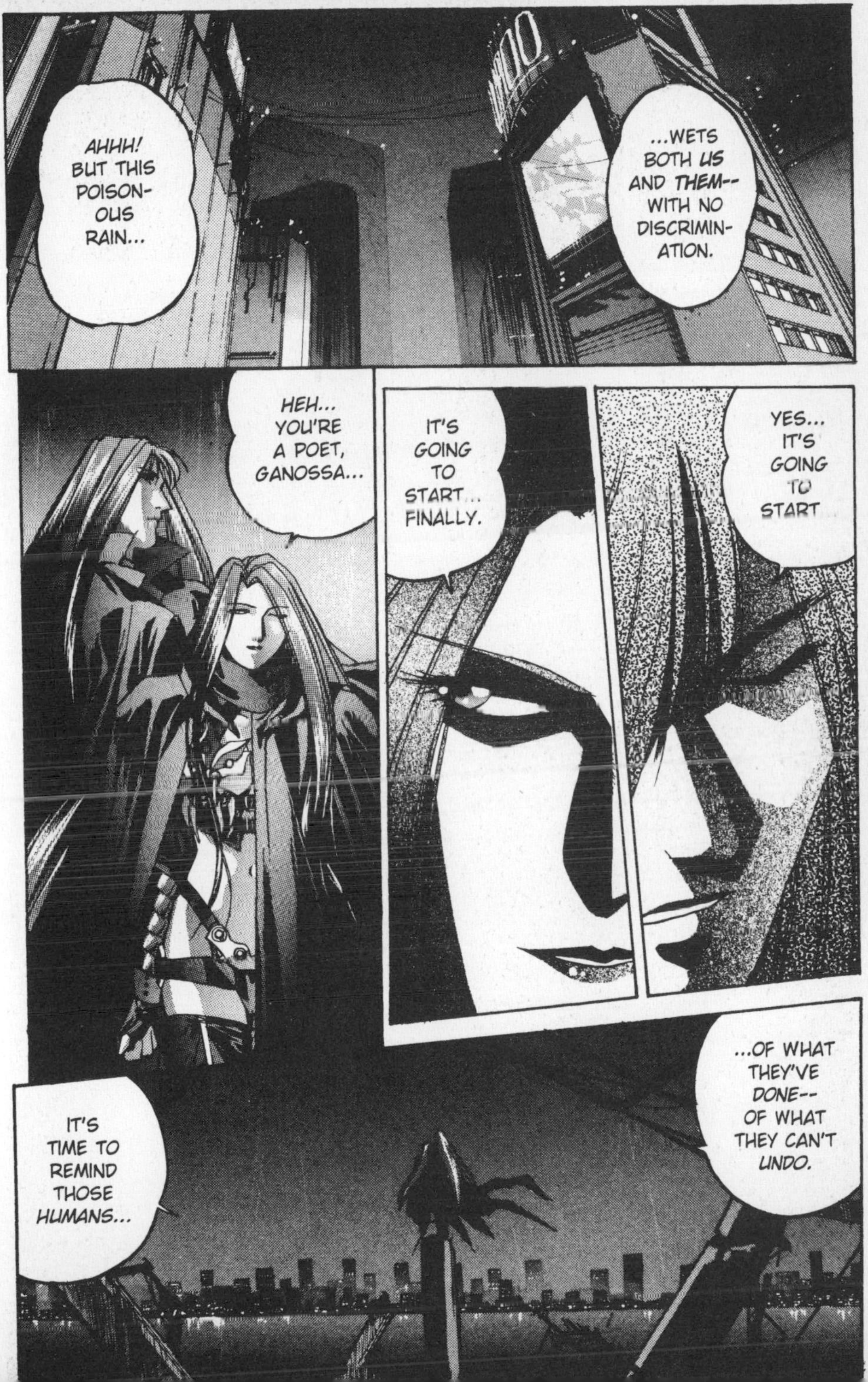
AHHH! BUT THIS POISON-OUS RAIN...
...WETS BOTH *US* AND *THEM*--WITH NO DISCRIMIN-ATION.
HEH... YOU'RE A POET, GANOSSA...
IT'S GOING TO START... FINALLY.
YES... IT'S GOING TO START...
IT'S TIME TO REMIND THOSE *HUMANS*...
...OF WHAT THEY'VE *DONE*--OF WHAT THEY CAN'T *UNDO*.

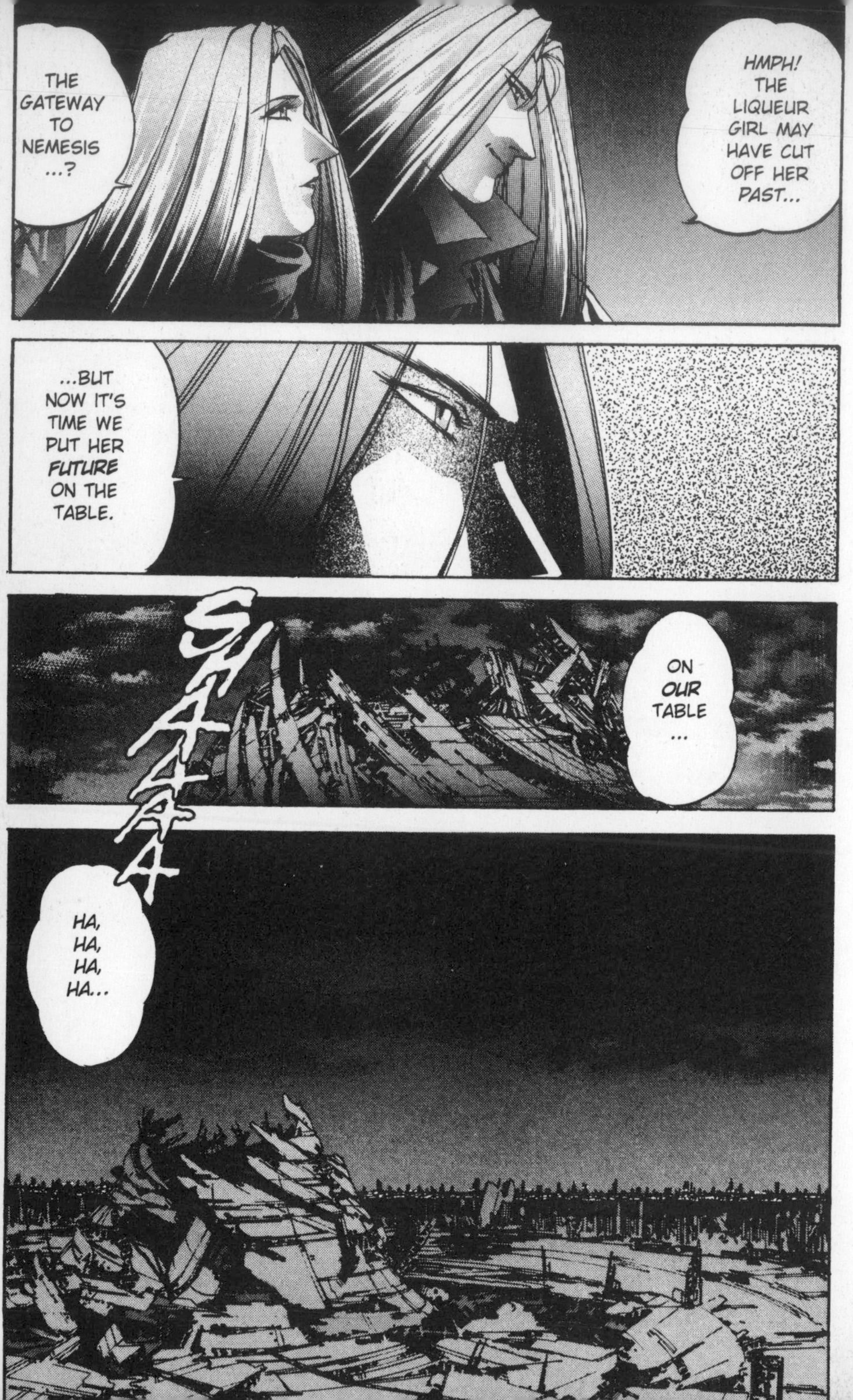
THE GATEWAY TO NEMESIS ...?
HMPH! THE LIQUEUR GIRL MAY HAVE CUT OFF HER PAST...
...BUT NOW IT'S TIME WE PUT HER FUTURE ON THE TABLE.
SHAAAA
ON OUR TABLE ...
HA, HA, HA, HA...

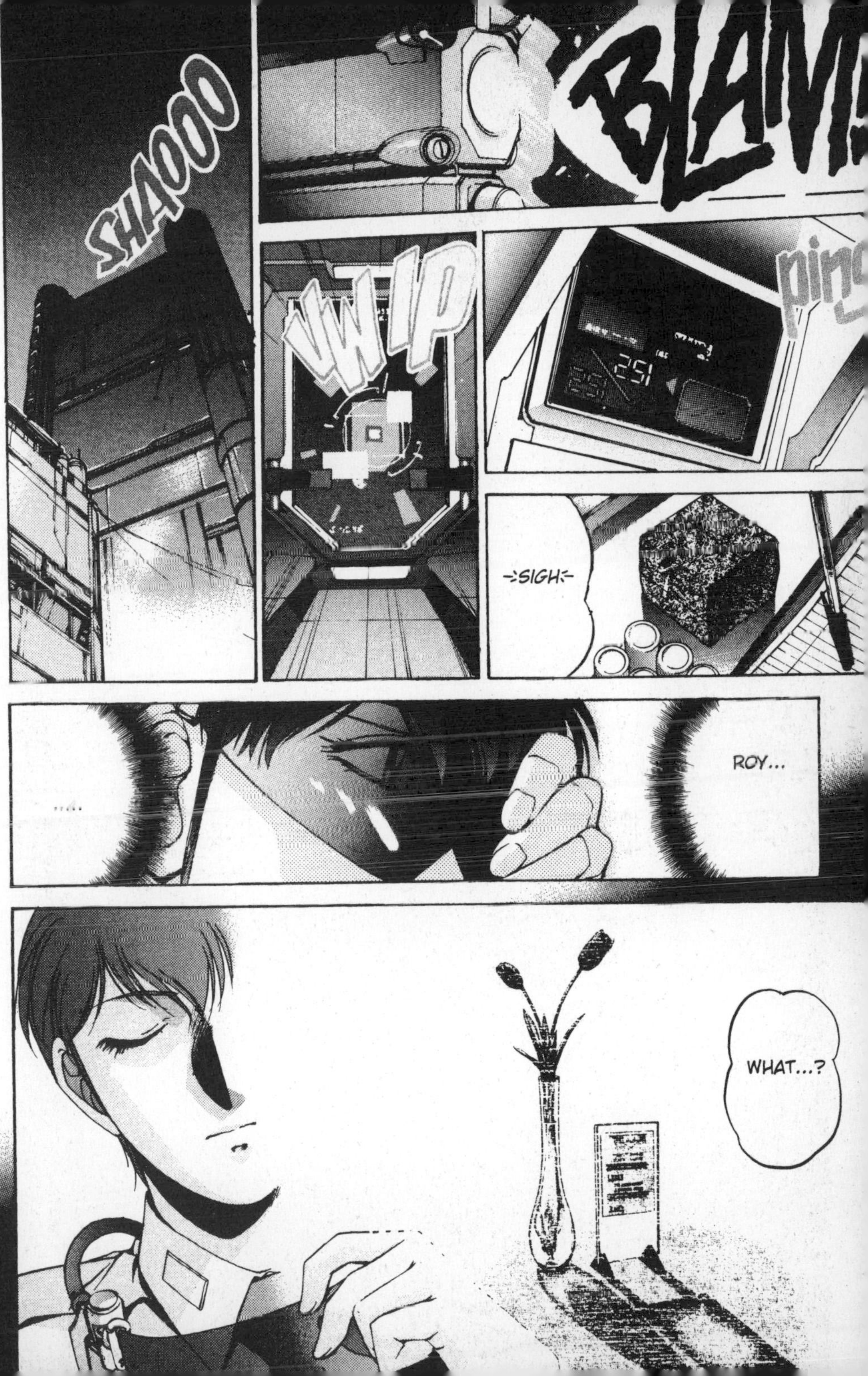
SHAOOO
BLAM!
VWIP
ping
SIGH
...
ROY...
WHAT...?

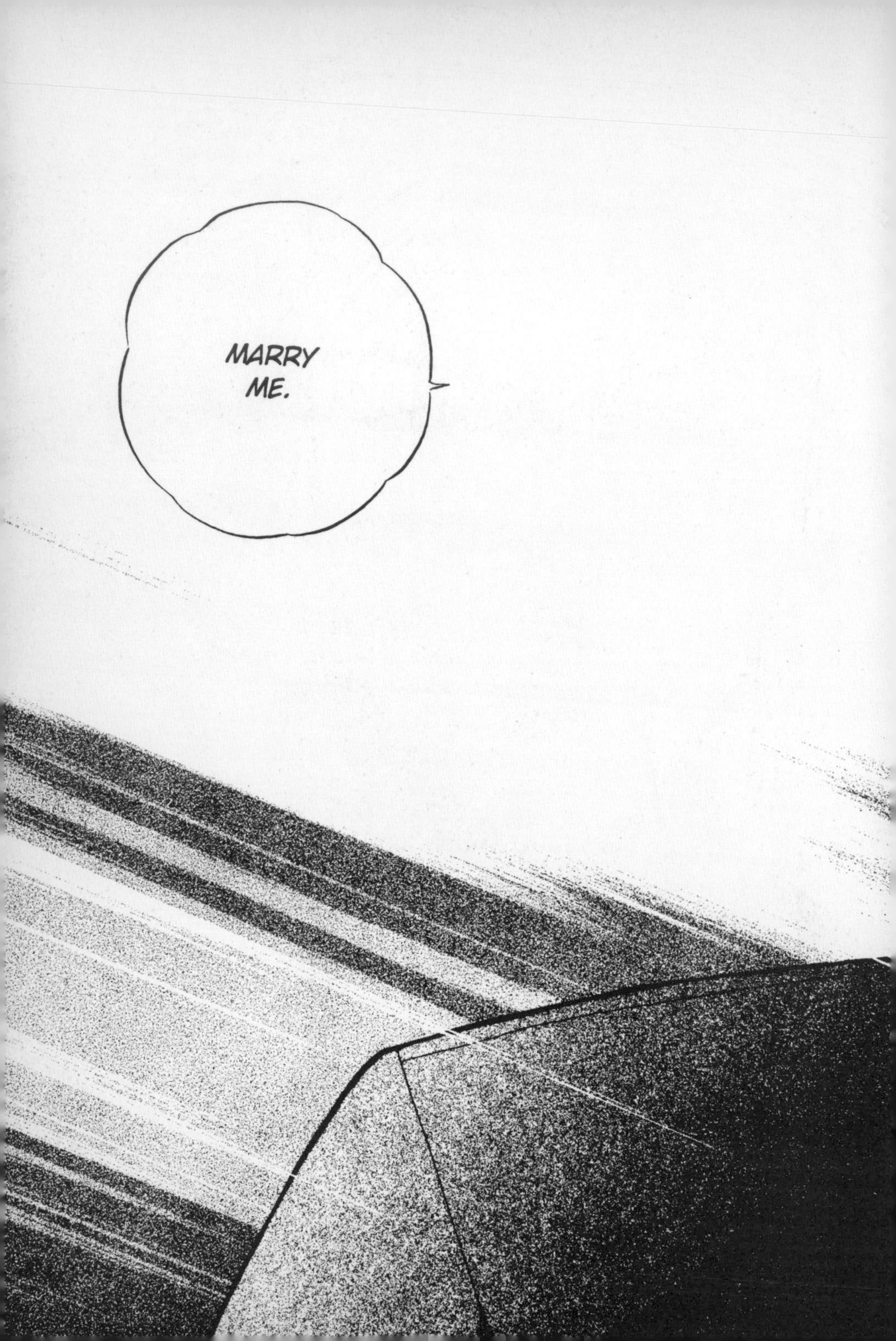
MARRY ME.

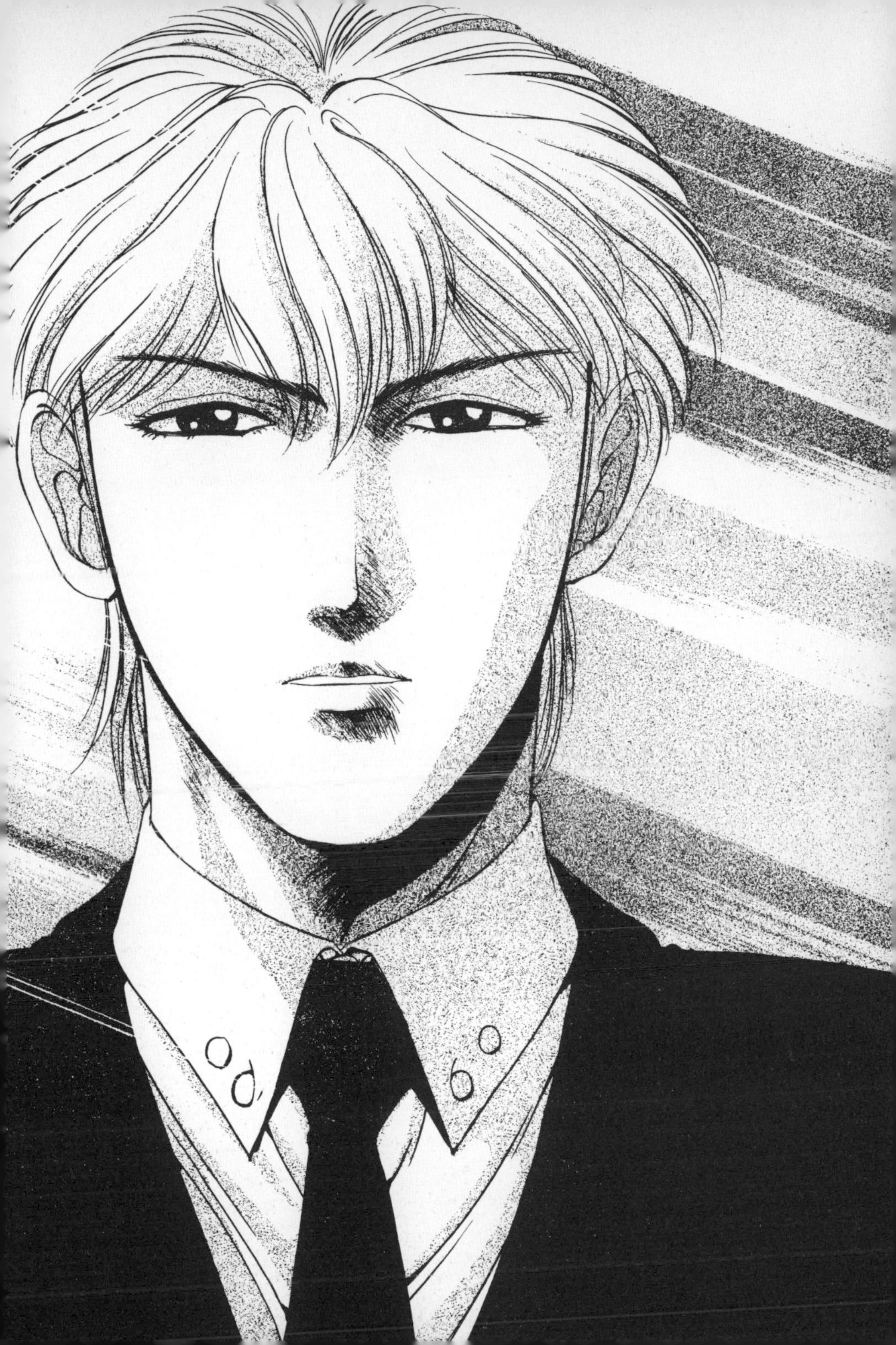

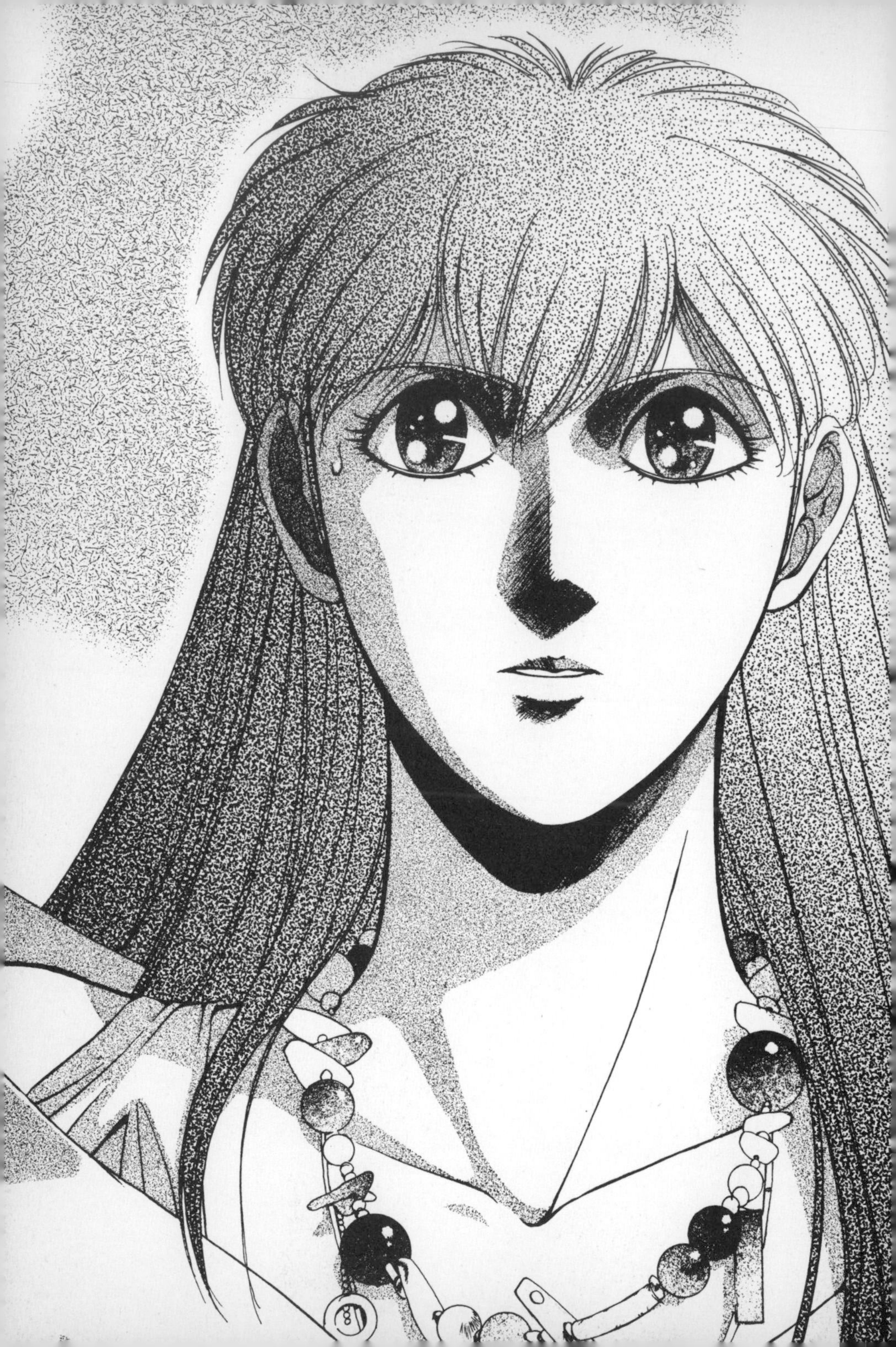

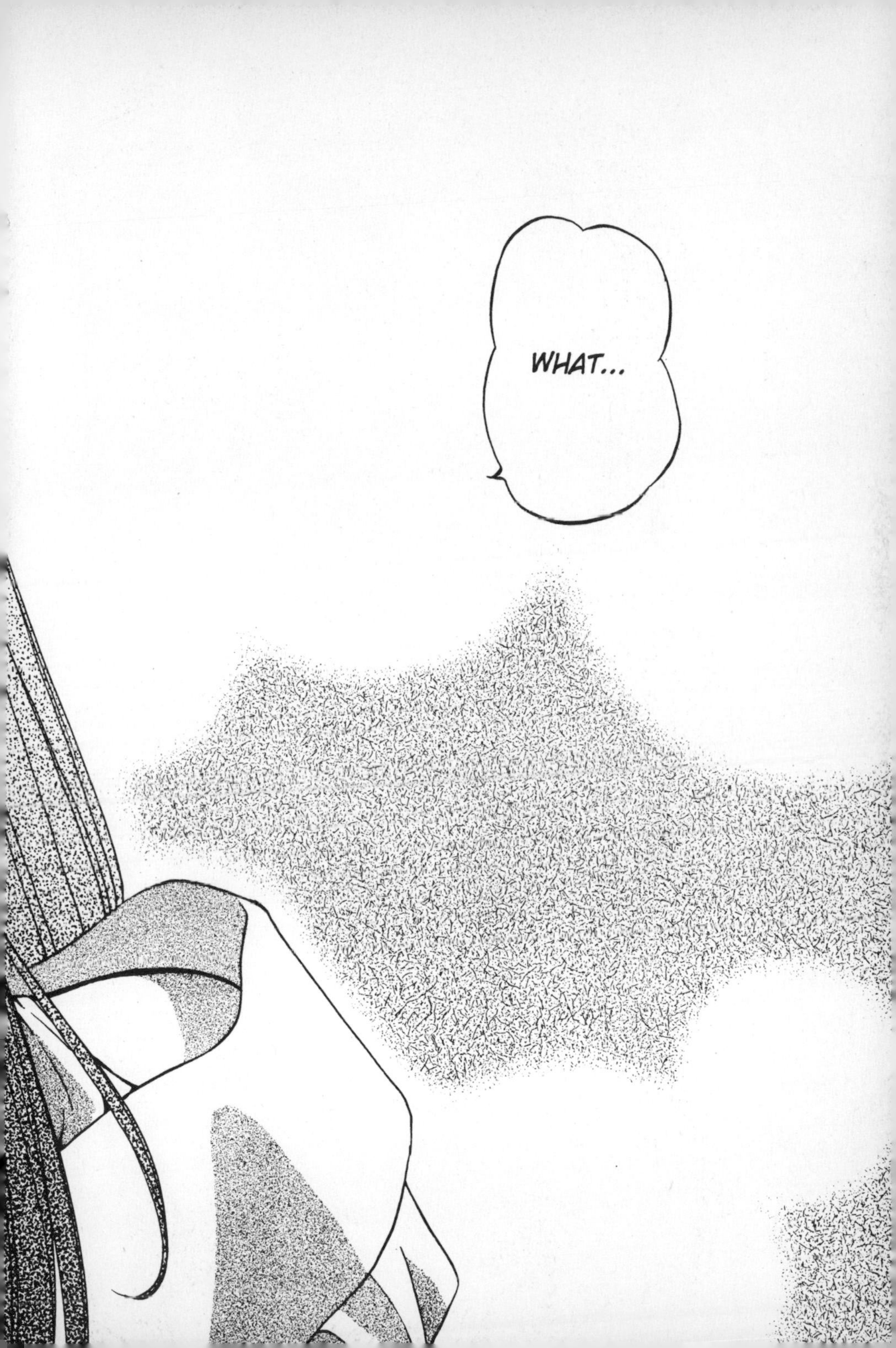
WHAT...

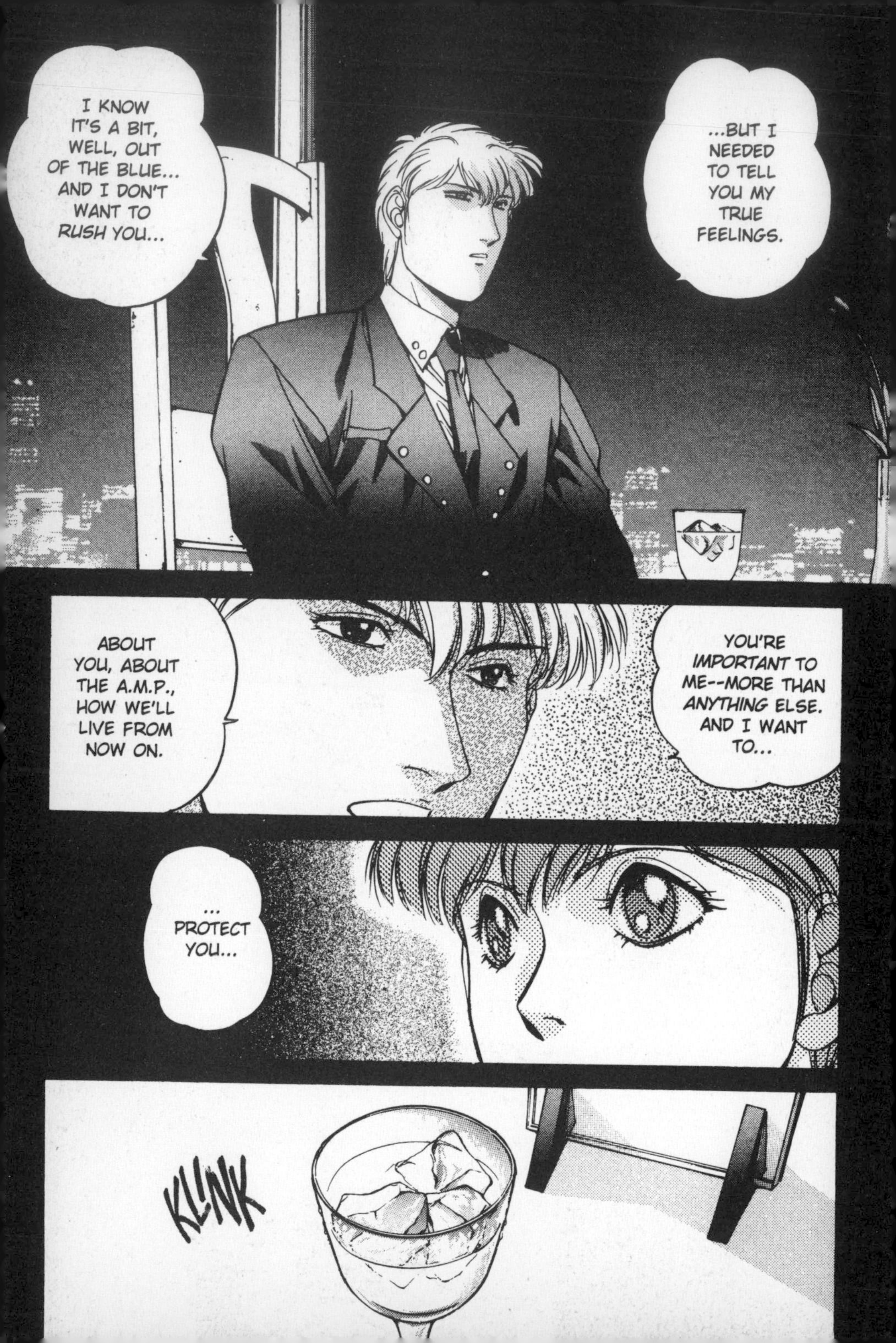
I KNOW IT'S A BIT, WELL, OUT OF THE BLUE... AND I DON'T WANT TO RUSH YOU...
...BUT I NEEDED TO TELL YOU MY TRUE FEELINGS.
ABOUT YOU, ABOUT THE A.M.P., HOW WE'LL LIVE FROM NOW ON.
YOU'RE IMPORTANT TO ME--MORE THAN ANYTHING ELSE. AND I WANT TO...
... PROTECT YOU...
KLINK

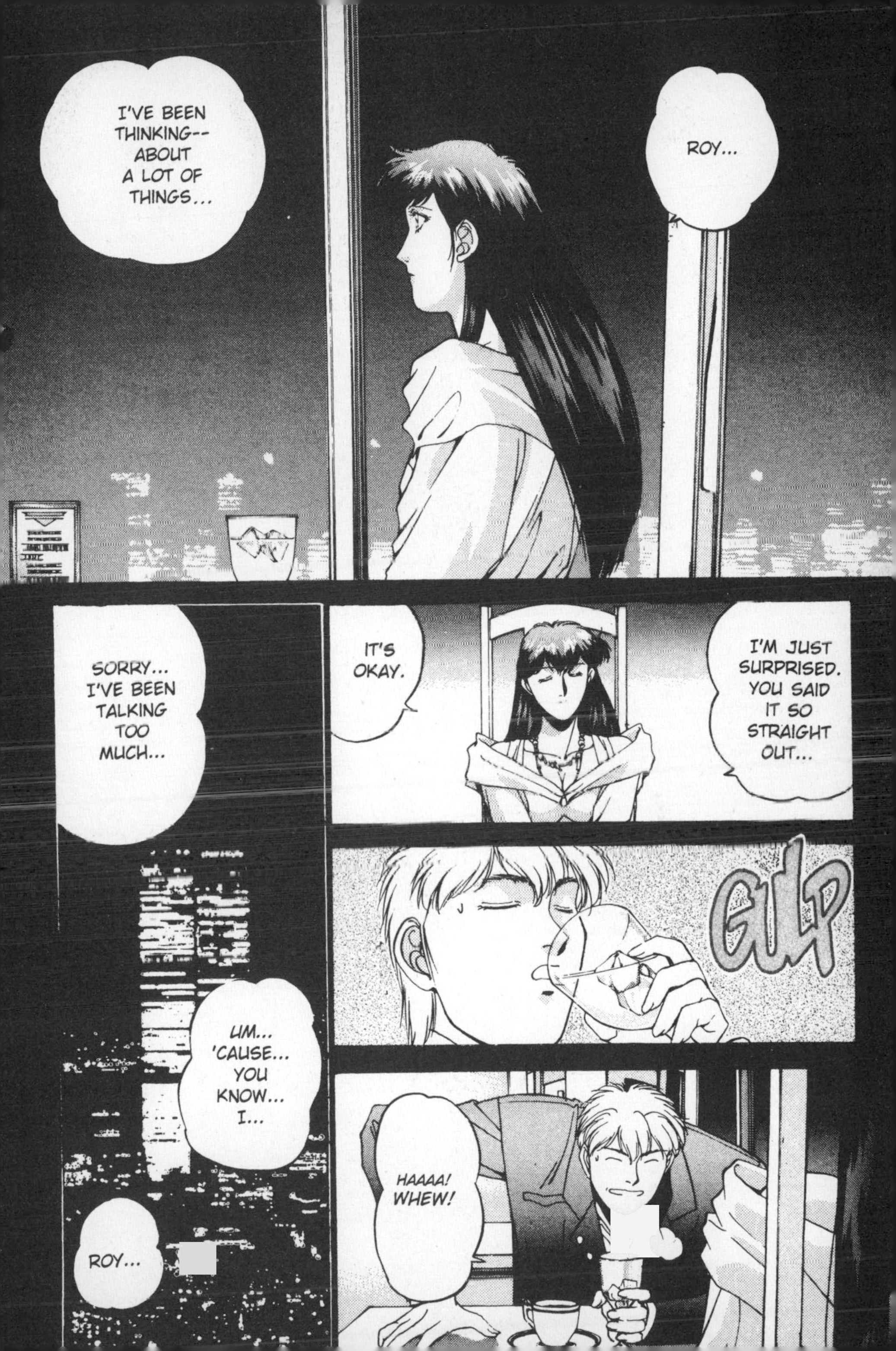
I'VE BEEN THINKING-- ABOUT A LOT OF THINGS...
ROY...
SORRY... I'VE BEEN TALKING TOO MUCH...
UM... 'CAUSE... YOU KNOW... I...
ROY...
IT'S OKAY.
I'M JUST SURPRISED. YOU SAID IT SO STRAIGHT OUT...
GULP
HAAAA! WHEW!

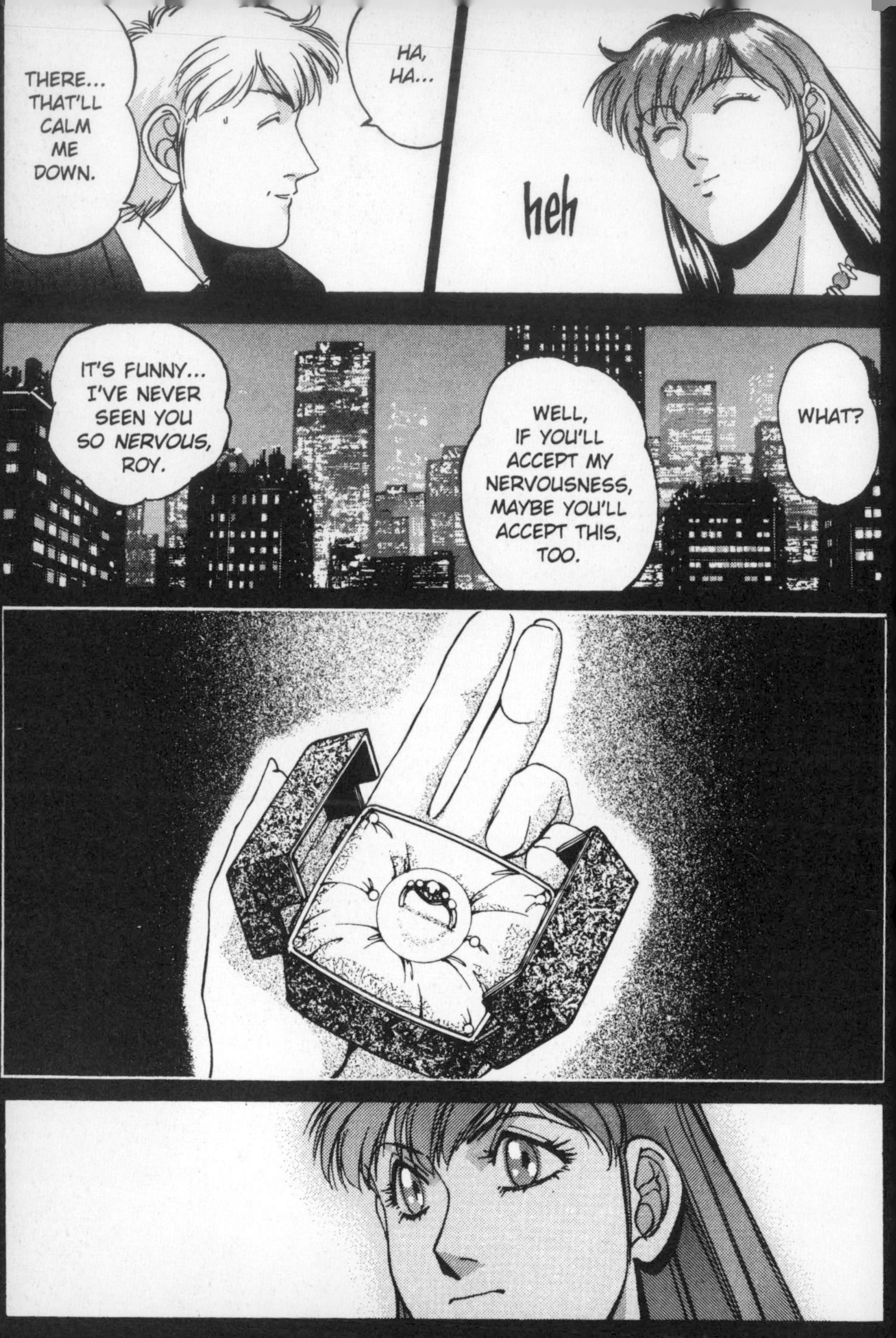
THERE... THAT'LL CALM ME DOWN.
HA, HA...
heh
IT'S FUNNY... I'VE NEVER SEEN YOU SO NERVOUS, ROY.
WELL, IF YOU'LL ACCEPT MY NERVOUSNESS, MAYBE YOU'LL ACCEPT THIS, TOO.
WHAT?

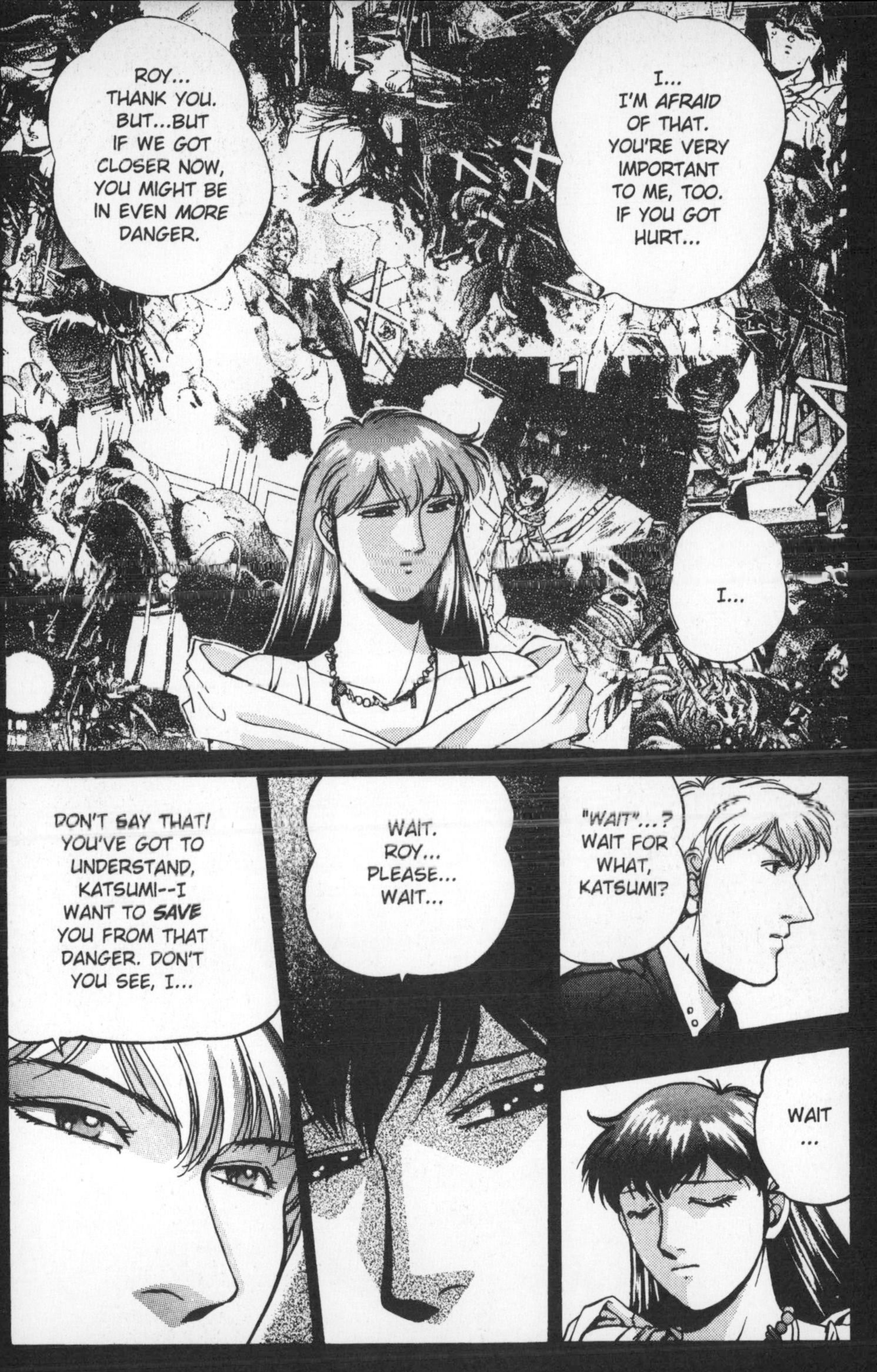
ROY... THANK YOU. BUT...BUT IF WE GOT CLOSER NOW, YOU MIGHT BE IN EVEN *MORE* DANGER.
I... I'M *AFRAID* OF THAT. YOU'RE VERY IMPORTANT TO ME, TOO. IF YOU GOT HURT...
I...
DON'T SAY THAT! YOU'VE GOT TO UNDERSTAND, KATSUMI--I WANT TO **SAVE** YOU FROM THAT DANGER. DON'T YOU SEE, I...
WAIT. ROY... PLEASE... WAIT...
"*WAIT*"...? WAIT FOR WHAT, KATSUMI?
WAIT ...

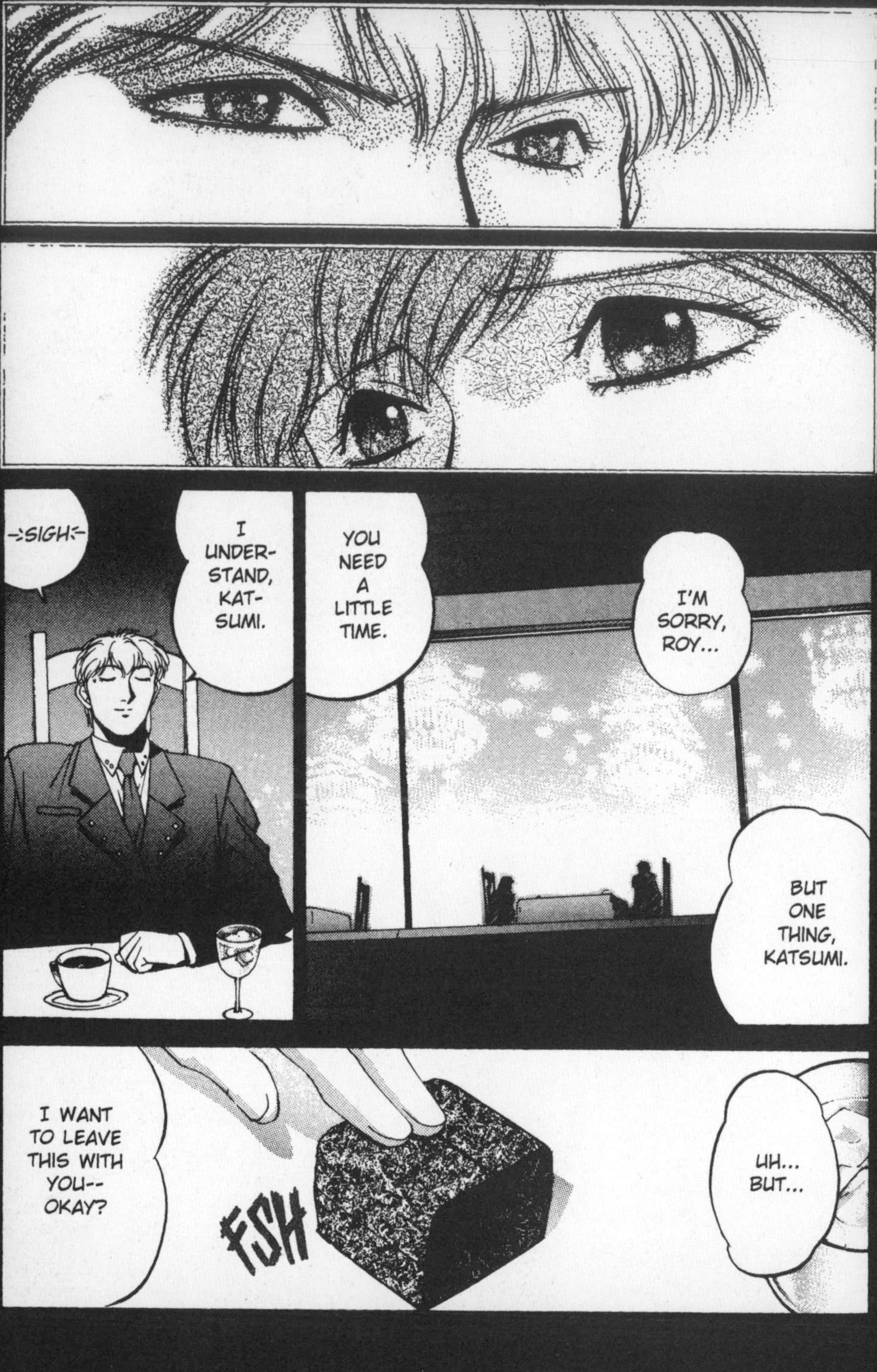

-SIGH-
I UNDERSTAND, KATSUMI.
YOU NEED A LITTLE TIME.
I'M SORRY, ROY...
BUT ONE THING, KATSUMI.
I WANT TO LEAVE THIS WITH YOU--OKAY?
FSH
UH... BUT...

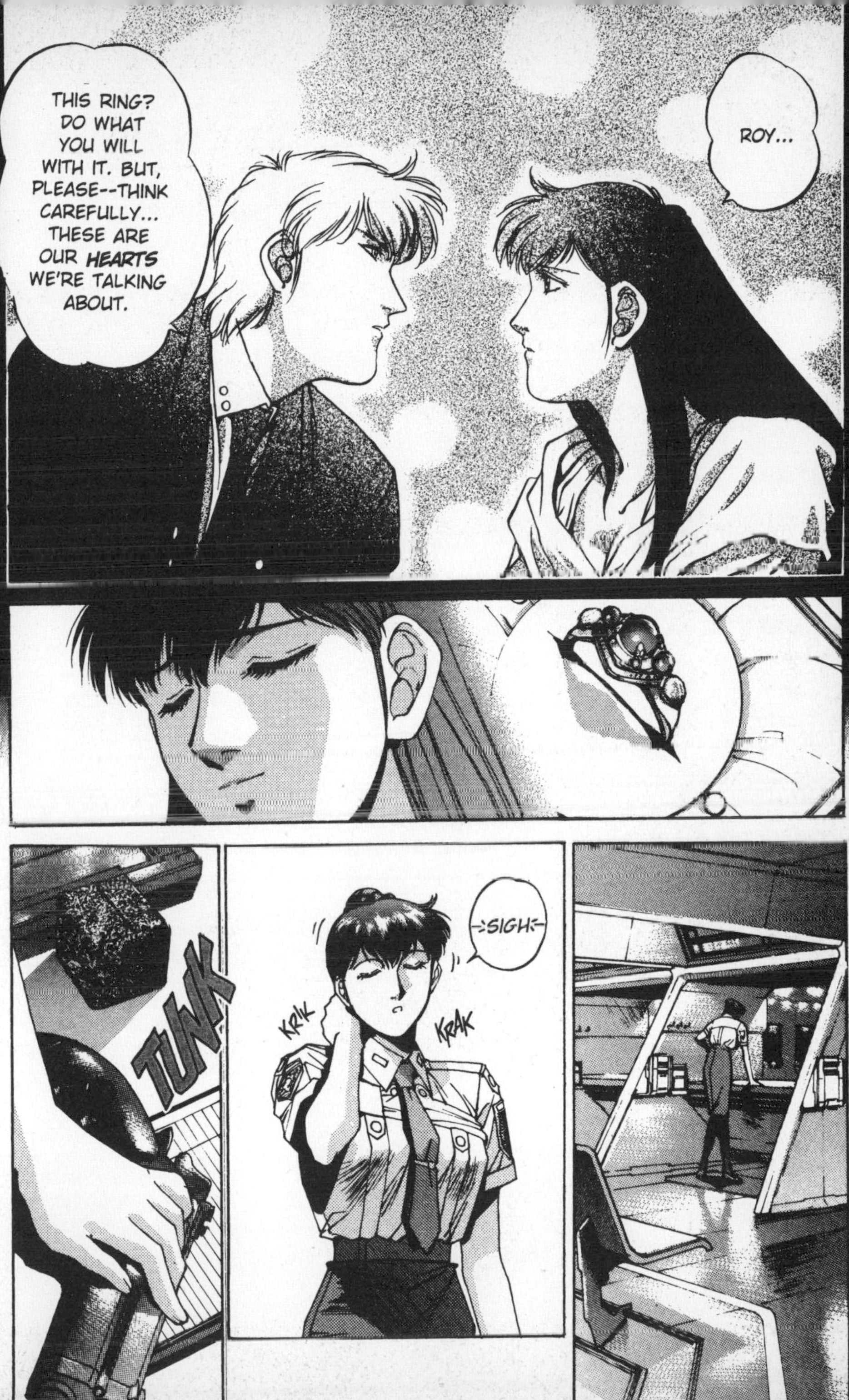
THIS RING? DO WHAT YOU WILL WITH IT. BUT, PLEASE--THINK CAREFULLY... THESE ARE OUR **HEARTS** WE'RE TALKING ABOUT.
ROY...
TUNK
-SIGH-
KRIK
KRAK

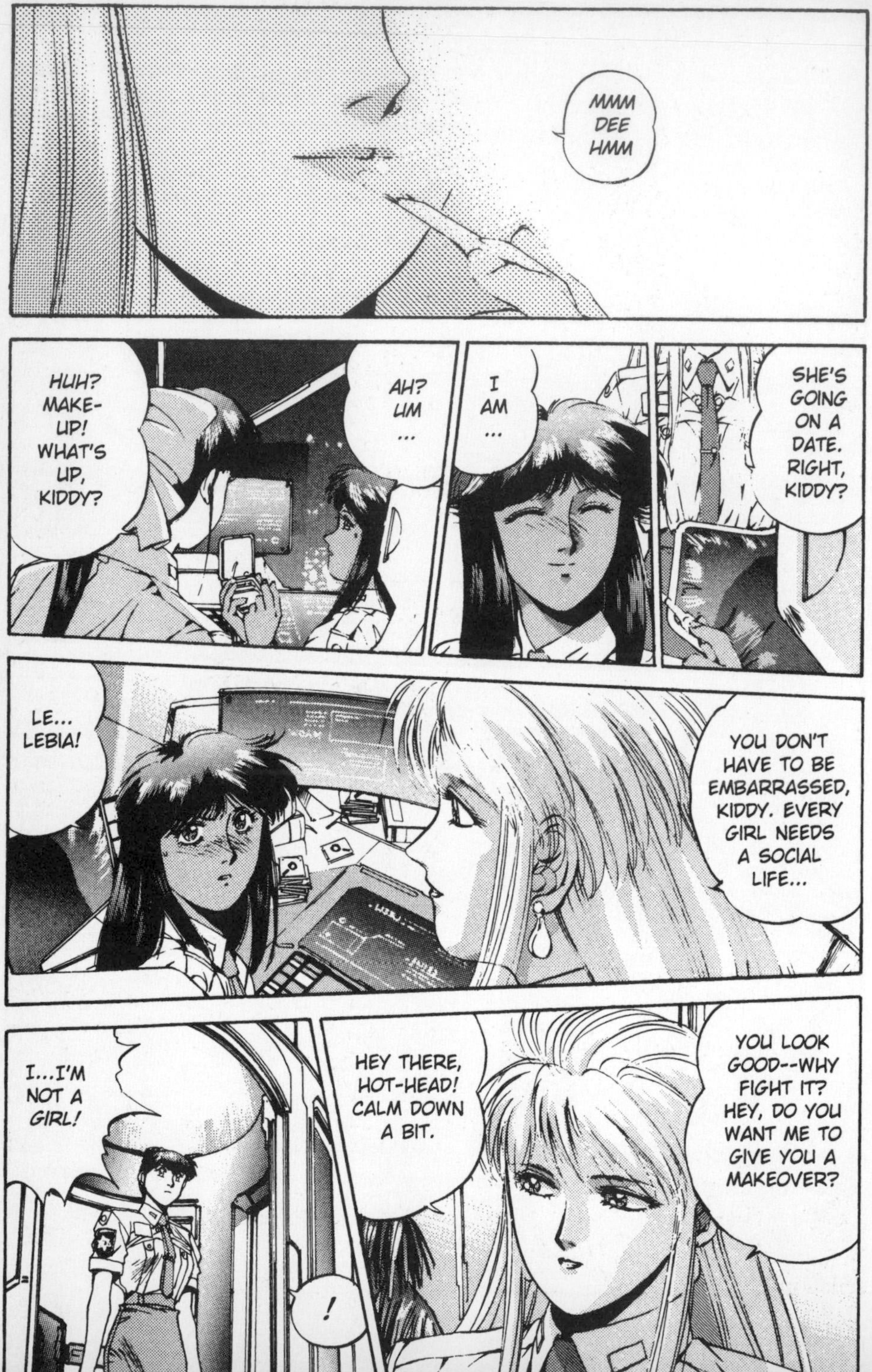
MMM DEE HMM
HUH? MAKE-UP! WHAT'S UP, KIDDY?
AH? UM ...
I AM ...
SHE'S GOING ON A DATE. RIGHT, KIDDY?
LE... LEBIA!
YOU DON'T HAVE TO BE EMBARRASSED, KIDDY. EVERY GIRL NEEDS A SOCIAL LIFE...
I...I'M NOT A GIRL!
!
HEY THERE, HOT-HEAD! CALM DOWN A BIT.
YOU LOOK GOOD--WHY FIGHT IT? HEY, DO YOU WANT ME TO GIVE YOU A MAKEOVER?

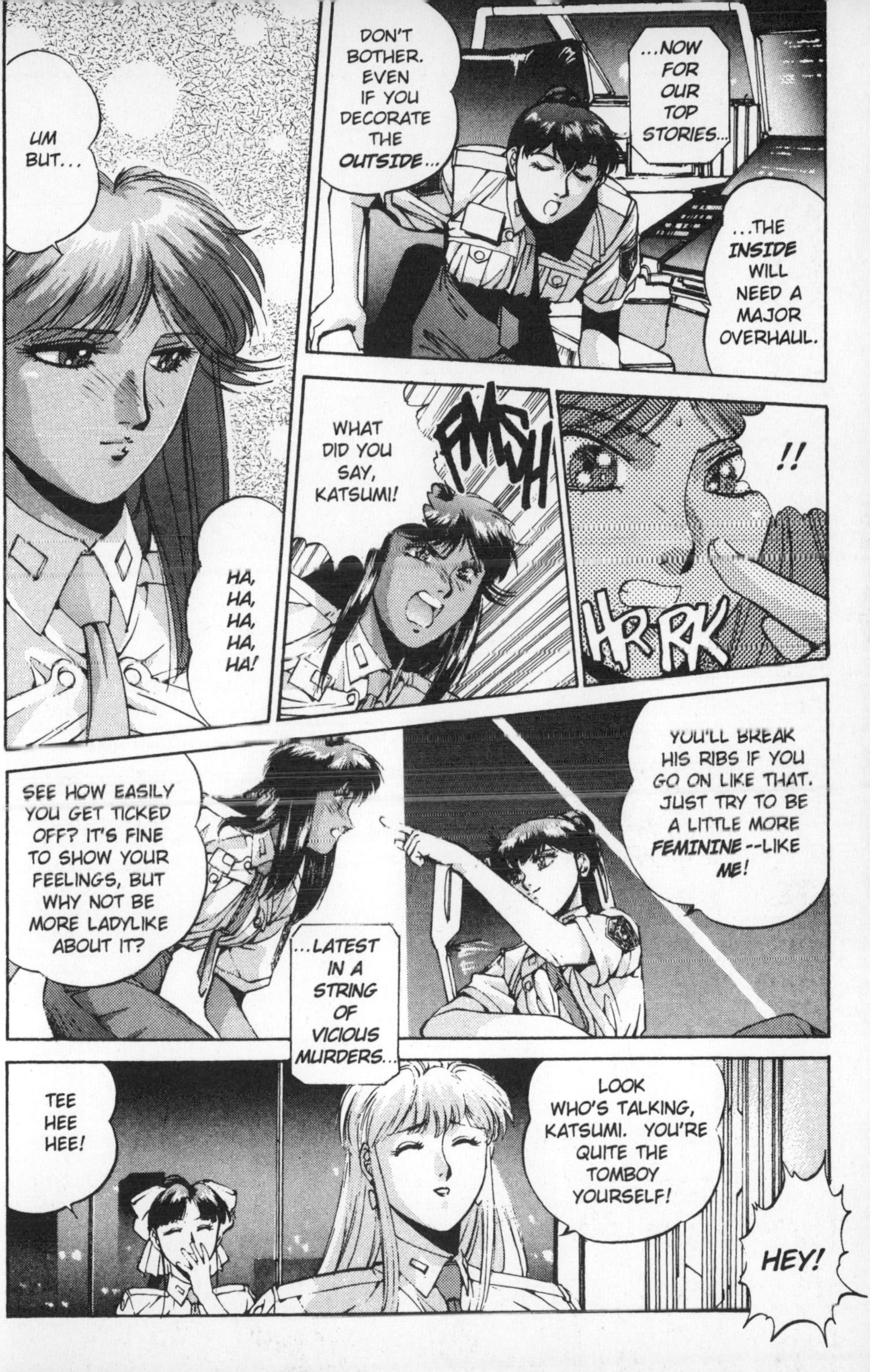
UM BUT...
HA, HA, HA, HA, HA!
DON'T BOTHER. EVEN IF YOU DECORATE THE OUTSIDE...
...NOW FOR OUR TOP STORIES...
...THE INSIDE WILL NEED A MAJOR OVERHAUL.
WHAT DID YOU SAY, KATSUMI!
FWSH
!!
HRRK
SEE HOW EASILY YOU GET TICKED OFF? IT'S FINE TO SHOW YOUR FEELINGS, BUT WHY NOT BE MORE LADYLIKE ABOUT IT?
YOU'LL BREAK HIS RIBS IF YOU GO ON LIKE THAT. JUST TRY TO BE A LITTLE MORE FEMININE--LIKE ME!
...LATEST IN A STRING OF VICIOUS MURDERS...
TEE HEE HEE!
LOOK WHO'S TALKING, KATSUMI. YOU'RE QUITE THE TOMBOY YOURSELF!
HEY!

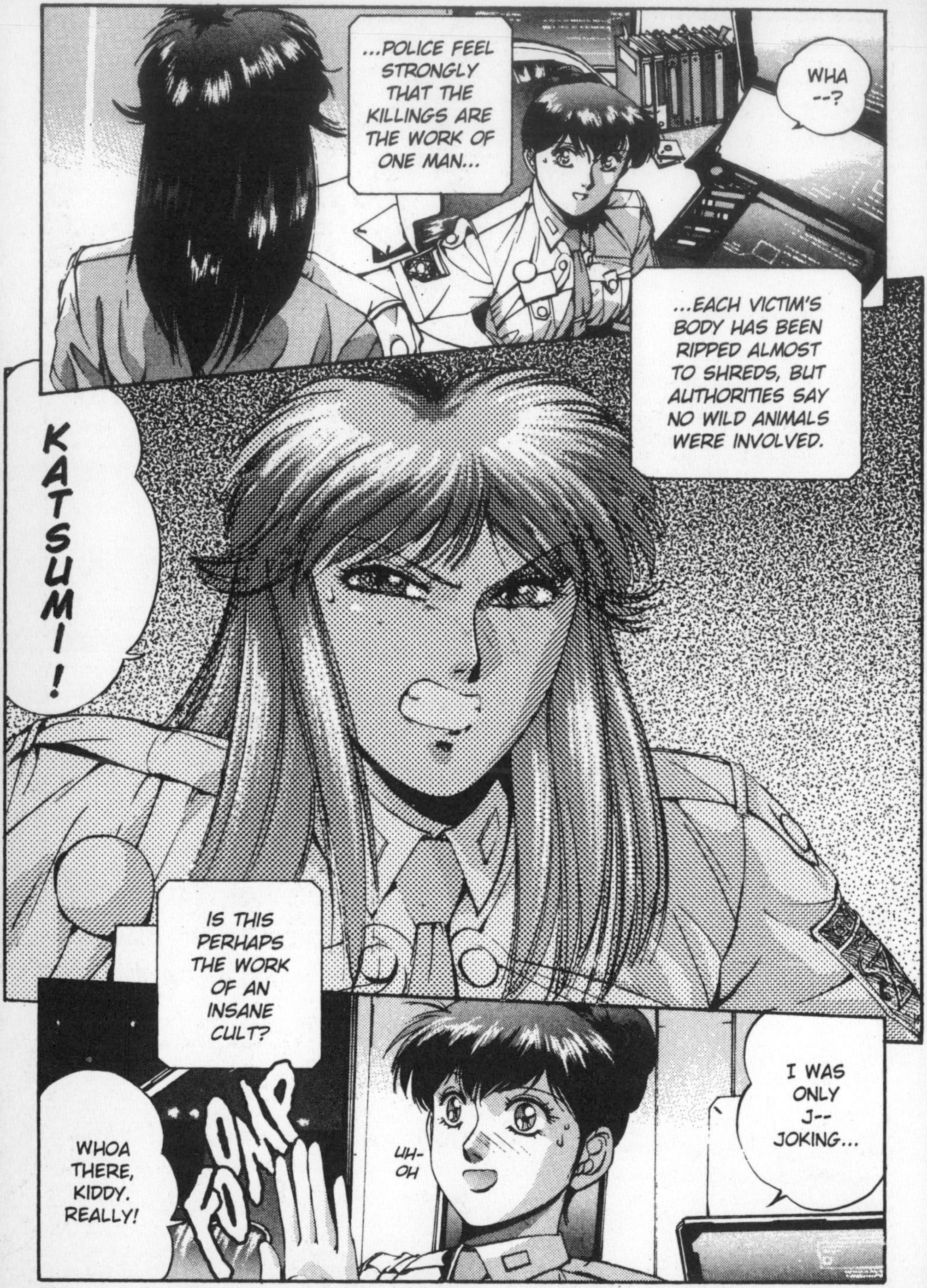
...POLICE FEEL STRONGLY THAT THE KILLINGS ARE THE WORK OF ONE MAN...
WHA --?
KATSUMI!
...EACH VICTIM'S BODY HAS BEEN RIPPED ALMOST TO SHREDS, BUT AUTHORITIES SAY NO WILD ANIMALS WERE INVOLVED.
IS THIS PERHAPS THE WORK OF AN INSANE CULT?
WHOA THERE, KIDDY. REALLY!
FOMP FOMP
UH-OH
I WAS ONLY J-- JOKING...

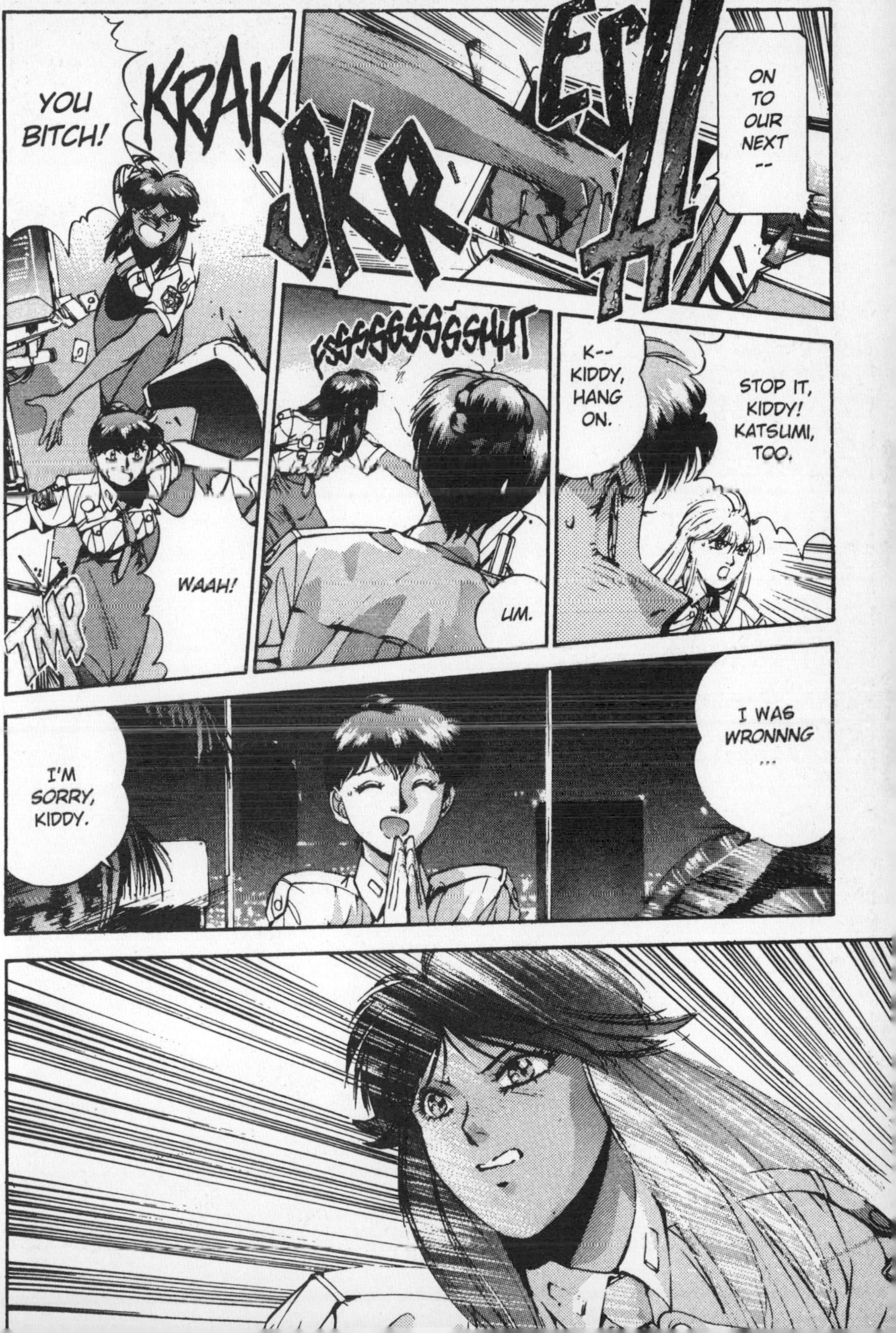
YOU BITCH!
KRAK
WAAH!
TMP
ON TO OUR NEXT --
K-- KIDDY, HANG ON.
UM.
STOP IT, KIDDY! KATSUMI, TOO.
I'M SORRY, KIDDY.
I WAS WRONNNG ...

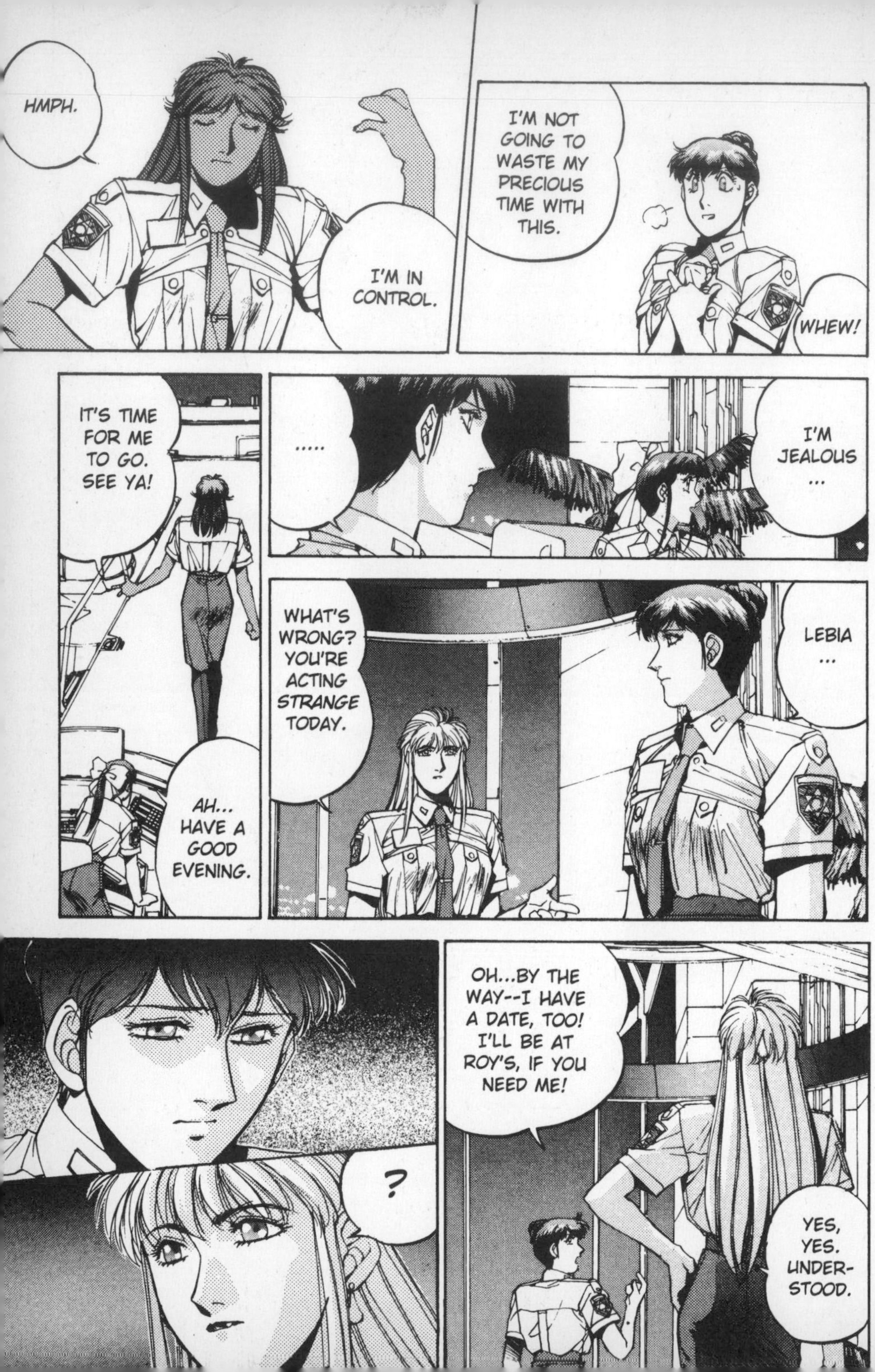
HMPH.
I'M IN CONTROL.
I'M NOT GOING TO WASTE MY PRECIOUS TIME WITH THIS.
WHEW!
IT'S TIME FOR ME TO GO. SEE YA!
AH... HAVE A GOOD EVENING.
.....
I'M JEALOUS ...
WHAT'S WRONG? YOU'RE ACTING STRANGE TODAY.
LEBIA ...
?
OH...BY THE WAY--I HAVE A DATE, TOO! I'LL BE AT ROY'S, IF YOU NEED ME!
YES, YES. UNDER-STOOD.

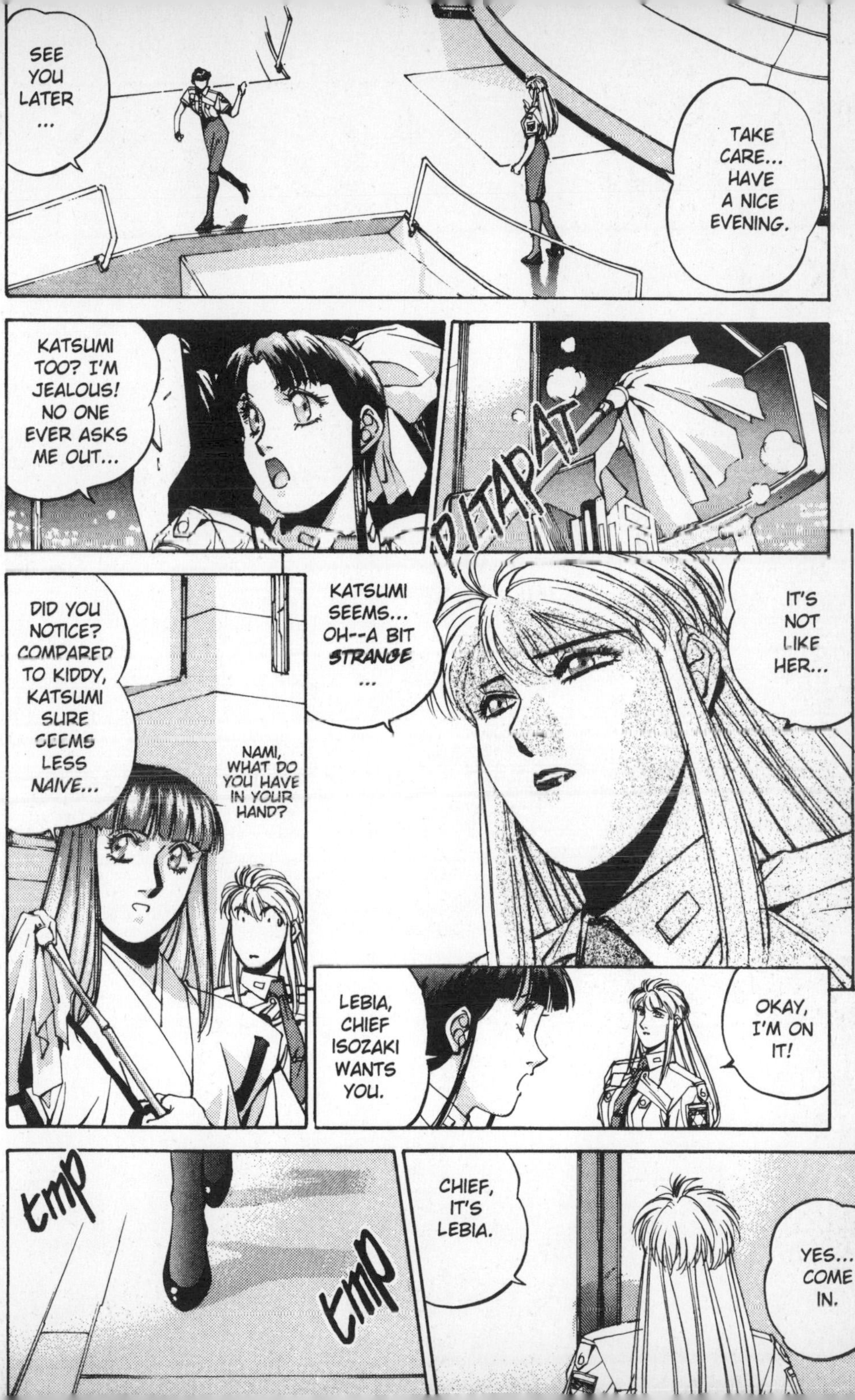
SEE YOU LATER ...
TAKE CARE... HAVE A NICE EVENING.
KATSUMI TOO? I'M JEALOUS! NO ONE EVER ASKS ME OUT...
PITAPAT
DID YOU NOTICE? COMPARED TO KIDDY, KATSUMI SURE SEEMS LESS NAIVE...
NAMI, WHAT DO YOU HAVE IN YOUR HAND?
KATSUMI SEEMS... OH--A BIT STRANGE ...
IT'S NOT LIKE HER...
LEBIA, CHIEF ISOZAKI WANTS YOU.
OKAY, I'M ON IT!
tmp
tmp
CHIEF, IT'S LEBIA.
YES... COME IN.

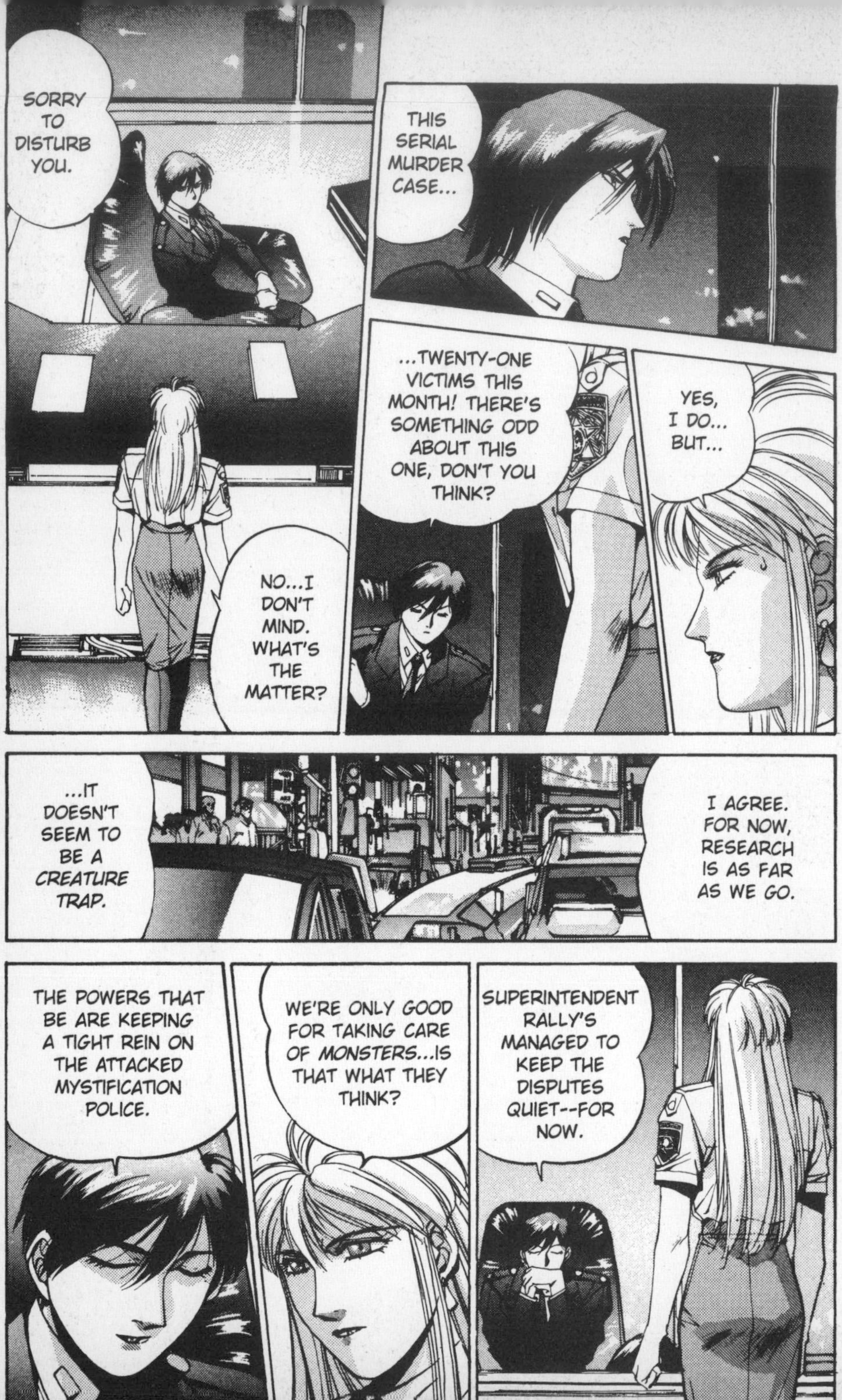
SORRY TO DISTURB YOU.
THIS SERIAL MURDER CASE...
NO...I DON'T MIND. WHAT'S THE MATTER?
...TWENTY-ONE VICTIMS THIS MONTH! THERE'S SOMETHING ODD ABOUT THIS ONE, DON'T YOU THINK?
YES, I DO... BUT...
...IT DOESN'T SEEM TO BE A CREATURE TRAP.
I AGREE. FOR NOW, RESEARCH IS AS FAR AS WE GO.
THE POWERS THAT BE ARE KEEPING A TIGHT REIN ON THE ATTACKED MYSTIFICATION POLICE.
WE'RE ONLY GOOD FOR TAKING CARE OF MONSTERS...IS THAT WHAT THEY THINK?
SUPERINTENDENT RALLY'S MANAGED TO KEEP THE DISPUTES QUIET--FOR NOW.

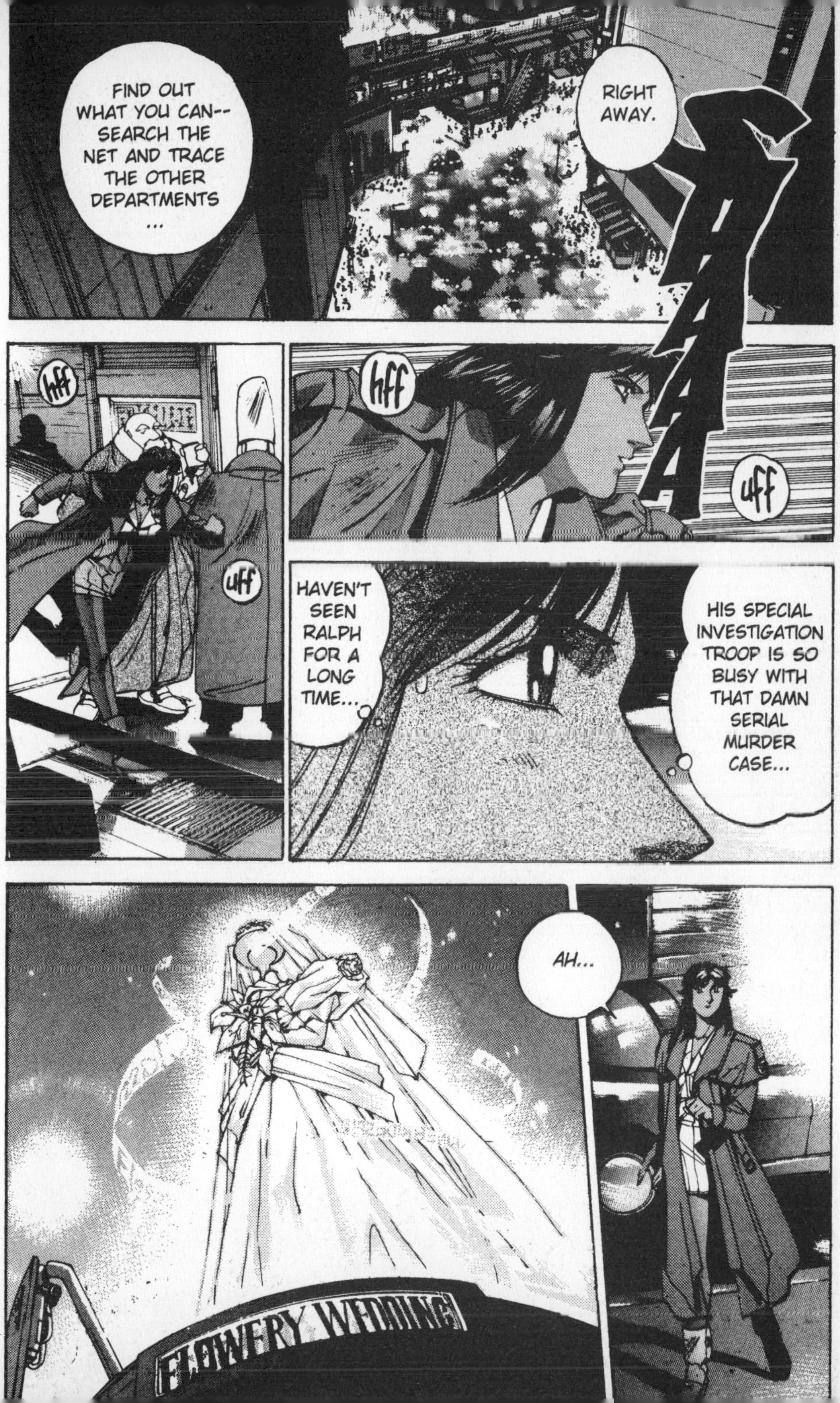
FIND OUT WHAT YOU CAN-- SEARCH THE NET AND TRACE THE OTHER DEPARTMENTS ...
RIGHT AWAY.
hff
uff
hff
uff
HAVEN'T SEEN RALPH FOR A LONG TIME...
HIS SPECIAL INVESTIGATION TROOP IS SO BUSY WITH THAT DAMN SERIAL MURDER CASE...
FLOWERY WEDDING
AH...

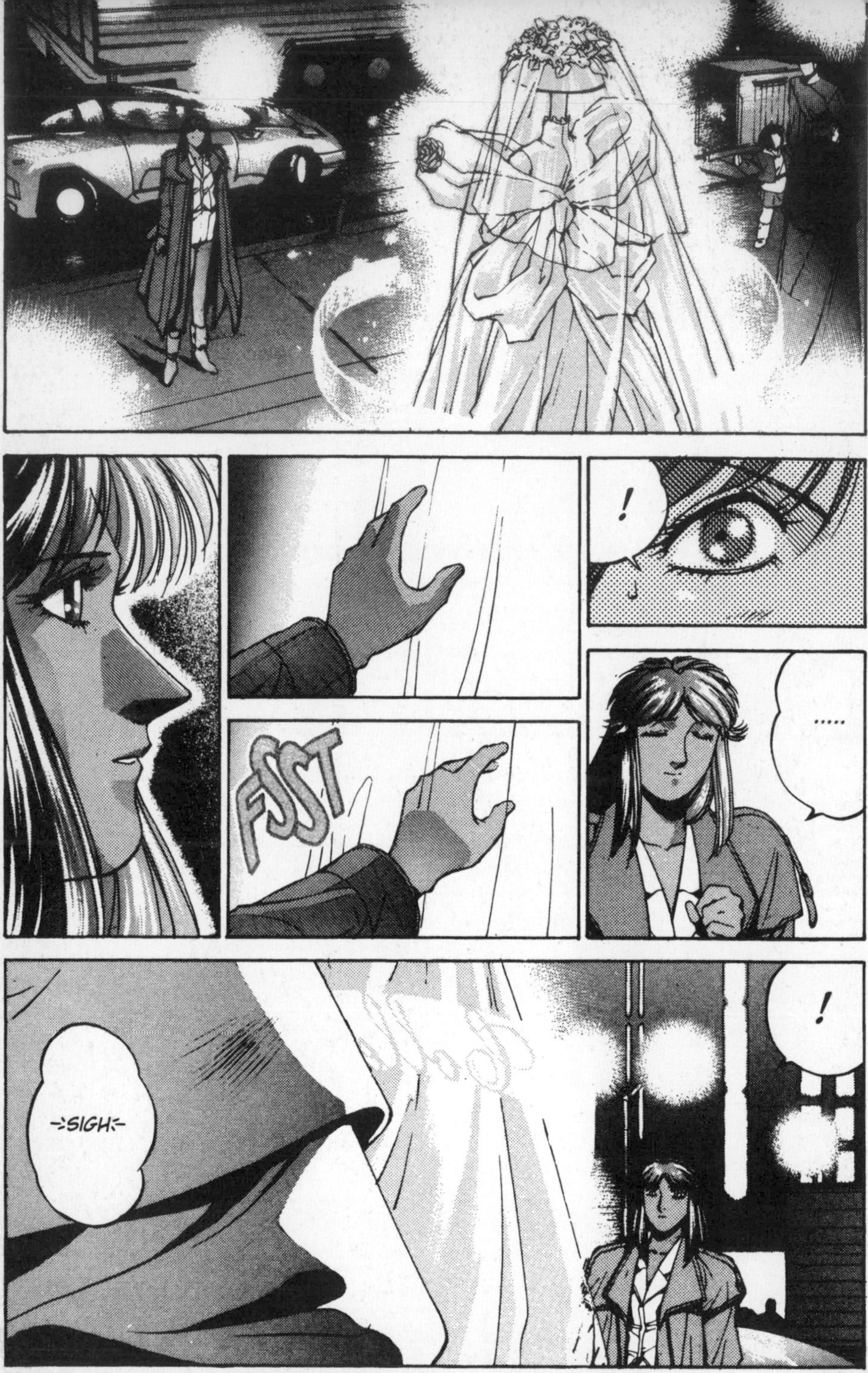
FSST
!
.....
-SIGH-
!

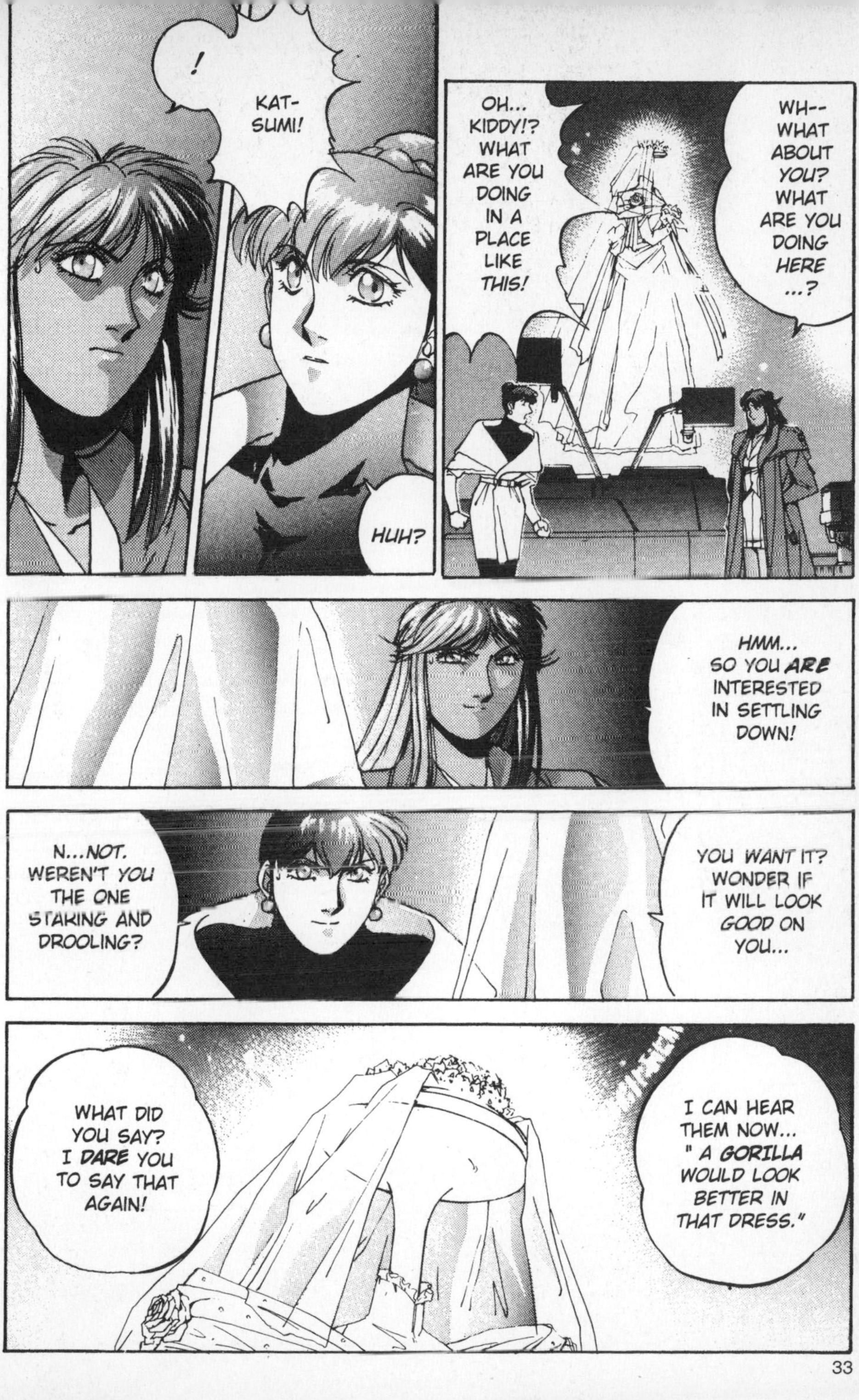
!
KAT-SUMI!
HUH?
OH... KIDDY!? WHAT ARE YOU DOING IN A PLACE LIKE THIS!
WH-- WHAT ABOUT *YOU?* WHAT ARE YOU DOING HERE ...?
HMM... SO YOU ***ARE*** INTERESTED IN SETTLING DOWN!
N...*NOT.* WEREN'T *YOU* THE ONE STARING AND DROOLING?
YOU *WANT* IT? WONDER IF IT WILL LOOK *GOOD* ON YOU...
WHAT DID YOU SAY? I ***DARE*** YOU TO SAY THAT AGAIN!
I CAN HEAR THEM NOW... " A ***GORILLA*** WOULD LOOK BETTER IN THAT DRESS."

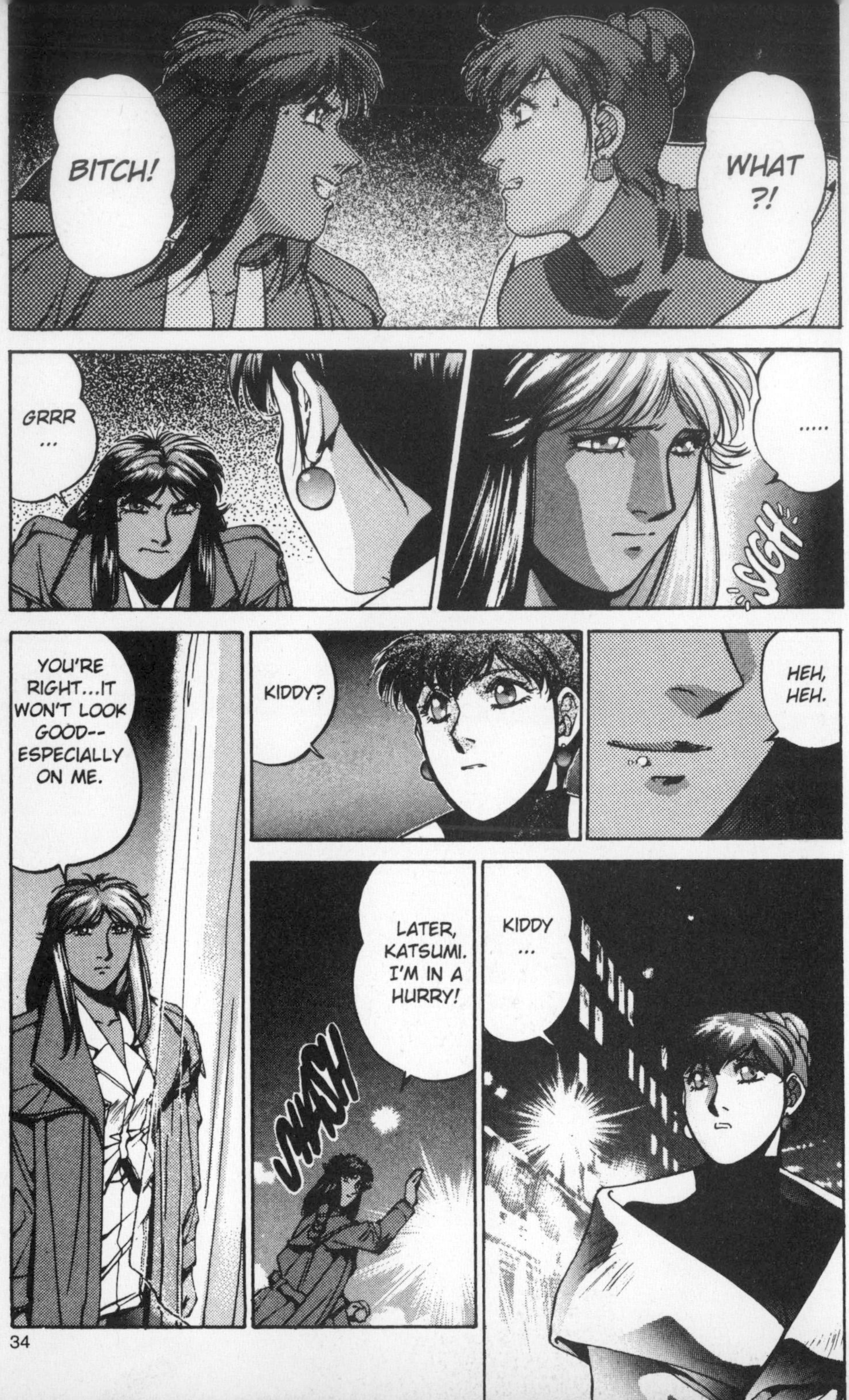
BITCH!
WHAT ?!
GRRR ...
.....
SIGH
YOU'RE RIGHT...IT WON'T LOOK GOOD-- ESPECIALLY ON ME.
KIDDY?
HEH, HEH.
LATER, KATSUMI. I'M IN A HURRY!
WHOOSH
KIDDY ...

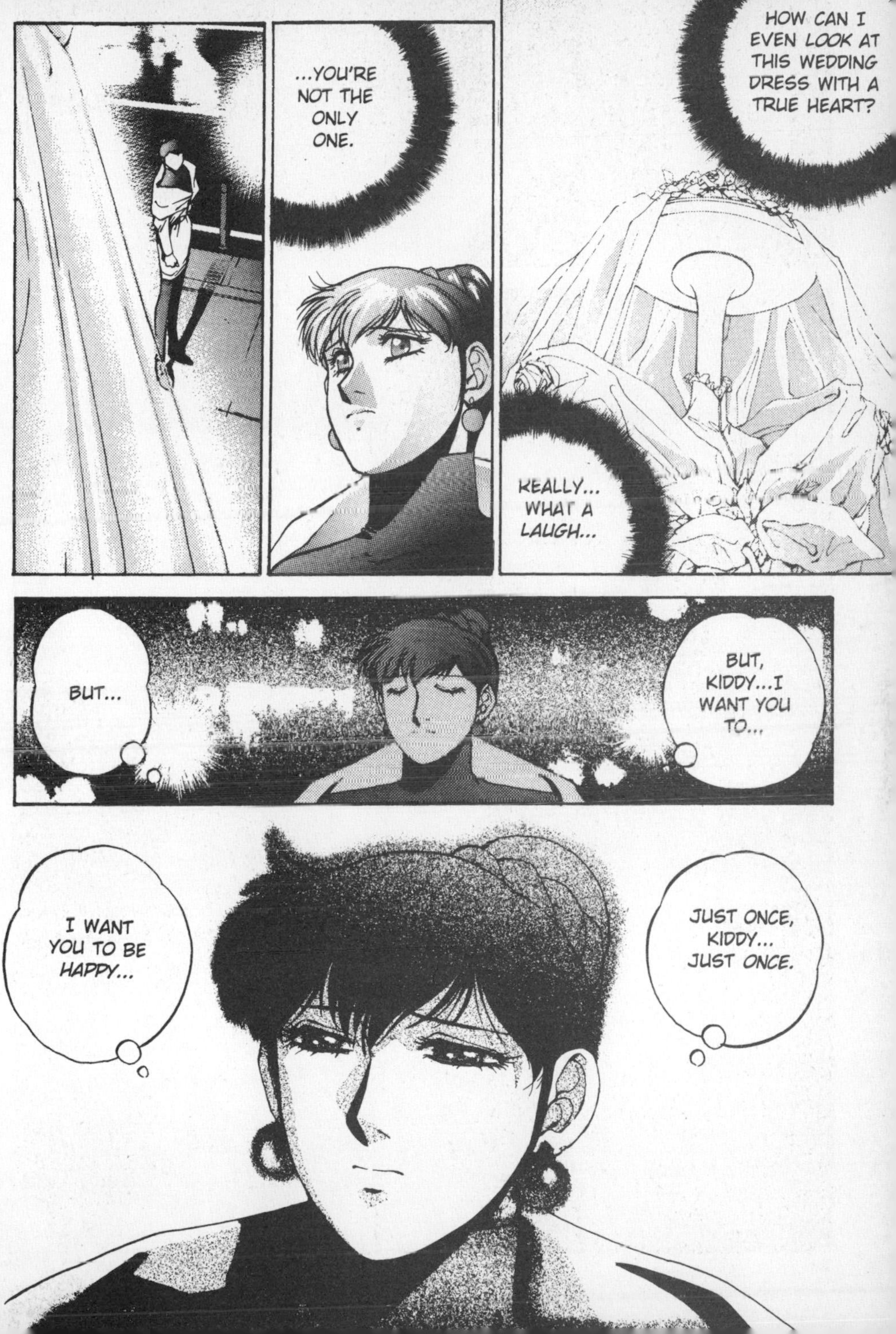
...YOU'RE NOT THE ONLY ONE.
HOW CAN I EVEN LOOK AT THIS WEDDING DRESS WITH A TRUE HEART?
REALLY... WHAT A LAUGH...
BUT...
BUT, KIDDY...I WANT YOU TO...
I WANT YOU TO BE HAPPY...
JUST ONCE, KIDDY... JUST ONCE.

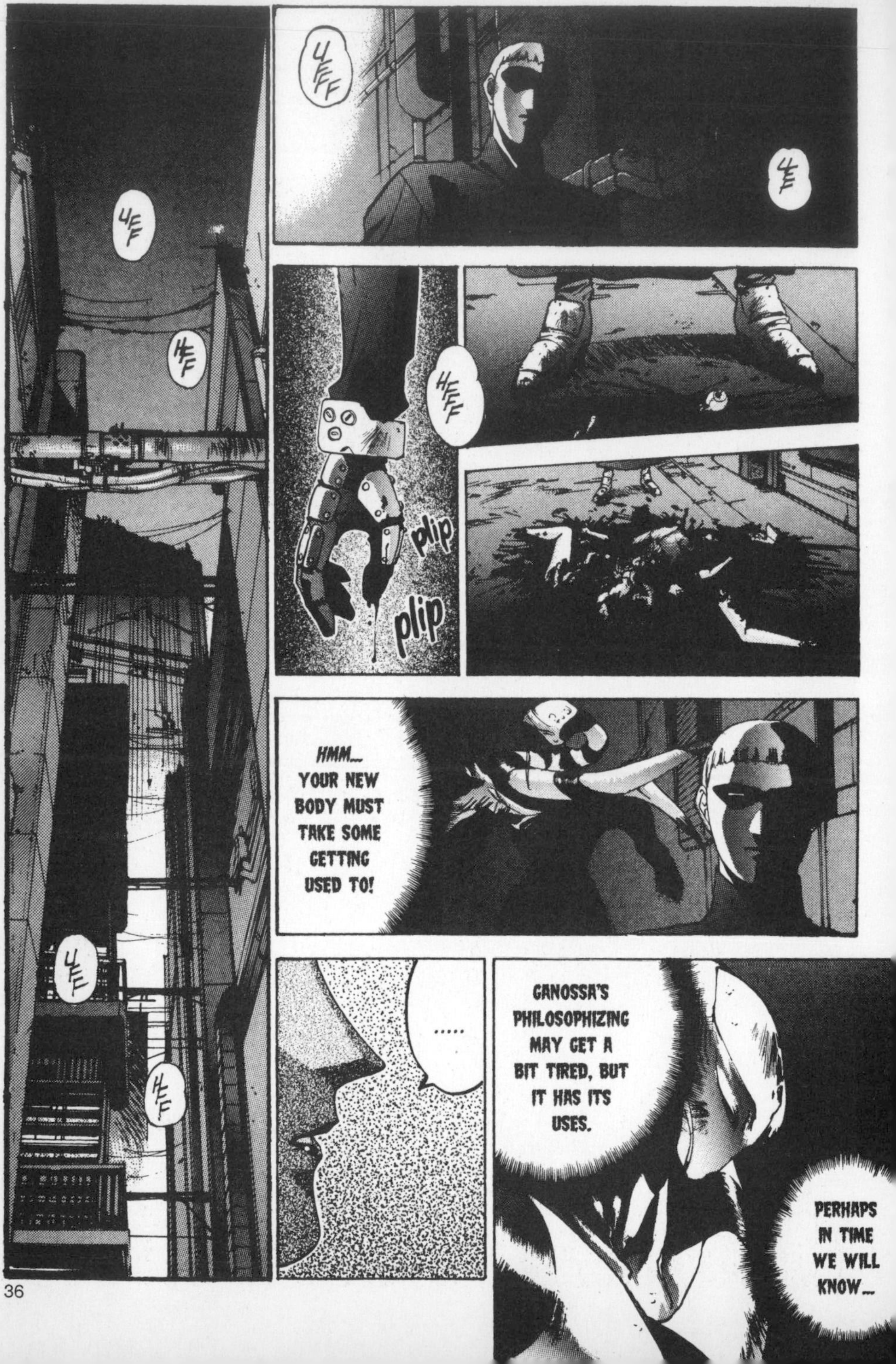

UFF
HEF
UFF
HEF
UFF
UFF
HEFF
plip
plip
HMM... YOUR NEW BODY MUST TAKE SOME GETTING USED TO!
.....
GANOSSA'S PHILOSOPHIZING MAY GET A BIT TIRED, BUT IT HAS ITS USES.
PERHAPS IN TIME WE WILL KNOW...

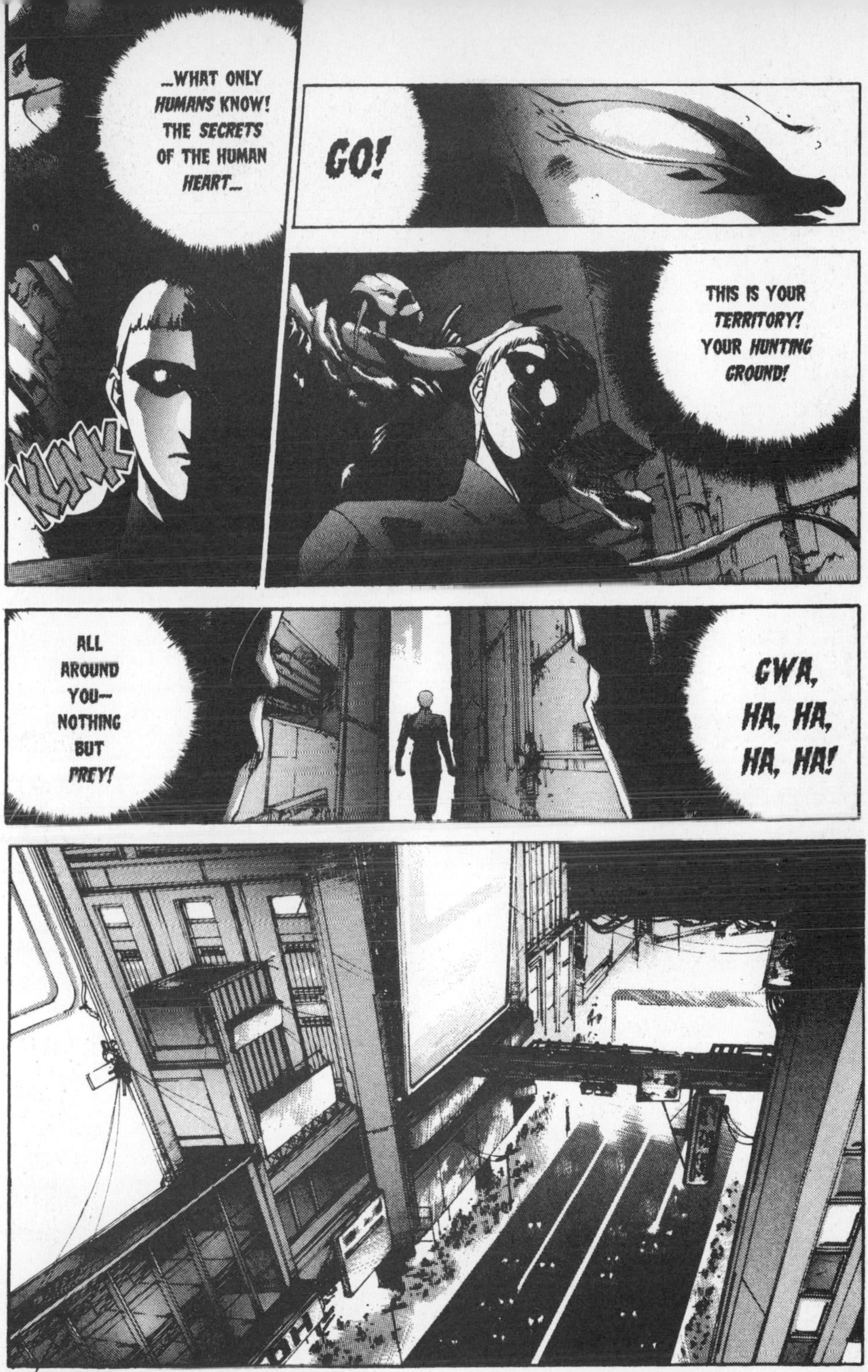
...WHAT ONLY HUMANS KNOW! THE SECRETS OF THE HUMAN HEART...
GO!
KLNK
THIS IS YOUR TERRITORY! YOUR HUNTING GROUND!
ALL AROUND YOU— NOTHING BUT PREY!
GWA, HA, HA, HA, HA!

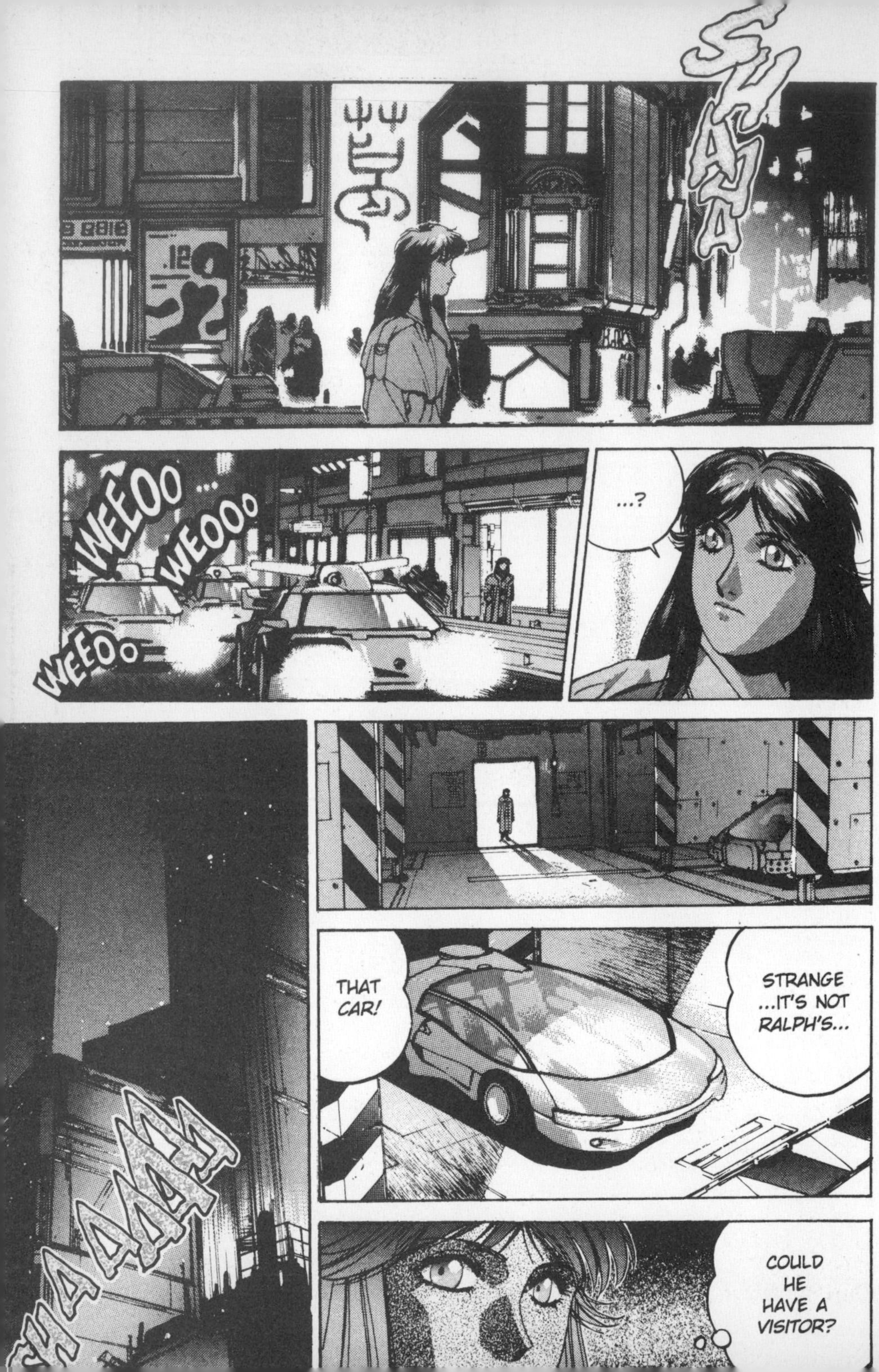
SHAA
WEEOO ...
WEOOo
WEEOo
...?
THAT CAR!
STRANGE ...IT'S NOT RALPH'S...
COULD HE HAVE A VISITOR?

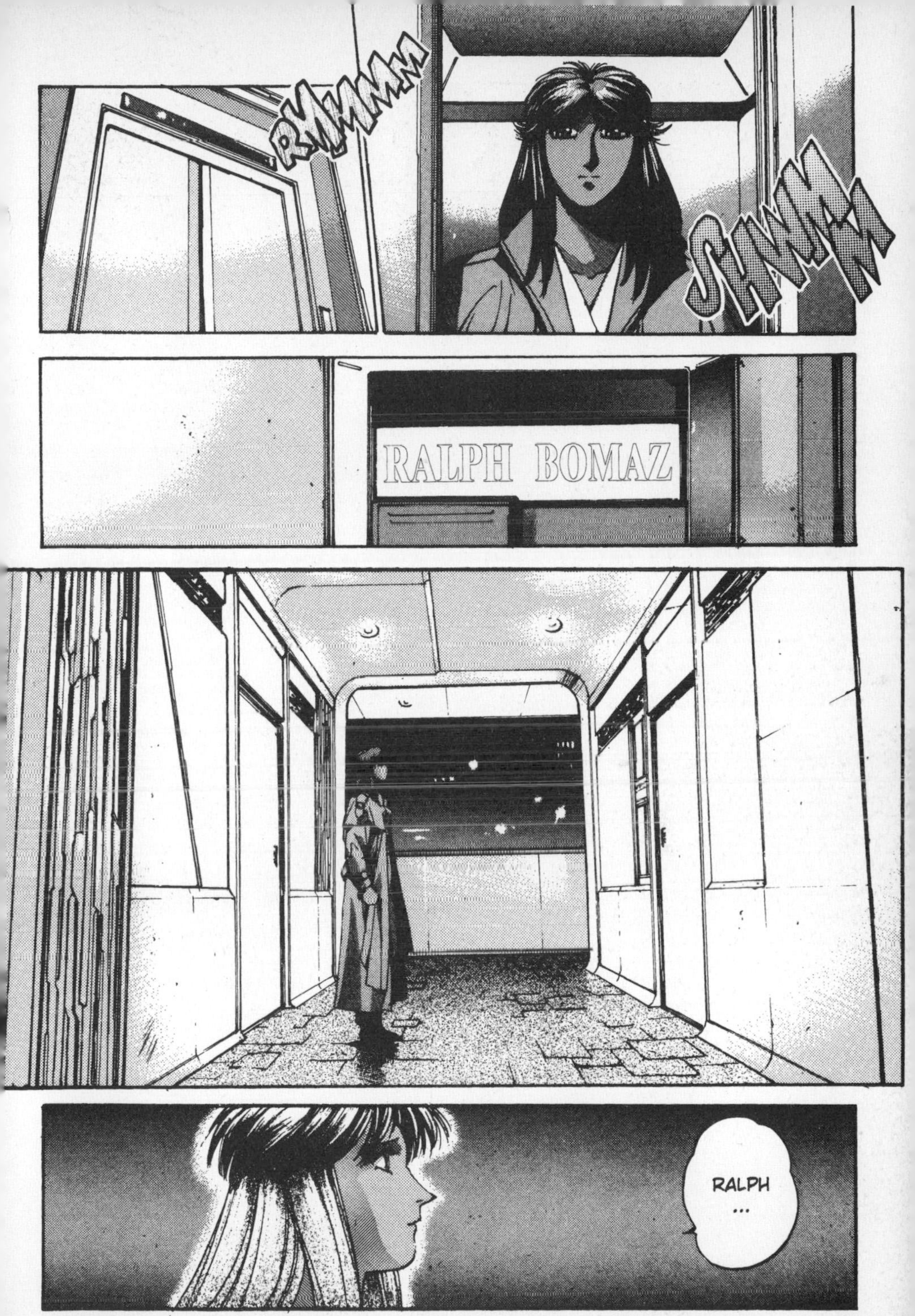
RALPH BOMAZ
RALPH ...

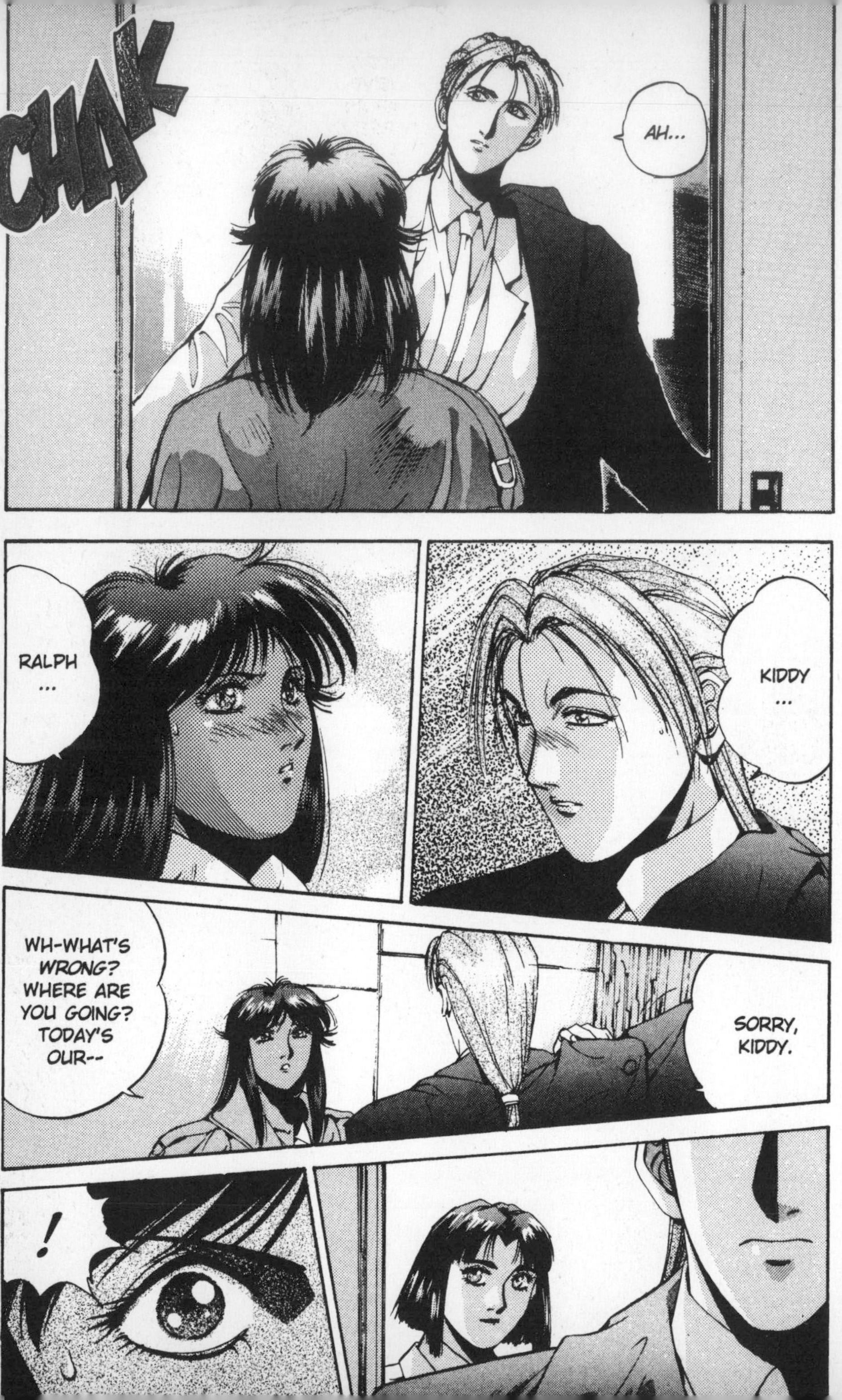
CHAK
AH...
RALPH ...
KIDDY ...
WH-WHAT'S WRONG? WHERE ARE YOU GOING? TODAY'S OUR--
SORRY, KIDDY.
!

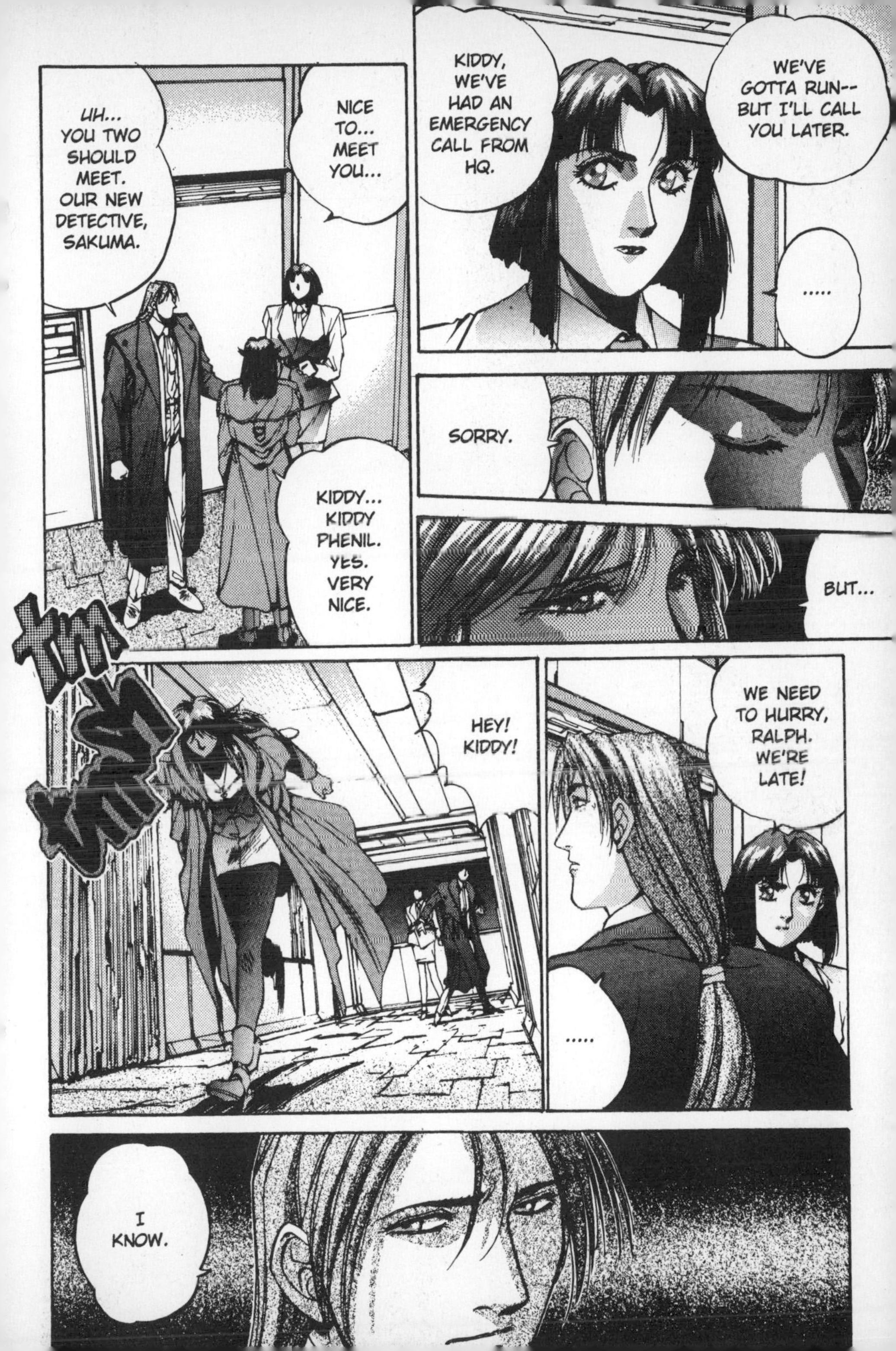
UH... YOU TWO SHOULD MEET. OUR NEW DETECTIVE, SAKUMA.
NICE TO... MEET YOU...
KIDDY... KIDDY PHENIL. YES. VERY NICE.
KIDDY, WE'VE HAD AN EMERGENCY CALL FROM HQ.
WE'VE GOTTA RUN-- BUT I'LL CALL YOU LATER.
.....
SORRY.
BUT...
HEY! KIDDY!
WE NEED TO HURRY, RALPH. WE'RE LATE!
.....
I KNOW.

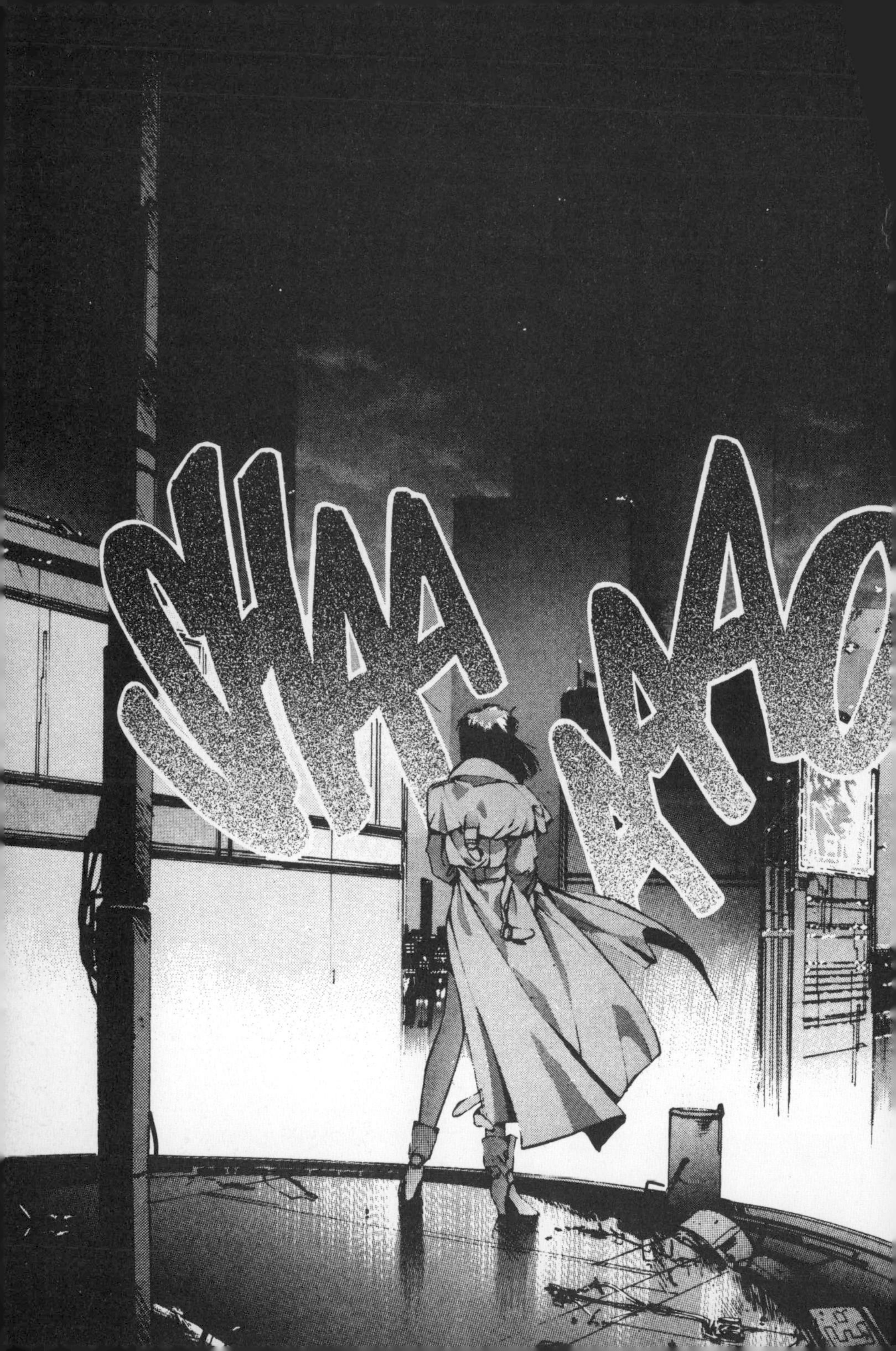
CHA KA

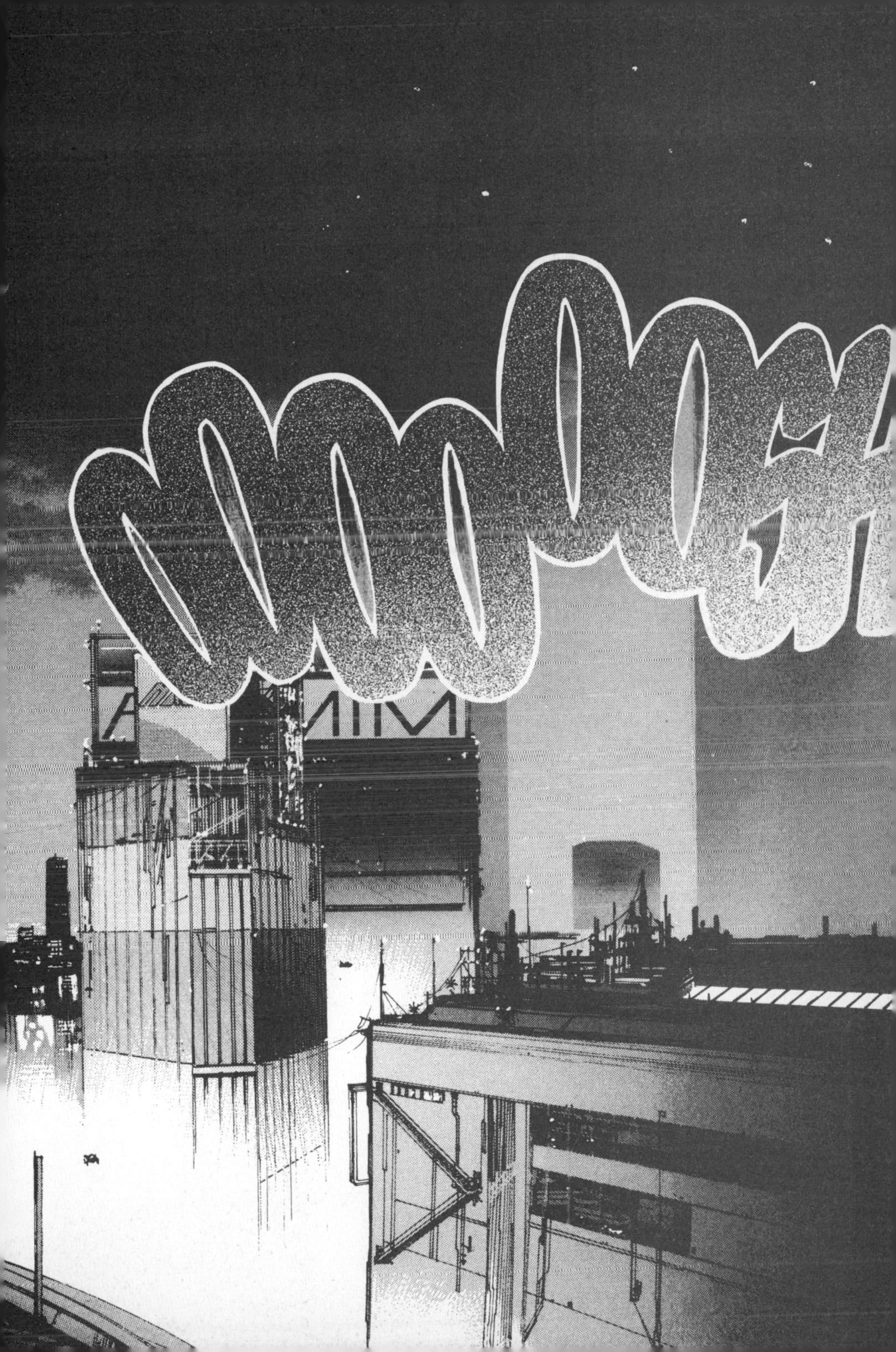

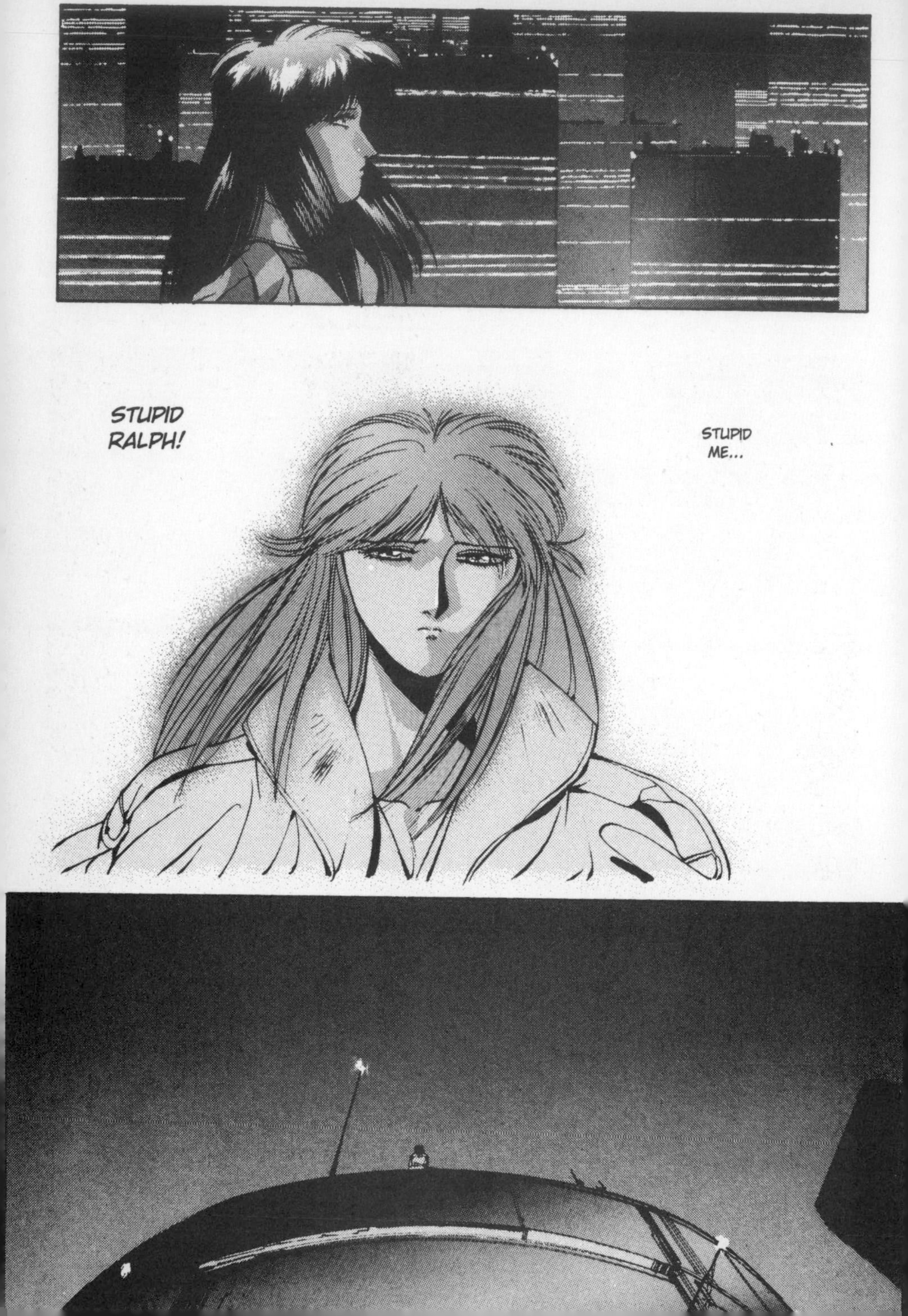
STUPID RALPH!
STUPID ME...

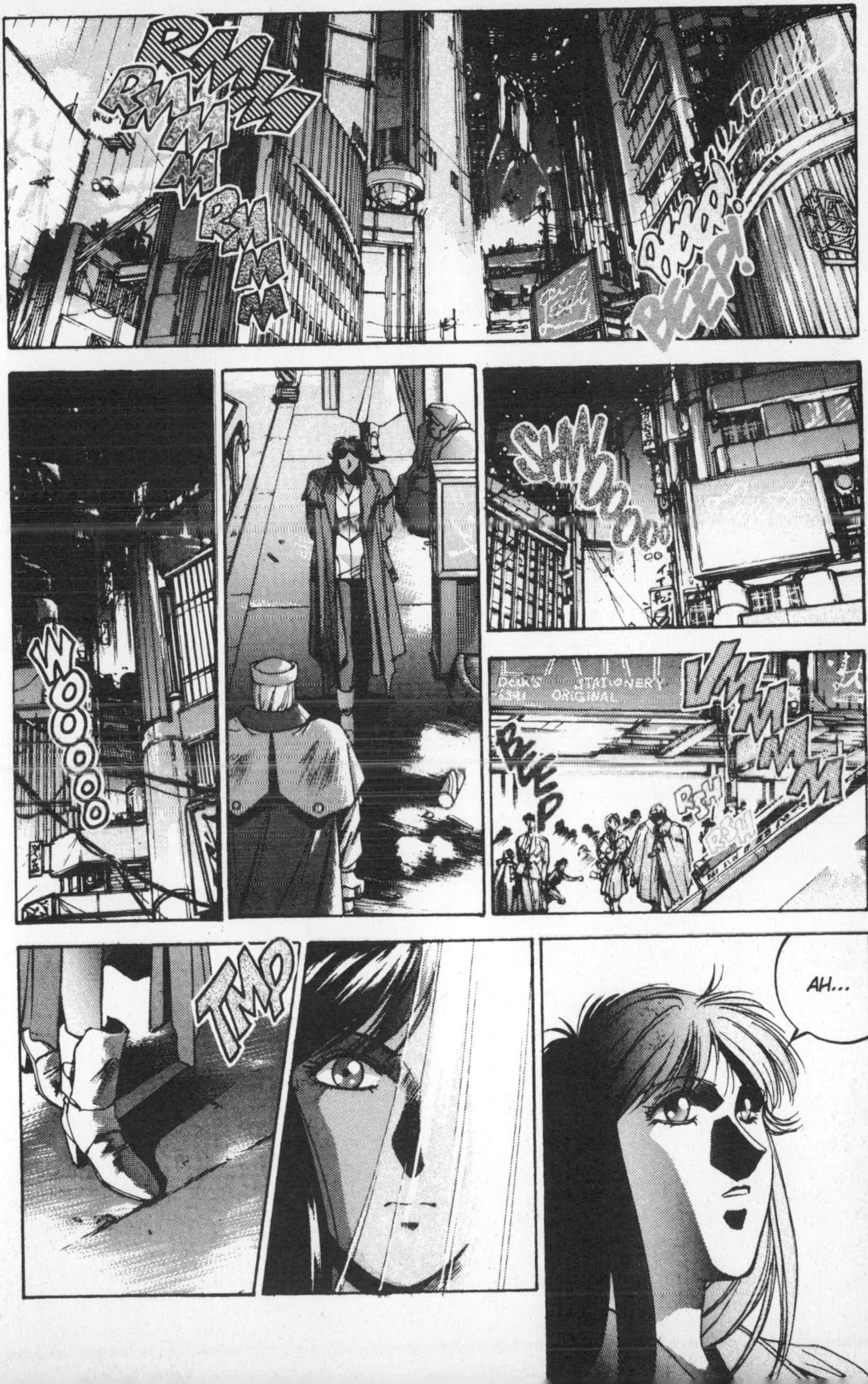
BEEP!
WOOOOOO
STATIONERY
ORIGINAL
BLEEP
TMP
AH...

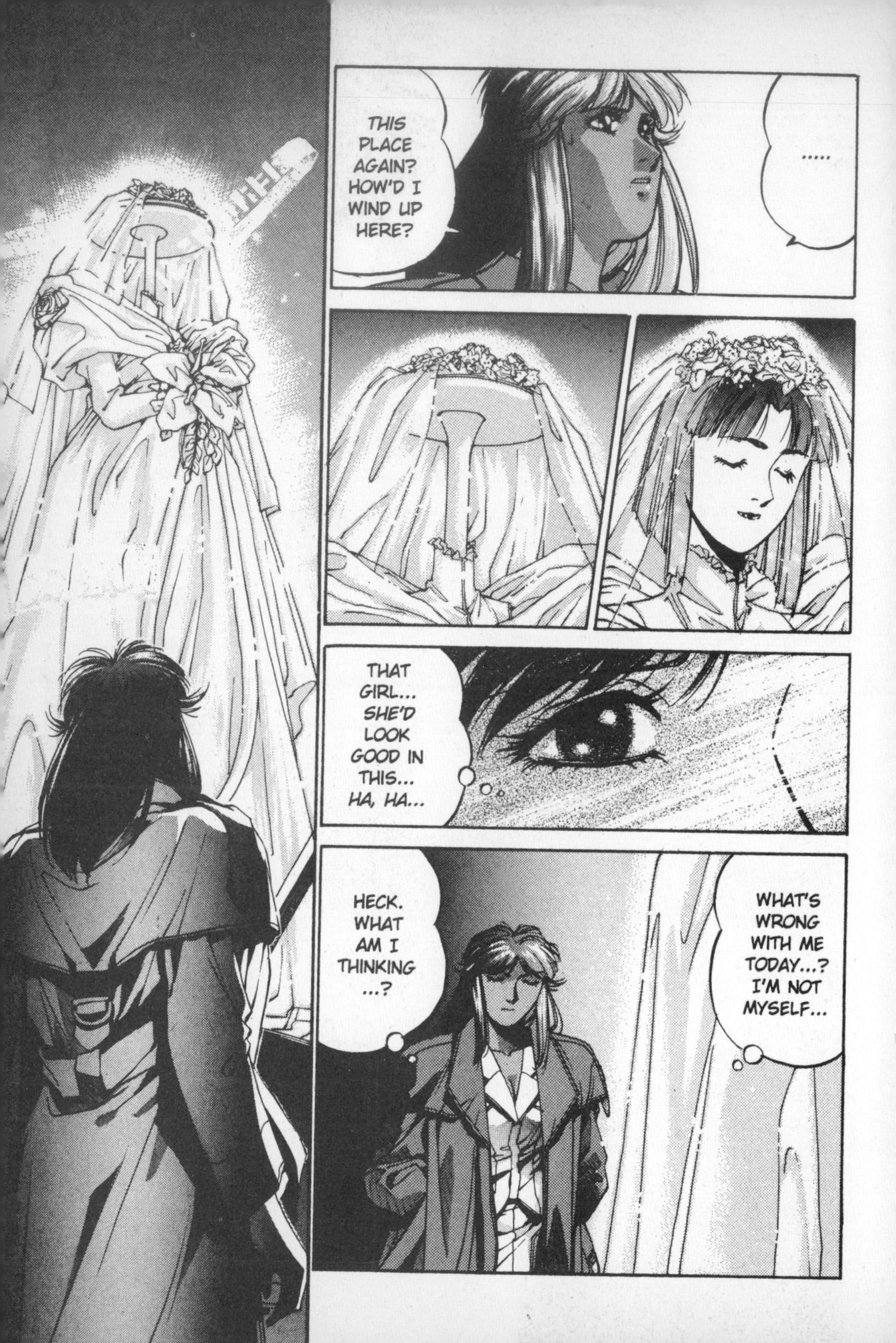
THIS PLACE AGAIN? HOW'D I WIND UP HERE?
.....
THAT GIRL... SHE'D LOOK GOOD IN THIS... HA, HA...
HECK. WHAT AM I THINKING ...?
WHAT'S WRONG WITH ME TODAY...? I'M NOT MYSELF...

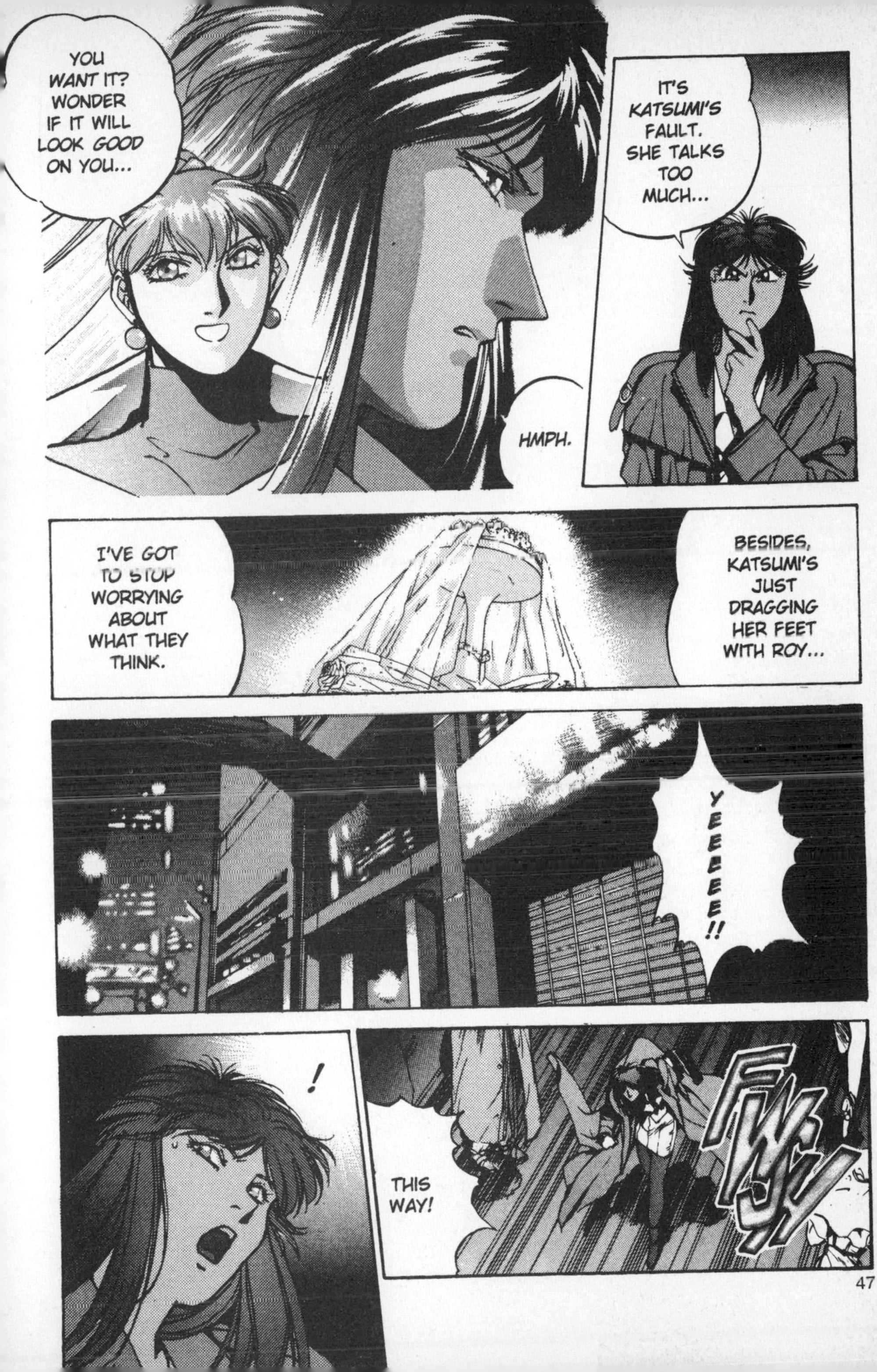
YOU WANT IT? WONDER IF IT WILL LOOK GOOD ON YOU...
HMPH.
IT'S KATSUMI'S FAULT. SHE TALKS TOO MUCH...
I'VE GOT TO STOP WORRYING ABOUT WHAT THEY THINK.
BESIDES, KATSUMI'S JUST DRAGGING HER FEET WITH ROY...
YEEEEEE!!
!
THIS WAY!
FWSSH

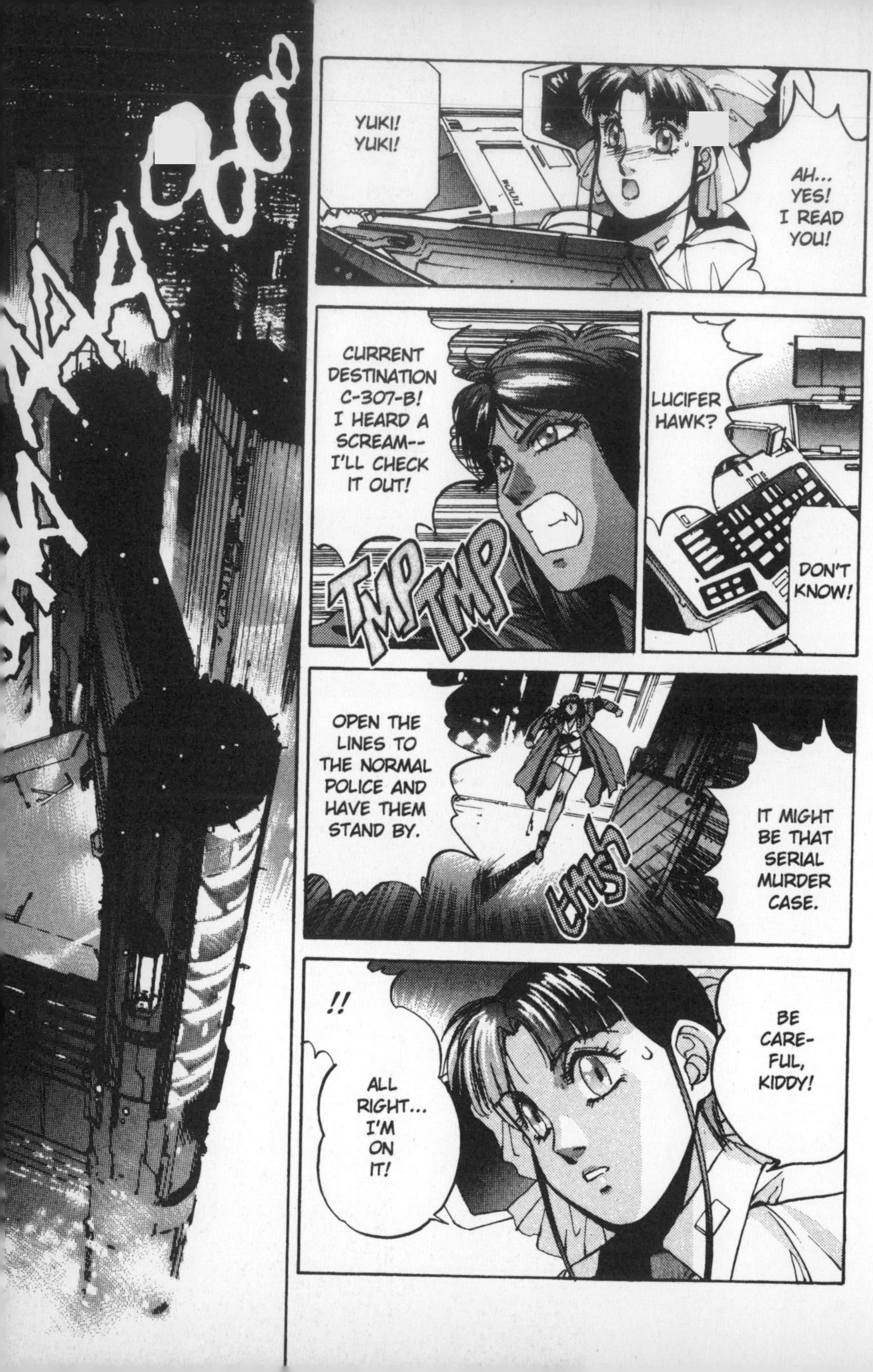
YUKI! YUKI!
AH... YES! I READ YOU!
CURRENT DESTINATION C-307-B! I HEARD A SCREAM--I'LL CHECK IT OUT!
TMP TMP
LUCIFER HAWK?
DON'T KNOW!
OPEN THE LINES TO THE NORMAL POLICE AND HAVE THEM STAND BY.
IT MIGHT BE THAT SERIAL MURDER CASE.
!!
BE CARE-FUL, KIDDY!
ALL RIGHT... I'M ON IT!

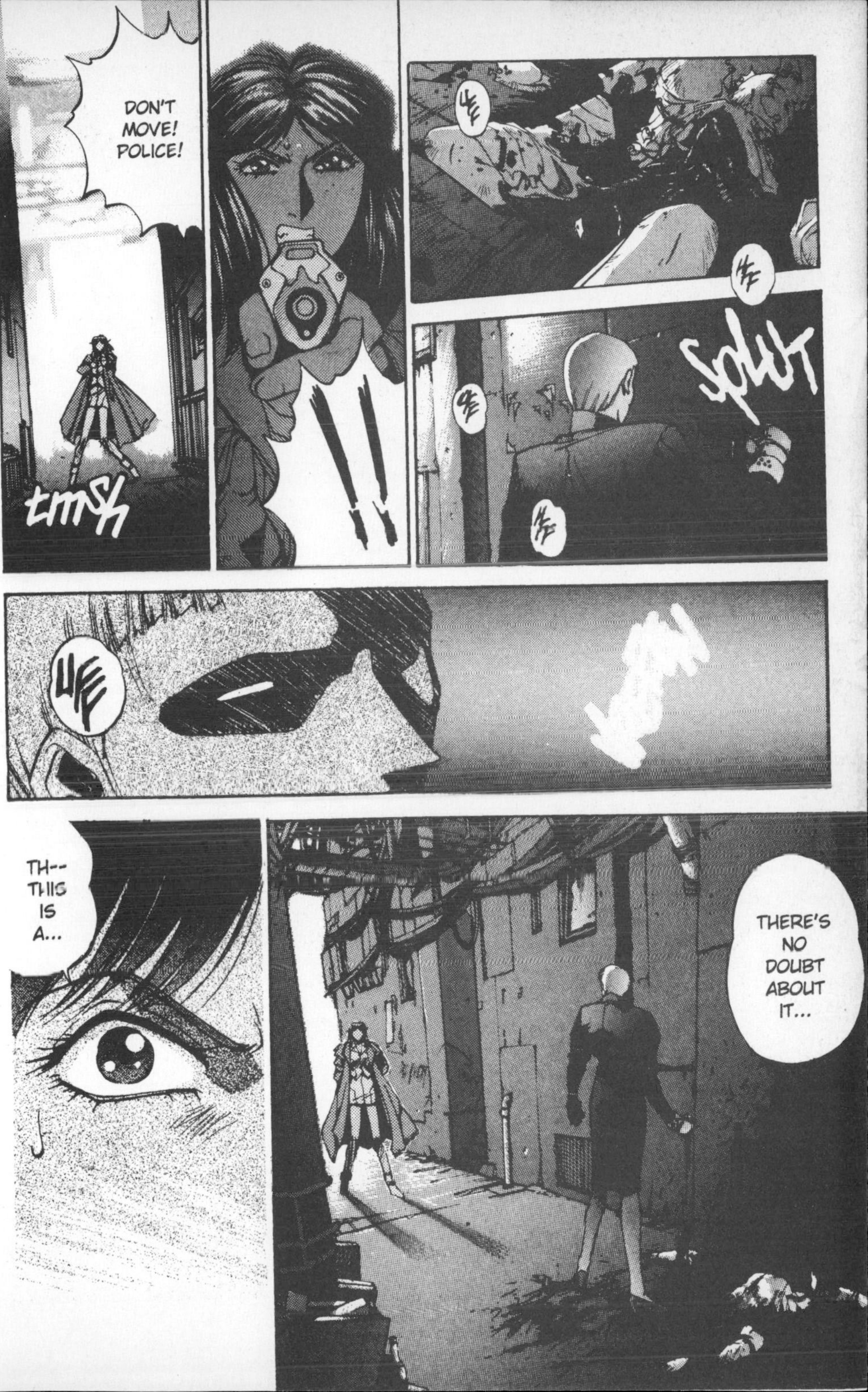
DON'T MOVE! POLICE!
tmsh
splut
UFF
TH-- THIS IS A...
THERE'S NO DOUBT ABOUT IT...

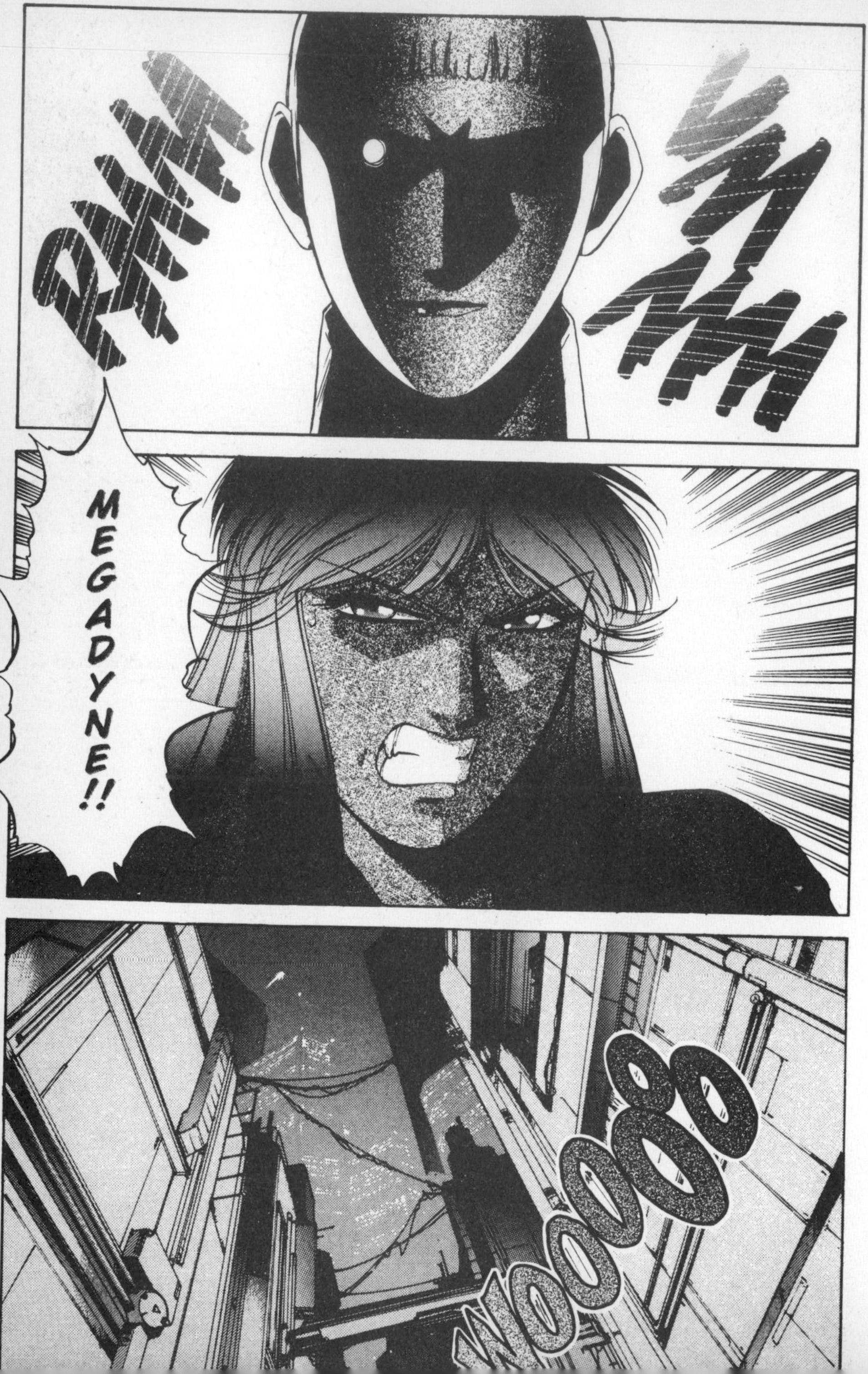
MEGADYNE!!

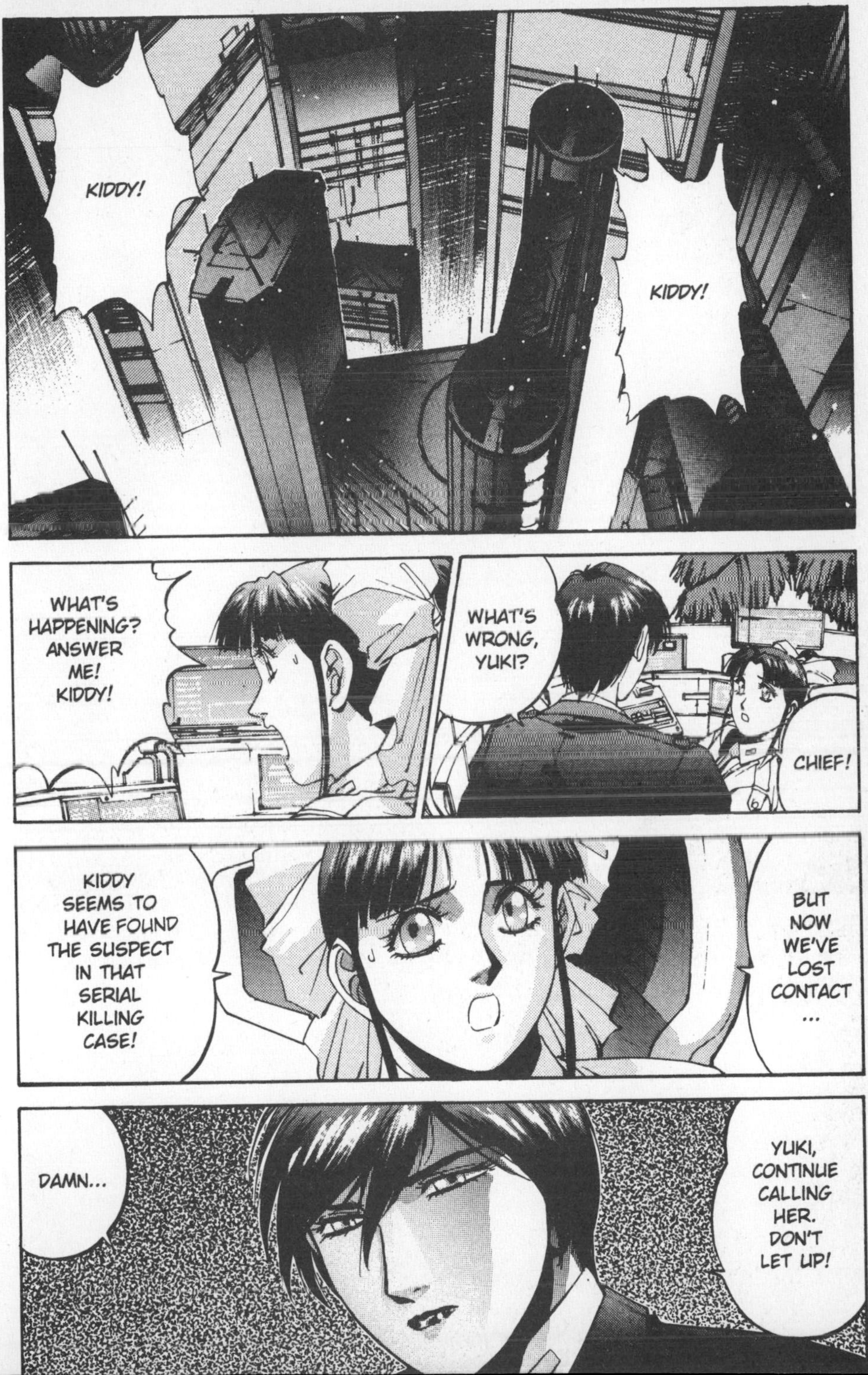
KIDDY!
KIDDY!
WHAT'S HAPPENING? ANSWER ME! KIDDY!
WHAT'S WRONG, YUKI?
CHIEF!
KIDDY SEEMS TO HAVE FOUND THE SUSPECT IN THAT SERIAL KILLING CASE!
BUT NOW WE'VE LOST CONTACT ...
DAMN...
YUKI, CONTINUE CALLING HER. DON'T LET UP!

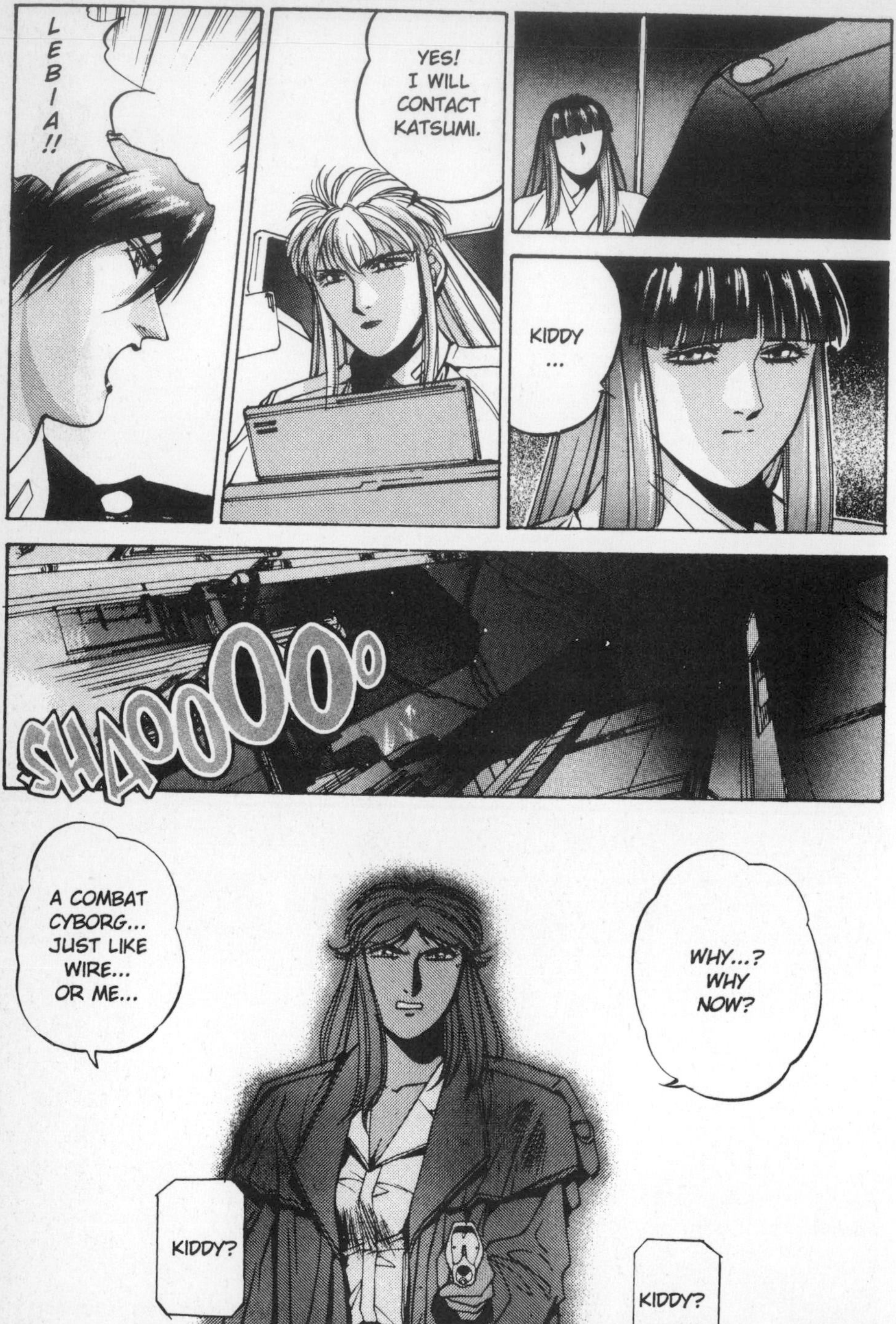
LEBIA!!
YES! I WILL CONTACT KATSUMI.
KIDDY ...
SHAOOOOO
A COMBAT CYBORG... JUST LIKE WIRE... OR ME...
WHY...? WHY NOW?
KIDDY?
KIDDY?

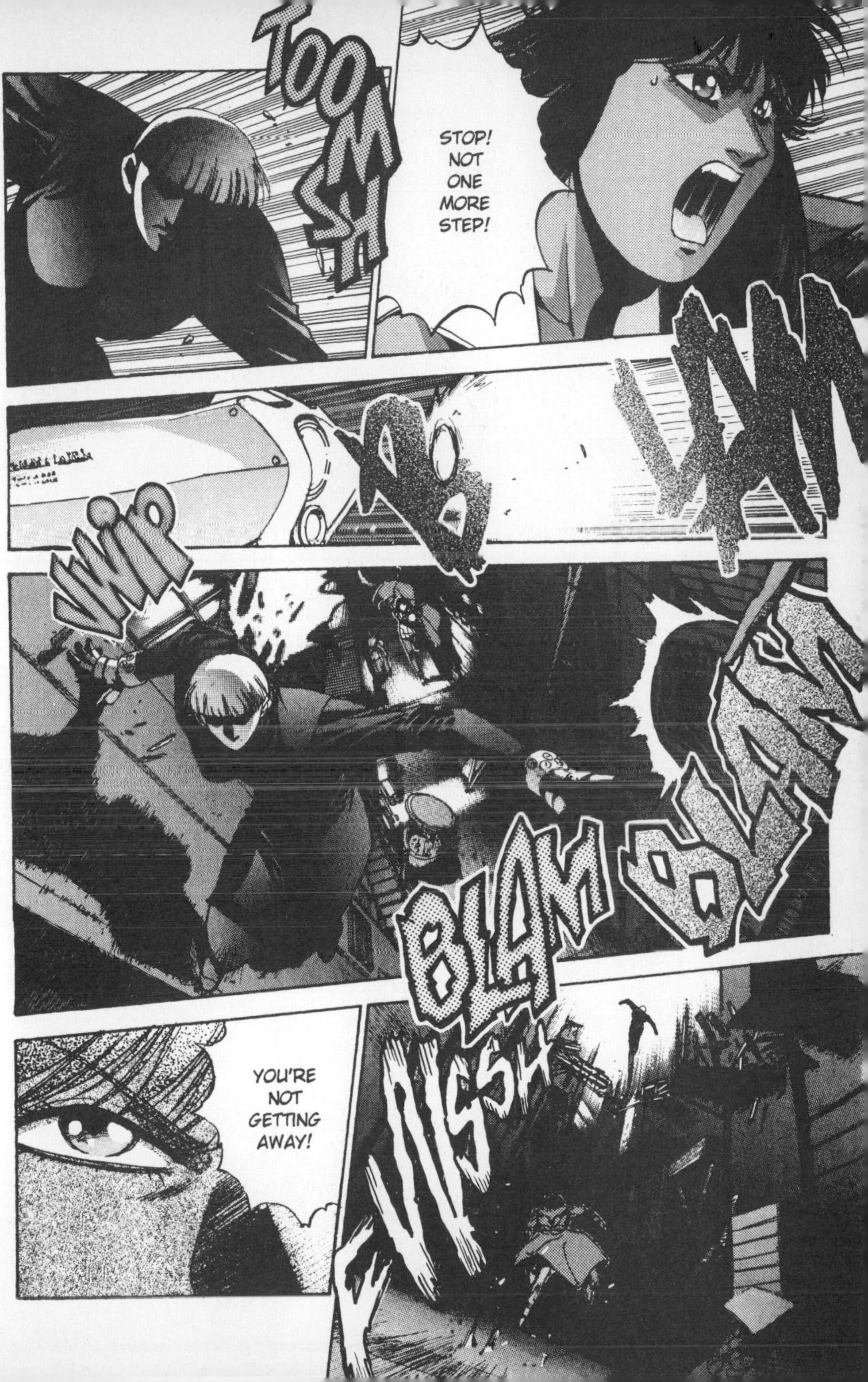
TOOMSH
STOP! NOT ONE MORE STEP!
BLAM BLAM
YOU'RE NOT GETTING AWAY!

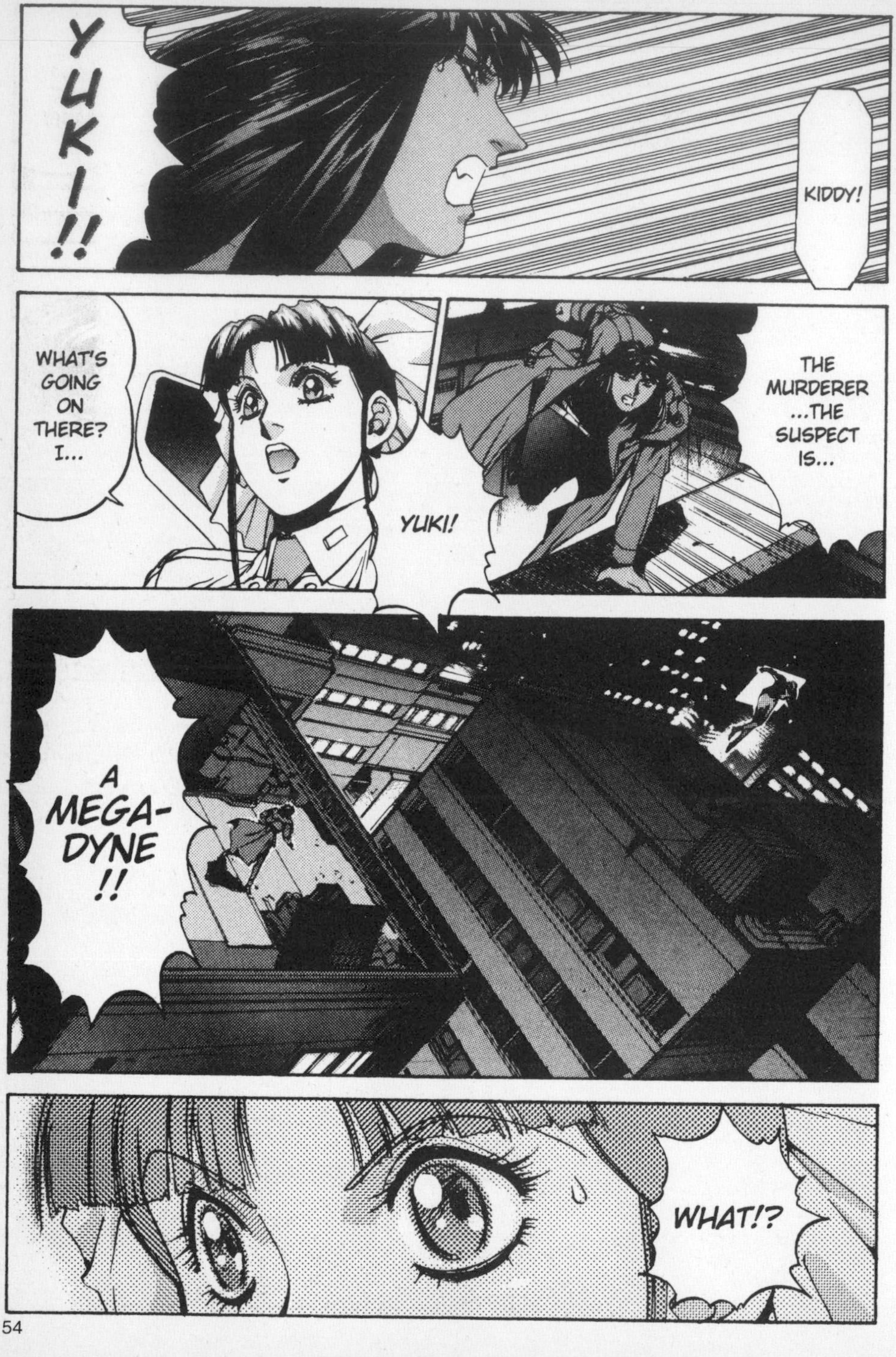
YUKI!!
KIDDY!
WHAT'S GOING ON THERE? I...
YUKI!
THE MURDERER ...THE SUSPECT IS...
A MEGA-DYNE!!
WHAT!?

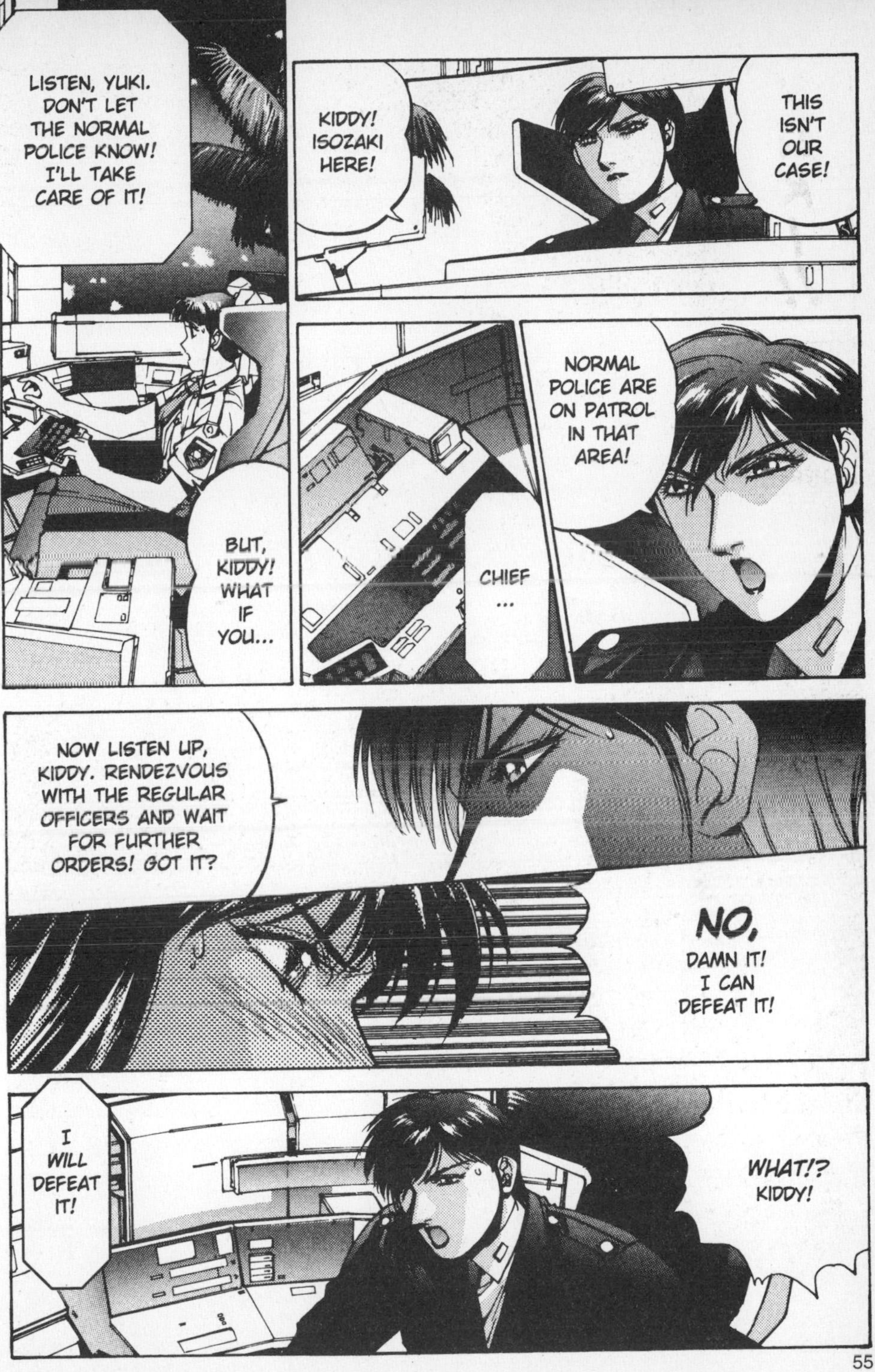
LISTEN, YUKI. DON'T LET THE NORMAL POLICE KNOW! I'LL TAKE CARE OF IT!
KIDDY! ISOZAKI HERE!
THIS ISN'T OUR CASE!
BUT, KIDDY! WHAT IF YOU...
CHIEF ...
NORMAL POLICE ARE ON PATROL IN THAT AREA!
NOW LISTEN UP, KIDDY. RENDEZVOUS WITH THE REGULAR OFFICERS AND WAIT FOR FURTHER ORDERS! GOT IT?
NO, DAMN IT! I CAN DEFEAT IT!
I WILL DEFEAT IT!
WHAT!? KIDDY!

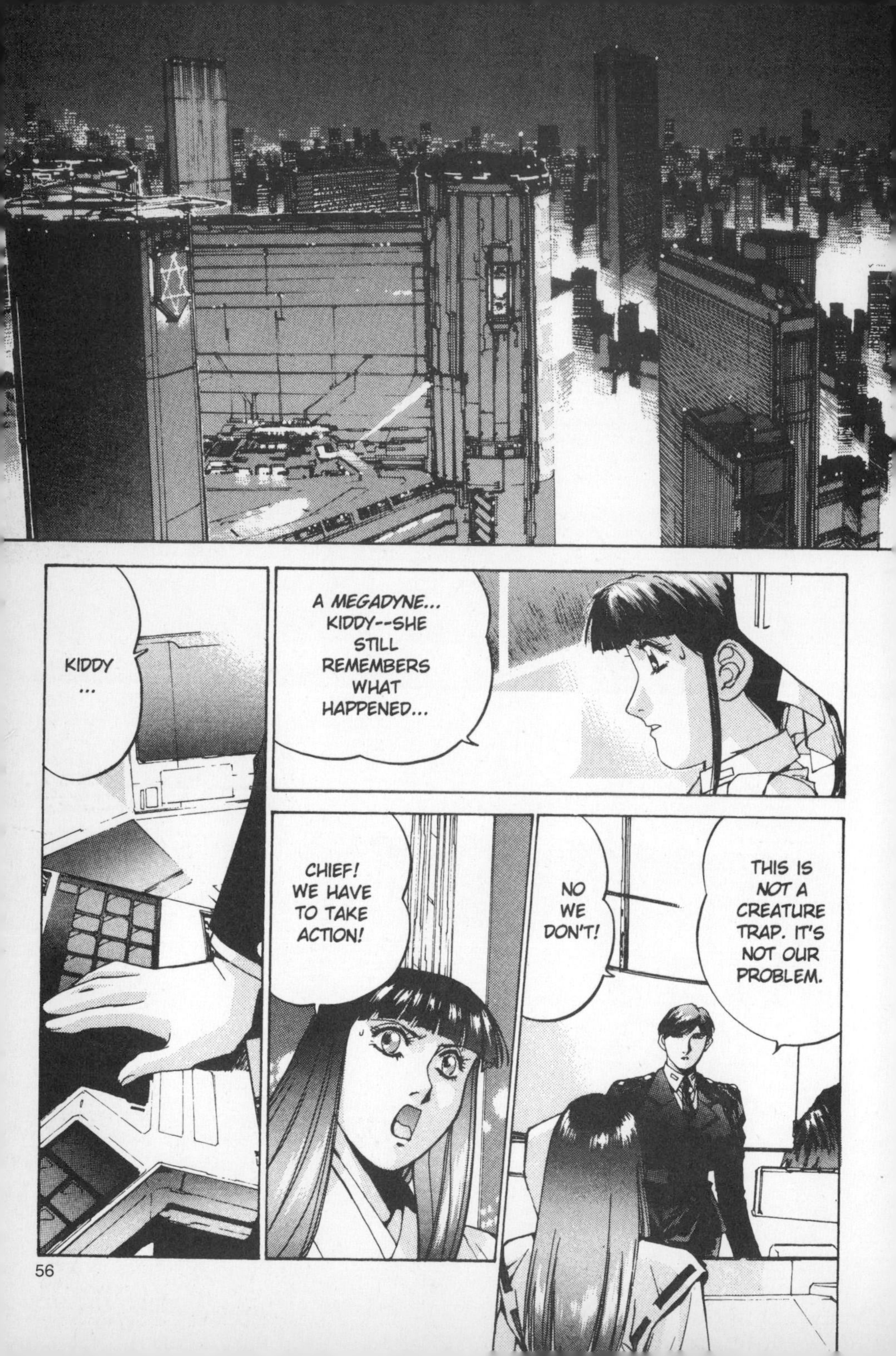

KIDDY ...
A MEGADYNE... KIDDY--SHE STILL REMEMBERS WHAT HAPPENED...
CHIEF! WE HAVE TO TAKE ACTION!
NO WE DON'T!
THIS IS NOT A CREATURE TRAP. IT'S NOT OUR PROBLEM.

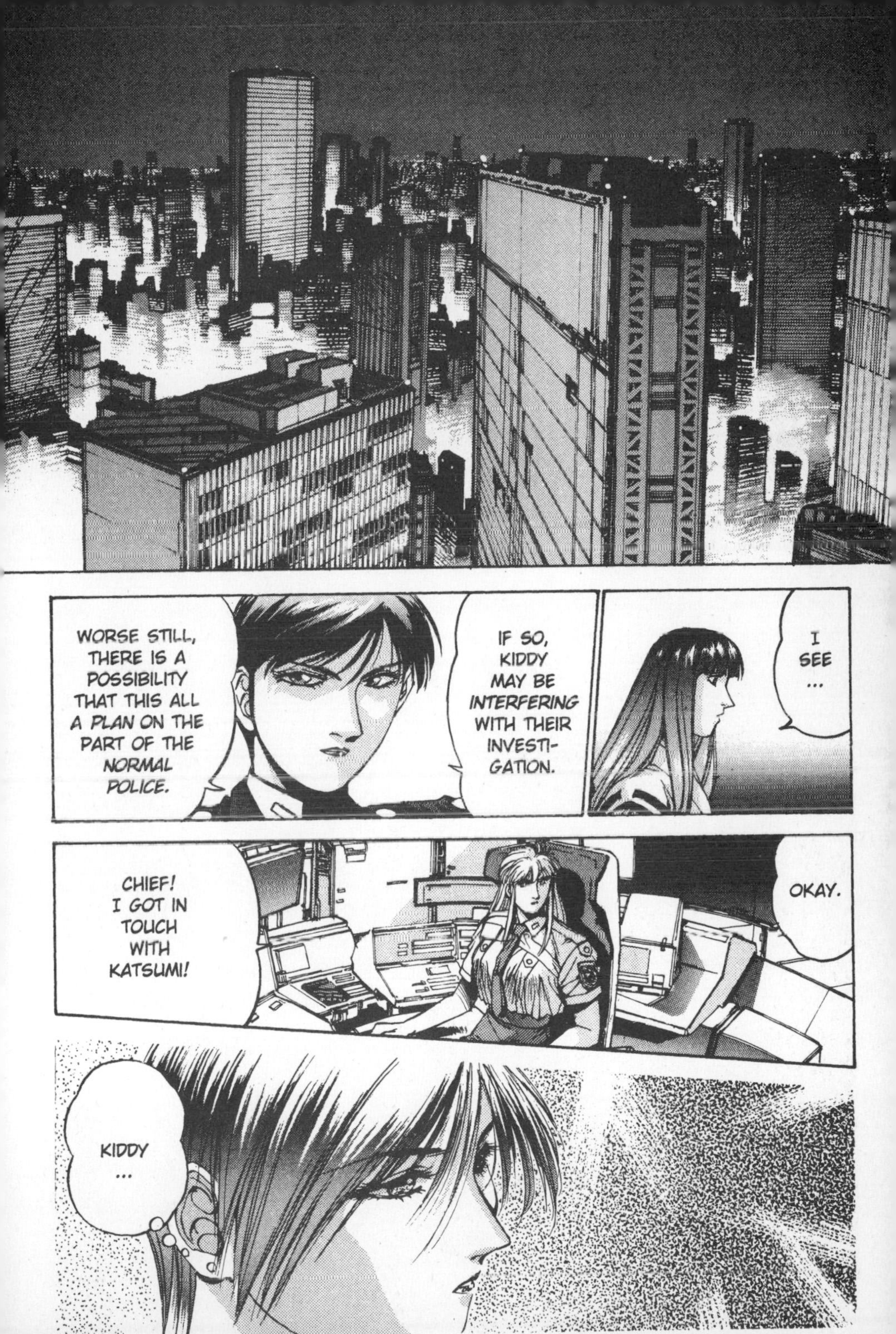
WORSE STILL, THERE IS A POSSIBILITY THAT THIS ALL A PLAN ON THE PART OF THE NORMAL POLICE.
IF SO, KIDDY MAY BE INTERFERING WITH THEIR INVESTI-GATION.
I SEE ...
CHIEF! I GOT IN TOUCH WITH KATSUMI!
OKAY.
KIDDY ...

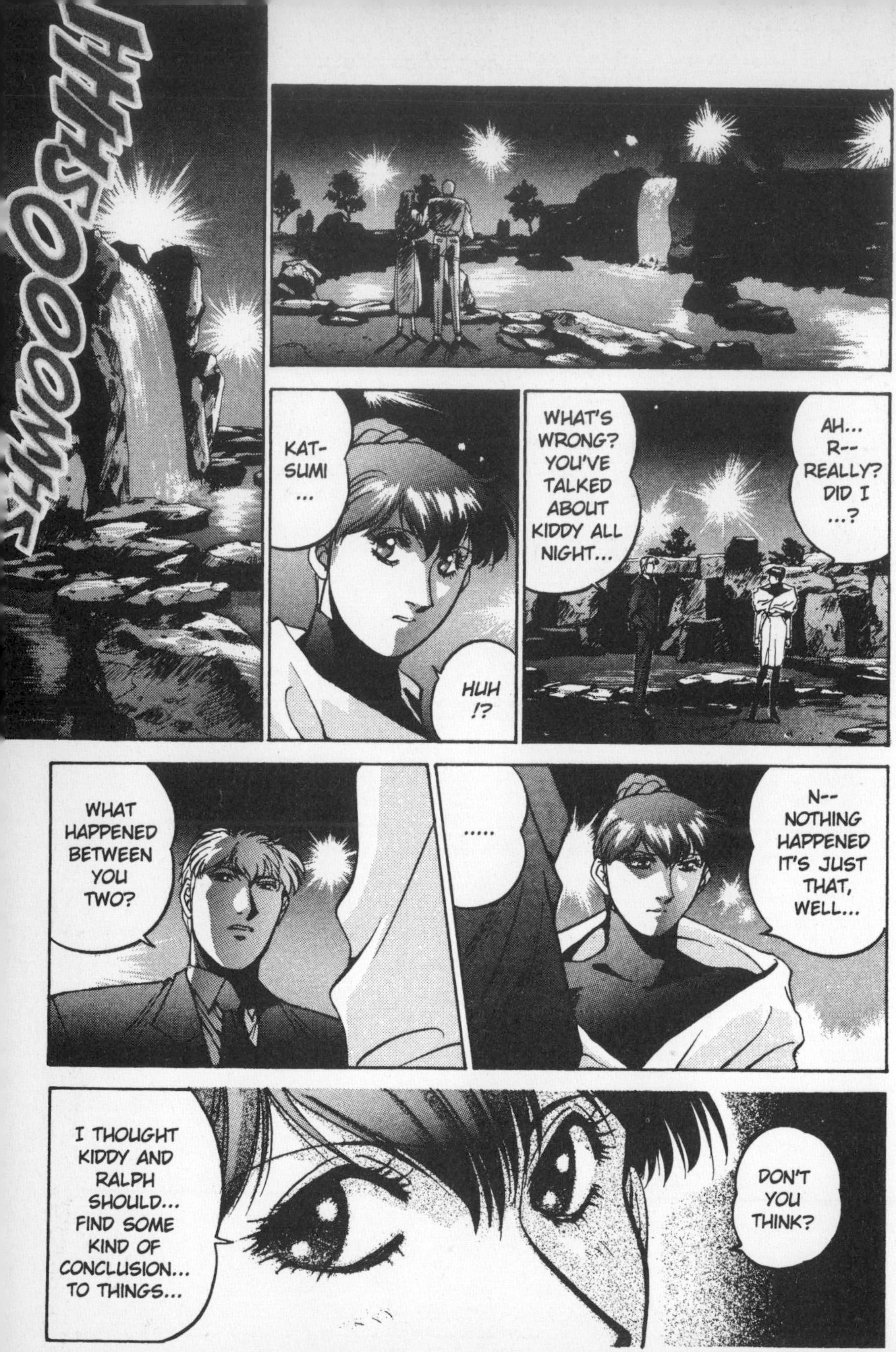
FHHSOOOMH
KAT-
SUMI
...
HUH
!?
WHAT'S WRONG? YOU'VE TALKED ABOUT KIDDY ALL NIGHT...
AH... R-- REALLY? DID I ...?
WHAT HAPPENED BETWEEN YOU TWO?
.....
N-- NOTHING HAPPENED IT'S JUST THAT, WELL...
I THOUGHT KIDDY AND RALPH SHOULD... FIND SOME KIND OF CONCLUSION... TO THINGS...
DON'T YOU THINK?

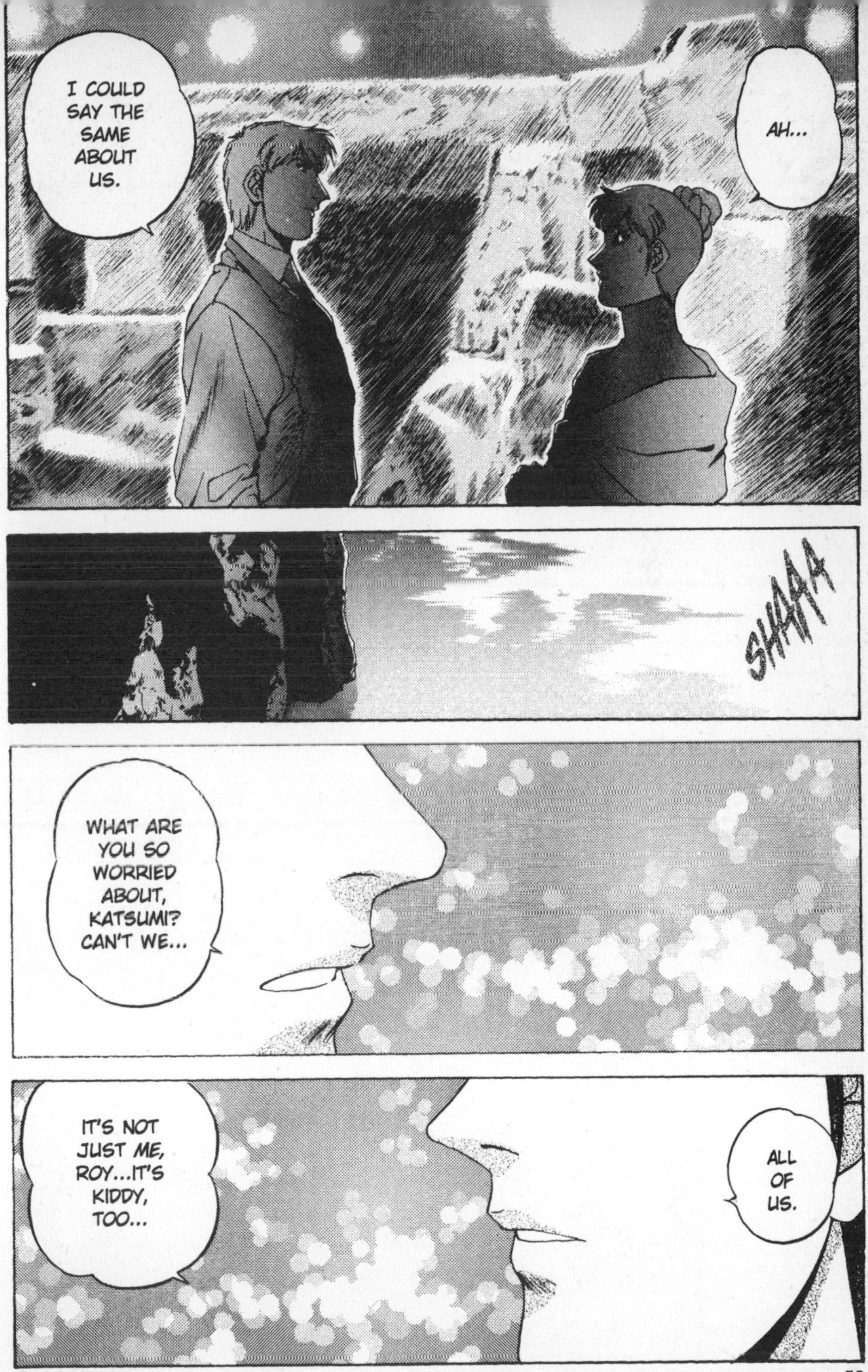
I COULD SAY THE SAME ABOUT US.
AH...
SHAAA
WHAT ARE YOU SO WORRIED ABOUT, KATSUMI? CAN'T WE...
IT'S NOT JUST ME, ROY...IT'S KIDDY, TOO...
ALL OF US.

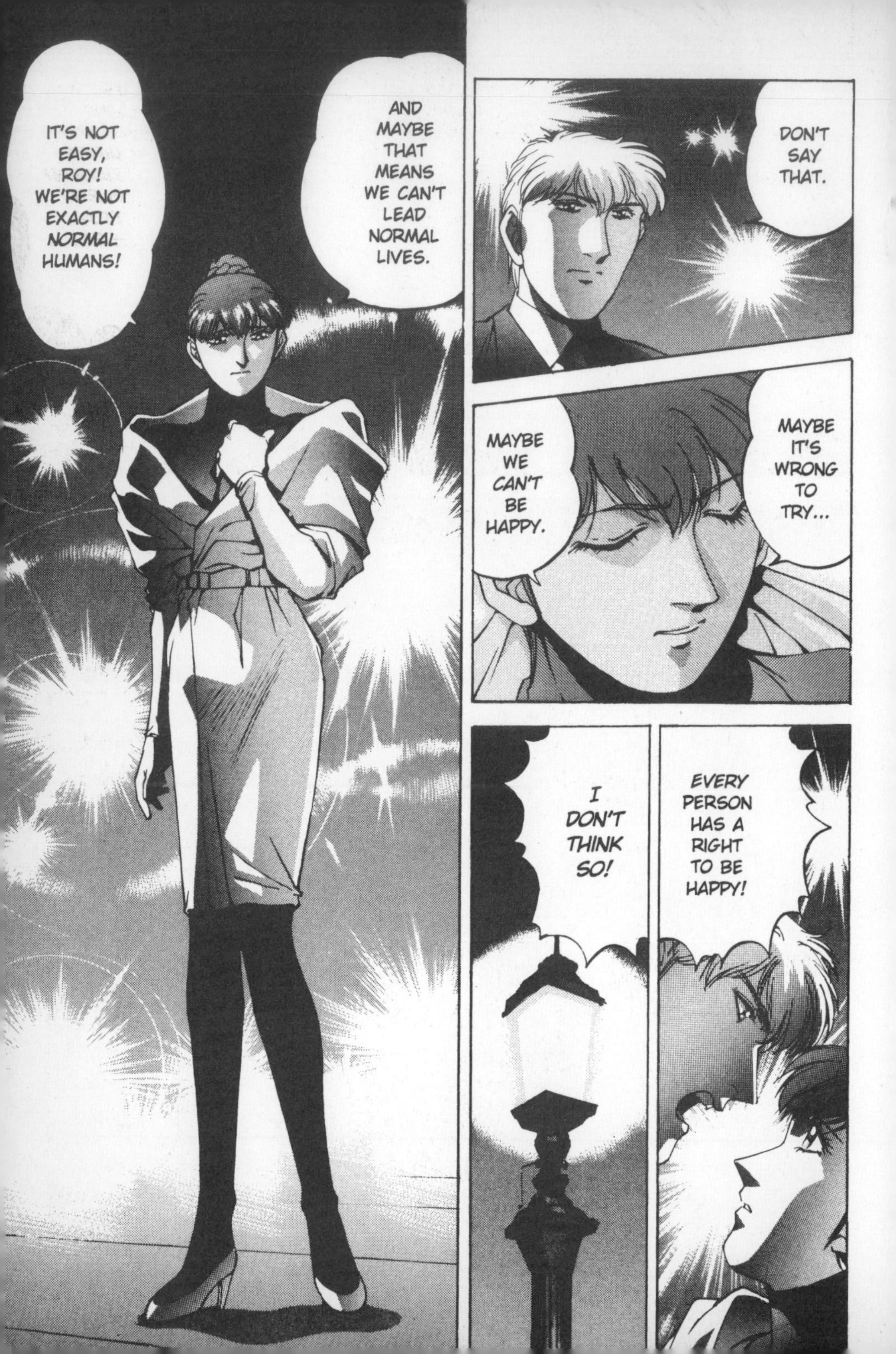
IT'S NOT EASY, ROY! WE'RE NOT EXACTLY NORMAL HUMANS!
AND MAYBE THAT MEANS WE CAN'T LEAD NORMAL LIVES.
DON'T SAY THAT.
MAYBE WE CAN'T BE HAPPY.
MAYBE IT'S WRONG TO TRY...
I DON'T THINK SO!
EVERY PERSON HAS A RIGHT TO BE HAPPY!

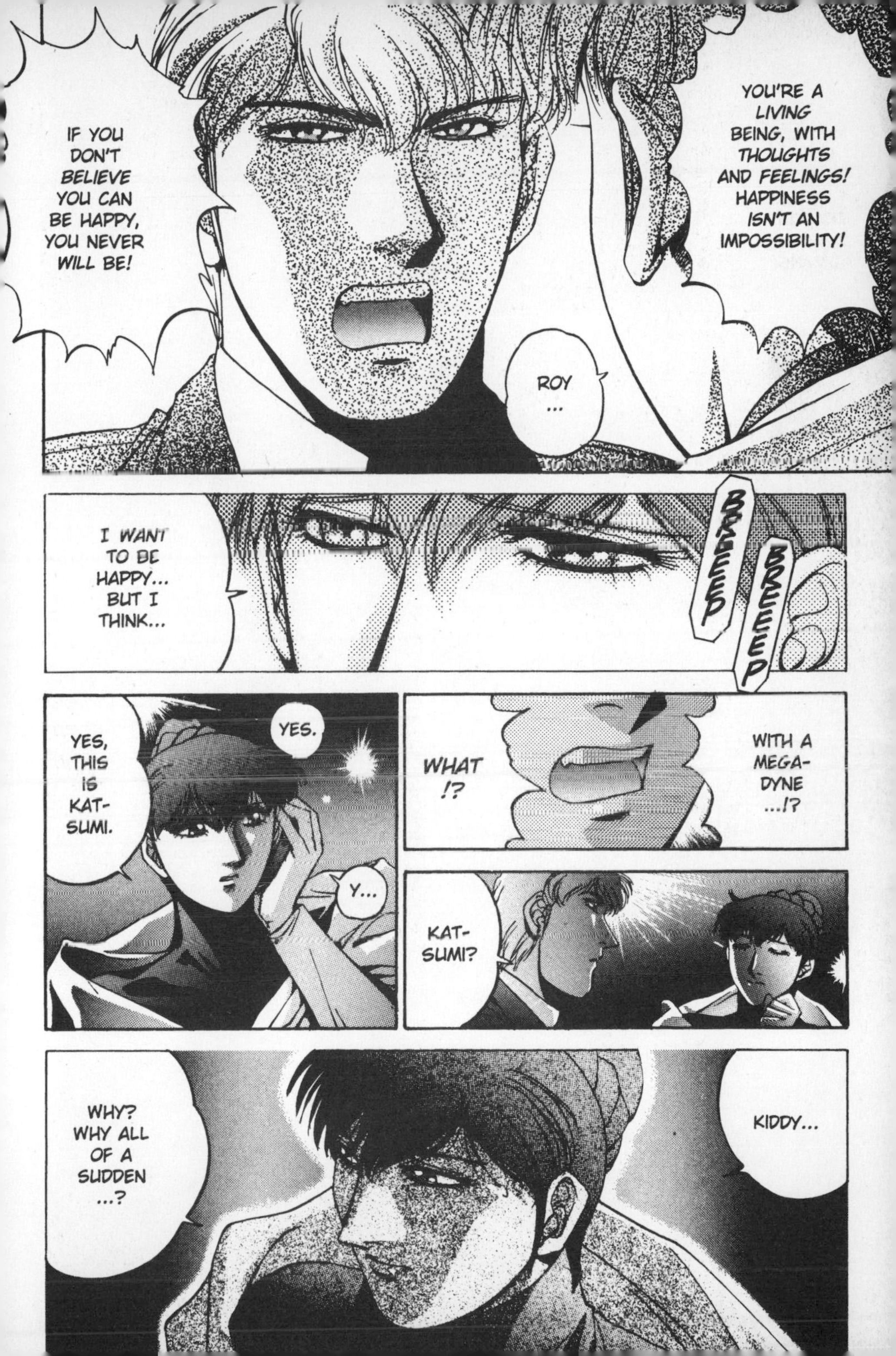
IF YOU DON'T BELIEVE YOU CAN BE HAPPY, YOU NEVER WILL BE!
YOU'RE A LIVING BEING, WITH THOUGHTS AND FEELINGS! HAPPINESS ISN'T AN IMPOSSIBILITY!
ROY ...
I WANT TO BE HAPPY... BUT I THINK...
BREEEP
BREEEP
YES, THIS IS KAT-SUMI.
YES.
Y...
WHAT !?
WITH A MEGA-DYNE ...!?
KAT-SUMI?
WHY? WHY ALL OF A SUDDEN ...?
KIDDY...

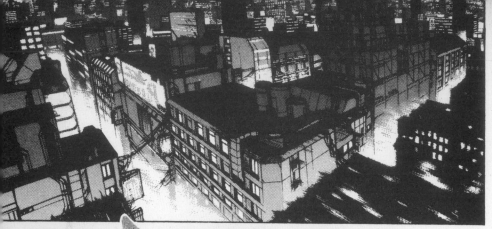

WIRE...

WHY NOW ...

...IN FRONT OF MY EYES ...!?

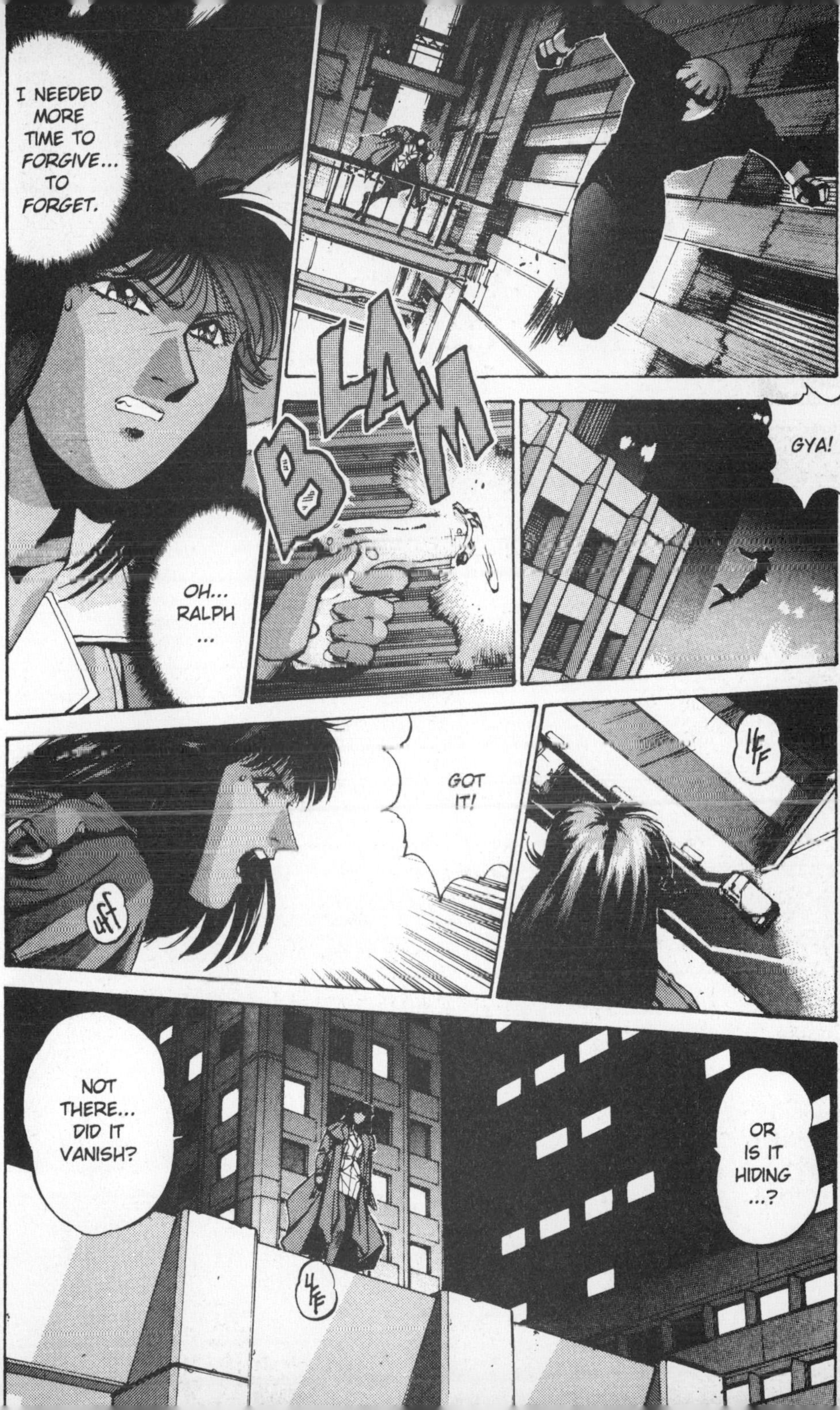
I NEEDED MORE TIME TO FORGIVE... TO FORGET.
OH... RALPH ...
BLAM
GYA!
GOT IT!
UFF
UFF
NOT THERE... DID IT VANISH?
UFF
OR IS IT HIDING ...?

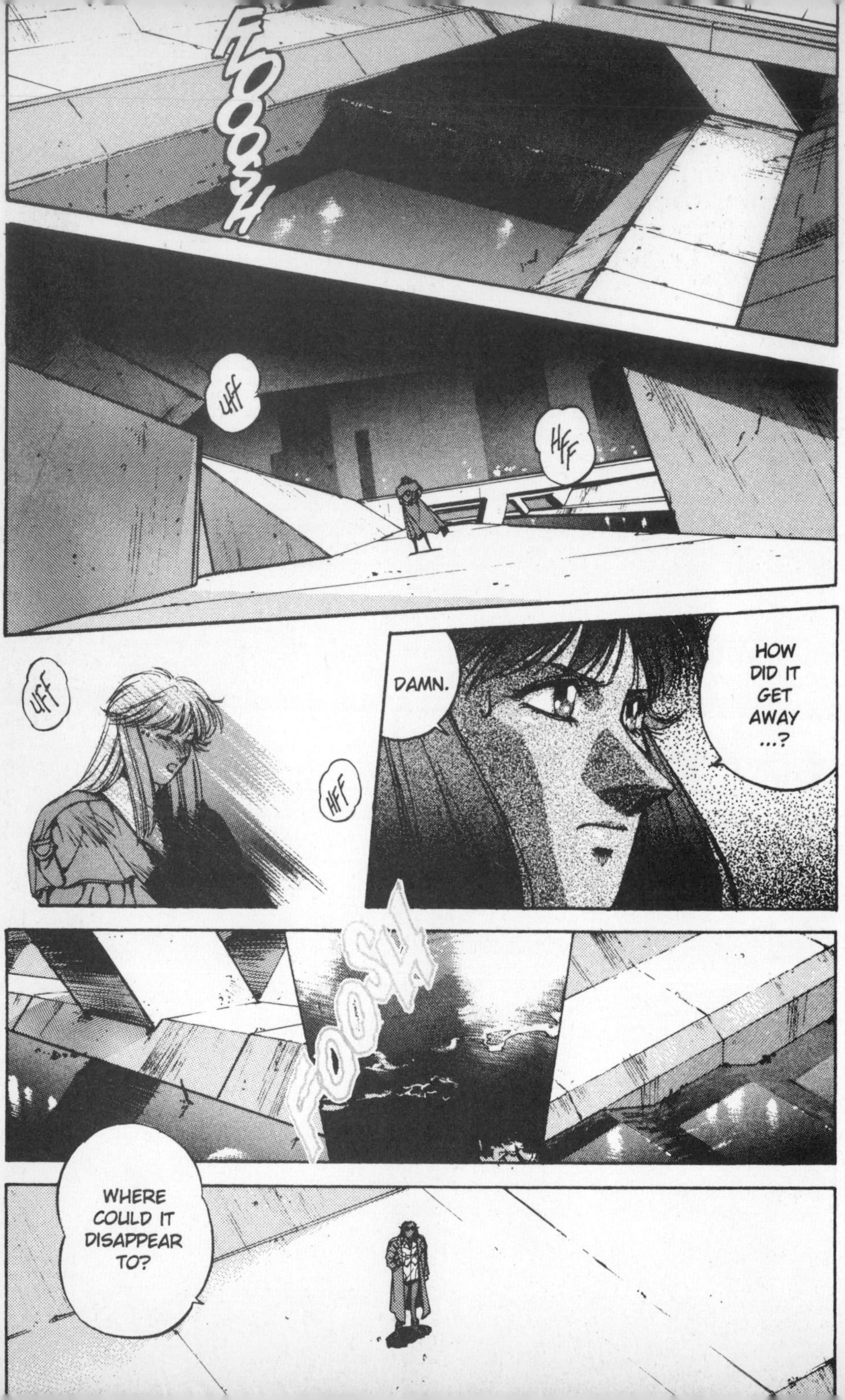

FLOOOSH
UFF
HFF
UFF
HFF
DAMN.
HOW DID IT GET AWAY ...?
FOOSH
WHERE COULD IT DISAPPEAR TO?

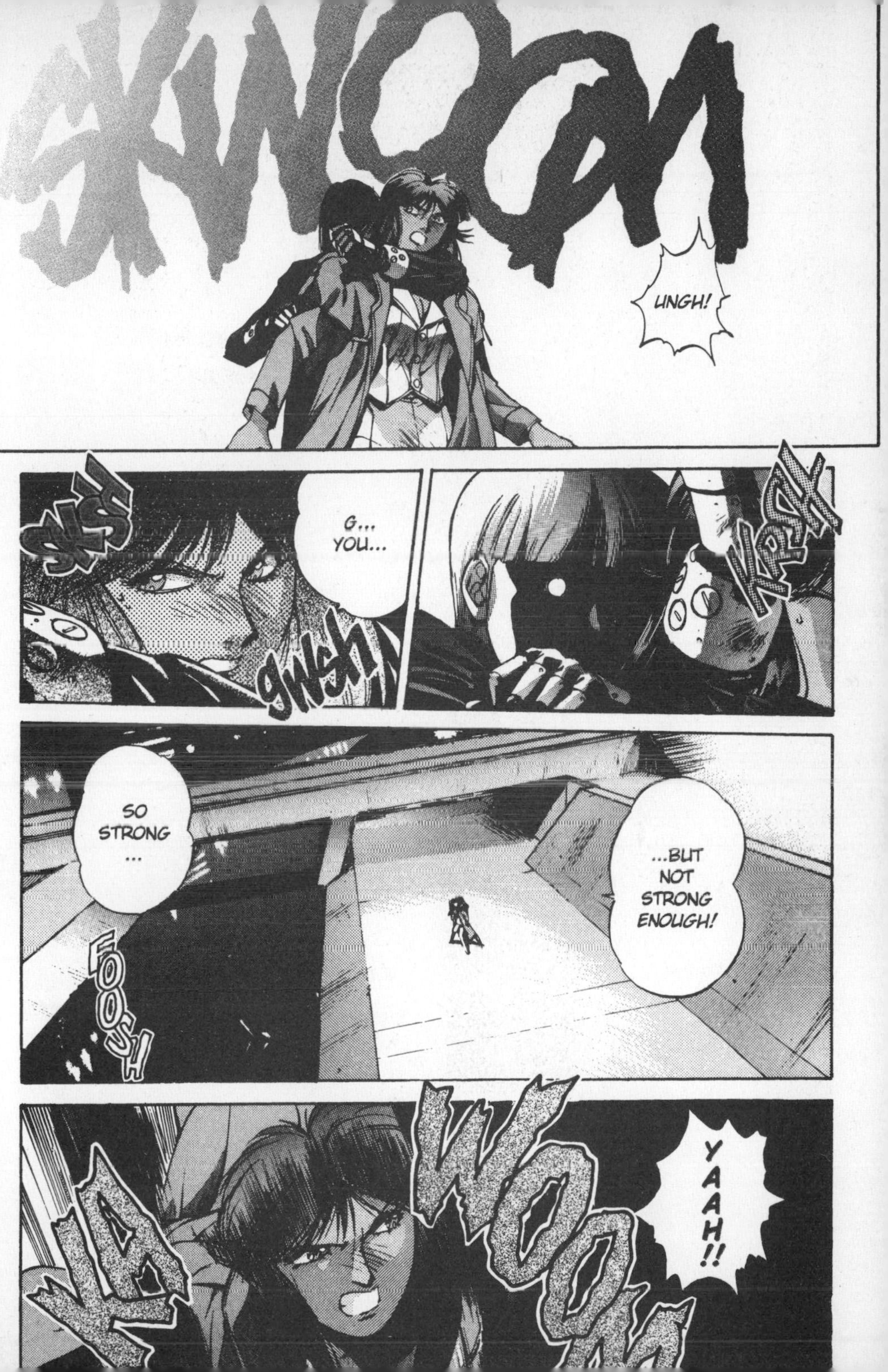

UNGH!
G... YOU...
gwsh
SO STRONG ...
...BUT NOT STRONG ENOUGH!
FOOSH
YAAAH!!

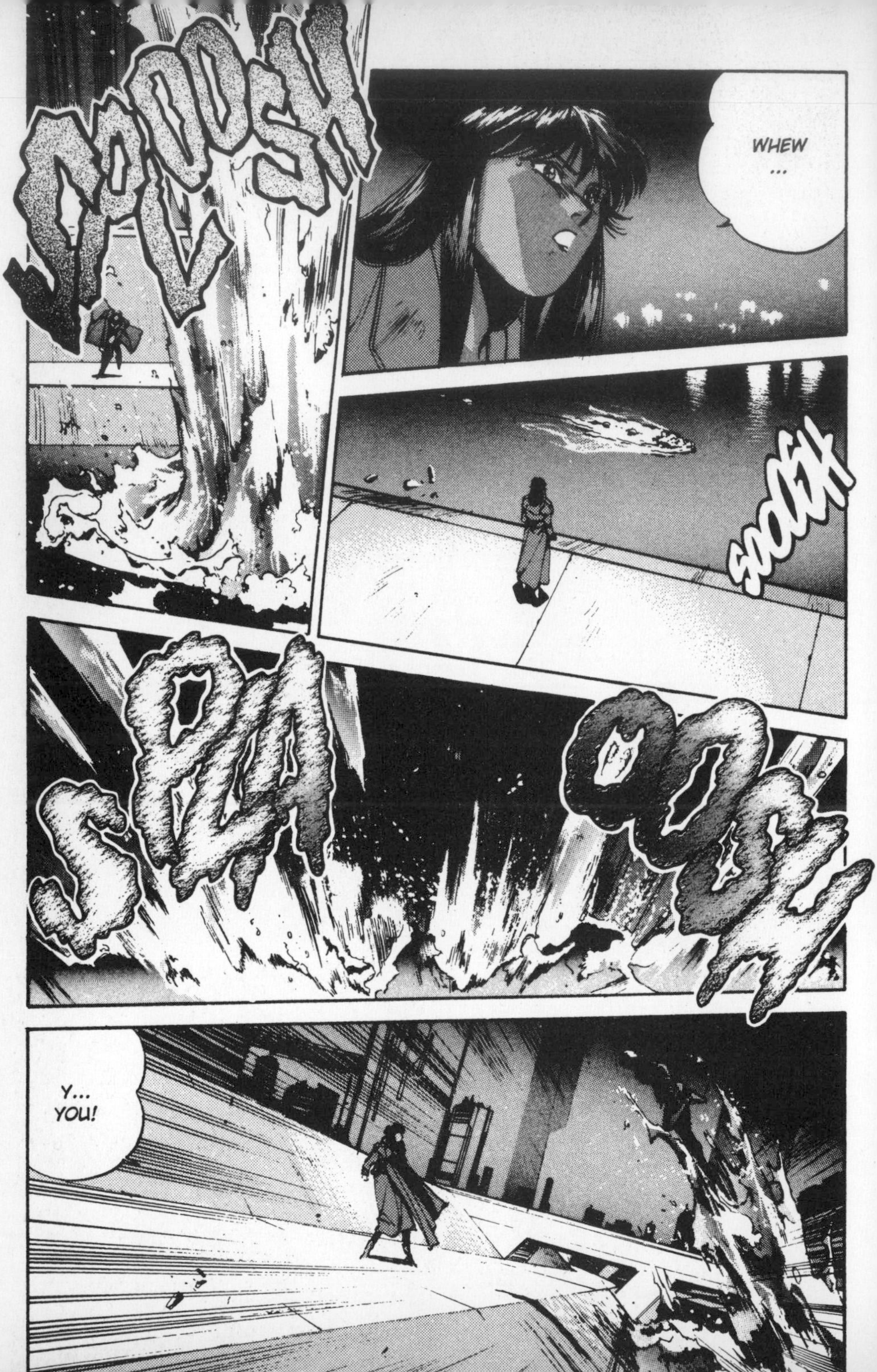
WHEW ...
Y... YOU!

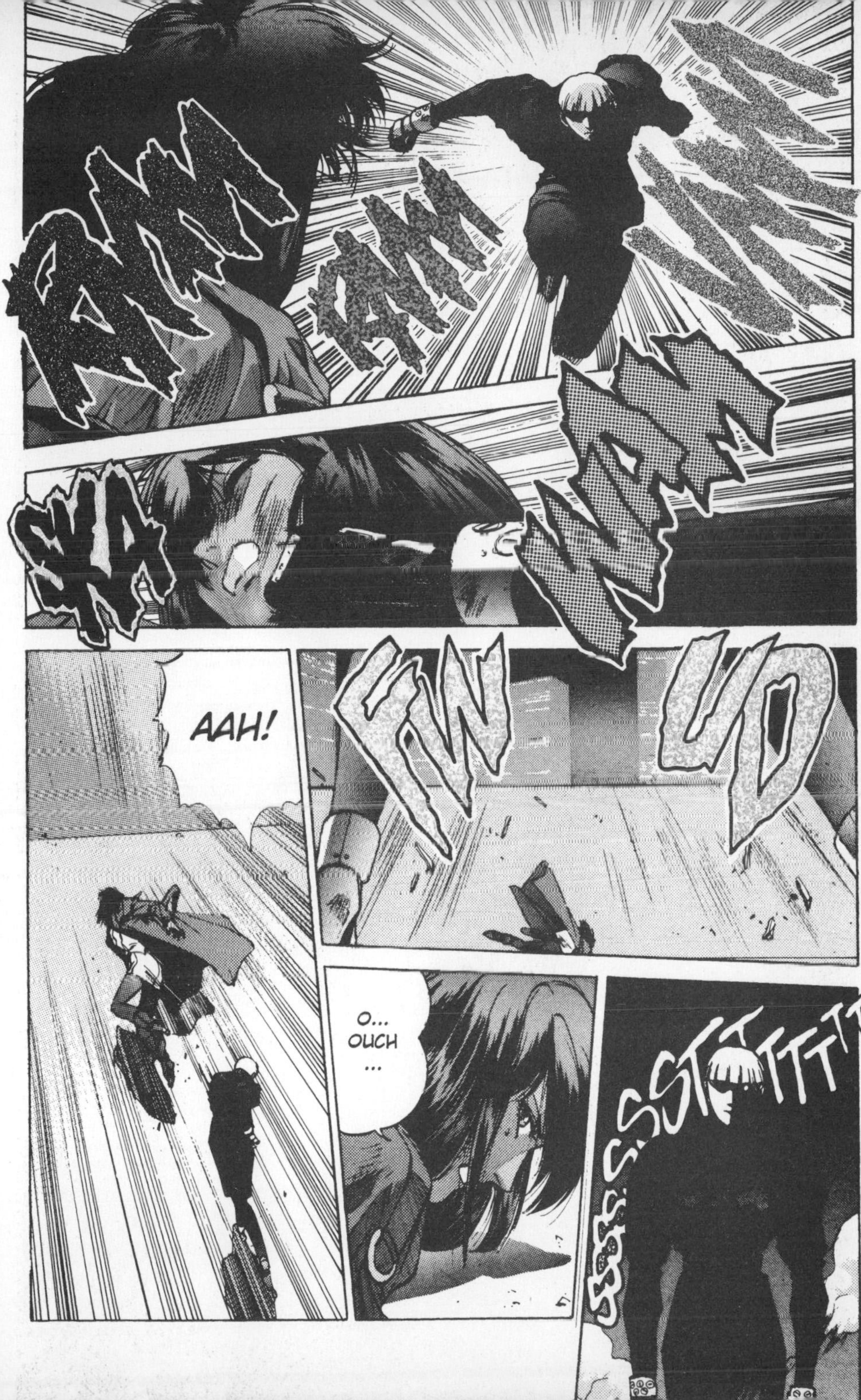
AAH!
O...
OUCH
...

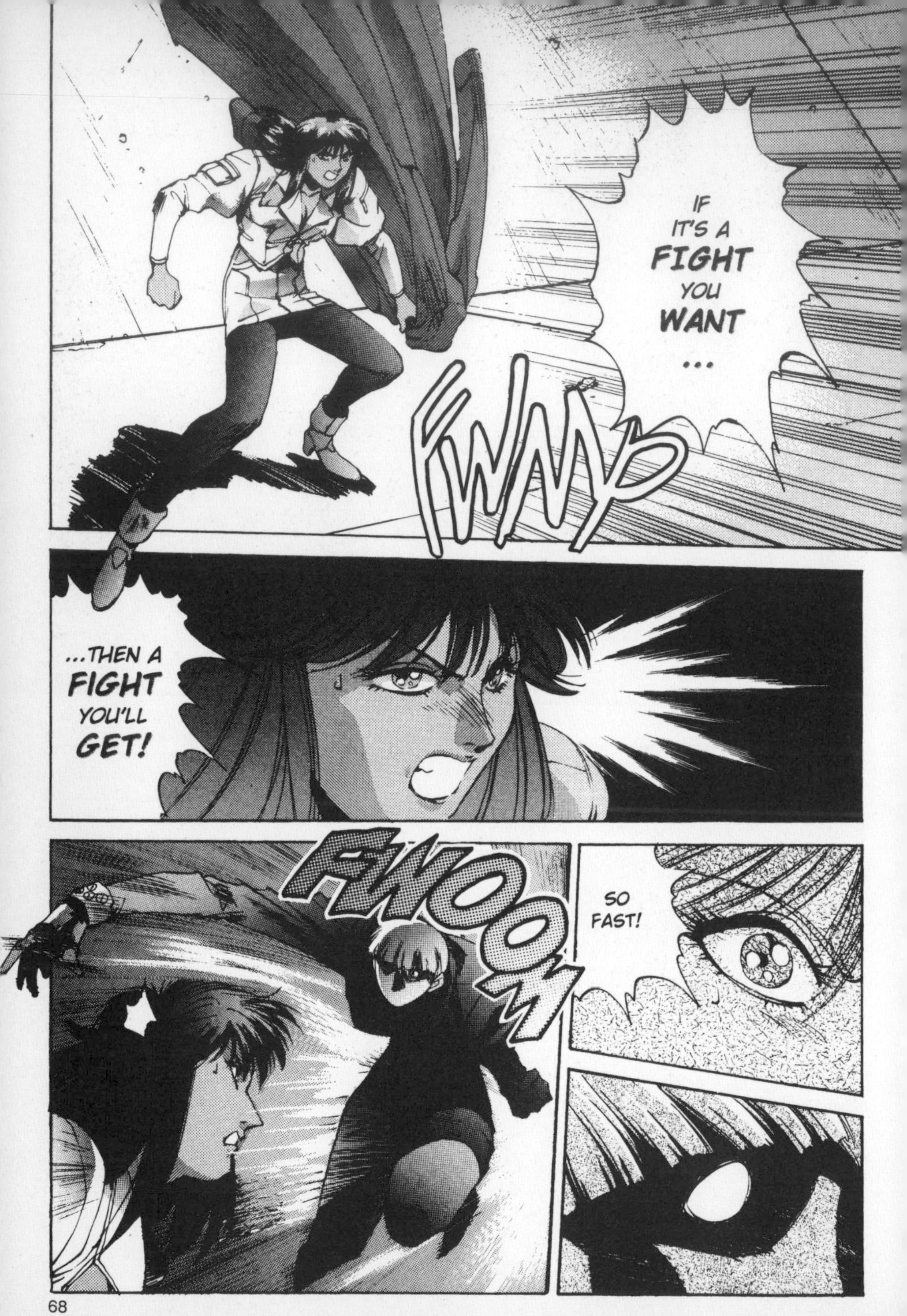
IF IT'S A FIGHT YOU WANT ...
FWMP
...THEN A FIGHT YOU'LL GET!
FWOOM
SO FAST!

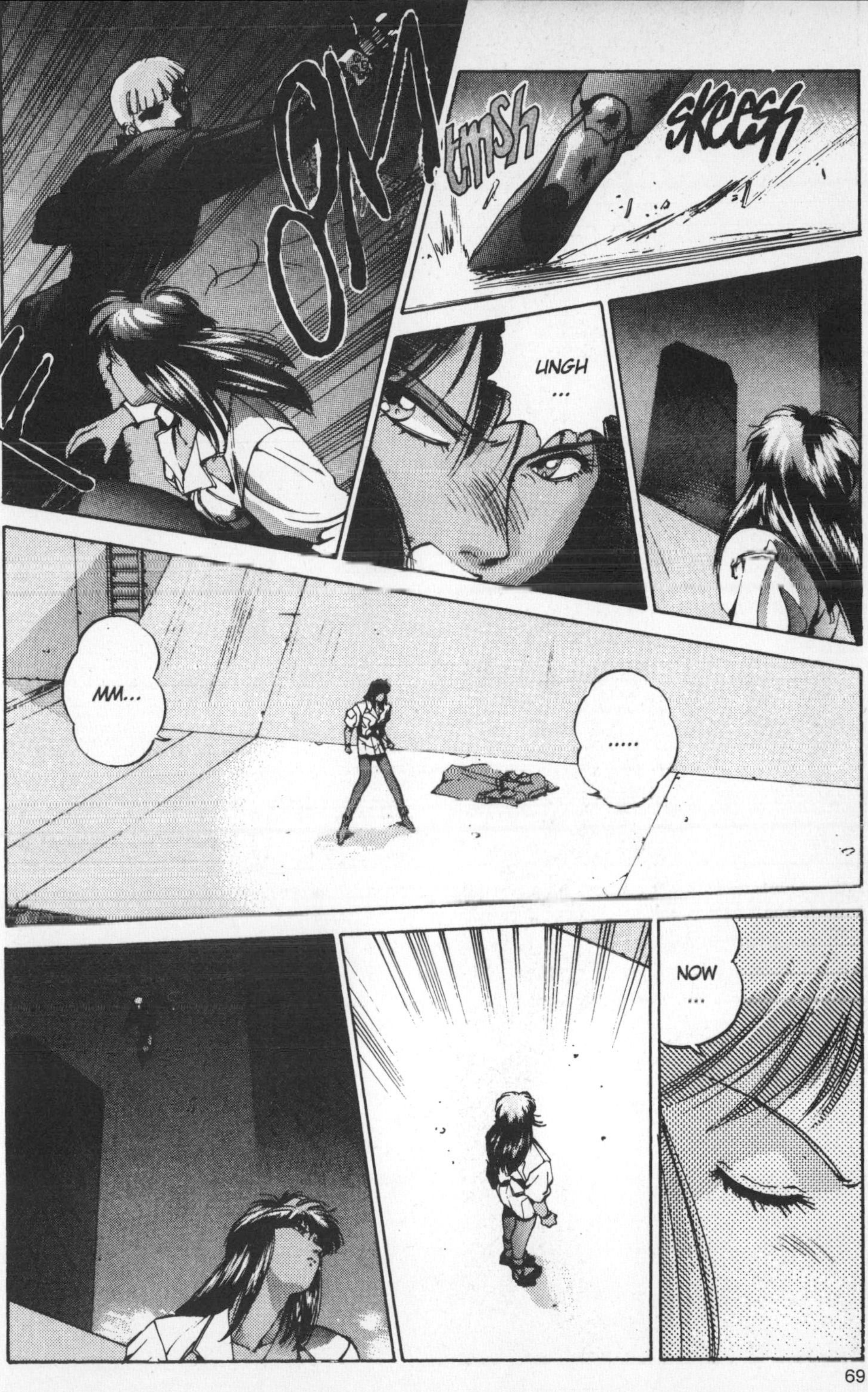

GM
thmsh
skeesh
UNGH ...
MM...
.....
NOW ...

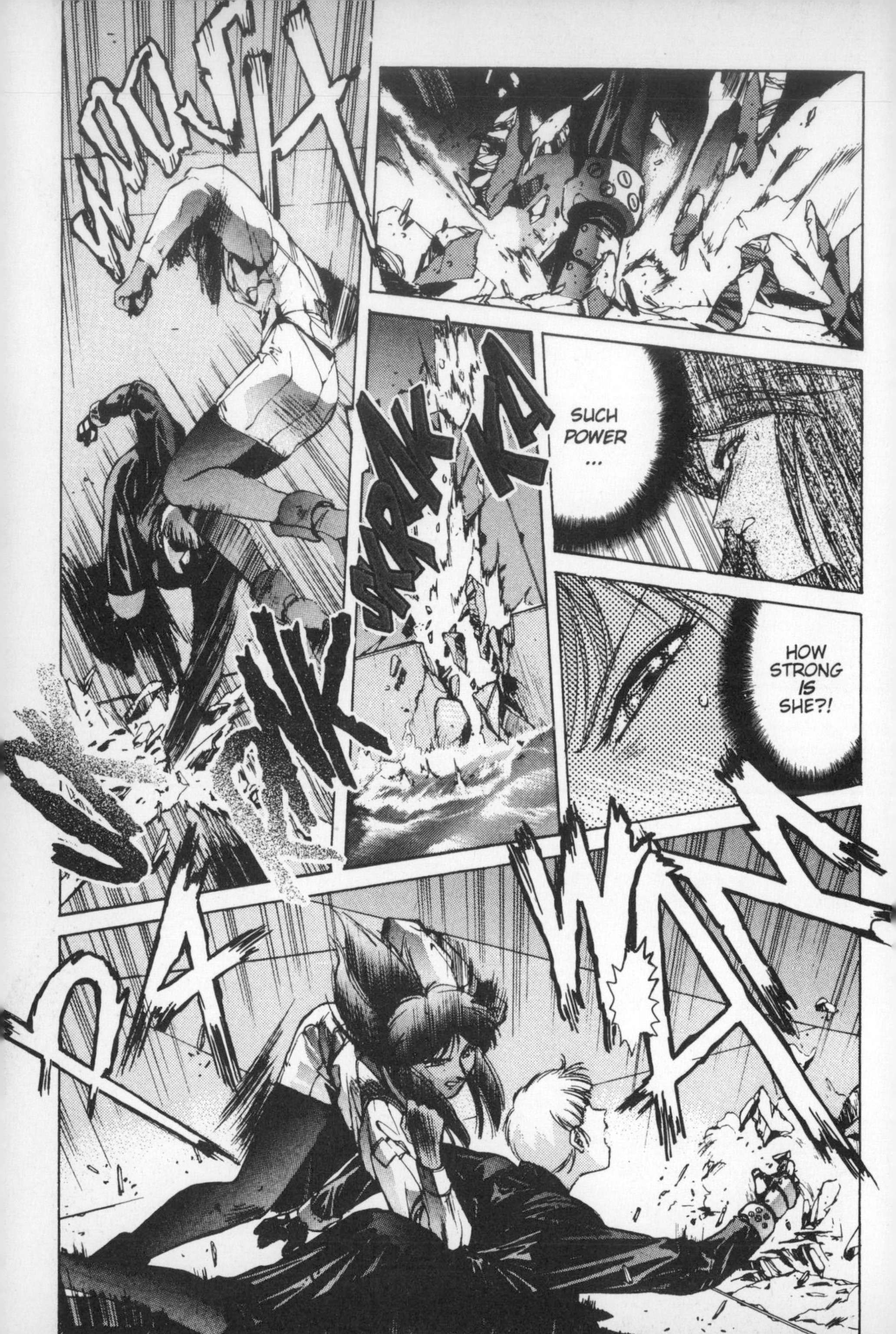
SUCH POWER ...
HOW STRONG IS SHE?!

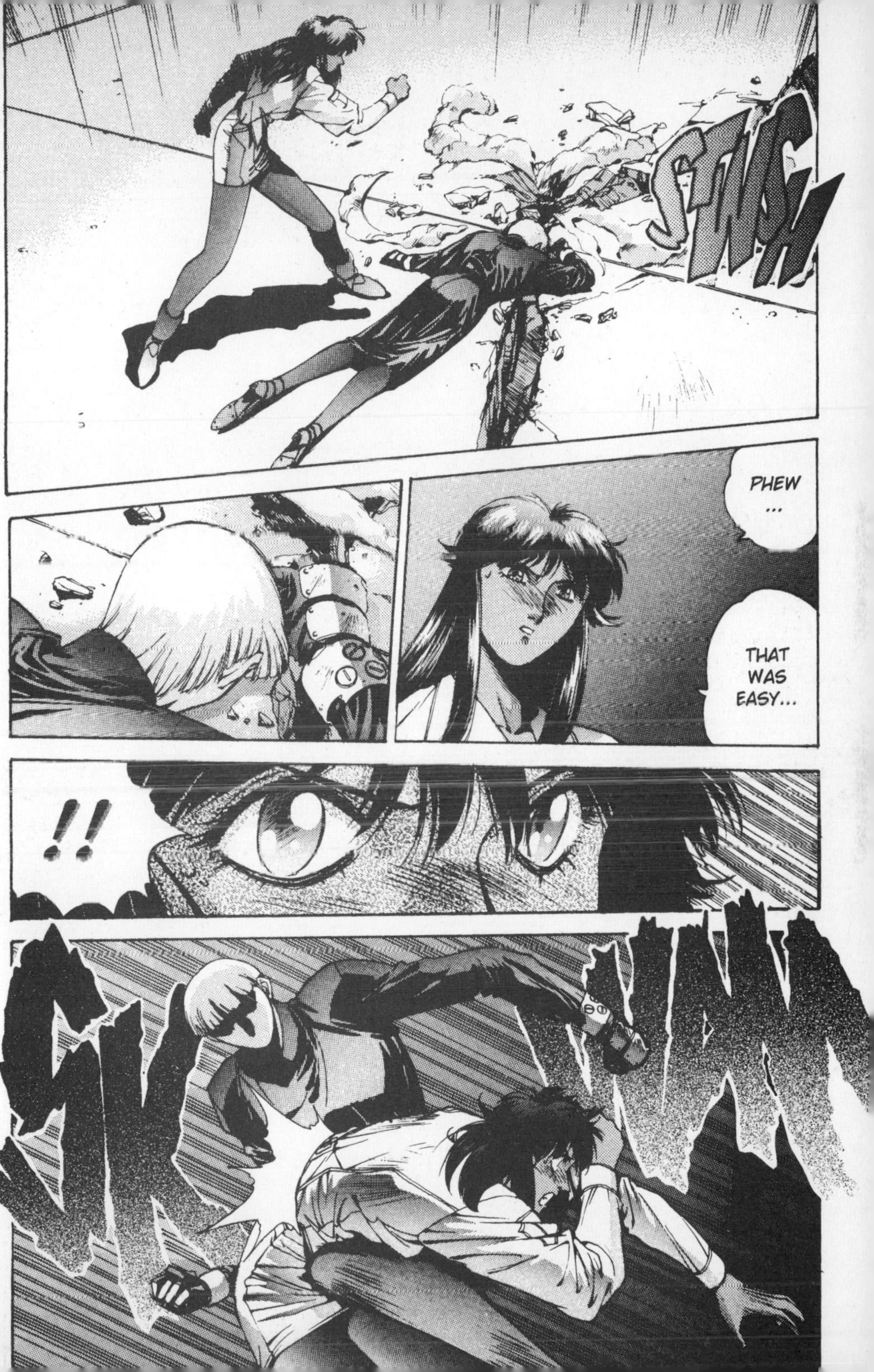

STASH
PHEW ...
THAT WAS EASY...
!!
SHWAM

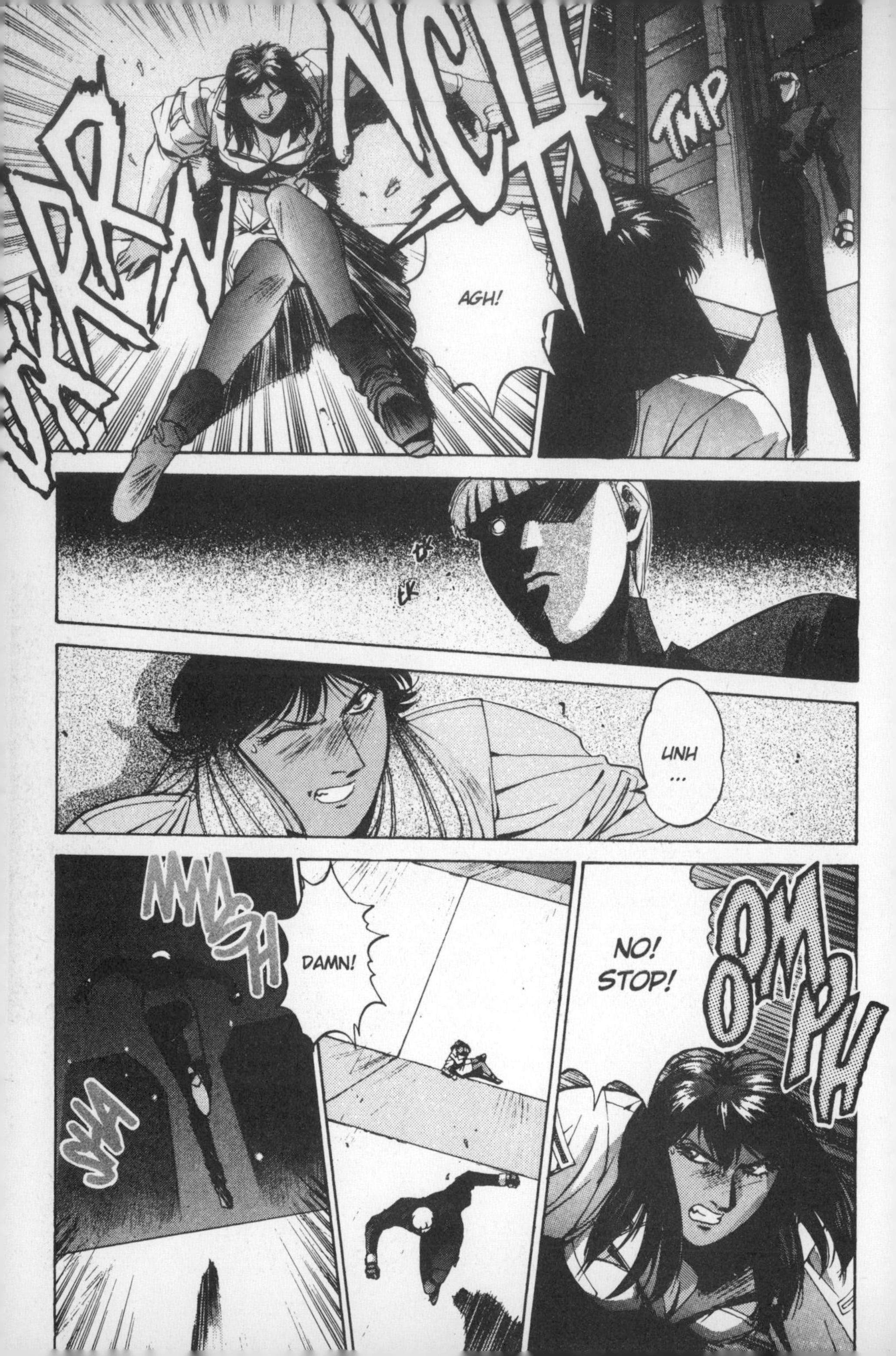

TMP
AGH!
EK
UNH ...
DAMN!
NO! STOP!
OOMPH

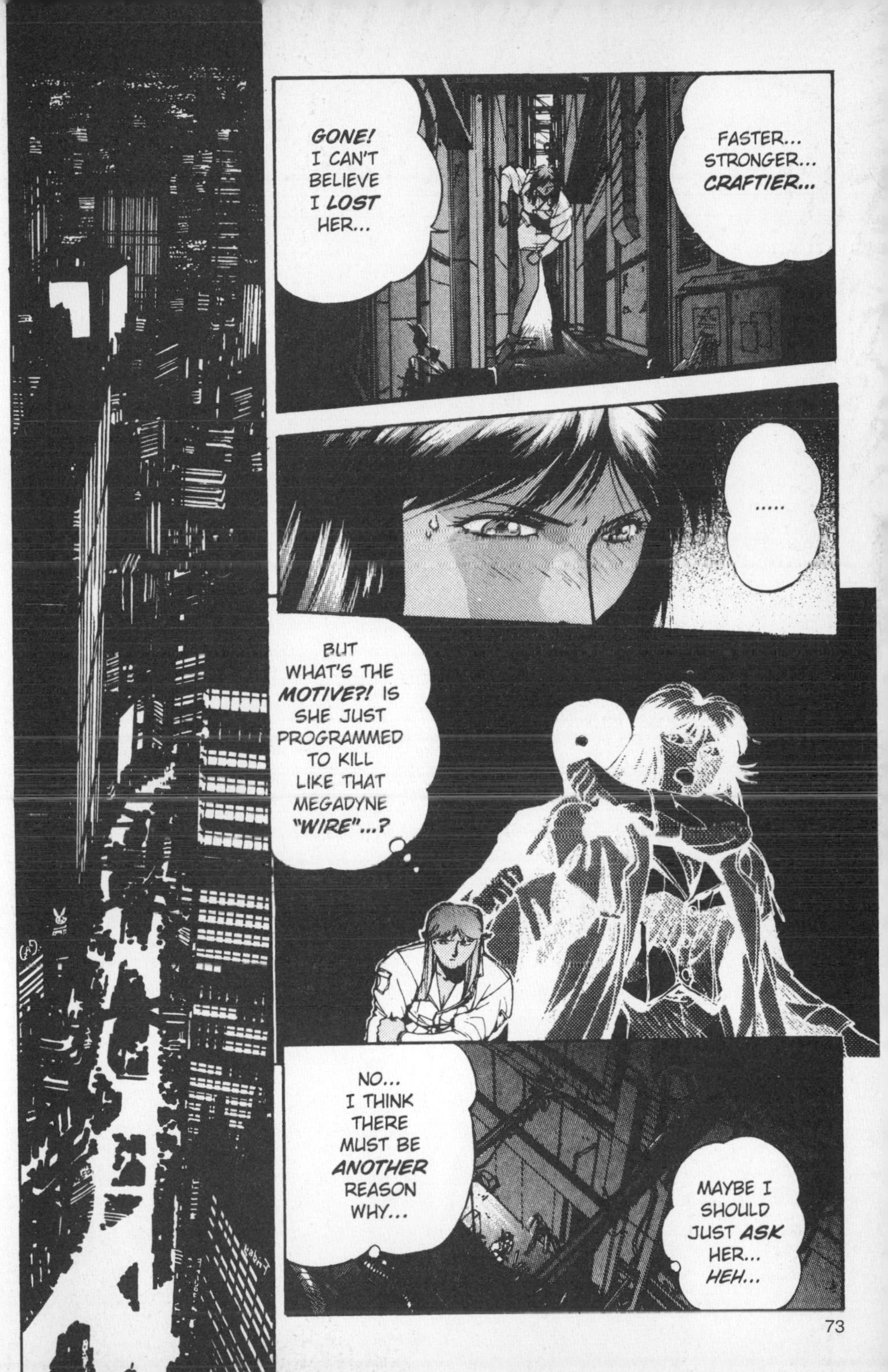

GONE! I CAN'T BELIEVE I LOST HER...
FASTER... STRONGER... CRAFTIER...
.....
BUT WHAT'S THE MOTIVE?! IS SHE JUST PROGRAMMED TO KILL LIKE THAT MEGADYNE "WIRE"...?
NO... I THINK THERE MUST BE ANOTHER REASON WHY...
MAYBE I SHOULD JUST ASK HER... HEH...

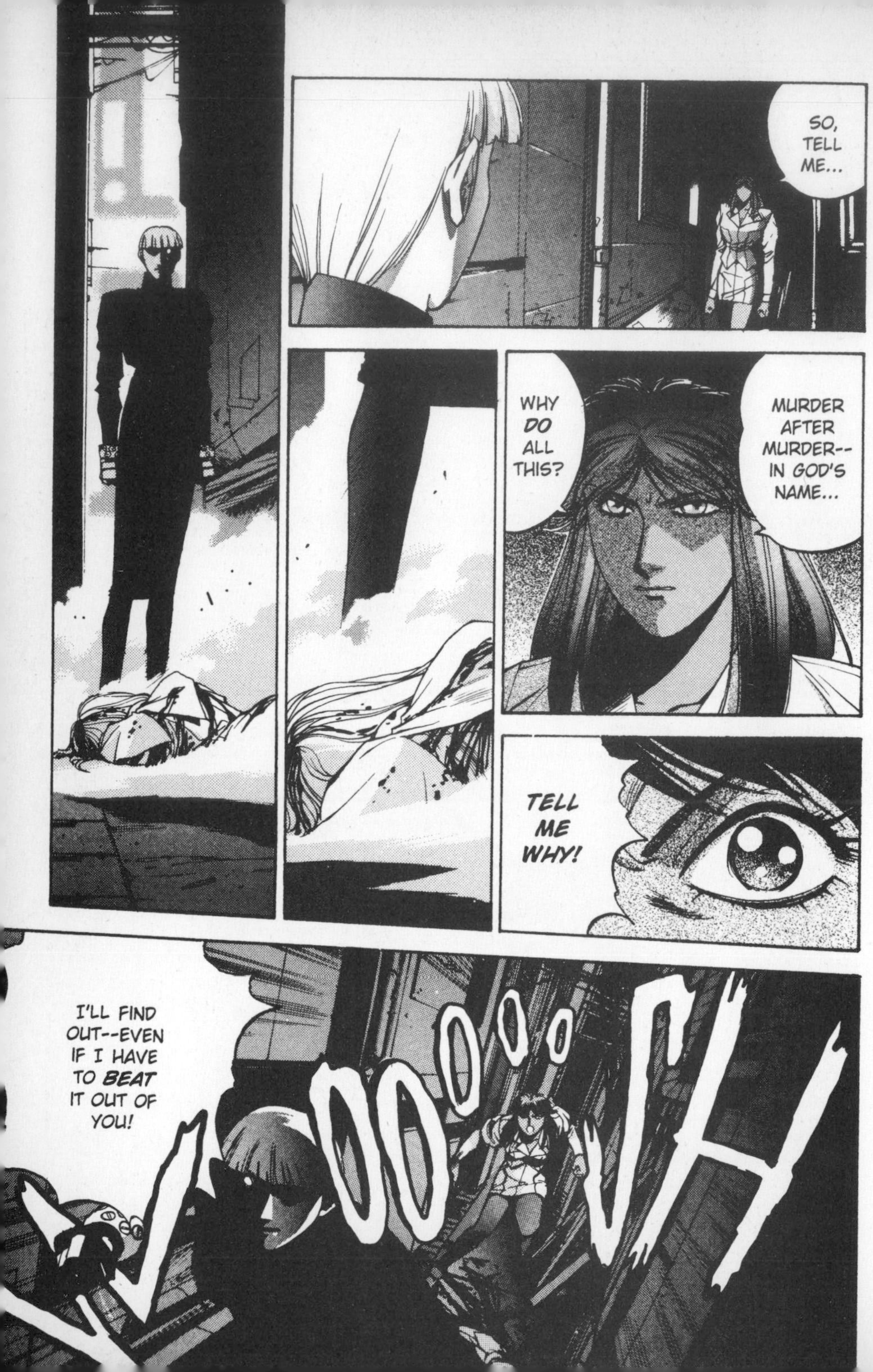
SO, TELL ME...
WHY DO ALL THIS?
MURDER AFTER MURDER-- IN GOD'S NAME...
TELL ME WHY!
I'LL FIND OUT--EVEN IF I HAVE TO BEAT IT OUT OF YOU!

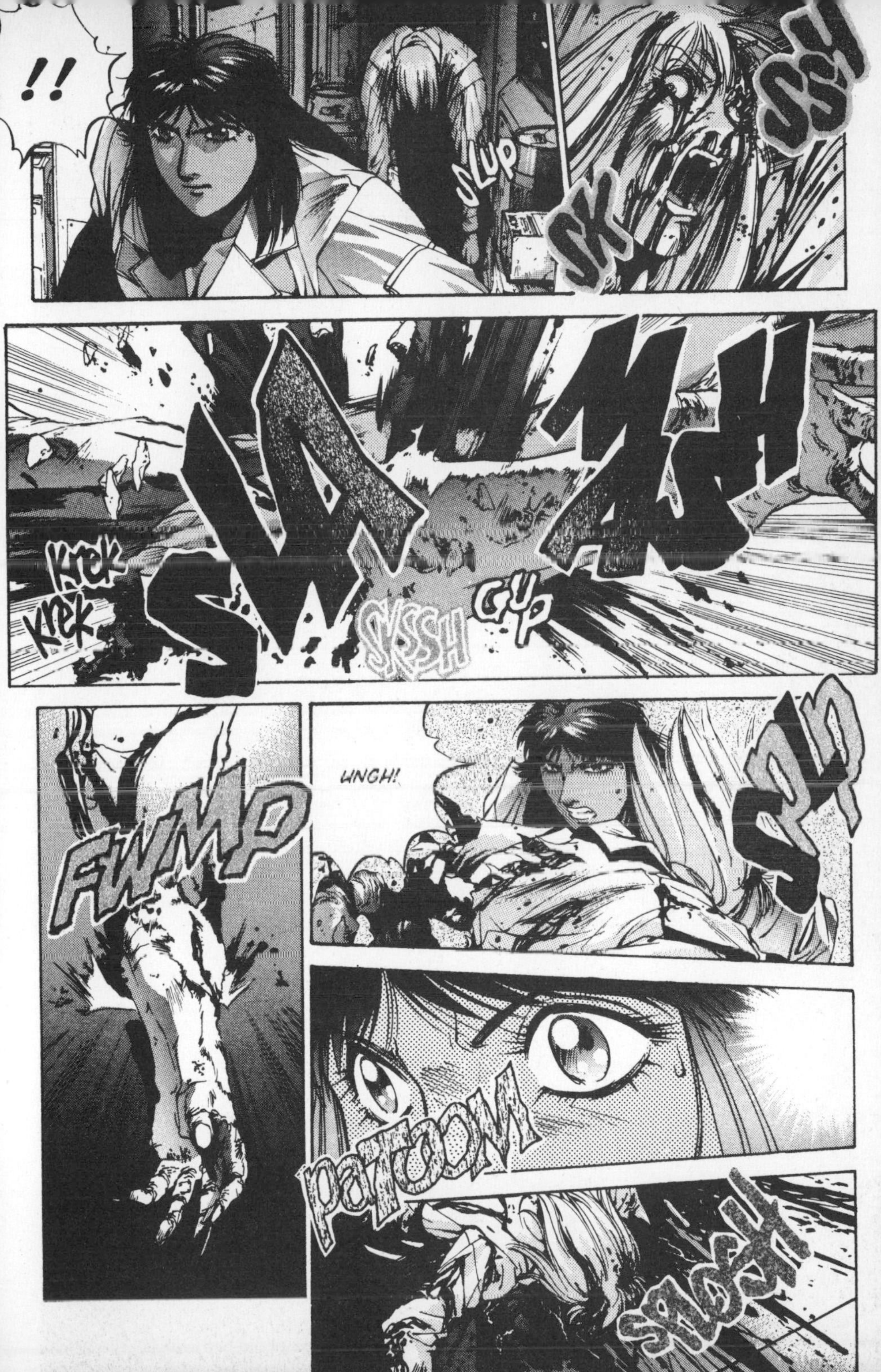
!!
SLUP
SK
krek
krek
SKSSH
GUP
FWMP
UNGH!
PATOOM

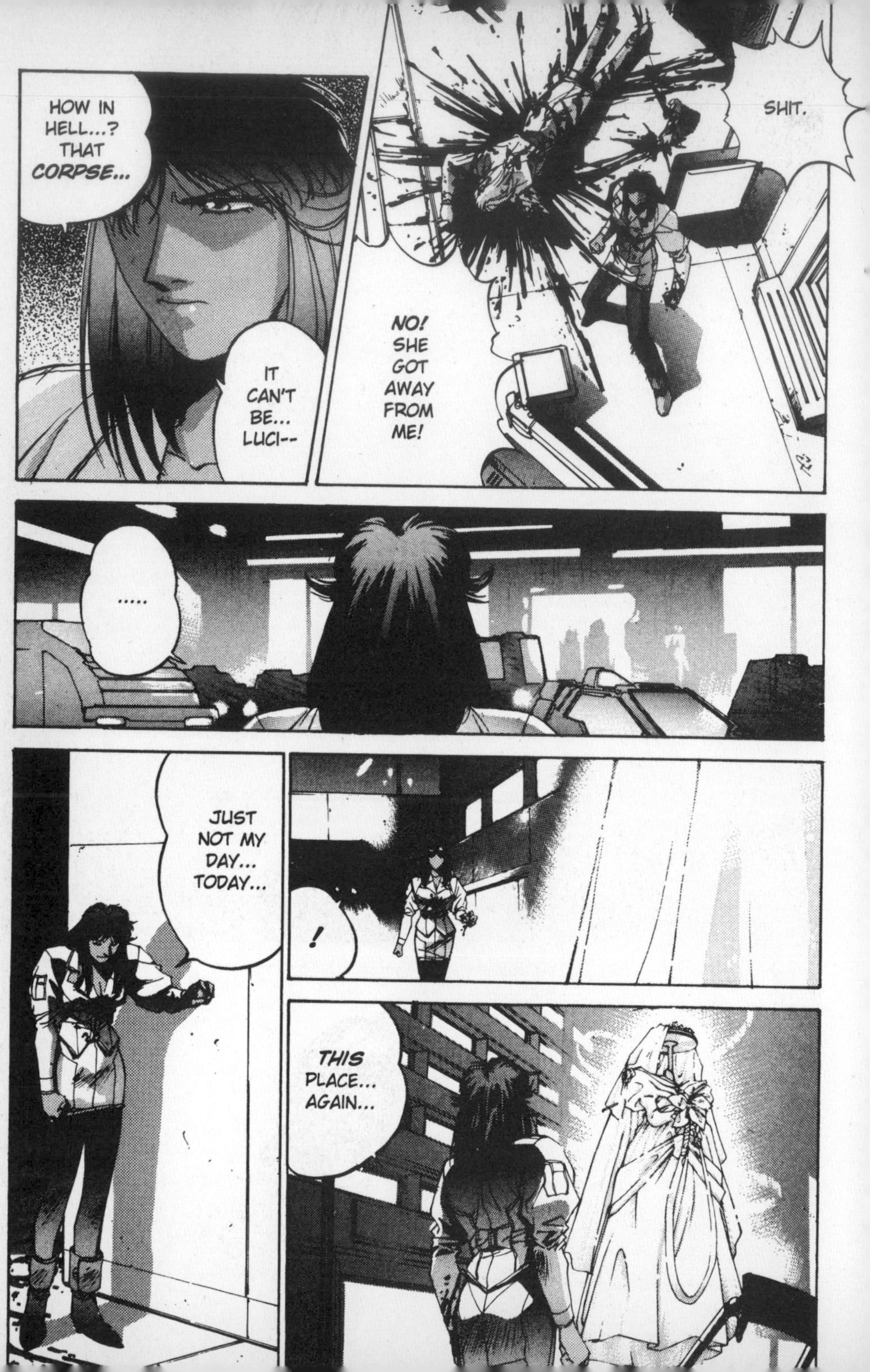
HOW IN HELL...? THAT CORPSE...
IT CAN'T BE... LUCI--
NO! SHE GOT AWAY FROM ME!
SHIT.
.....
JUST NOT MY DAY... TODAY...
!
THIS PLACE... AGAIN...

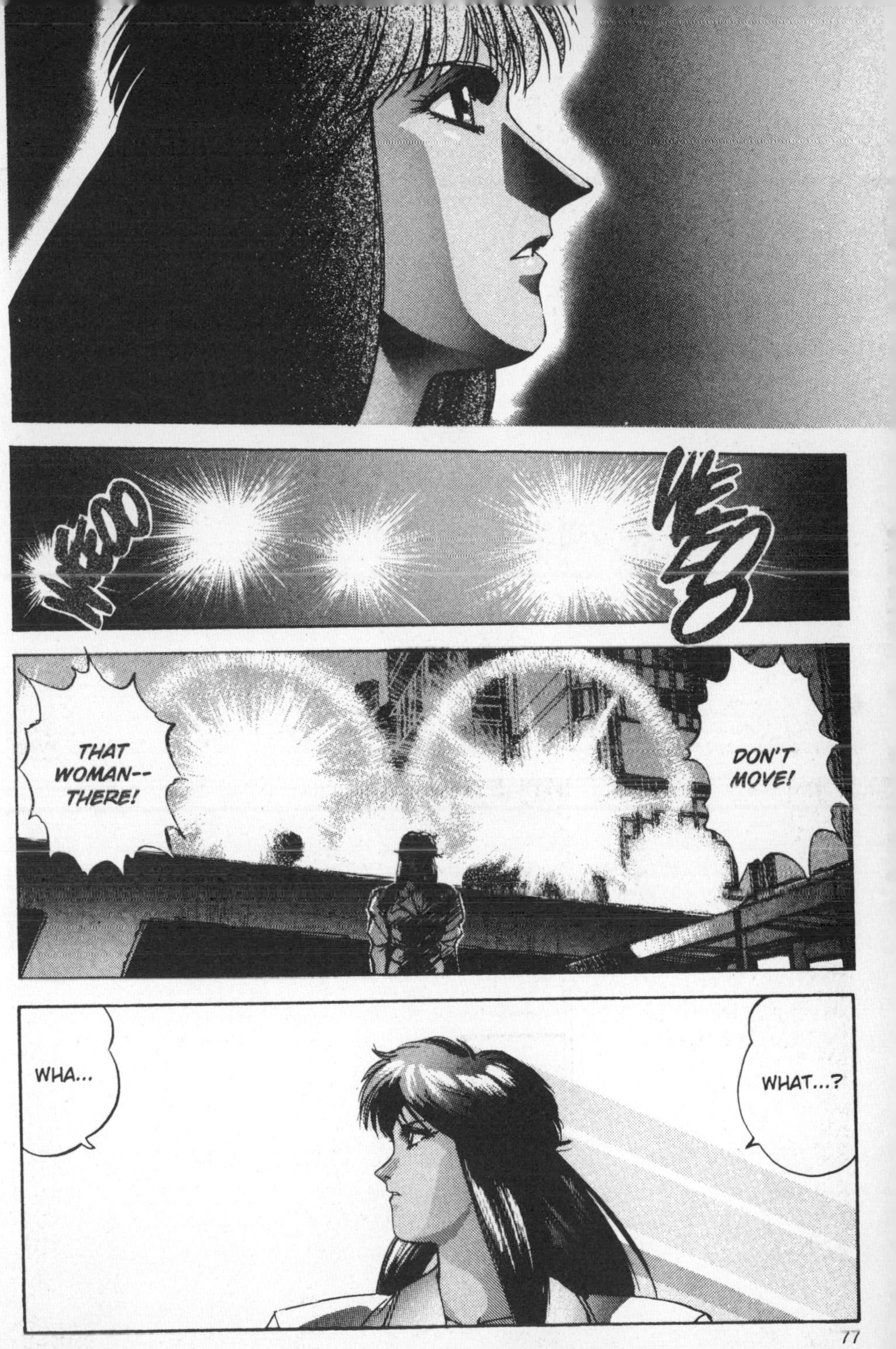
DON'T MOVE!
THAT WOMAN-- THERE!
WHAT...?
WHA...

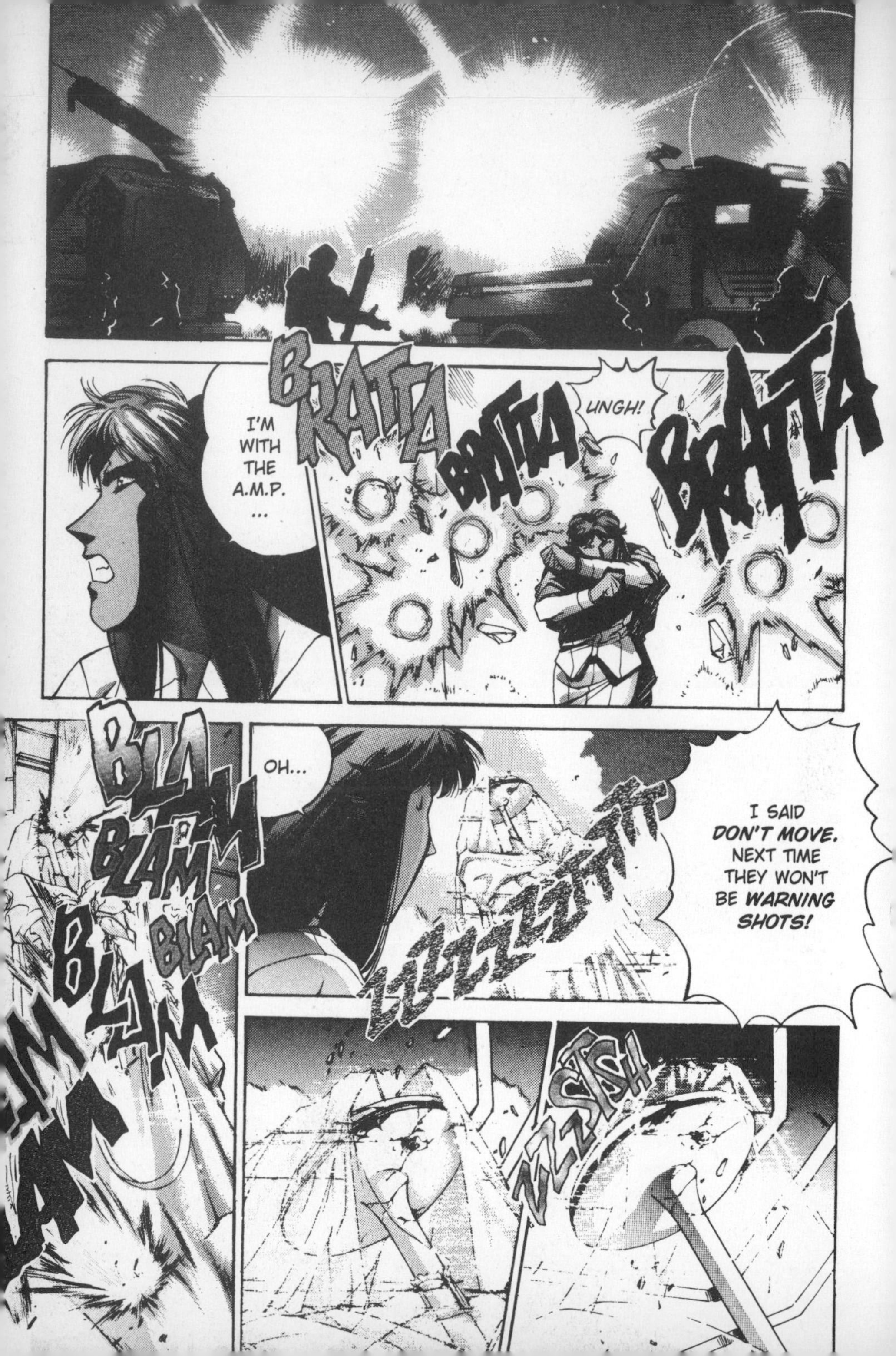

BRATTA
I'M WITH THE A.M.P. ...
BRATTA
UNGH!
BRATTA
BLAM BLAM BLAM BLAM
OH...
ZZZZZZTTT
I SAID *DON'T MOVE.* NEXT TIME THEY WON'T BE *WARNING SHOTS!*
ZZSSH

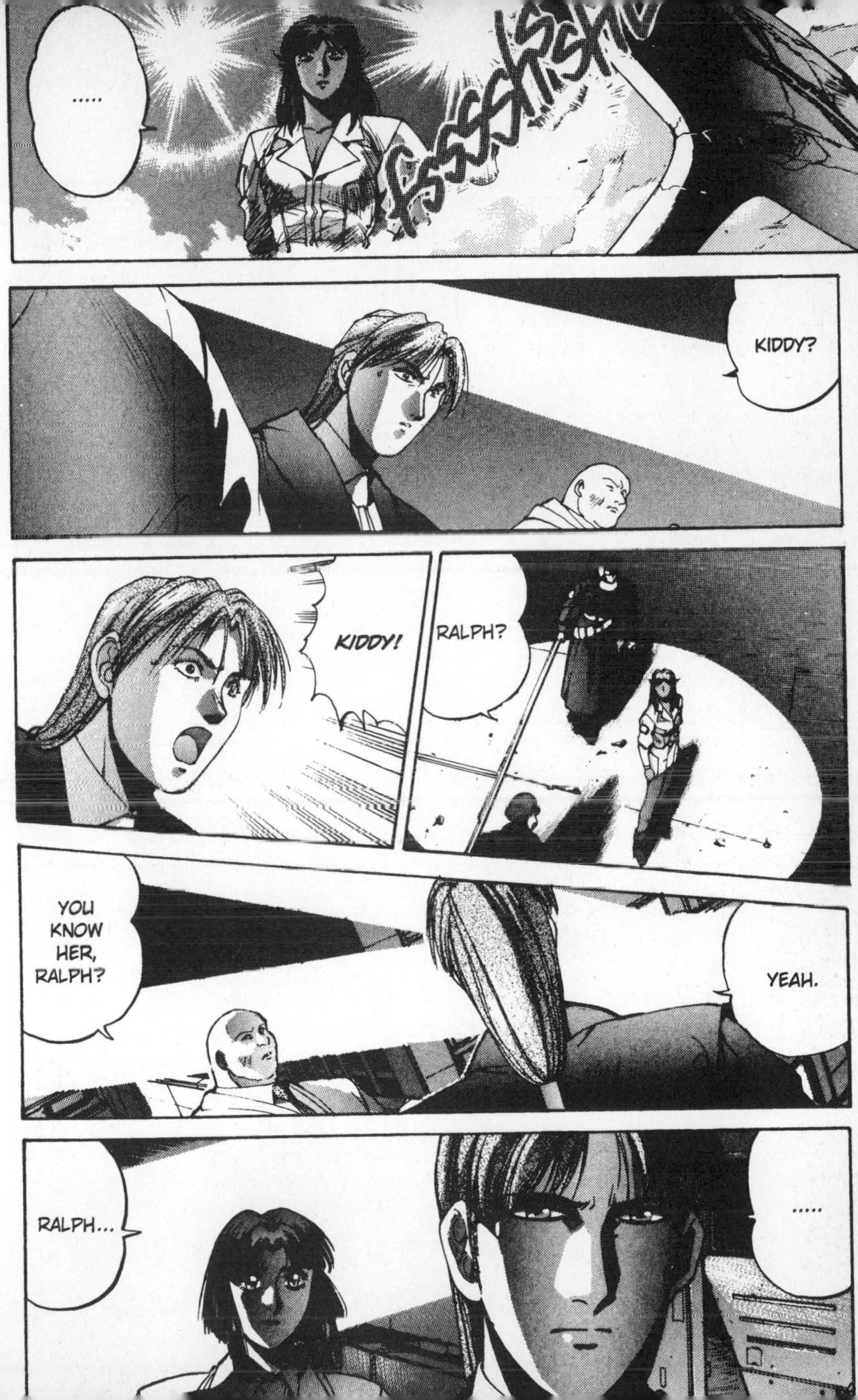
.....
KIDDY?
KIDDY!
RALPH?
YOU KNOW HER, RALPH?
YEAH.
RALPH...
.....

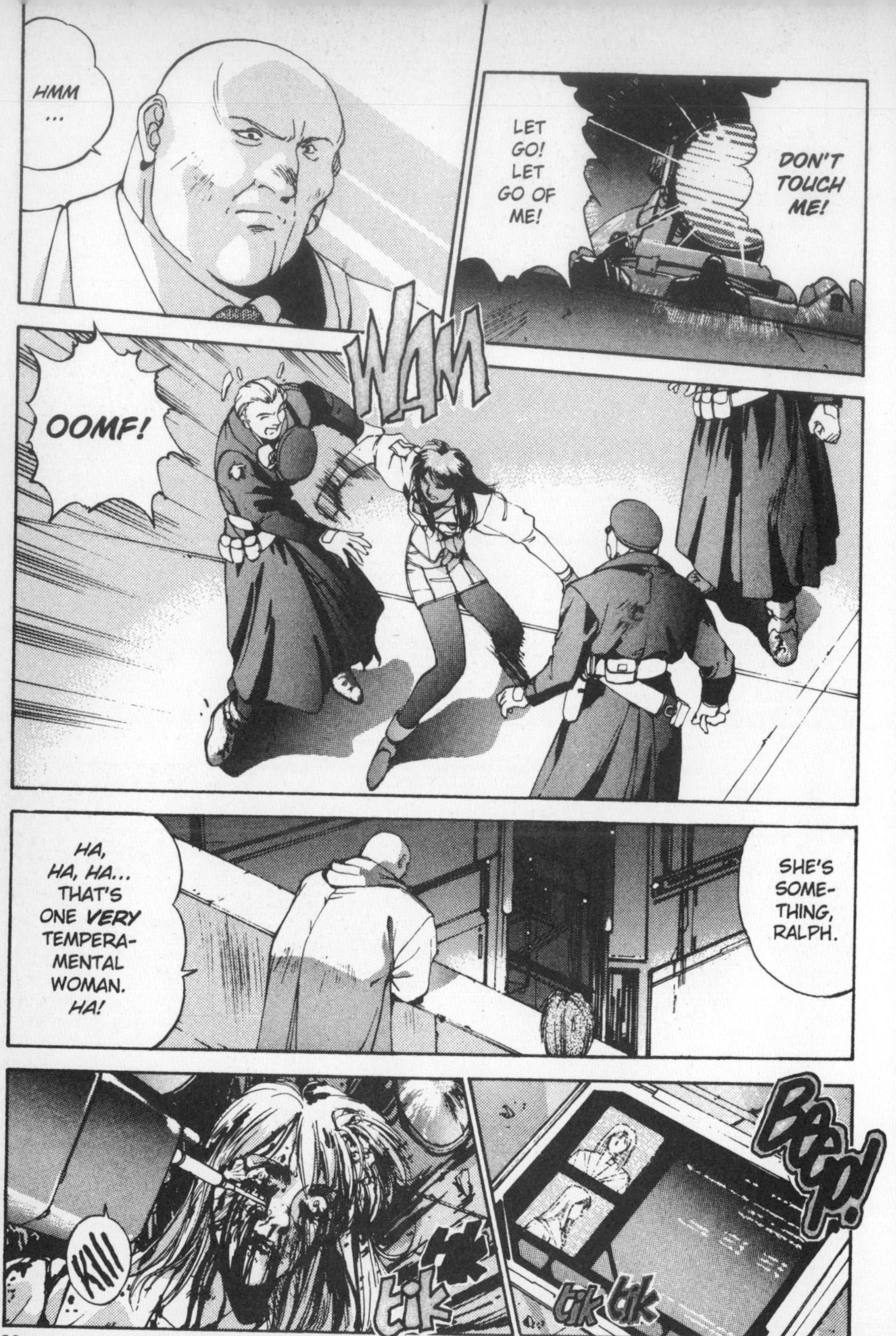
HMM ...
LET GO! LET GO OF ME!
DON'T TOUCH ME!
WAM
OOMF!
HA, HA, HA... THAT'S ONE *VERY* TEMPERAMENTAL WOMAN. HA!
SHE'S SOME-THING, RALPH.
KIII
tik
tik tik
Beep!

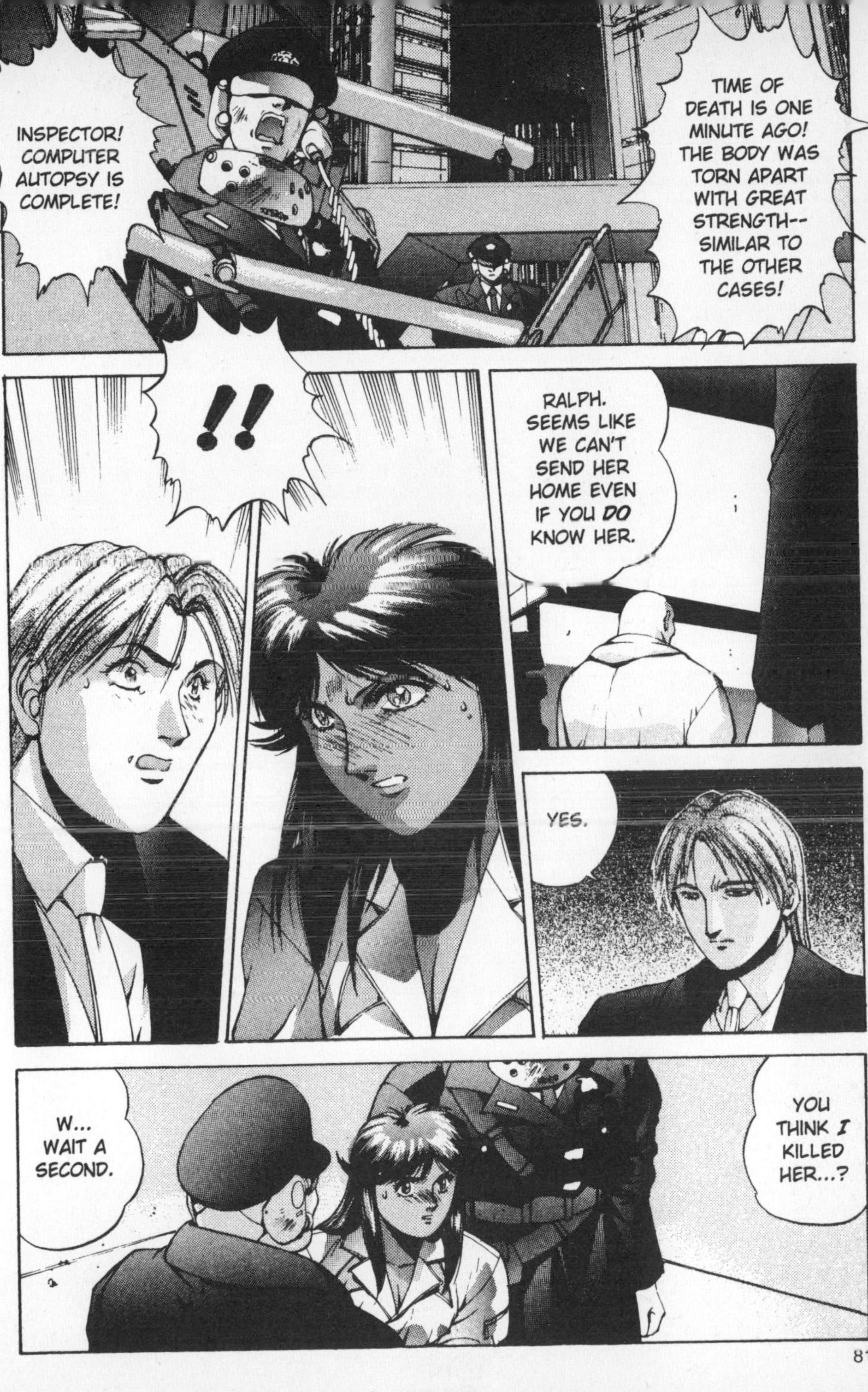
INSPECTOR! COMPUTER AUTOPSY IS COMPLETE!
TIME OF DEATH IS ONE MINUTE AGO! THE BODY WAS TORN APART WITH GREAT STRENGTH-- SIMILAR TO THE OTHER CASES!
!!
RALPH. SEEMS LIKE WE CAN'T SEND HER HOME EVEN IF YOU *DO* KNOW HER.
YES.
W... WAIT A SECOND.
YOU THINK *I* KILLED HER...?

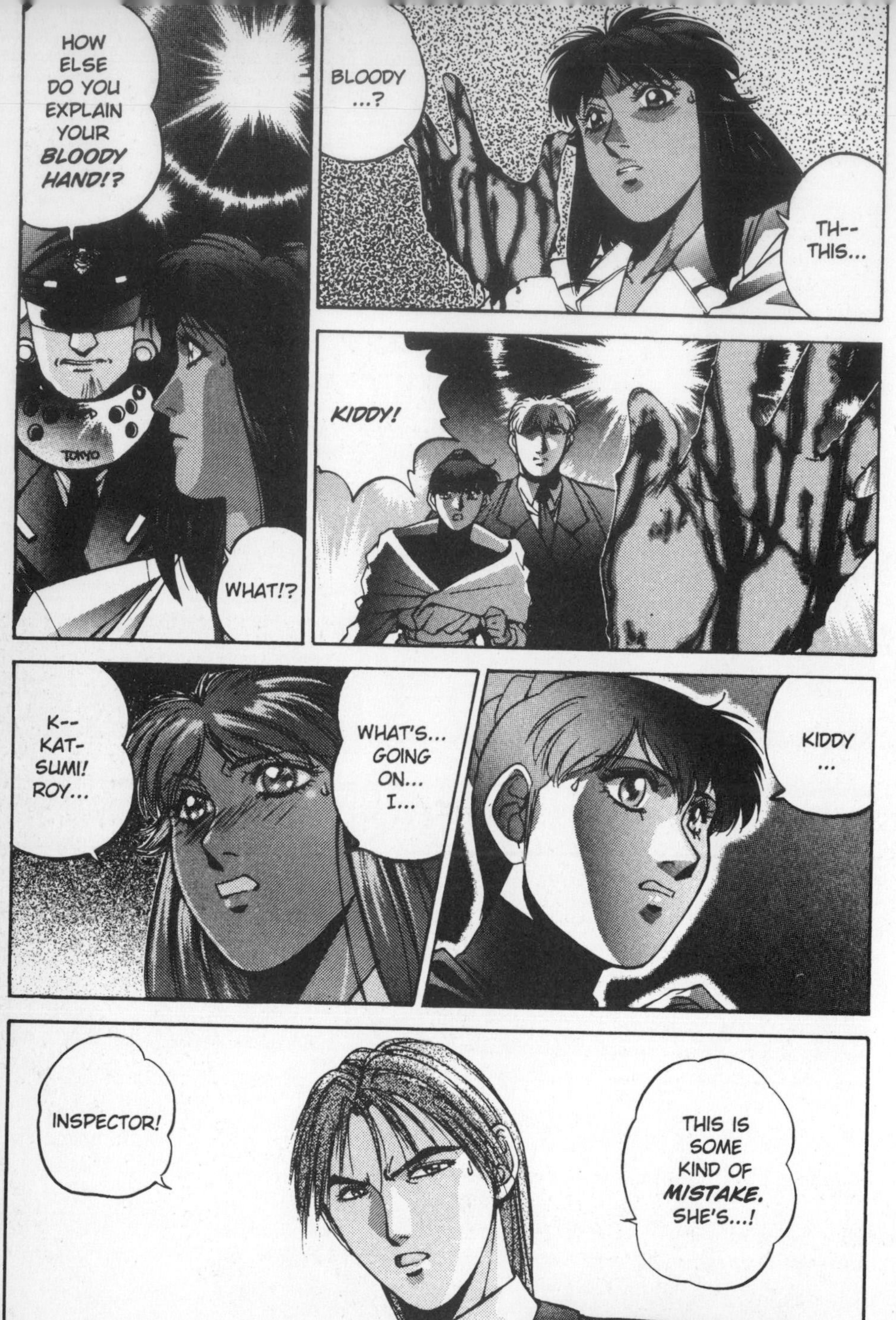
HOW ELSE DO YOU EXPLAIN YOUR *BLOODY HAND!?*
TOKYO
WHAT!?
BLOODY ...?
TH-- THIS...
KIDDY!
K-- KAT-SUMI! ROY...
WHAT'S... GOING ON... I...
KIDDY ...
INSPECTOR!
THIS IS SOME KIND OF *MISTAKE.* SHE'S...!

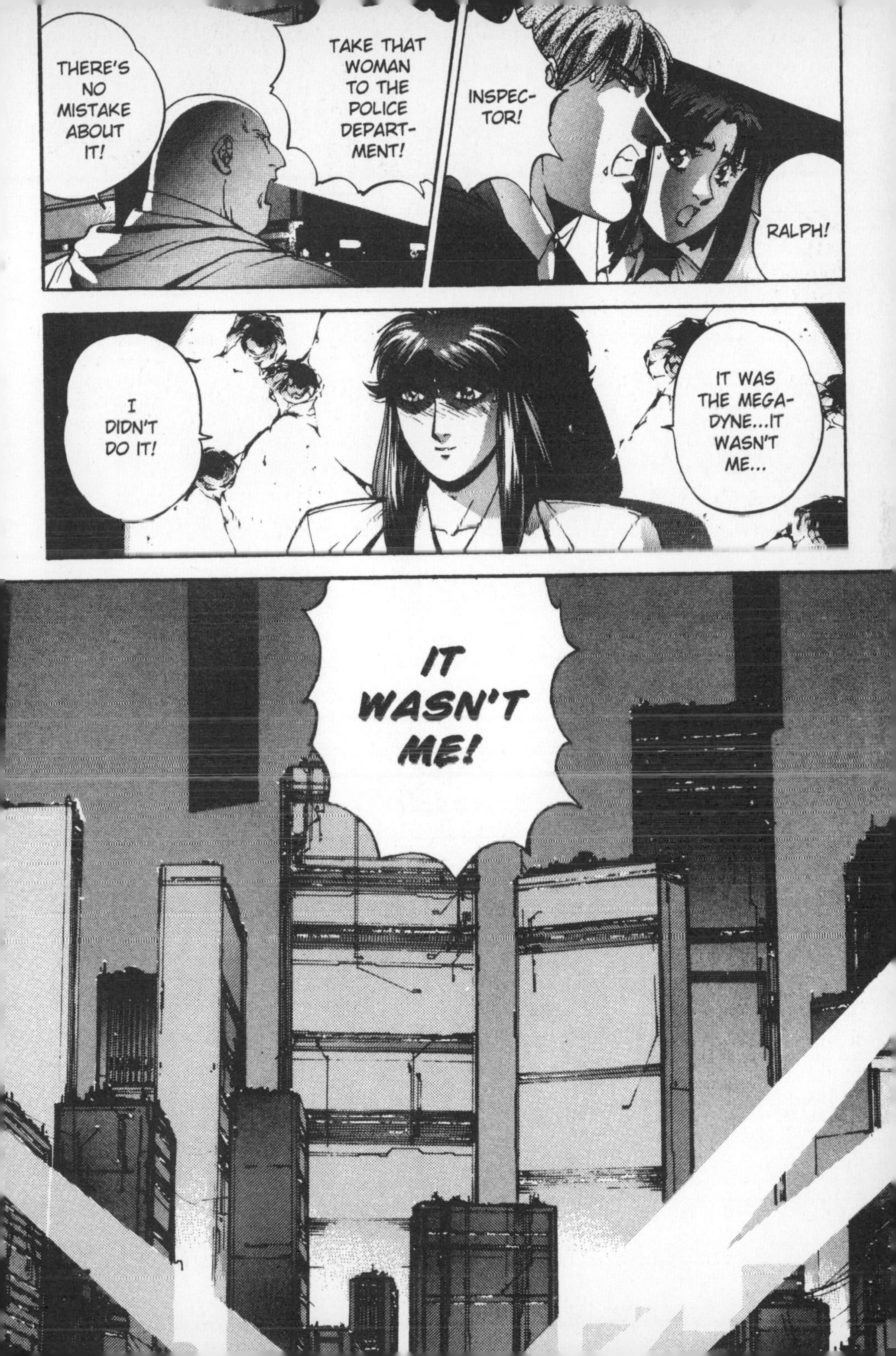
THERE'S NO MISTAKE ABOUT IT!
TAKE THAT WOMAN TO THE POLICE DEPARTMENT!
INSPECTOR!
RALPH!
I DIDN'T DO IT!
IT WAS THE MEGA-DYNE...IT WASN'T ME...
IT WASN'T ME!

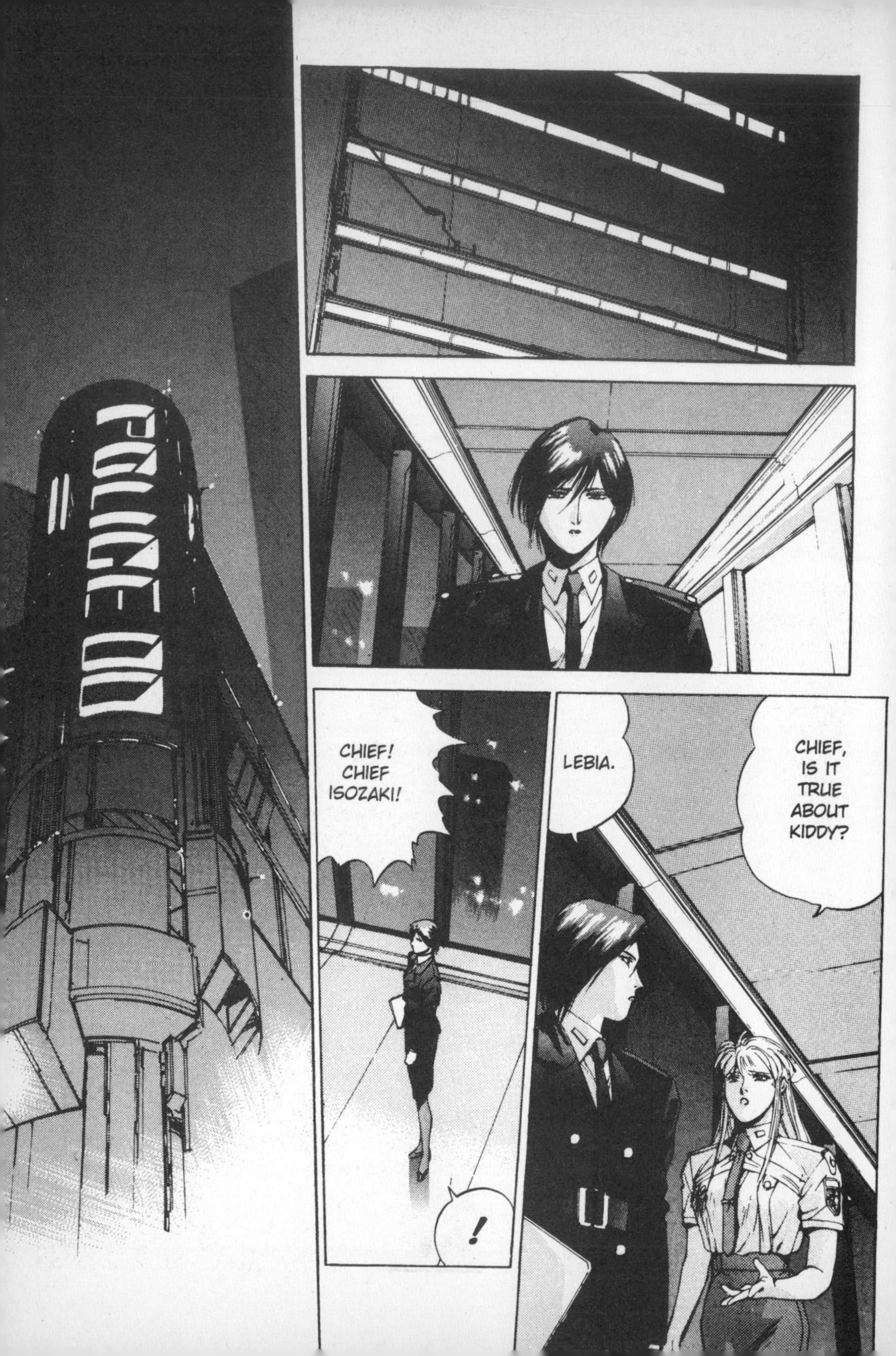
CHIEF! CHIEF ISOZAKI!
!
LEBIA.
CHIEF, IS IT TRUE ABOUT KIDDY?

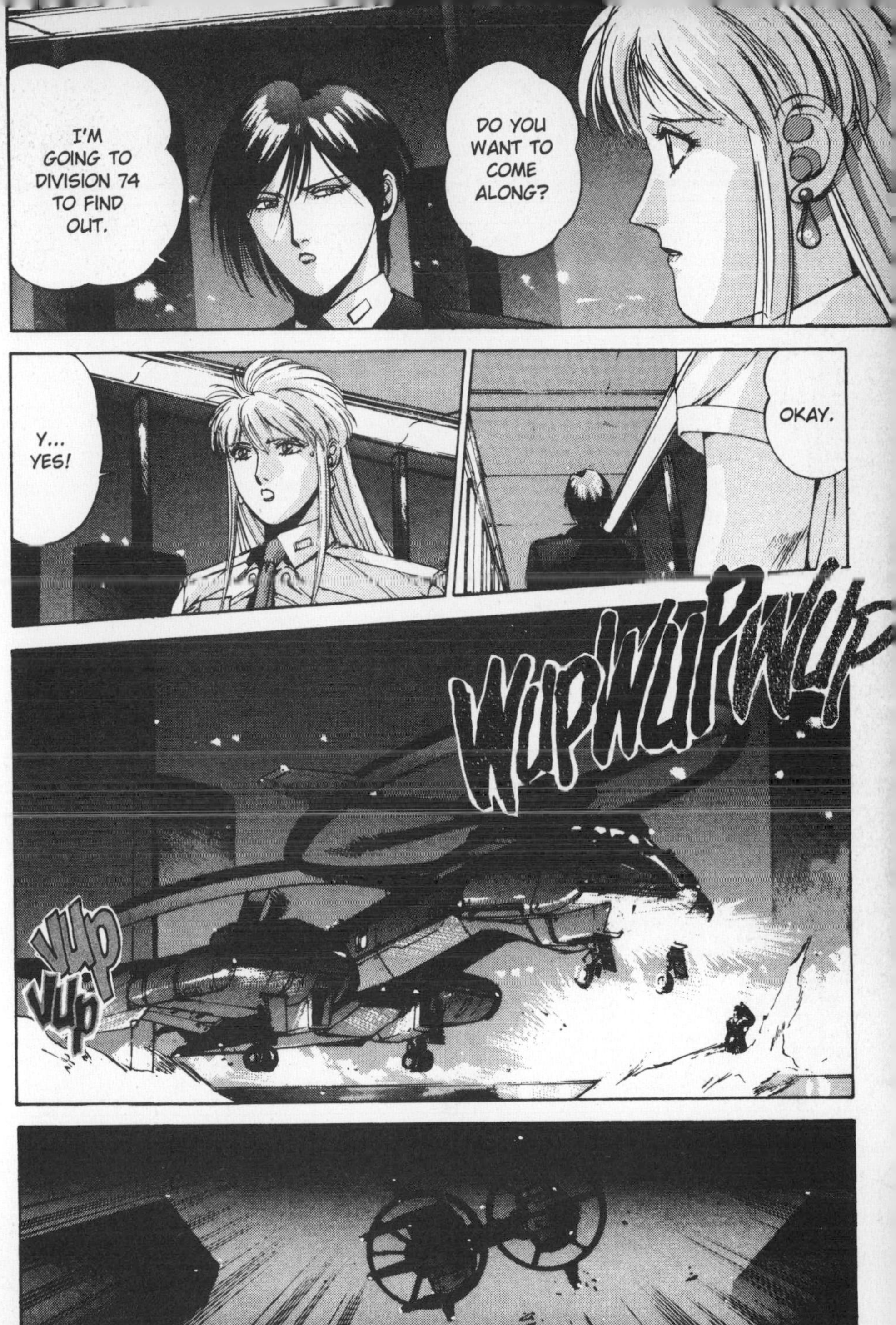
I'M GOING TO DIVISION 74 TO FIND OUT.
DO YOU WANT TO COME ALONG?
Y... YES!
OKAY.
WUPWUPWUP
VUP VUP

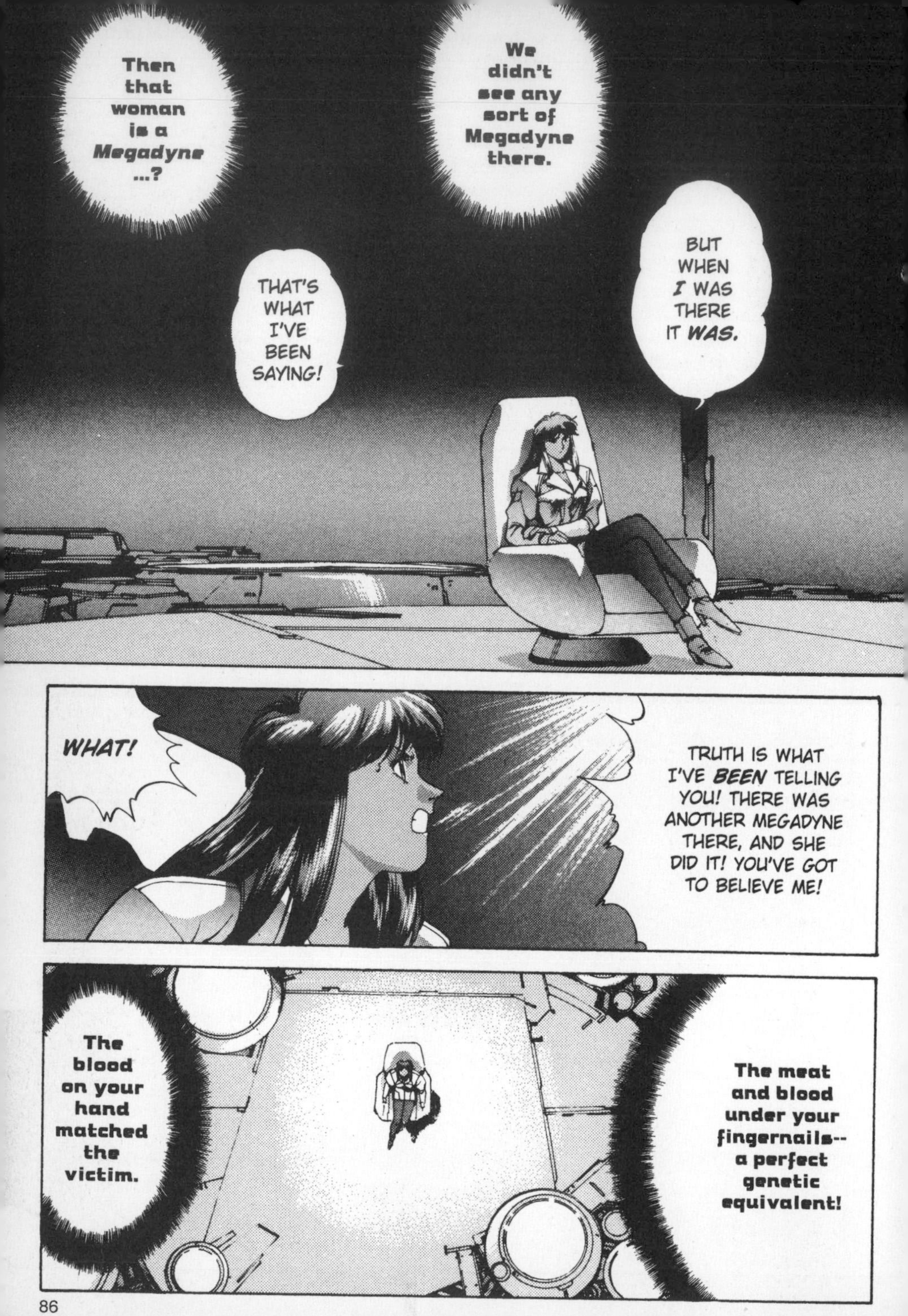

Then that woman is a *Megadyne* ...?
We didn't see any sort of Megadyne there.
THAT'S WHAT I'VE BEEN SAYING!
BUT WHEN *I* WAS THERE IT ***WAS.***
WHAT!
TRUTH IS WHAT I'VE ***BEEN*** TELLING YOU! THERE WAS ANOTHER MEGADYNE THERE, AND SHE DID IT! YOU'VE GOT TO BELIEVE ME!
The blood on your hand matched the victim.
The meat and blood under your fingernails-- a perfect genetic equivalent!

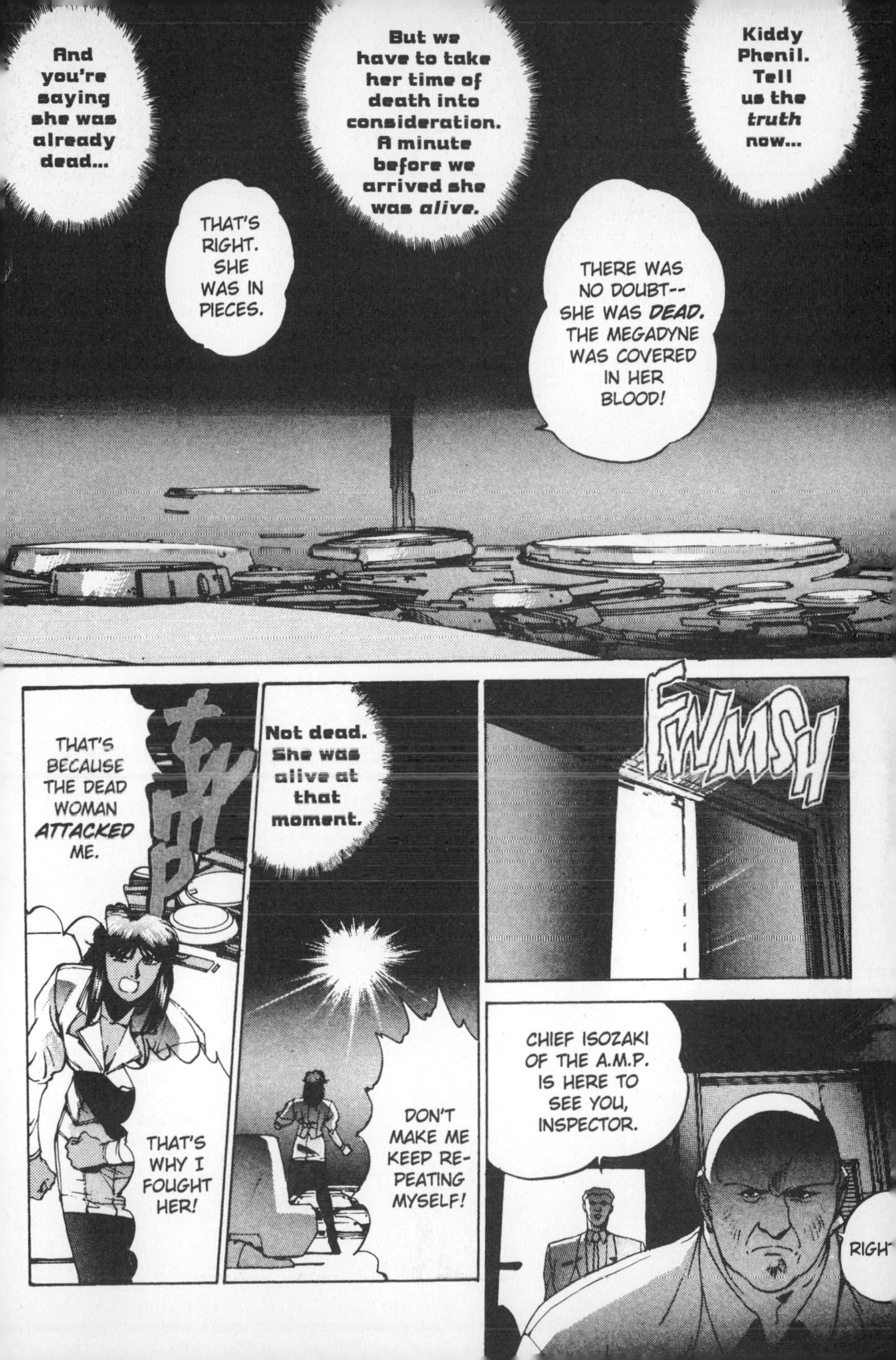
And you're saying she was already dead...
But we have to take her time of death into consideration. A minute before we arrived she was *alive.*
Kiddy Phenil. Tell us the *truth* now...
THAT'S RIGHT. SHE WAS IN PIECES.
THERE WAS NO DOUBT-- SHE WAS *DEAD.* THE MEGADYNE WAS COVERED IN HER BLOOD!
THAT'S BECAUSE THE DEAD WOMAN *ATTACKED* ME.
THAT'S WHY I FOUGHT HER!
Not dead. She was alive at that moment.
DON'T MAKE ME KEEP RE-PEATING MYSELF!
FWMSH
CHIEF ISOZAKI OF THE A.M.P. IS HERE TO SEE YOU, INSPECTOR.
RIGH

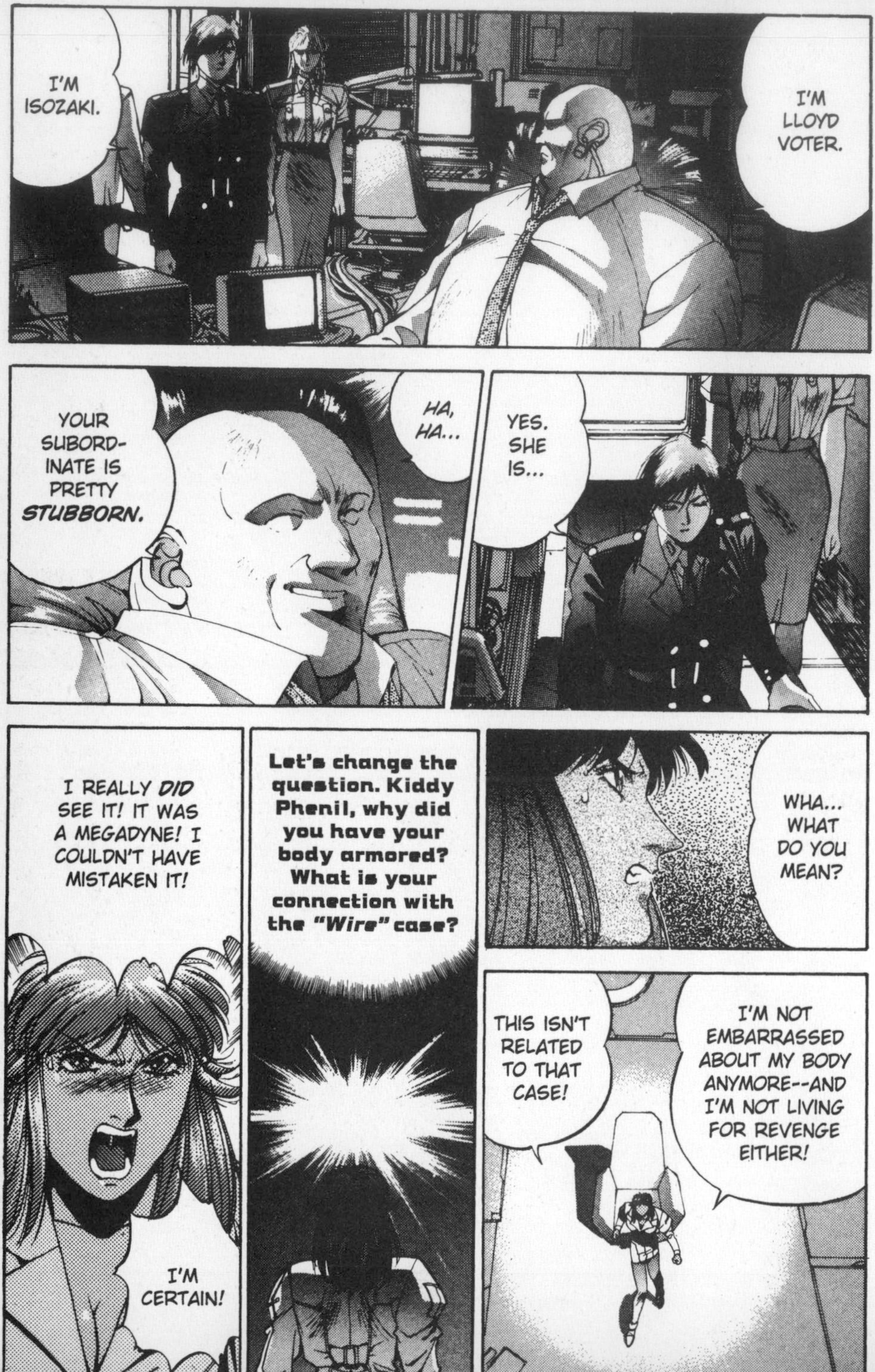
I'M ISOZAKI.
I'M LLOYD VOTER.
YOUR SUBORD-INATE IS PRETTY *STUBBORN.*
HA, HA...
YES. SHE IS...
I REALLY *DID* SEE IT! IT WAS A MEGADYNE! I COULDN'T HAVE MISTAKEN IT!
I'M CERTAIN!
Let's change the question. Kiddy Phenil, why did you have your body armored? What is your connection with the *"Wire"* case?
WHA... WHAT DO YOU MEAN?
THIS ISN'T RELATED TO THAT CASE!
I'M NOT EMBARRASSED ABOUT MY BODY ANYMORE--AND I'M NOT LIVING FOR REVENGE EITHER!

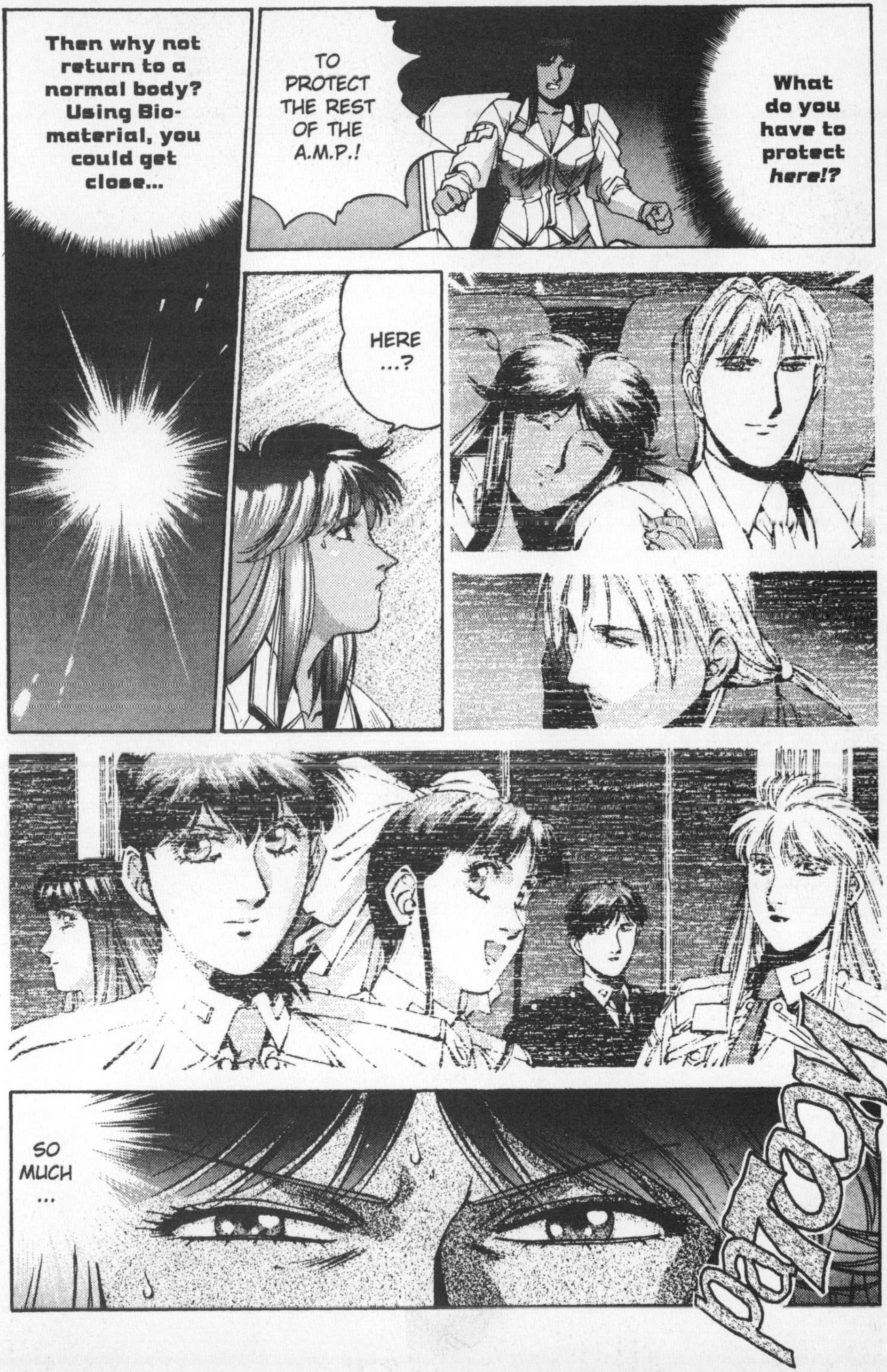
Then why not return to a normal body? Using Bio-material, you could get close...
TO PROTECT THE REST OF THE A.M.P.!
What do you have to protect *here!?*
HERE ...?
SO MUCH ...

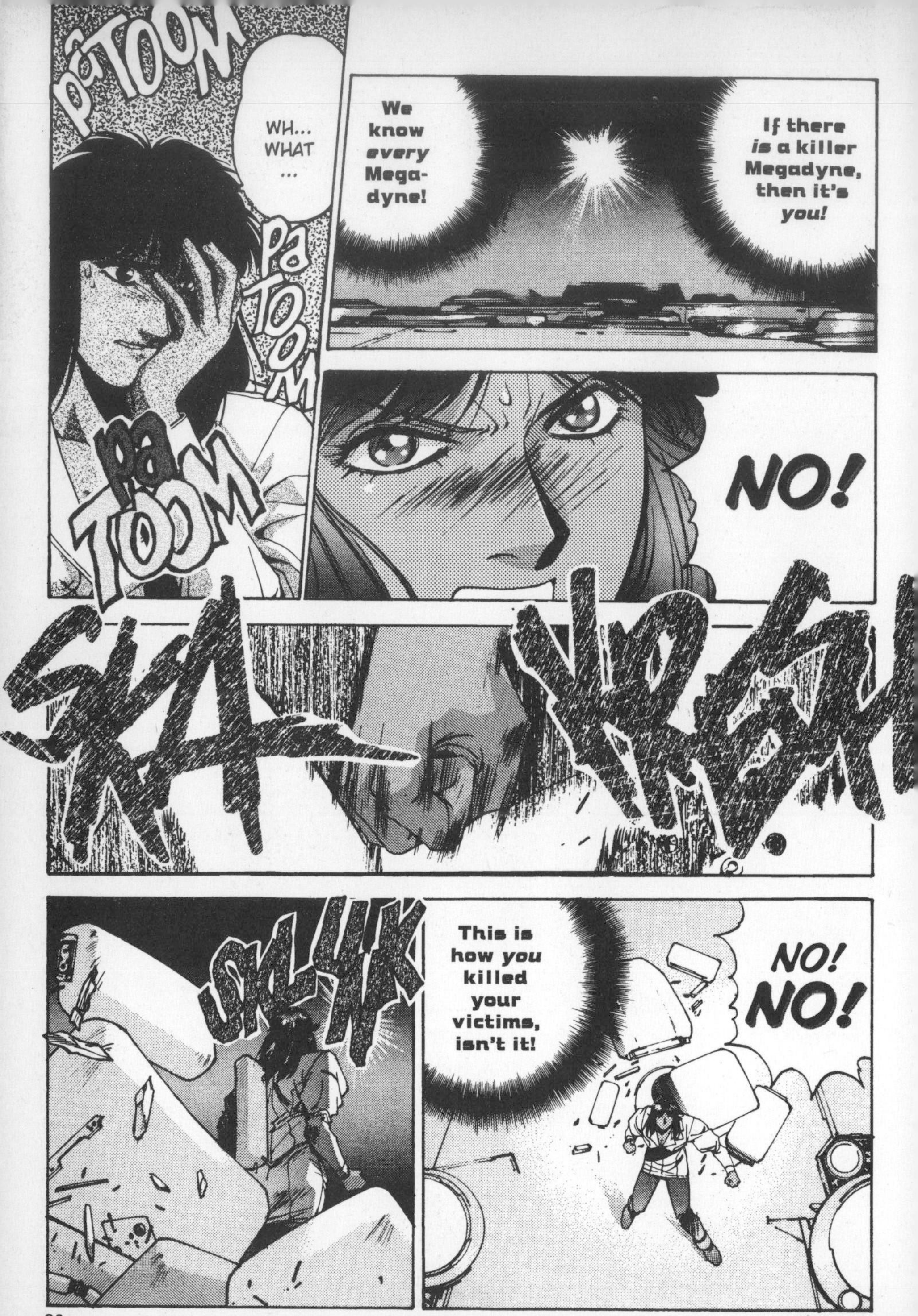
pa TOOM
WH... WHAT ...
pa TOO OM
pa TOOM
We know every Mega-dyne!
If there is a killer Megadyne, then it's you!
NO!
SKA KRASH
SPLUK
This is how you killed your victims, isn't it!
NO! NO!

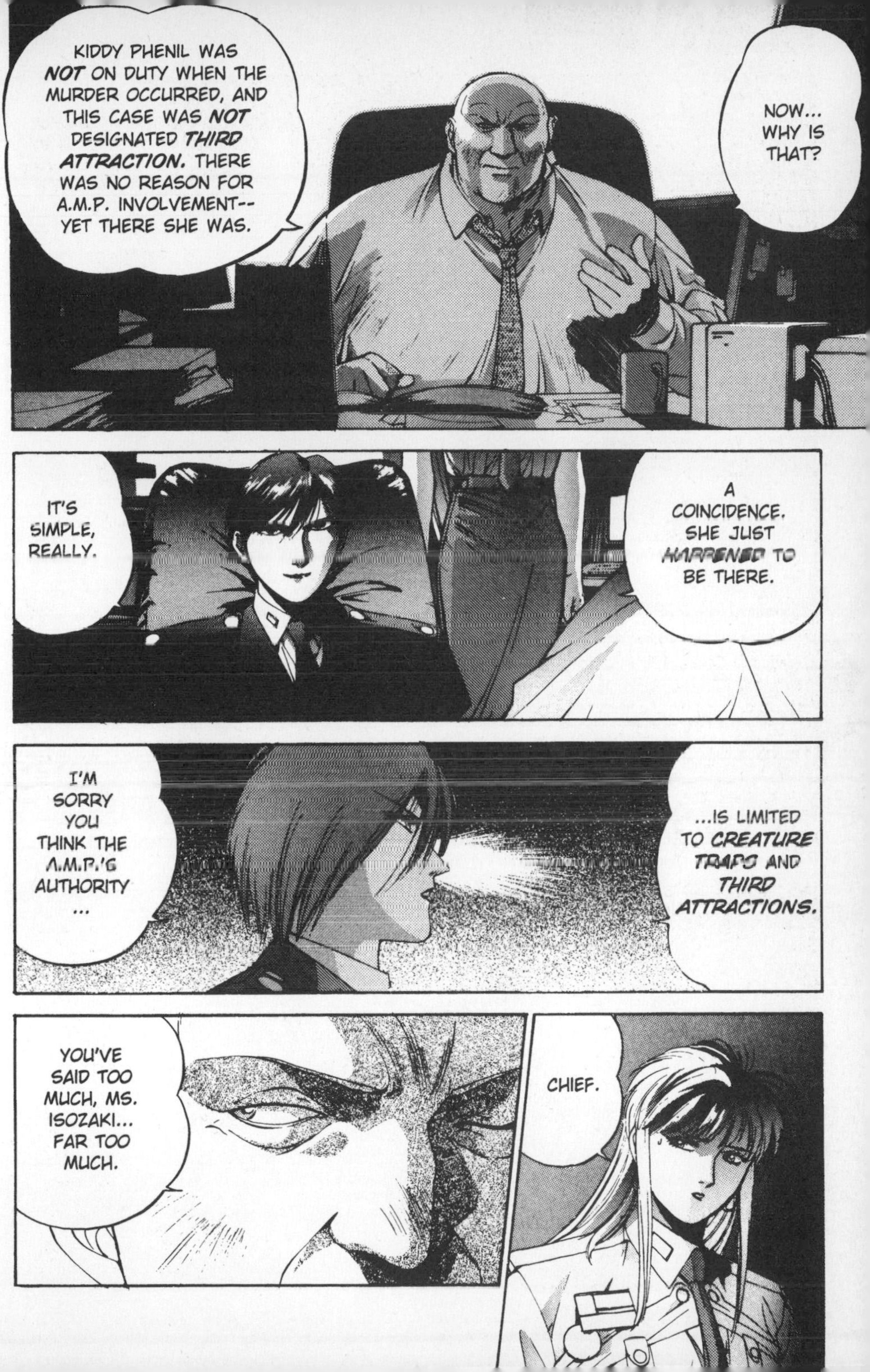
KIDDY PHENIL WAS *NOT* ON DUTY WHEN THE MURDER OCCURRED, AND THIS CASE WAS *NOT* DESIGNATED *THIRD ATTRACTION.* THERE WAS NO REASON FOR A.M.P. INVOLVEMENT--YET THERE SHE WAS.
NOW... WHY IS THAT?
IT'S SIMPLE, REALLY.
A COINCIDENCE. SHE JUST *HAPPENED* TO BE THERE.
I'M SORRY YOU THINK THE A.M.P.'S AUTHORITY ...
...IS LIMITED TO *CREATURE TRAPS* AND *THIRD ATTRACTIONS.*
YOU'VE SAID TOO MUCH, MS. ISOZAKI... FAR TOO MUCH.
CHIEF.

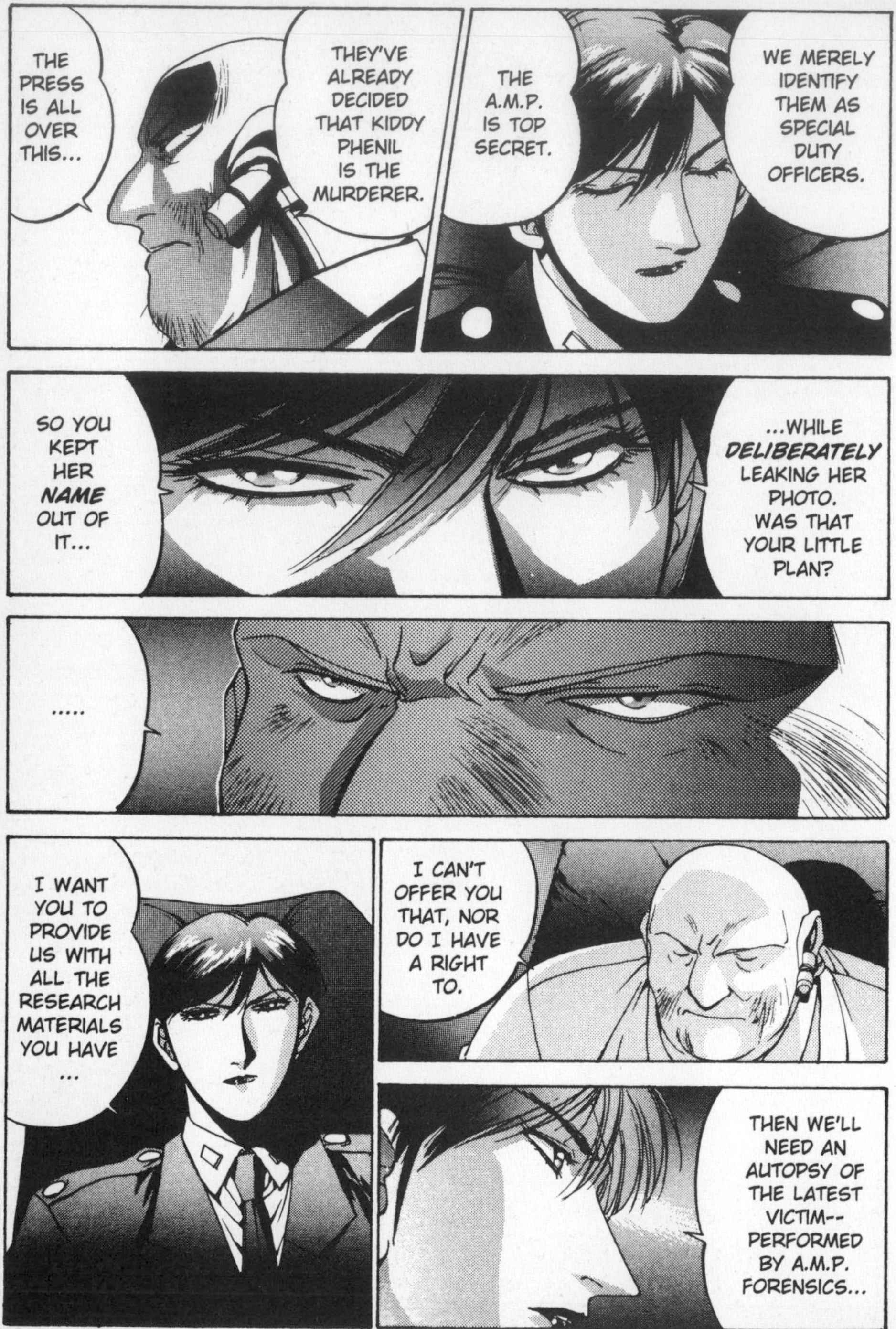
THE PRESS IS ALL OVER THIS...
THEY'VE ALREADY DECIDED THAT KIDDY PHENIL IS THE MURDERER.
THE A.M.P. IS TOP SECRET.
WE MERELY IDENTIFY THEM AS SPECIAL DUTY OFFICERS.
SO YOU KEPT HER NAME OUT OF IT...
...WHILE DELIBERATELY LEAKING HER PHOTO. WAS THAT YOUR LITTLE PLAN?
.....
I WANT YOU TO PROVIDE US WITH ALL THE RESEARCH MATERIALS YOU HAVE ...
I CAN'T OFFER YOU THAT, NOR DO I HAVE A RIGHT TO.
THEN WE'LL NEED AN AUTOPSY OF THE LATEST VICTIM--PERFORMED BY A.M.P. FORENSICS...

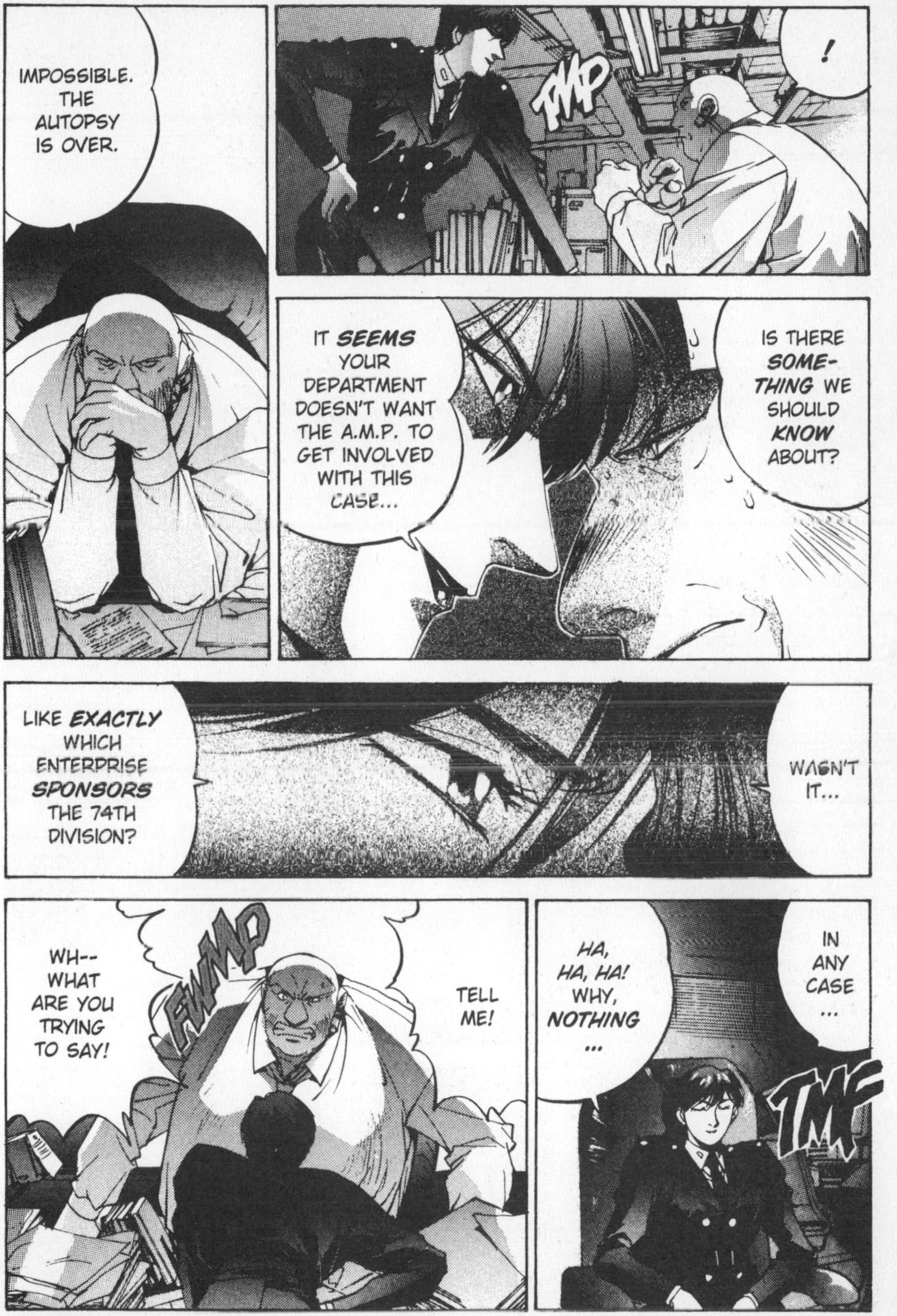
IMPOSSIBLE. THE AUTOPSY IS OVER.
TMP
!
IT SEEMS YOUR DEPARTMENT DOESN'T WANT THE A.M.P. TO GET INVOLVED WITH THIS CASE...
IS THERE SOMETHING WE SHOULD KNOW ABOUT?
LIKE EXACTLY WHICH ENTERPRISE SPONSORS THE 74TH DIVISION?
WASN'T IT...
WH-- WHAT ARE YOU TRYING TO SAY!
FWMP
TELL ME!
HA, HA, HA! WHY, NOTHING...
IN ANY CASE...
TMF

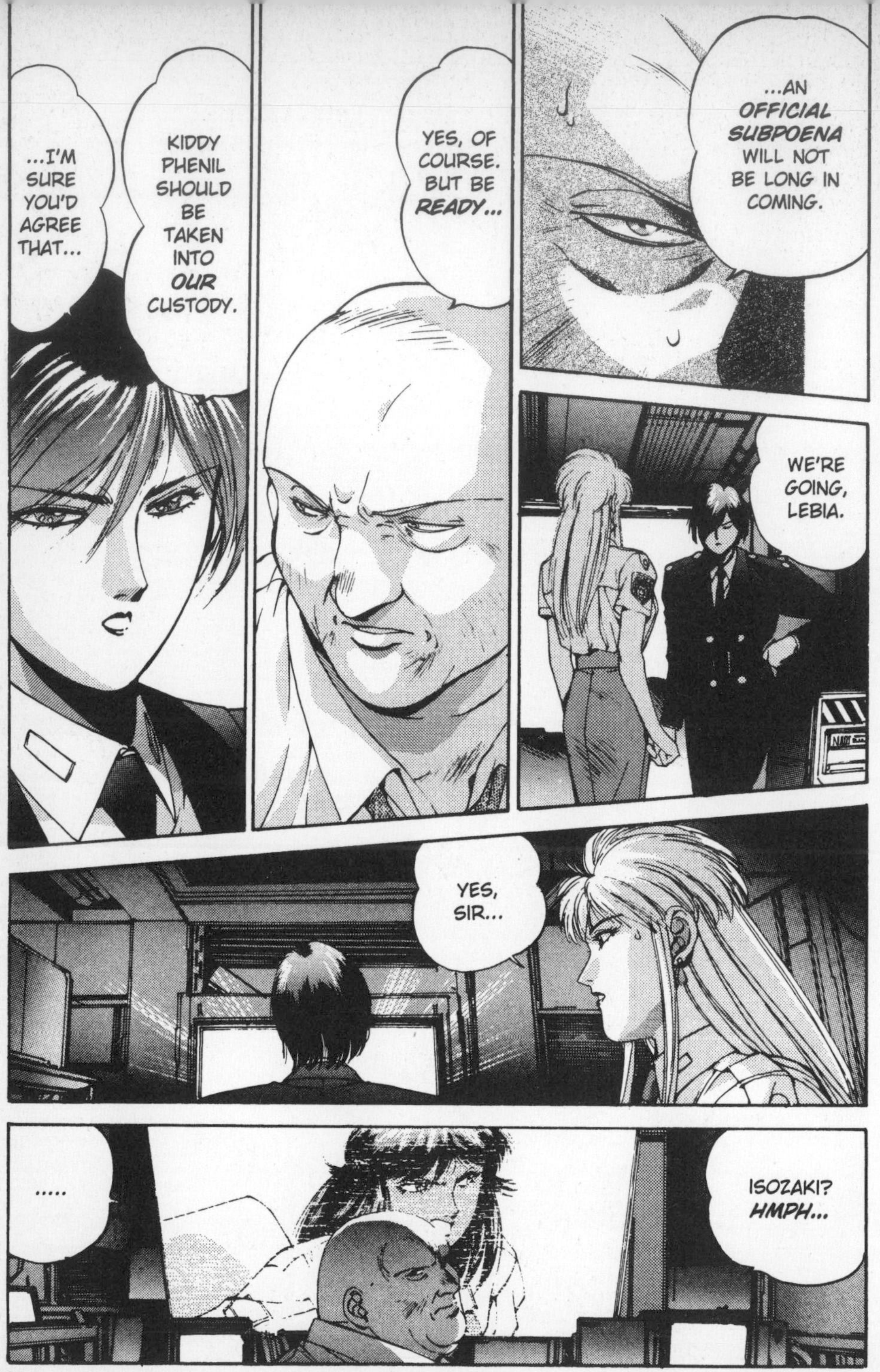
...I'M SURE YOU'D AGREE THAT...
KIDDY PHENIL SHOULD BE TAKEN INTO OUR CUSTODY.
YES, OF COURSE. BUT BE READY...
...AN OFFICIAL SUBPOENA WILL NOT BE LONG IN COMING.
WE'RE GOING, LEBIA.
YES, SIR...
.....
ISOZAKI? HMPH...

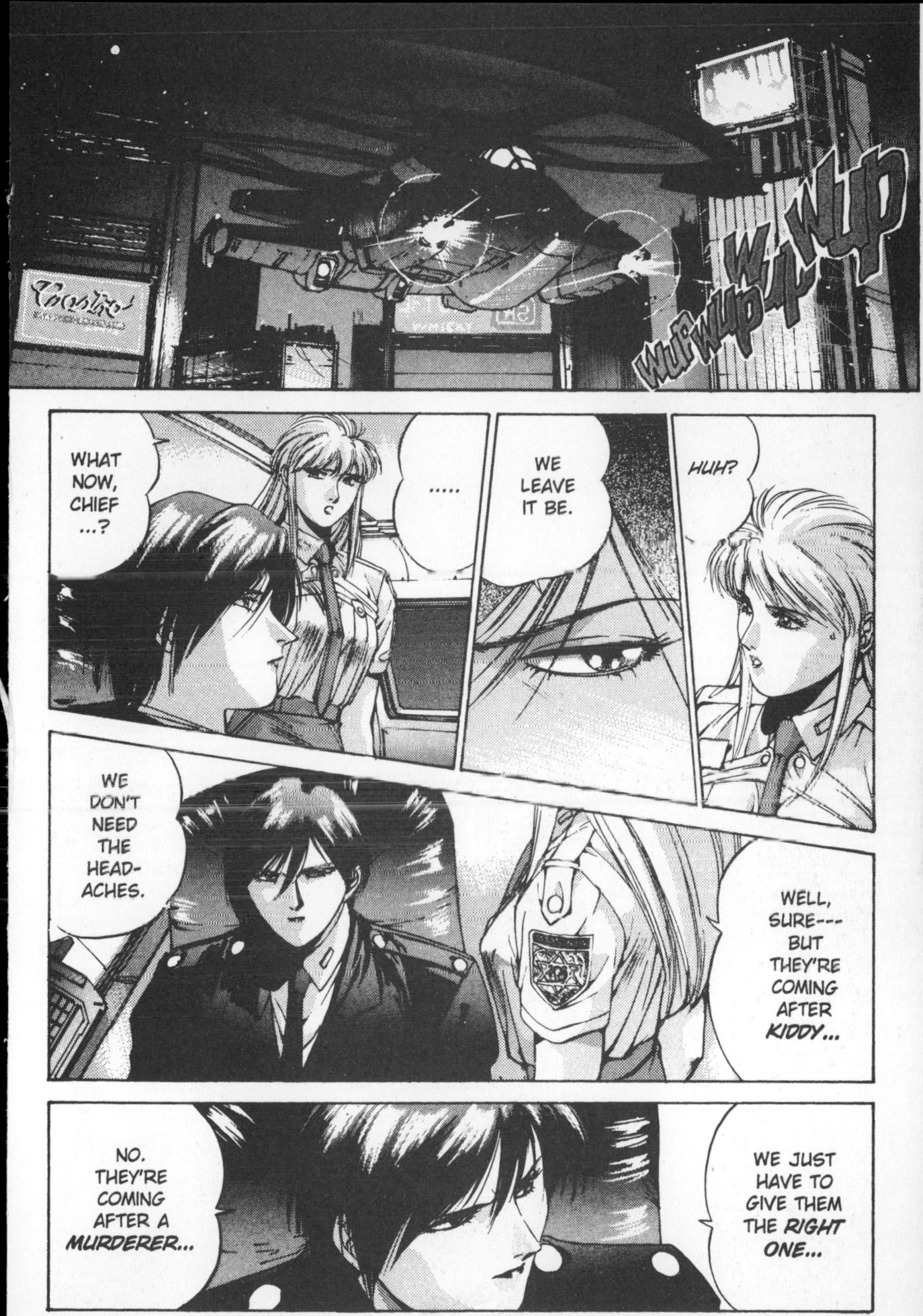
WUP WUP WUP WUP
WHAT NOW, CHIEF ...?
.....
WE LEAVE IT BE.
HUH?
WE DON'T NEED THE HEAD-ACHES.
WELL, SURE--- BUT THEY'RE COMING AFTER *KIDDY*...
NO. THEY'RE COMING AFTER A *MURDERER*...
WE JUST HAVE TO GIVE THEM THE *RIGHT ONE*...

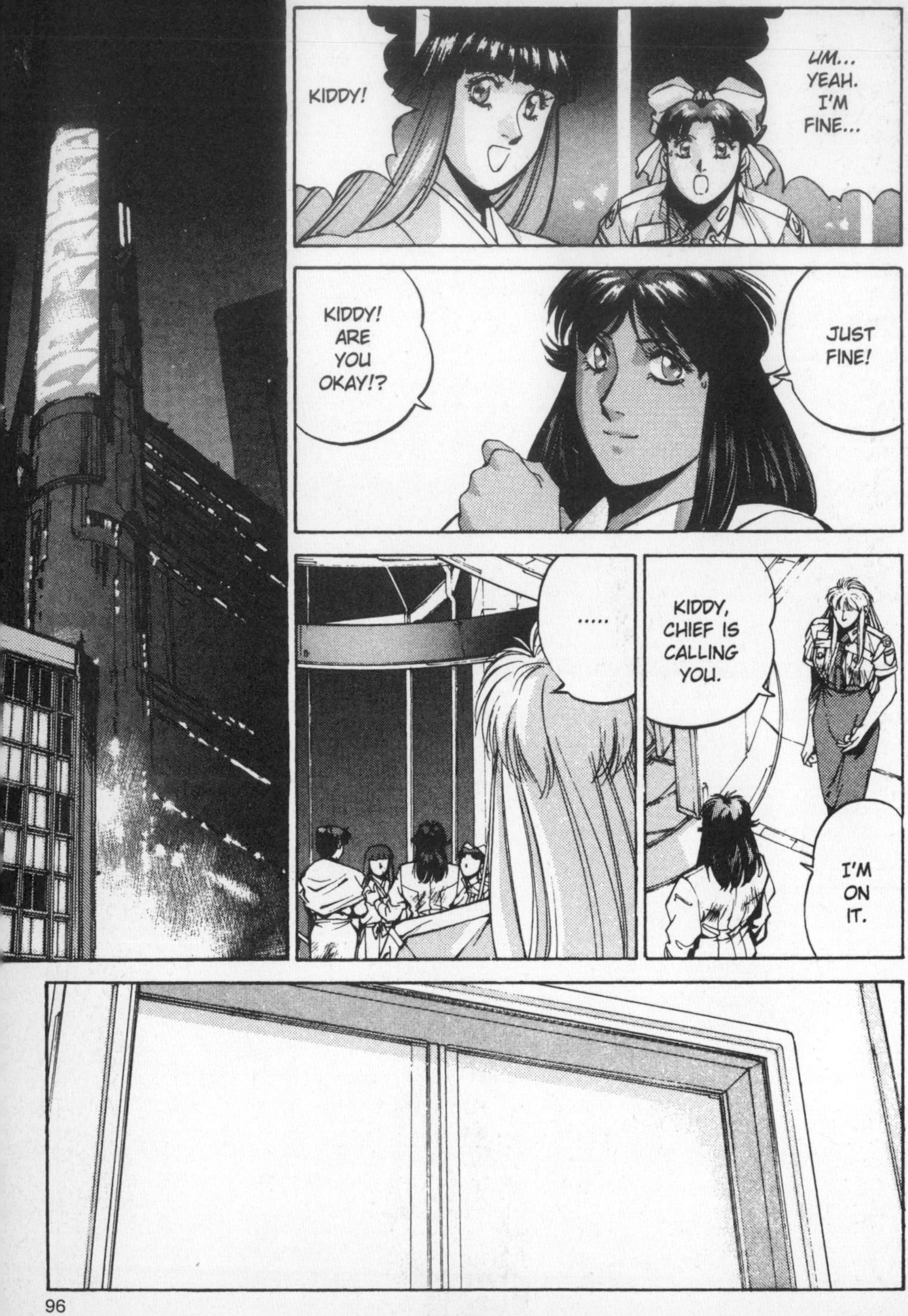
KIDDY!
UM... YEAH. I'M FINE...
KIDDY! ARE YOU OKAY!?
JUST FINE!
.....
KIDDY, CHIEF IS CALLING YOU.
I'M ON IT.

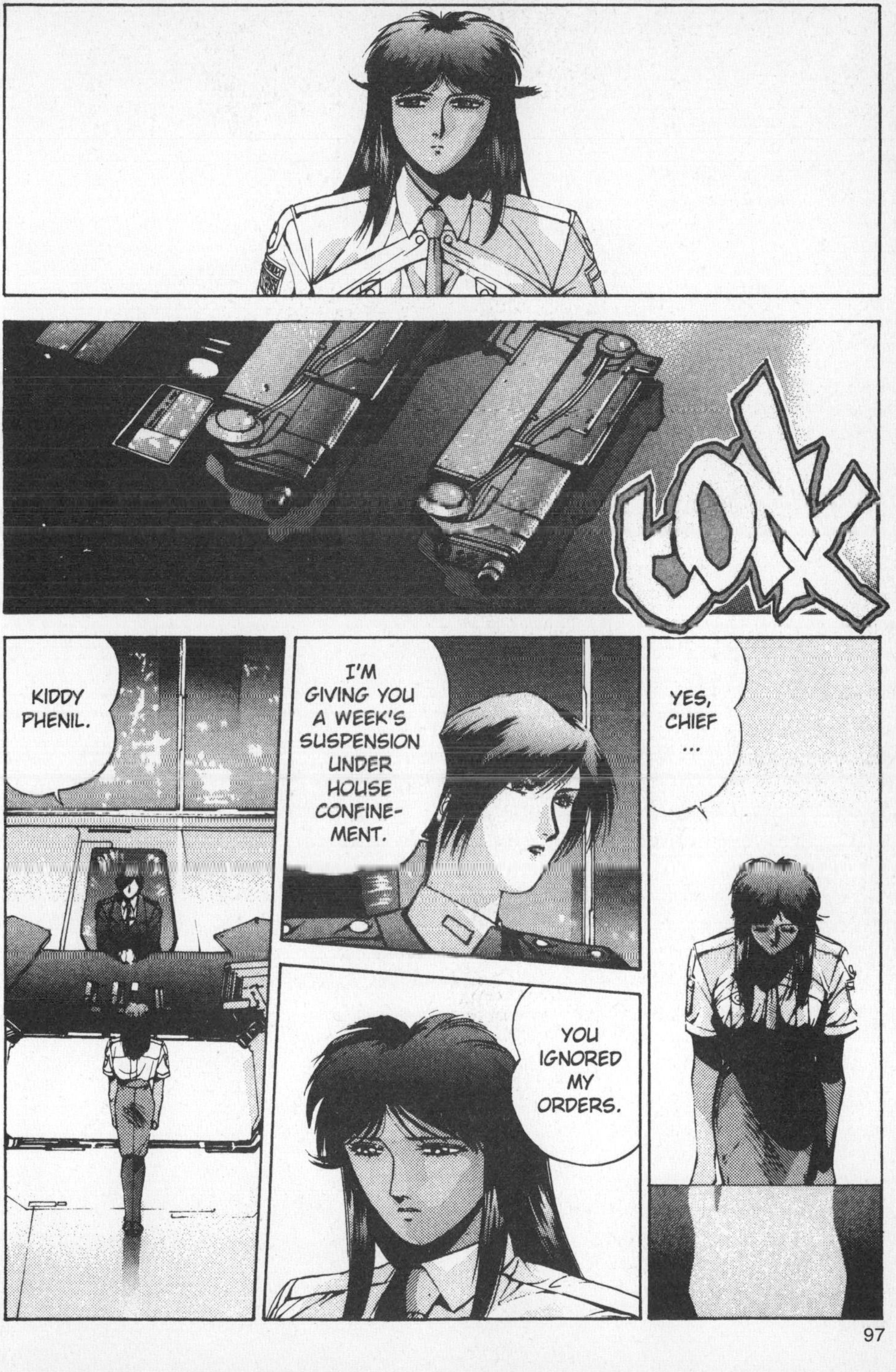
COK
KIDDY PHENIL.
I'M GIVING YOU A WEEK'S SUSPENSION UNDER HOUSE CONFINE-MENT.
YOU IGNORED MY ORDERS.
YES, CHIEF ...

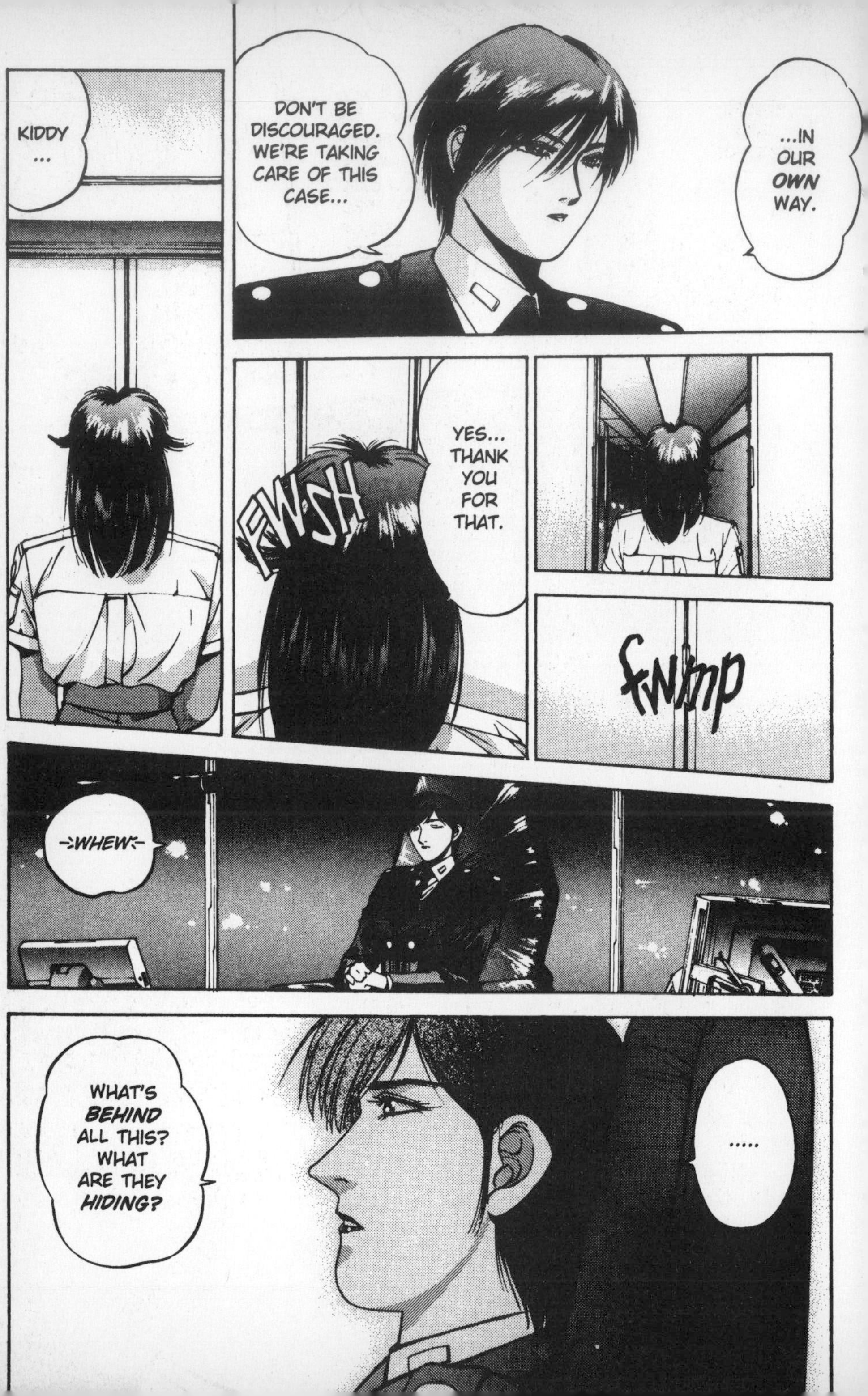

KIDDY ...
DON'T BE DISCOURAGED. WE'RE TAKING CARE OF THIS CASE...
...IN OUR OWN WAY.
YES... THANK YOU FOR THAT.
FWSH
fwimp
-WHEW-
WHAT'S BEHIND ALL THIS? WHAT ARE THEY HIDING?
.....

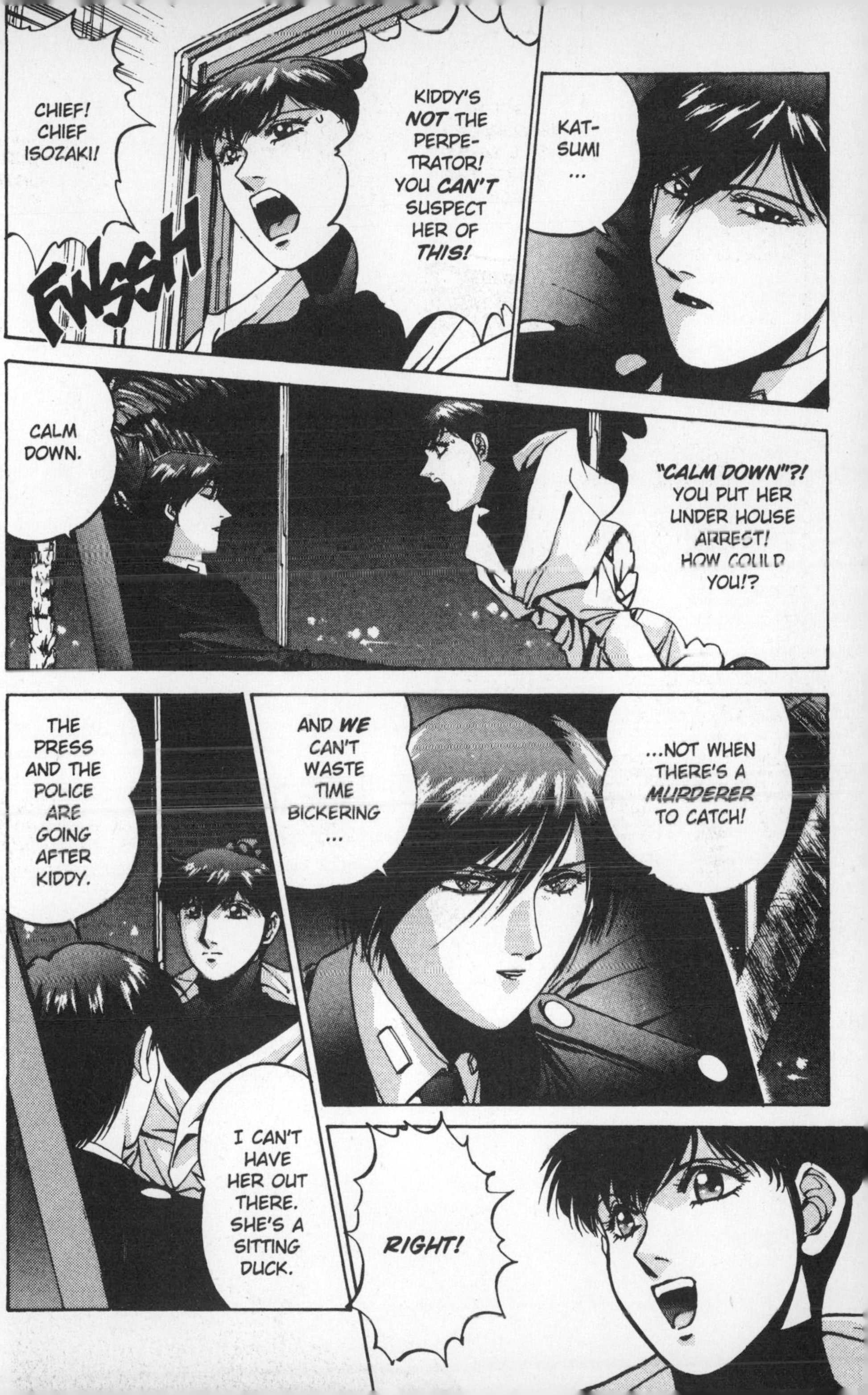
CHIEF! CHIEF ISOZAKI!
FWSSH
KIDDY'S *NOT* THE PERPETRATOR! YOU *CAN'T* SUSPECT HER OF *THIS!*
KATSUMI ...
CALM DOWN.
"CALM DOWN"?! YOU PUT HER UNDER HOUSE ARREST! HOW COULD YOU!?
THE PRESS AND THE POLICE ARE GOING AFTER KIDDY.
AND *WE* CAN'T WASTE TIME BICKERING ...
...NOT WHEN THERE'S A *MURDERER* TO CATCH!
I CAN'T HAVE HER OUT THERE. SHE'S A SITTING DUCK.
RIGHT!

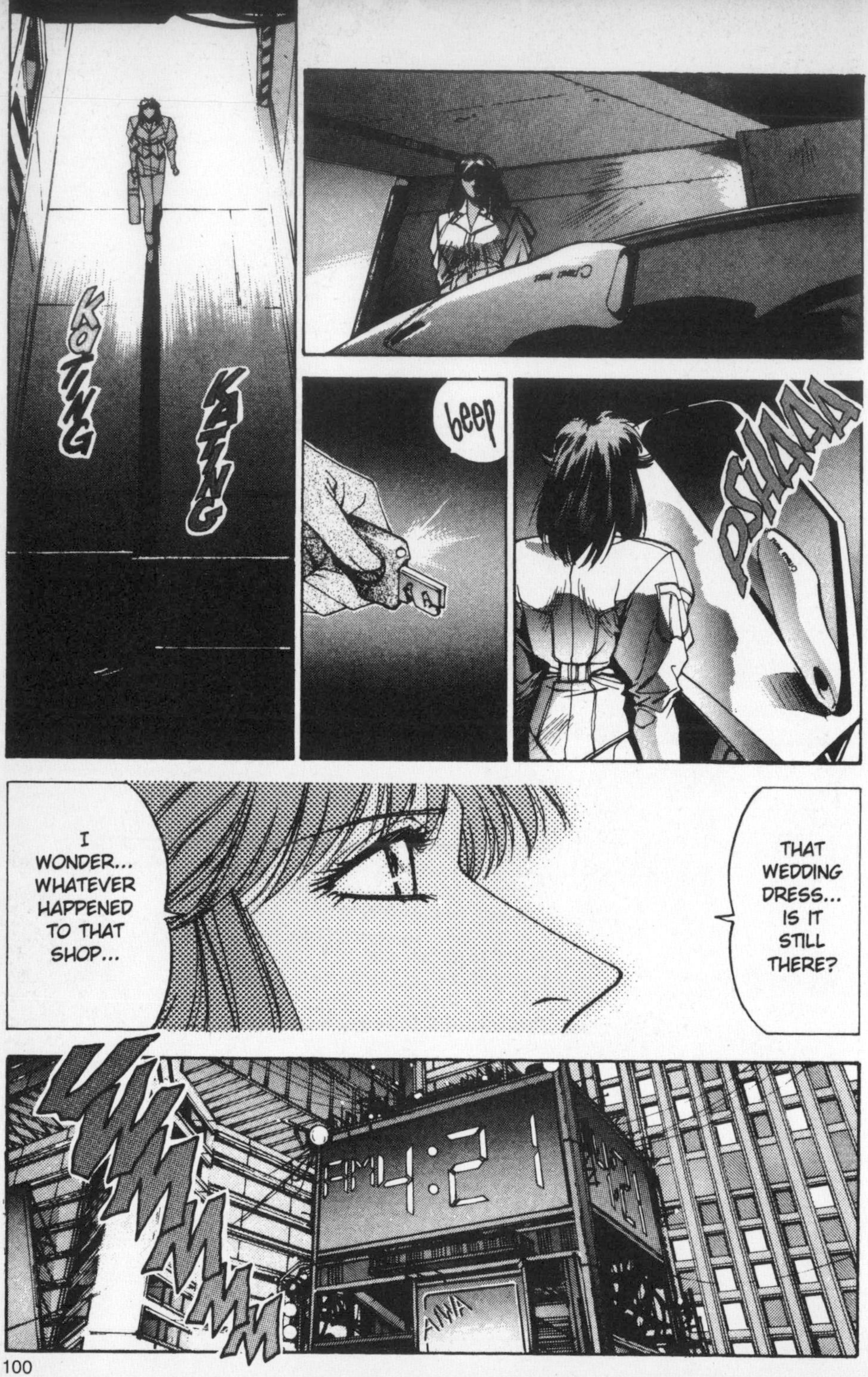
KOTING
KATING
beep
PSHAAA
I WONDER... WHATEVER HAPPENED TO THAT SHOP...
THAT WEDDING DRESS... IS IT STILL THERE?
AM4:21

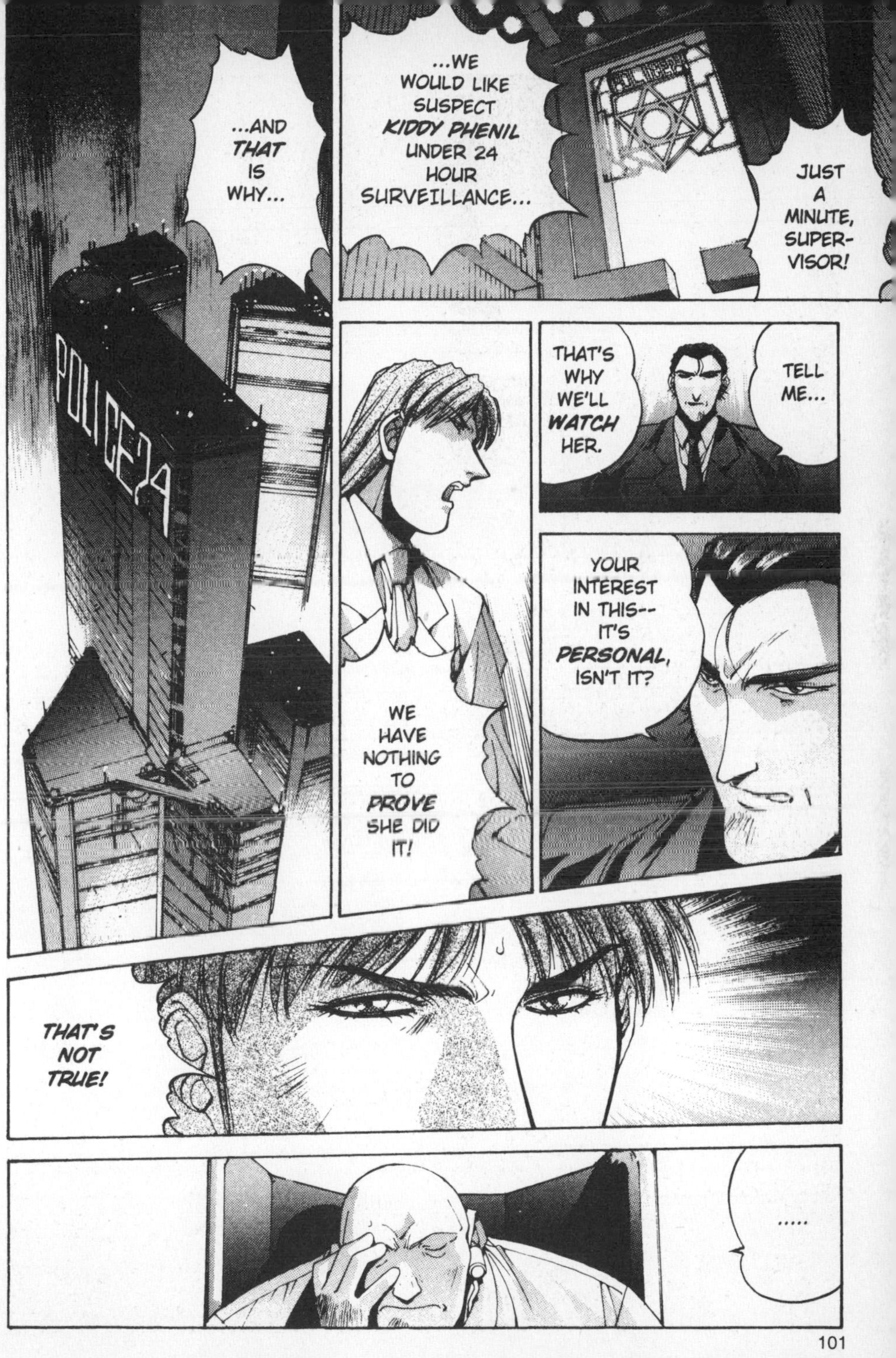
...AND THAT IS WHY...
POLICE24
...WE WOULD LIKE SUSPECT KIDDY PHENIL UNDER 24 HOUR SURVEILLANCE...
JUST A MINUTE, SUPER-VISOR!
WE HAVE NOTHING TO PROVE SHE DID IT!
THAT'S WHY WE'LL WATCH HER.
TELL ME...
YOUR INTEREST IN THIS-- IT'S PERSONAL, ISN'T IT?
THAT'S NOT TRUE!
.....

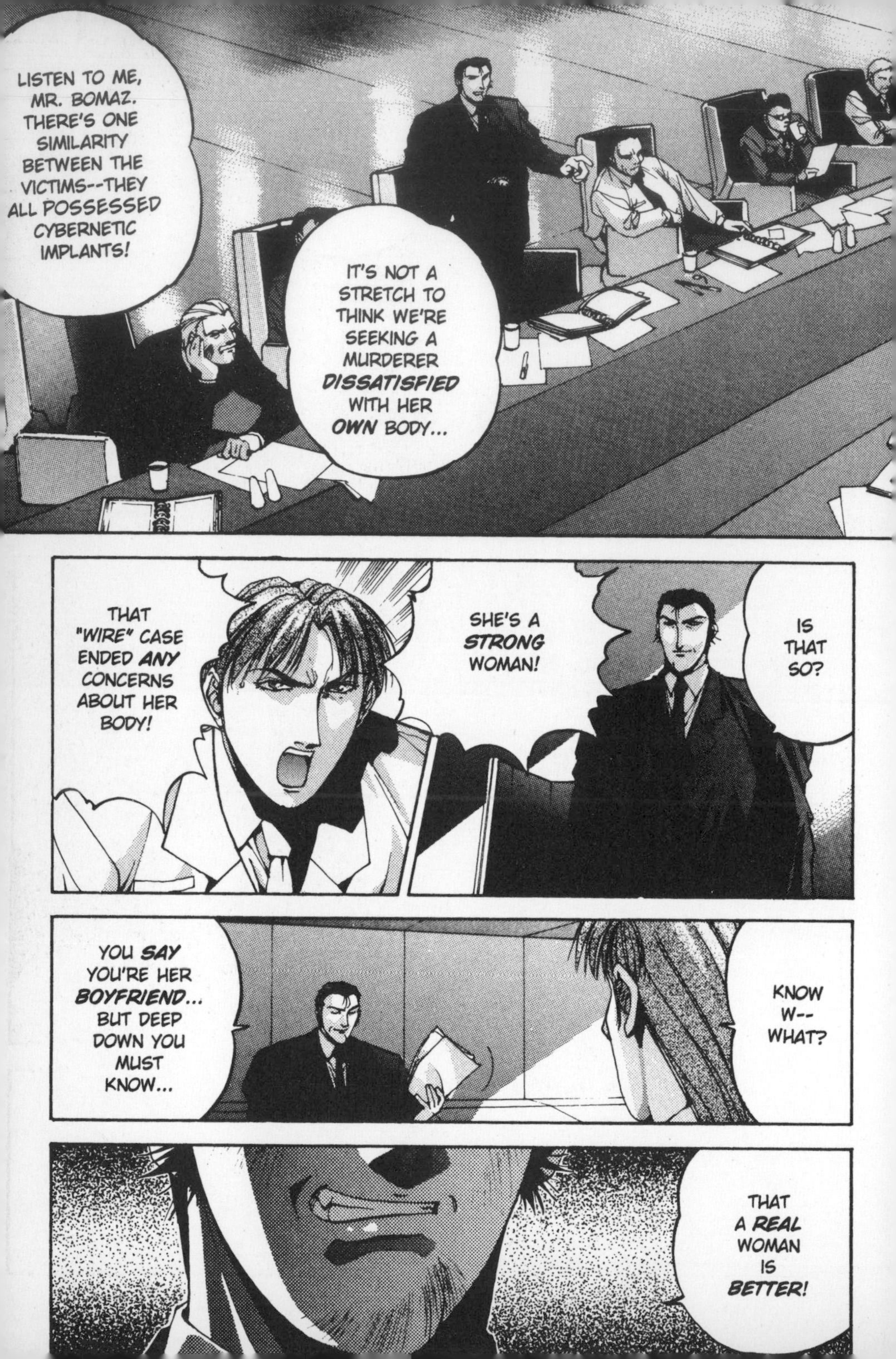
LISTEN TO ME, MR. BOMAZ. THERE'S ONE SIMILARITY BETWEEN THE VICTIMS--THEY ALL POSSESSED CYBERNETIC IMPLANTS!
IT'S NOT A STRETCH TO THINK WE'RE SEEKING A MURDERER DISSATISFIED WITH HER OWN BODY...
THAT "WIRE" CASE ENDED ANY CONCERNS ABOUT HER BODY!
SHE'S A STRONG WOMAN!
IS THAT SO?
YOU SAY YOU'RE HER BOYFRIEND... BUT DEEP DOWN YOU MUST KNOW...
KNOW W-- WHAT?
THAT A REAL WOMAN IS BETTER!

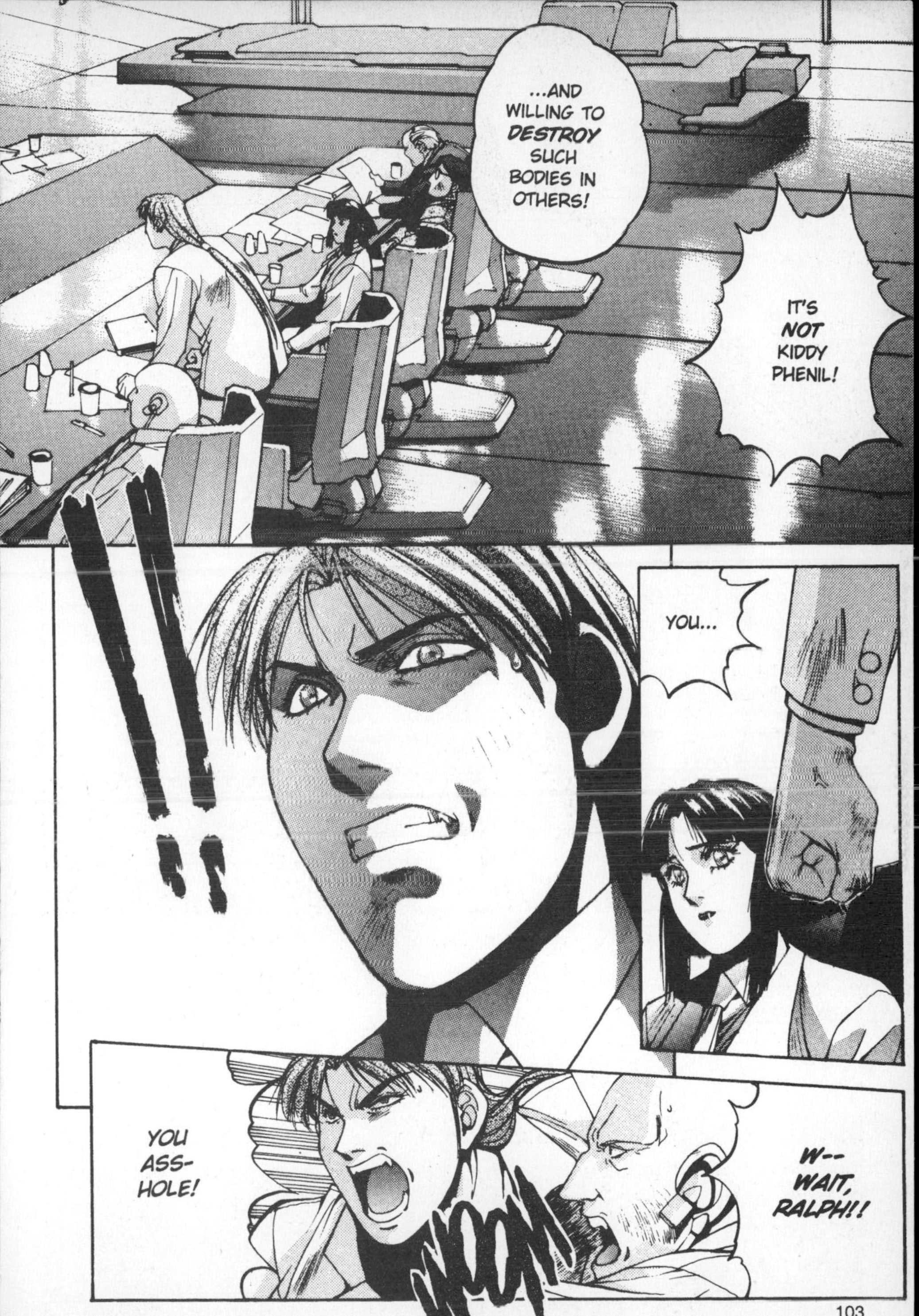
...AND WILLING TO DESTROY SUCH BODIES IN OTHERS!
IT'S NOT KIDDY PHENIL!
YOU...
YOU ASS-HOLE!
W-- WAIT, RALPH!!

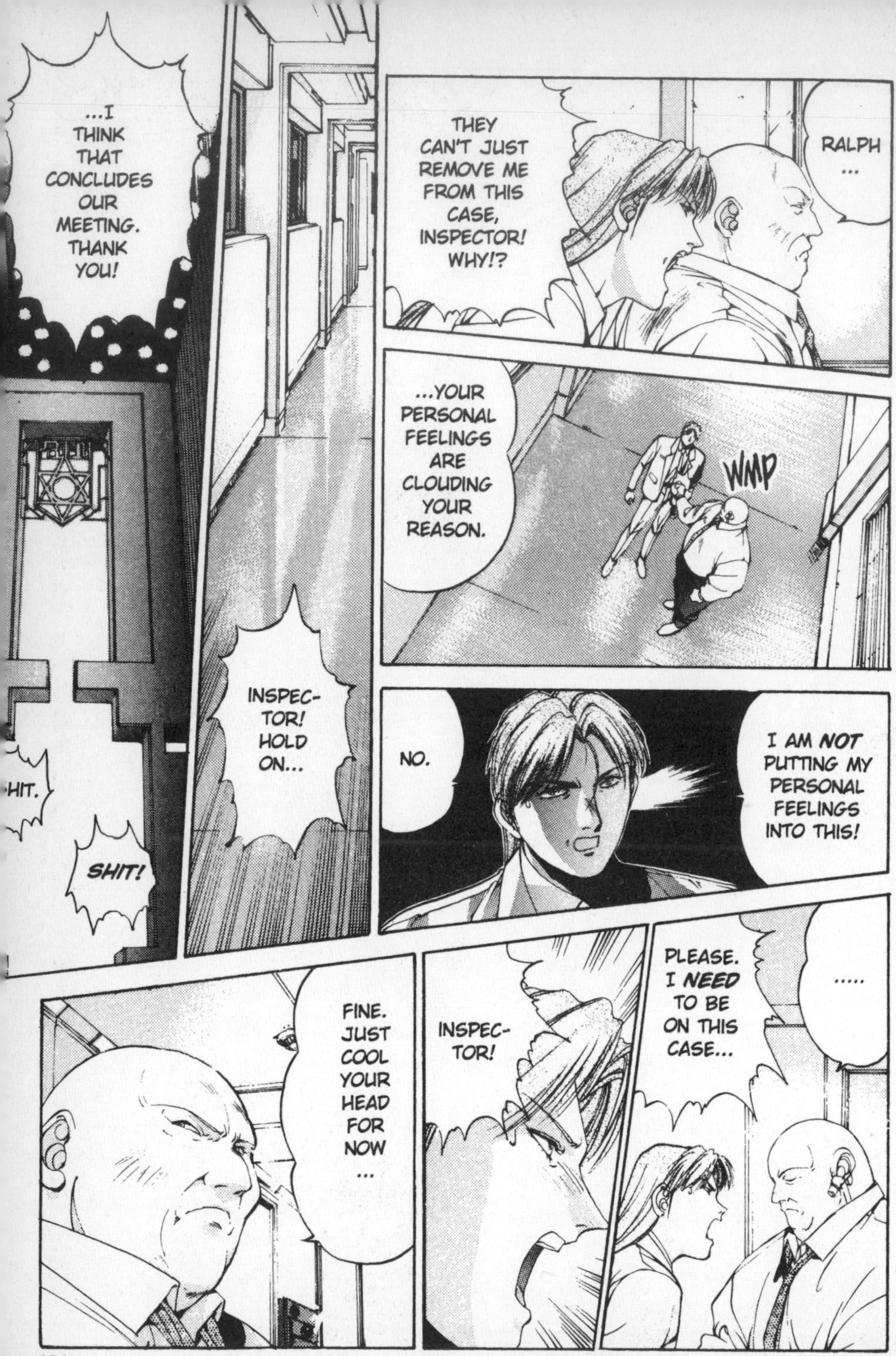
...I THINK THAT CONCLUDES OUR MEETING. THANK YOU!
HIT.
SHIT!
INSPECTOR! HOLD ON...
THEY CAN'T JUST REMOVE ME FROM THIS CASE, INSPECTOR! WHY!?
RALPH...
...YOUR PERSONAL FEELINGS ARE CLOUDING YOUR REASON.
WMP
NO.
I AM NOT PUTTING MY PERSONAL FEELINGS INTO THIS!
FINE. JUST COOL YOUR HEAD FOR NOW...
INSPECTOR!
PLEASE. I NEED TO BE ON THIS CASE...
.....

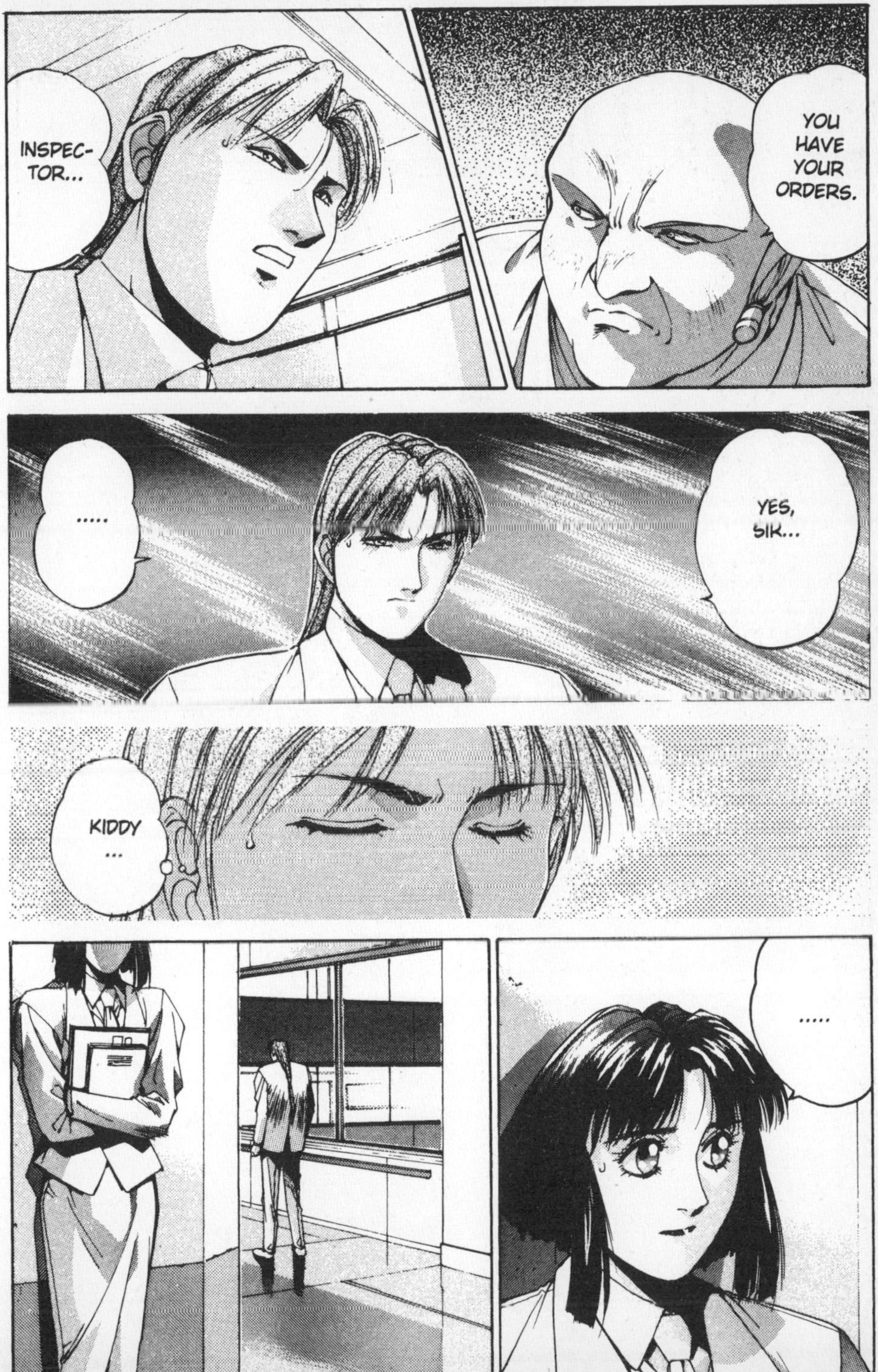
INSPECTOR...
YOU HAVE YOUR ORDERS.
.....
YES, SIR...
KIDDY ...
.....

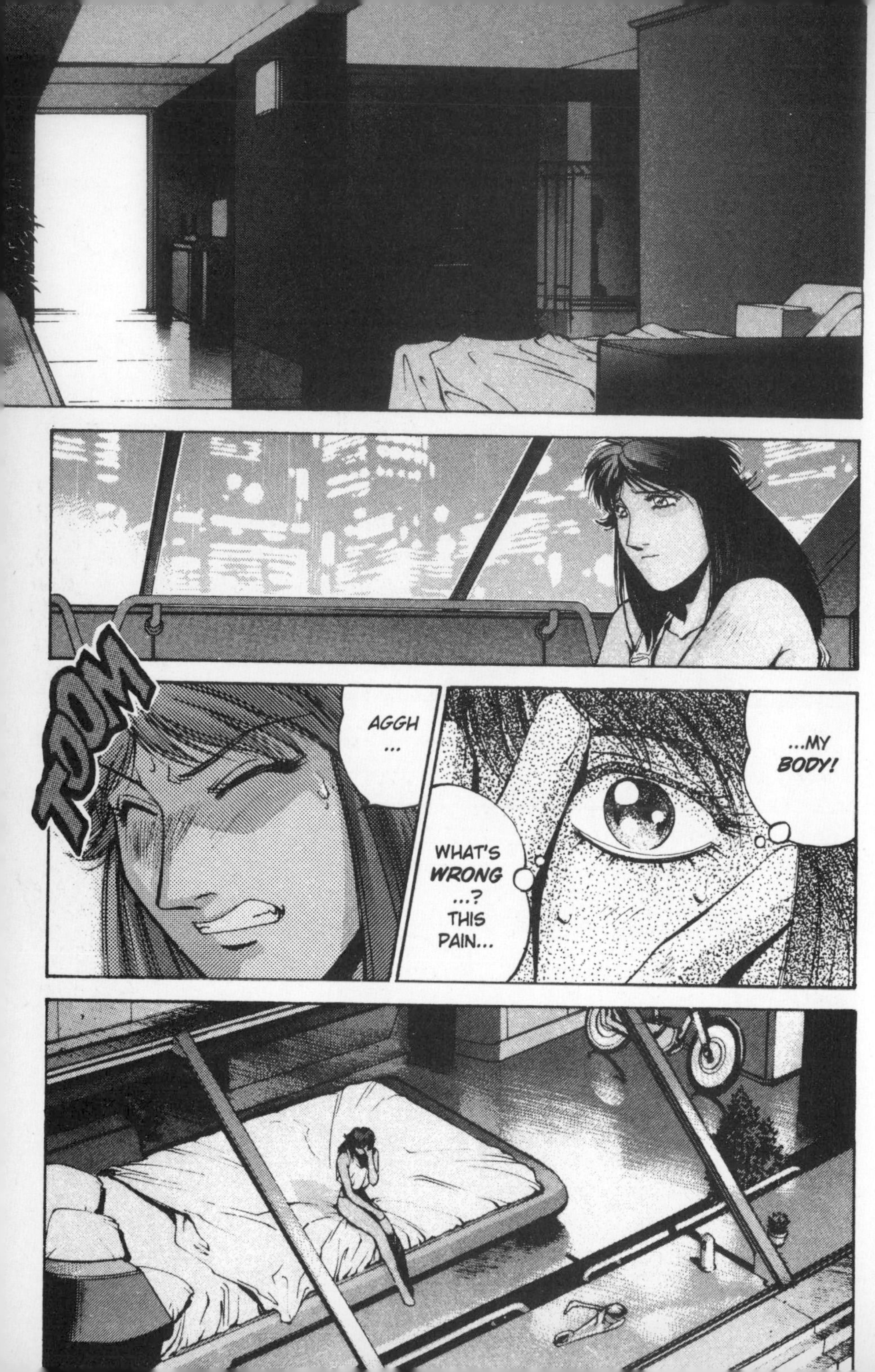
AGGH ...
WHAT'S WRONG ...? THIS PAIN...
...MY BODY!

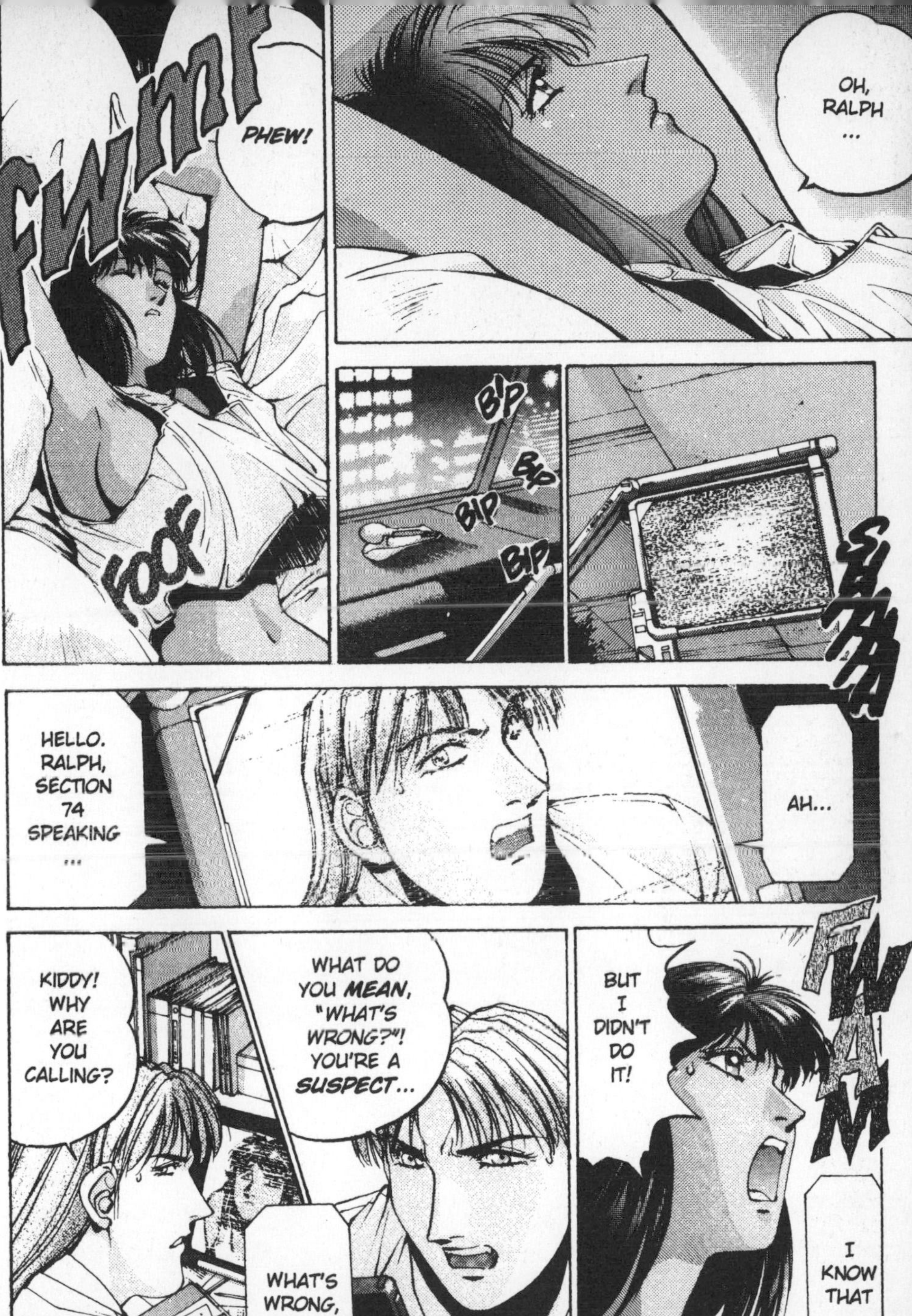
FWMF
PHEW!
FOOF
OH, RALPH ...
BIP
BIP
BIP
BIP
SHHH
HELLO. RALPH, SECTION 74 SPEAKING ...
AH...
KIDDY! WHY ARE YOU CALLING?
WHAT'S WRONG, RALPH?
WHAT DO YOU MEAN, "WHAT'S WRONG?"! YOU'RE A SUSPECT...
BUT I DIDN'T DO IT!
FWAM
I KNOW THAT ...

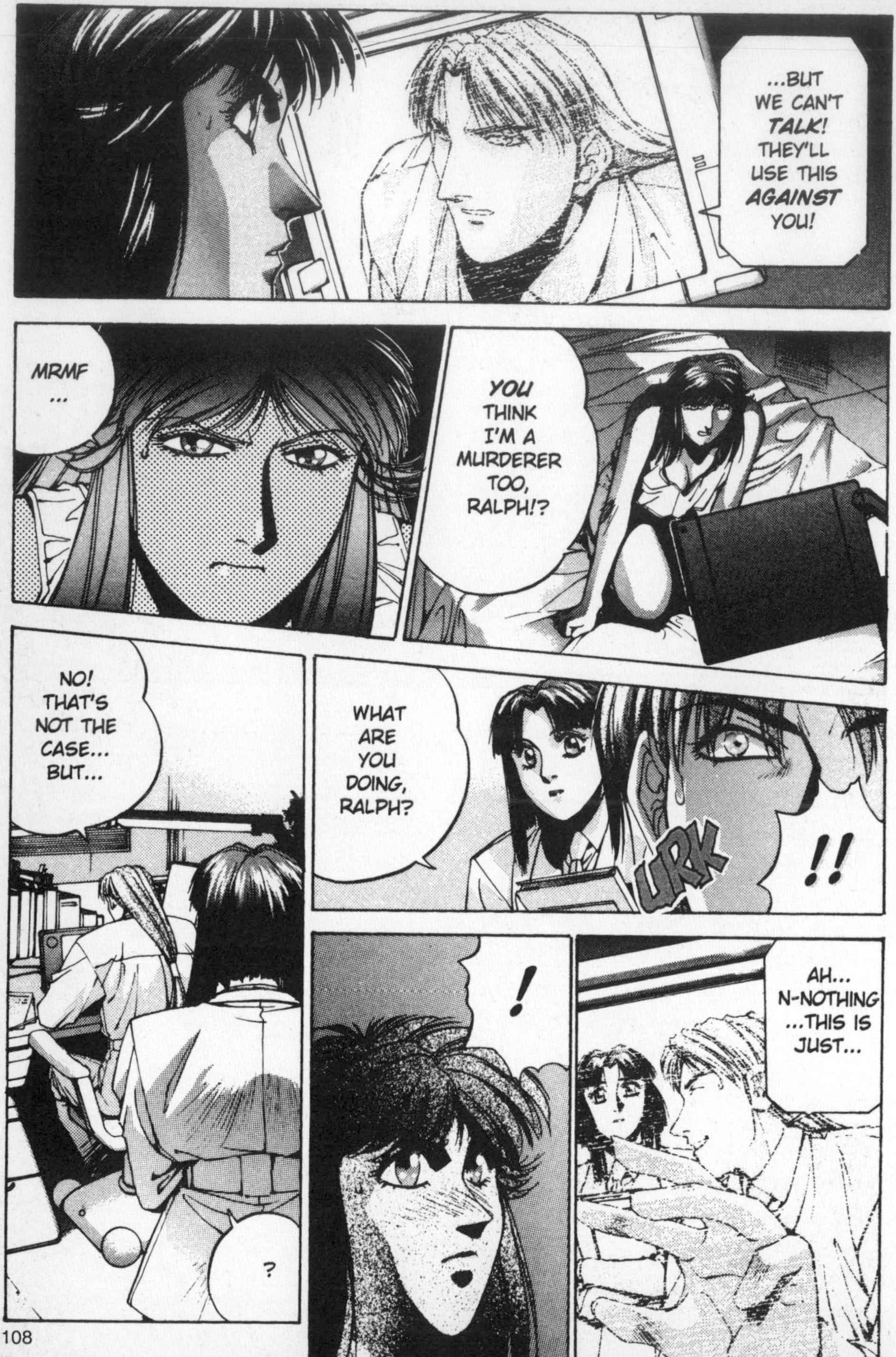
...BUT WE CAN'T TALK! THEY'LL USE THIS AGAINST YOU!
MRMF ...
YOU THINK I'M A MURDERER TOO, RALPH!?
NO! THAT'S NOT THE CASE... BUT...
?
WHAT ARE YOU DOING, RALPH?
URK
!!
!
AH... N-NOTHING ...THIS IS JUST...

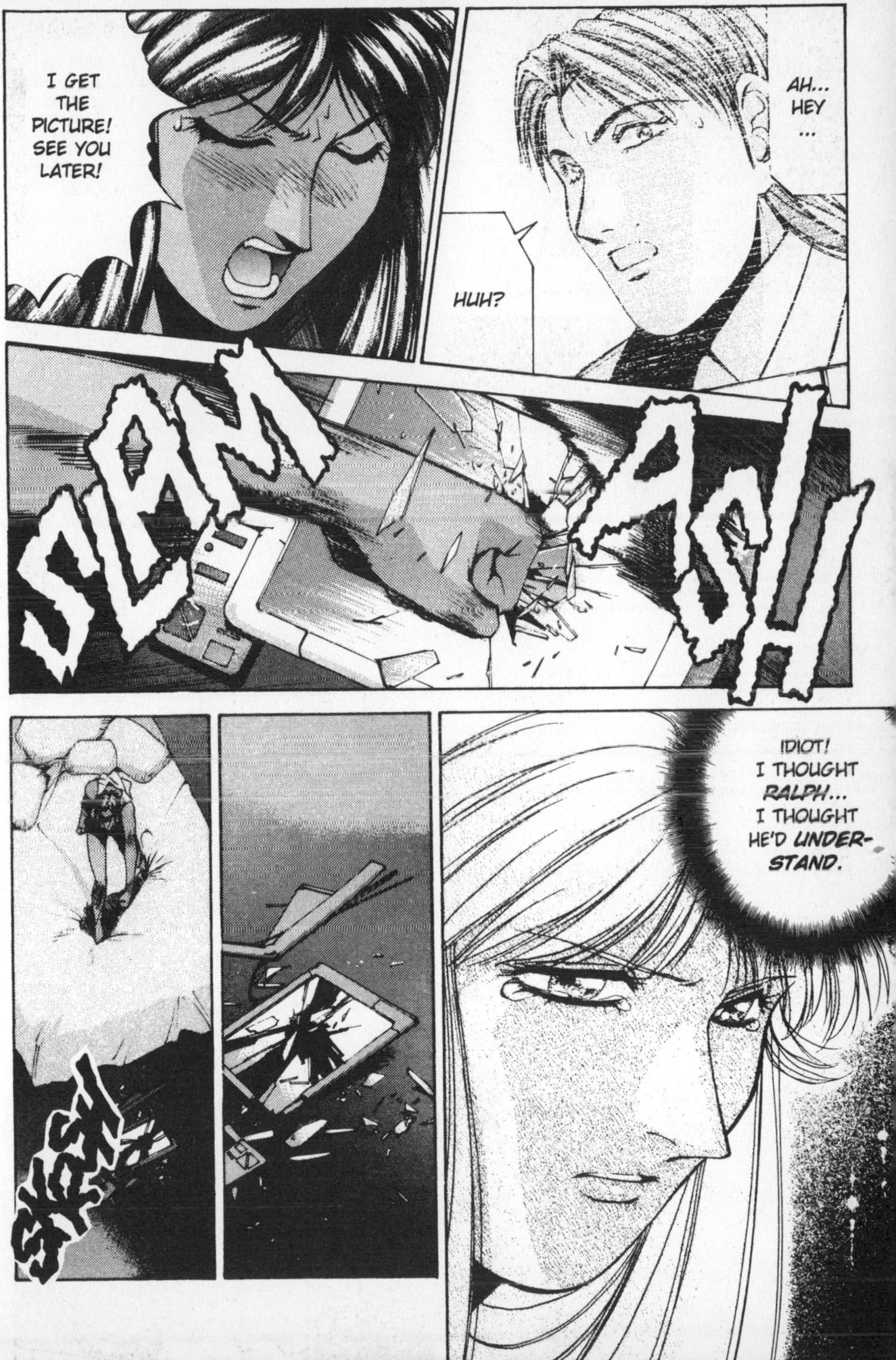

I GET THE PICTURE! SEE YOU LATER!
HUH?
AH... HEY ...
SLAM
ASH!
!DIOT! I THOUGHT *RALPH*... I THOUGHT HE'D *UNDER-STAND*.

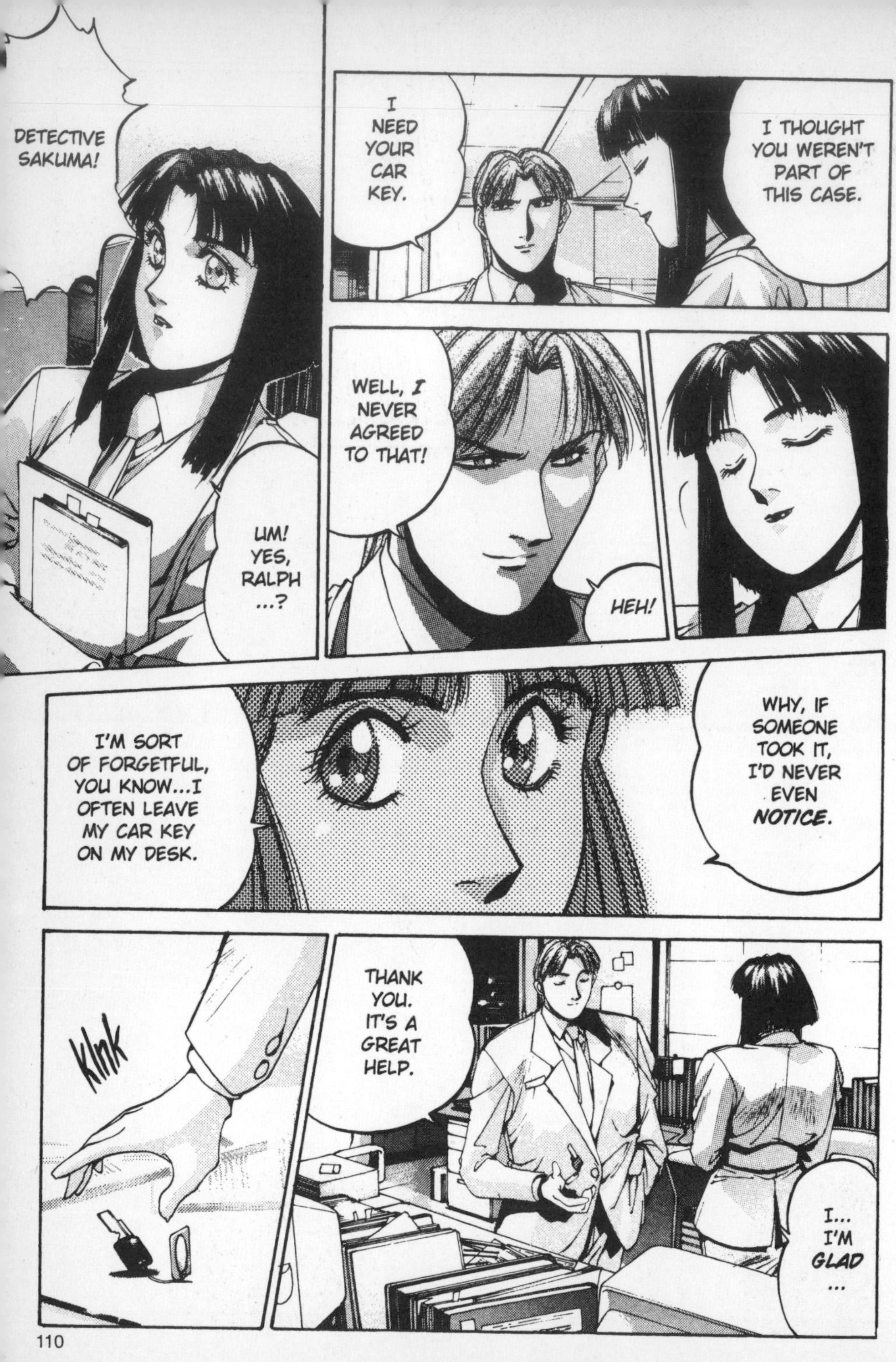

DETECTIVE SAKUMA!
UM! YES, RALPH ...?
I NEED YOUR CAR KEY.
I THOUGHT YOU WEREN'T PART OF THIS CASE.
WELL, *I* NEVER AGREED TO THAT!
HEH!
I'M SORT OF FORGETFUL, YOU KNOW...I OFTEN LEAVE MY CAR KEY ON MY DESK.
WHY, IF SOMEONE TOOK IT, I'D NEVER EVEN ***NOTICE***.
klnk
THANK YOU. IT'S A GREAT HELP.
I... I'M ***GLAD*** ...

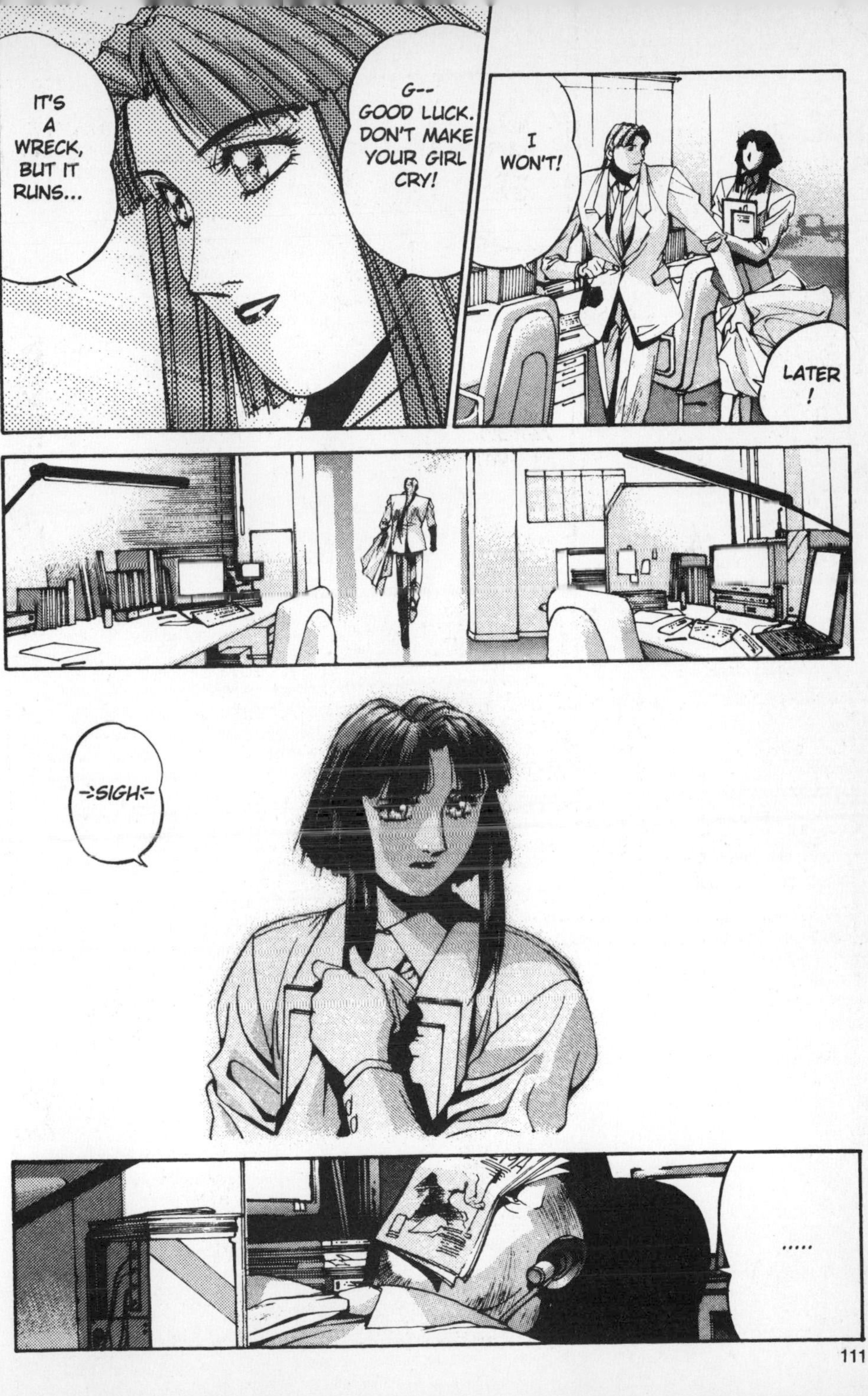
IT'S A WRECK, BUT IT RUNS...
G-- GOOD LUCK. DON'T MAKE YOUR GIRL CRY!
I WON'T!
LATER!
-SIGH-
.....

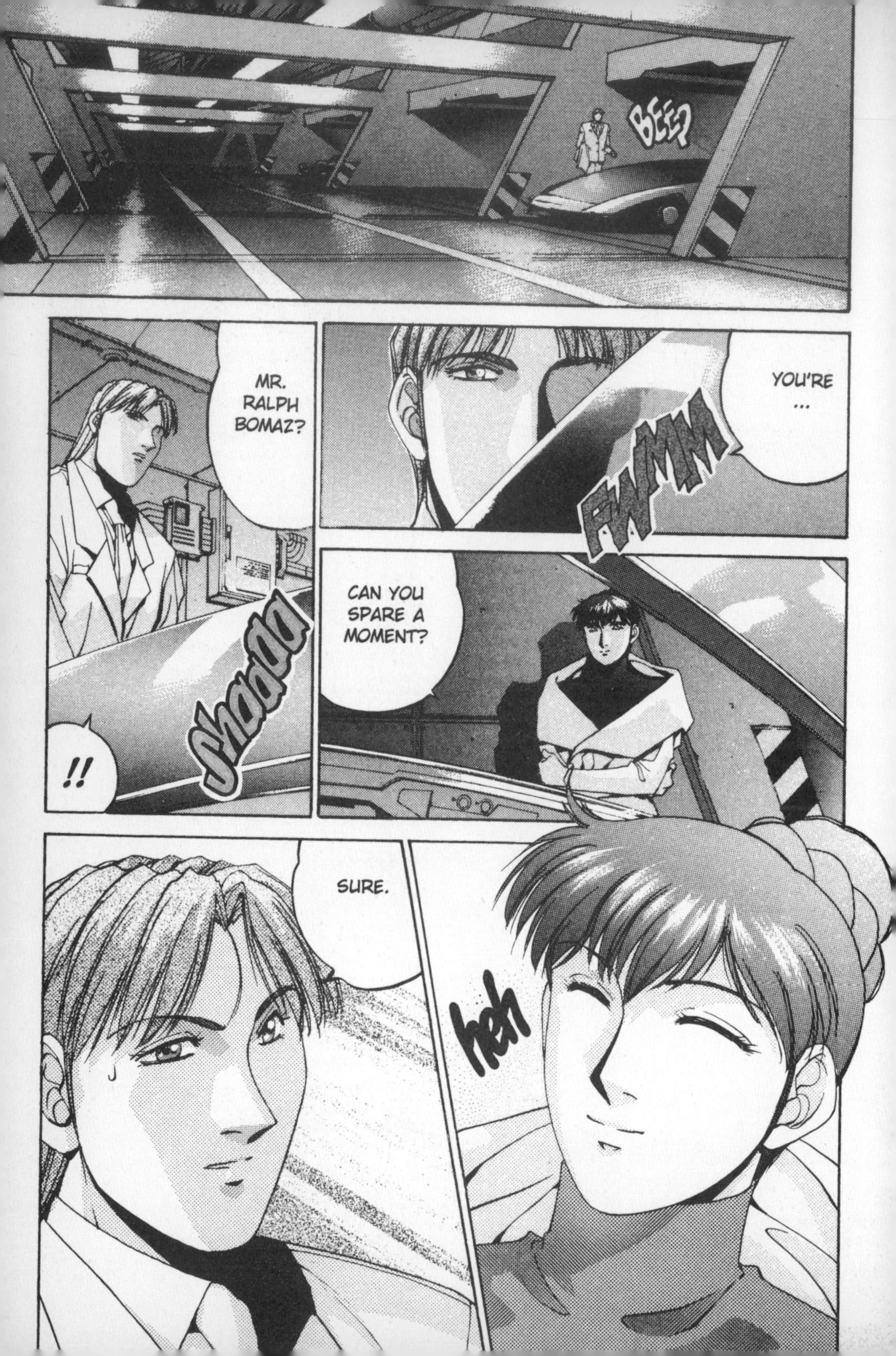

BEEP
MR. RALPH BOMAZ?
shaaa
!!
YOU'RE ...
FWMM
CAN YOU SPARE A MOMENT?
SURE.
heh

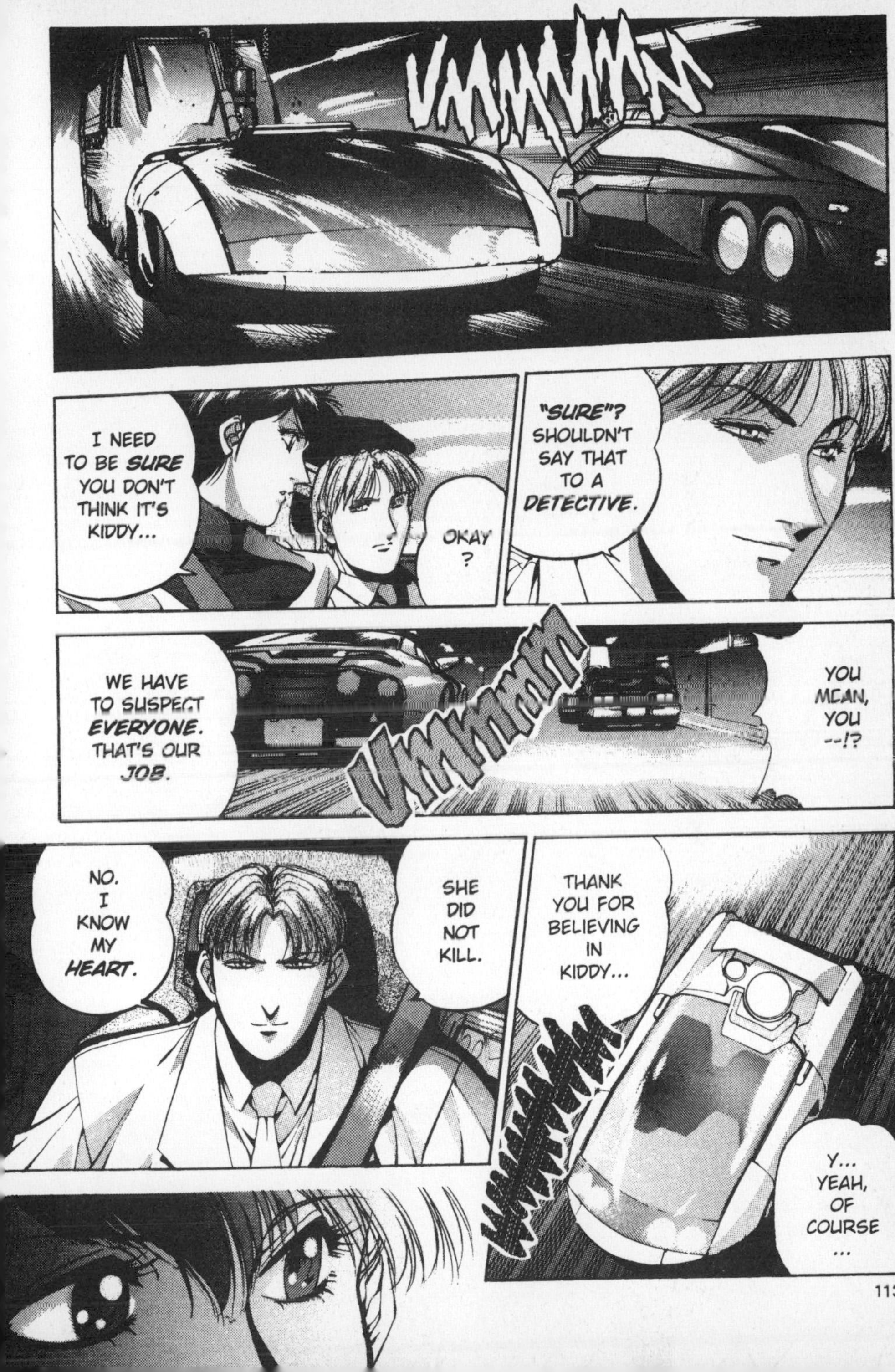

I NEED TO BE SURE YOU DON'T THINK IT'S KIDDY...
OKAY?
"SURE"? SHOULDN'T SAY THAT TO A DETECTIVE.
WE HAVE TO SUSPECT EVERYONE. THAT'S OUR JOB.
YOU MEAN, YOU --!?
NO. I KNOW MY HEART.
SHE DID NOT KILL.
THANK YOU FOR BELIEVING IN KIDDY...
Y... YEAH, OF COURSE ...

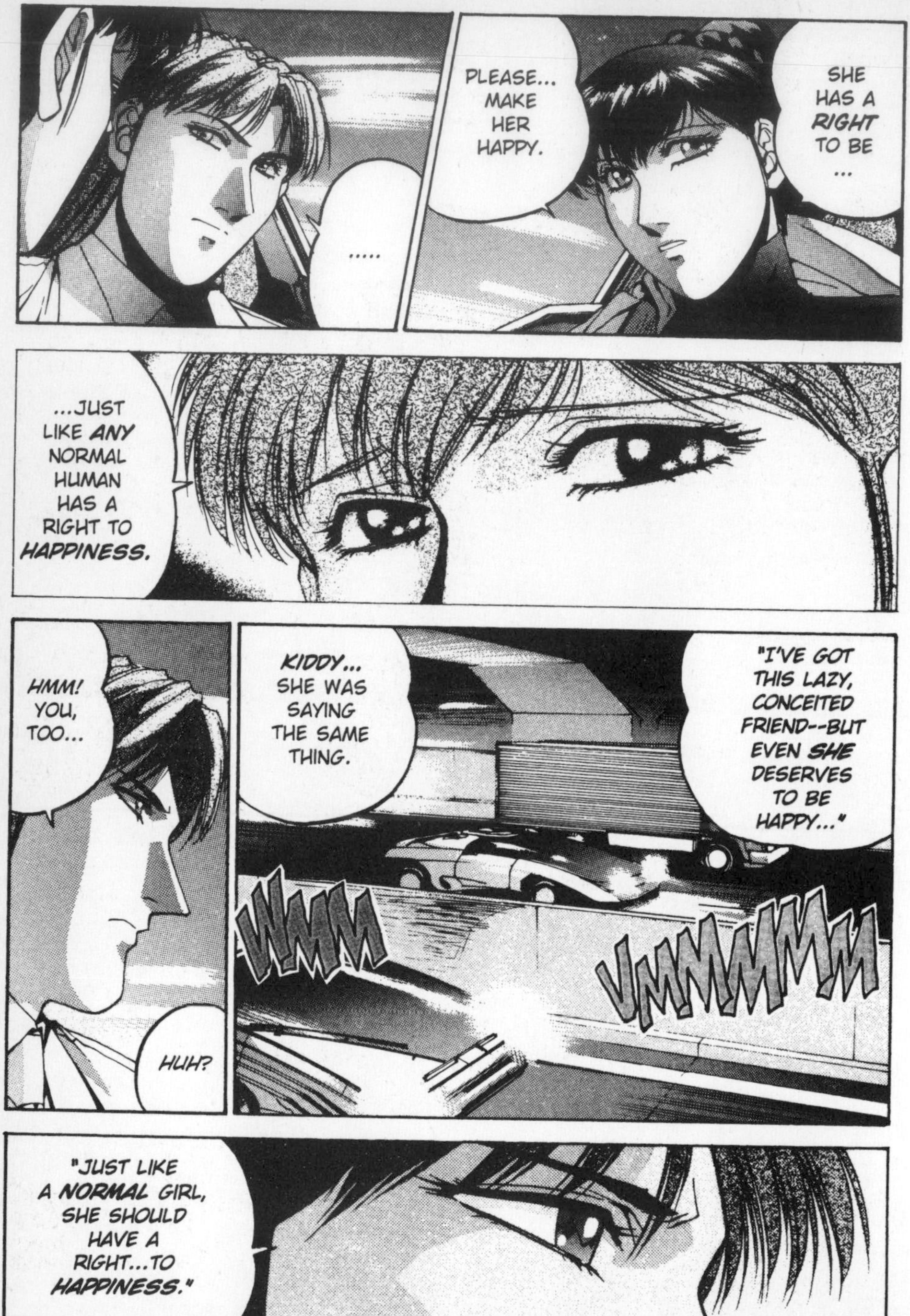
.....
PLEASE... MAKE HER HAPPY.
SHE HAS A RIGHT TO BE ...
...JUST LIKE ANY NORMAL HUMAN HAS A RIGHT TO HAPPINESS.
HMM! YOU, TOO...
HUH?
KIDDY... SHE WAS SAYING THE SAME THING.
"I'VE GOT THIS LAZY, CONCEITED FRIEND--BUT EVEN SHE DESERVES TO BE HAPPY..."
WMM
VMMMMMM
"JUST LIKE A NORMAL GIRL, SHE SHOULD HAVE A RIGHT...TO HAPPINESS."

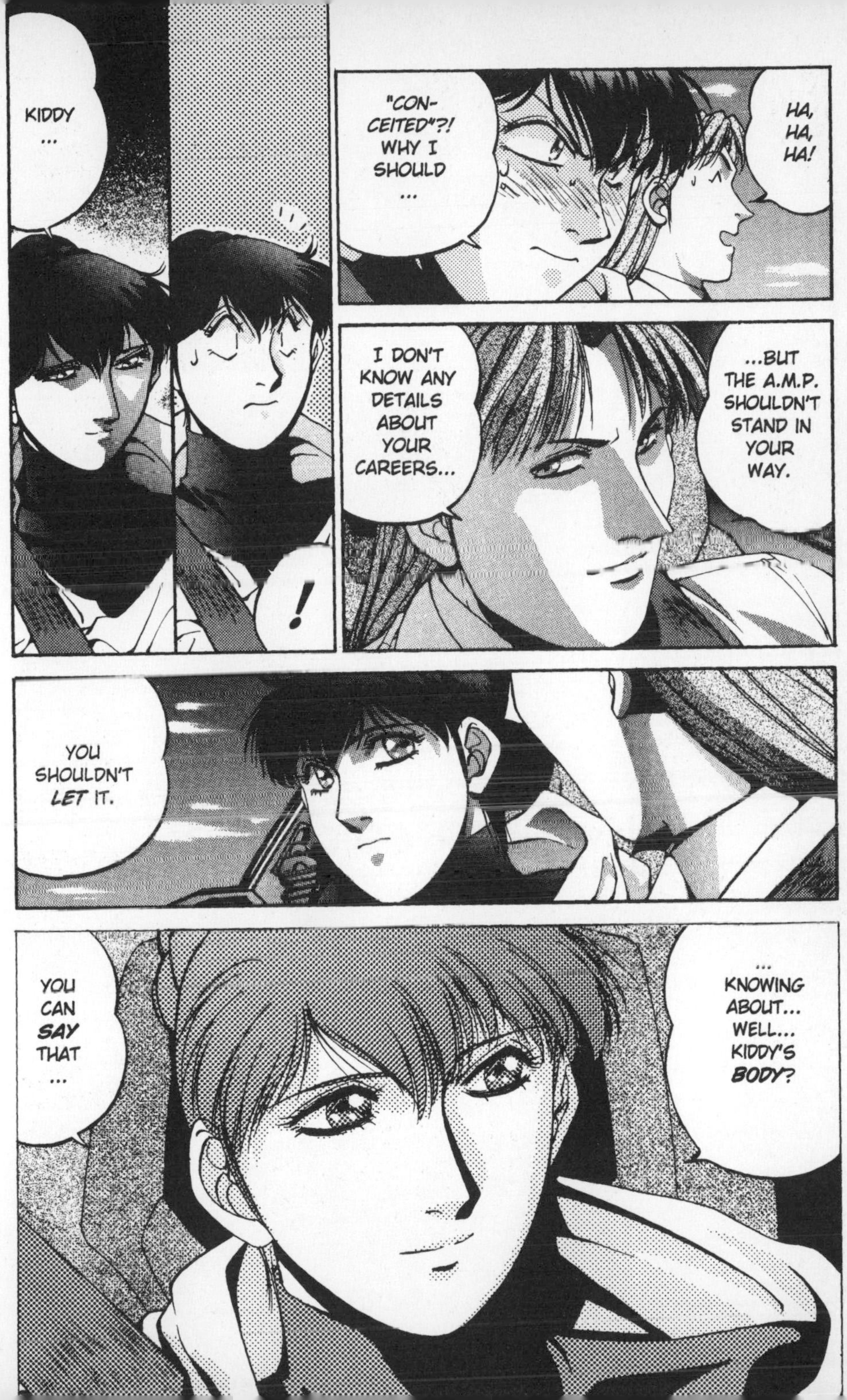
KIDDY ...
"CON-CEITED"?! WHY I SHOULD ...
HA, HA, HA!
!
I DON'T KNOW ANY DETAILS ABOUT YOUR CAREERS...
...BUT THE A.M.P. SHOULDN'T STAND IN YOUR WAY.
YOU SHOULDN'T *LET* IT.
YOU CAN *SAY* THAT ...
... KNOWING ABOUT... WELL... KIDDY'S *BODY*?

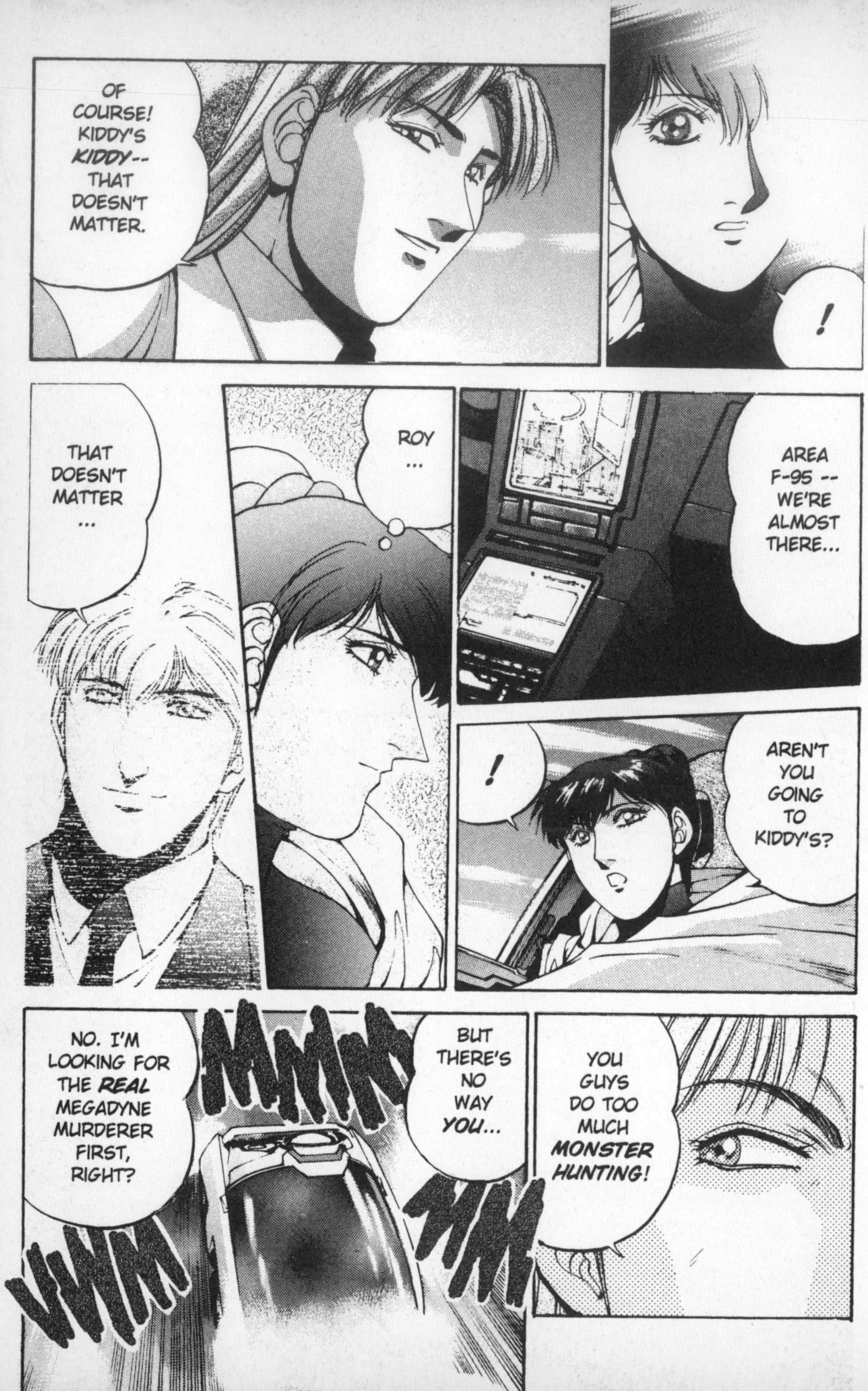
OF COURSE! KIDDY'S *KIDDY*-- THAT DOESN'T MATTER.
!
THAT DOESN'T MATTER ...
ROY ...
AREA F-95 -- WE'RE ALMOST THERE...
!
AREN'T YOU GOING TO KIDDY'S?
NO. I'M LOOKING FOR THE *REAL* MEGADYNE MURDERER FIRST, RIGHT?
BUT THERE'S NO WAY *YOU*...
YOU GUYS DO TOO MUCH *MONSTER HUNTING*!

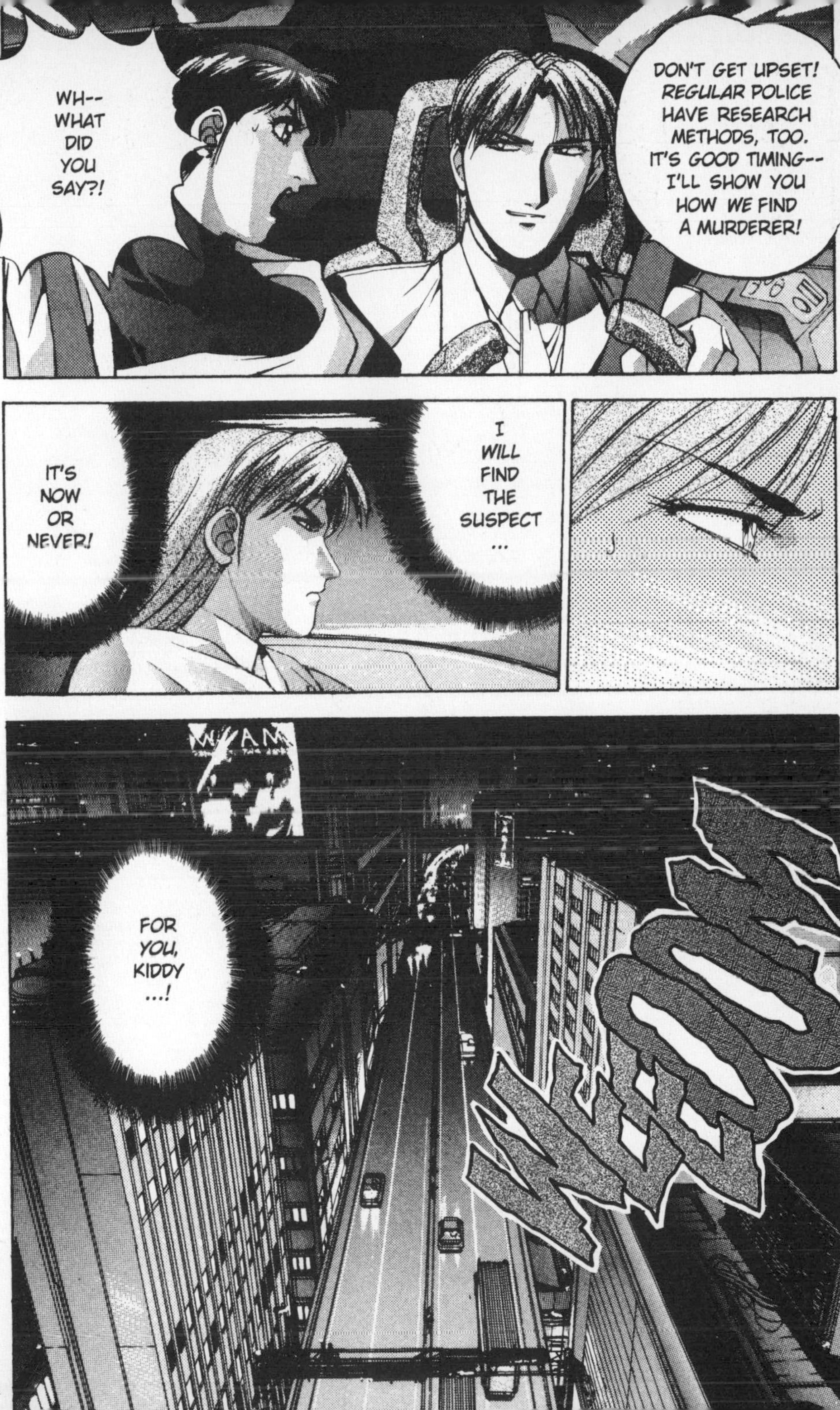
WH-- WHAT DID YOU SAY?!
DON'T GET UPSET! REGULAR POLICE HAVE RESEARCH METHODS, TOO. IT'S GOOD TIMING-- I'LL SHOW YOU HOW WE FIND A MURDERER!
IT'S NOW OR NEVER!
I WILL FIND THE SUSPECT ...
FOR YOU, KIDDY ...!

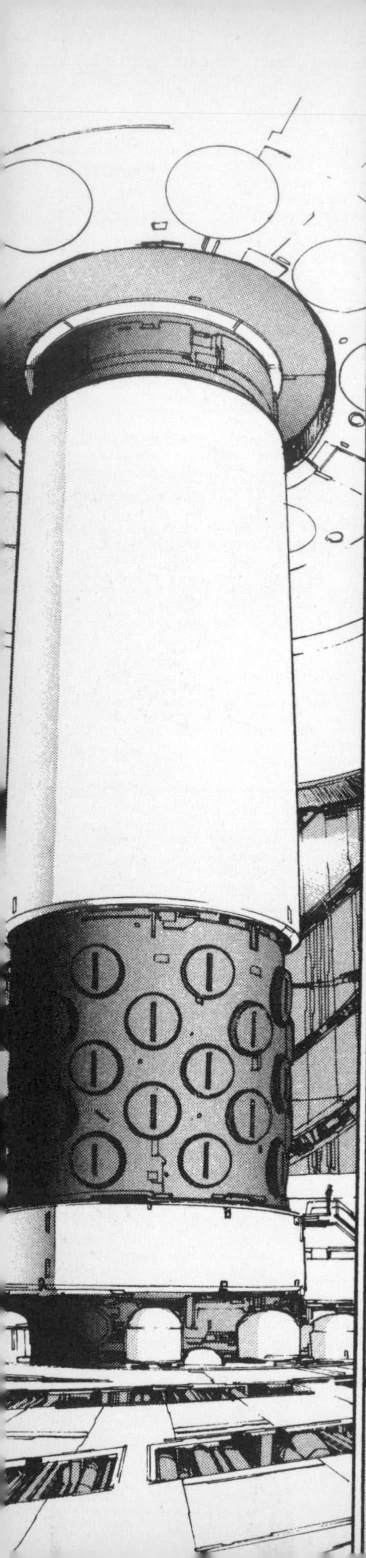

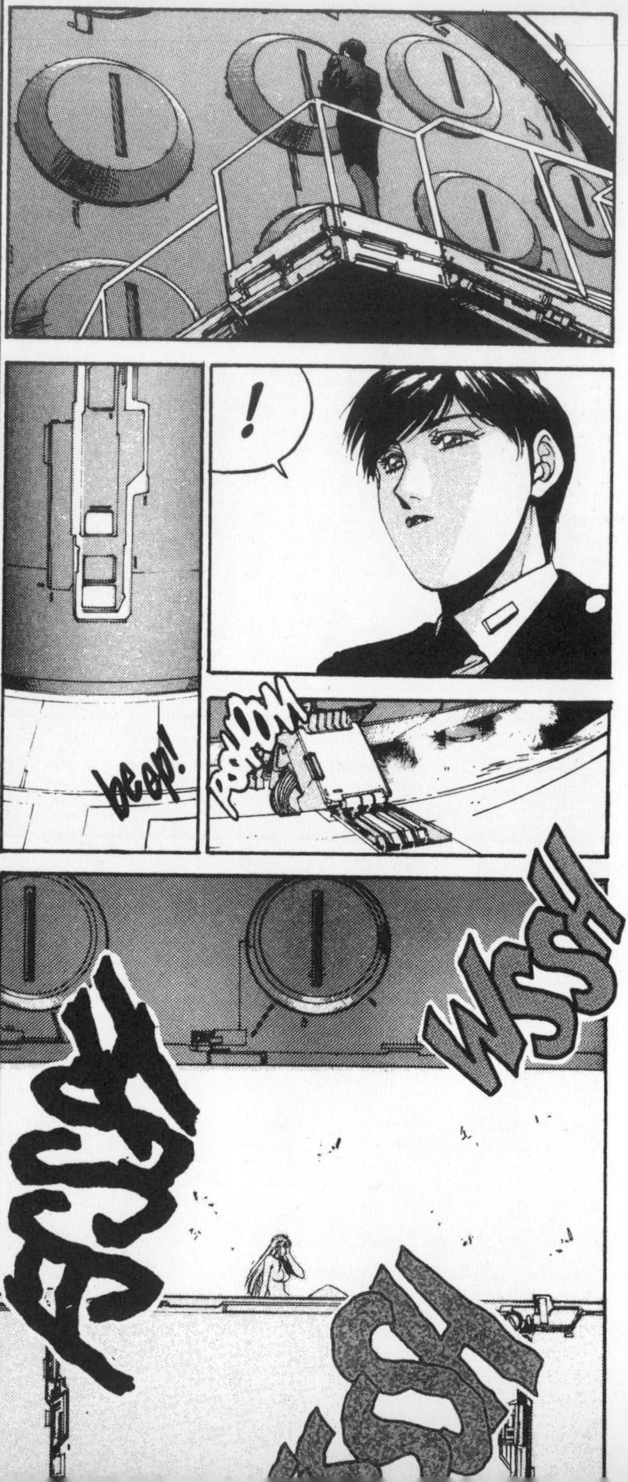

!
beep!
WSSH

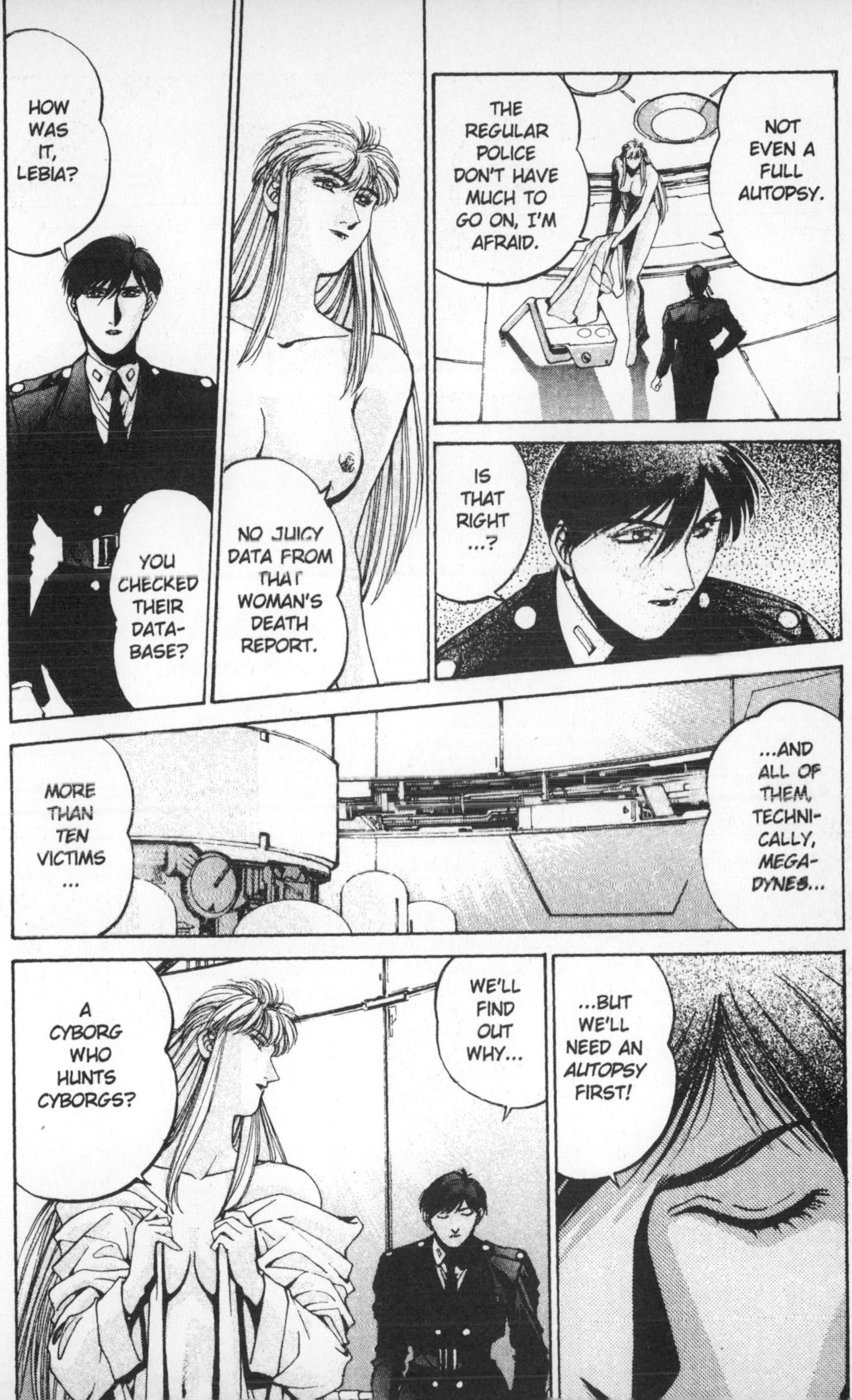
HOW WAS IT, LEBIA?
YOU CHECKED THEIR DATA-BASE?
NO JUICY DATA FROM THAT WOMAN'S DEATH REPORT.
THE REGULAR POLICE DON'T HAVE MUCH TO GO ON, I'M AFRAID.
NOT EVEN A FULL AUTOPSY.
IS THAT RIGHT ...?
MORE THAN TEN VICTIMS ...
...AND ALL OF THEM, TECHNI-CALLY, MEGA-DYNES...
A CYBORG WHO HUNTS CYBORGS?
WE'LL FIND OUT WHY...
...BUT WE'LL NEED AN AUTOPSY FIRST!

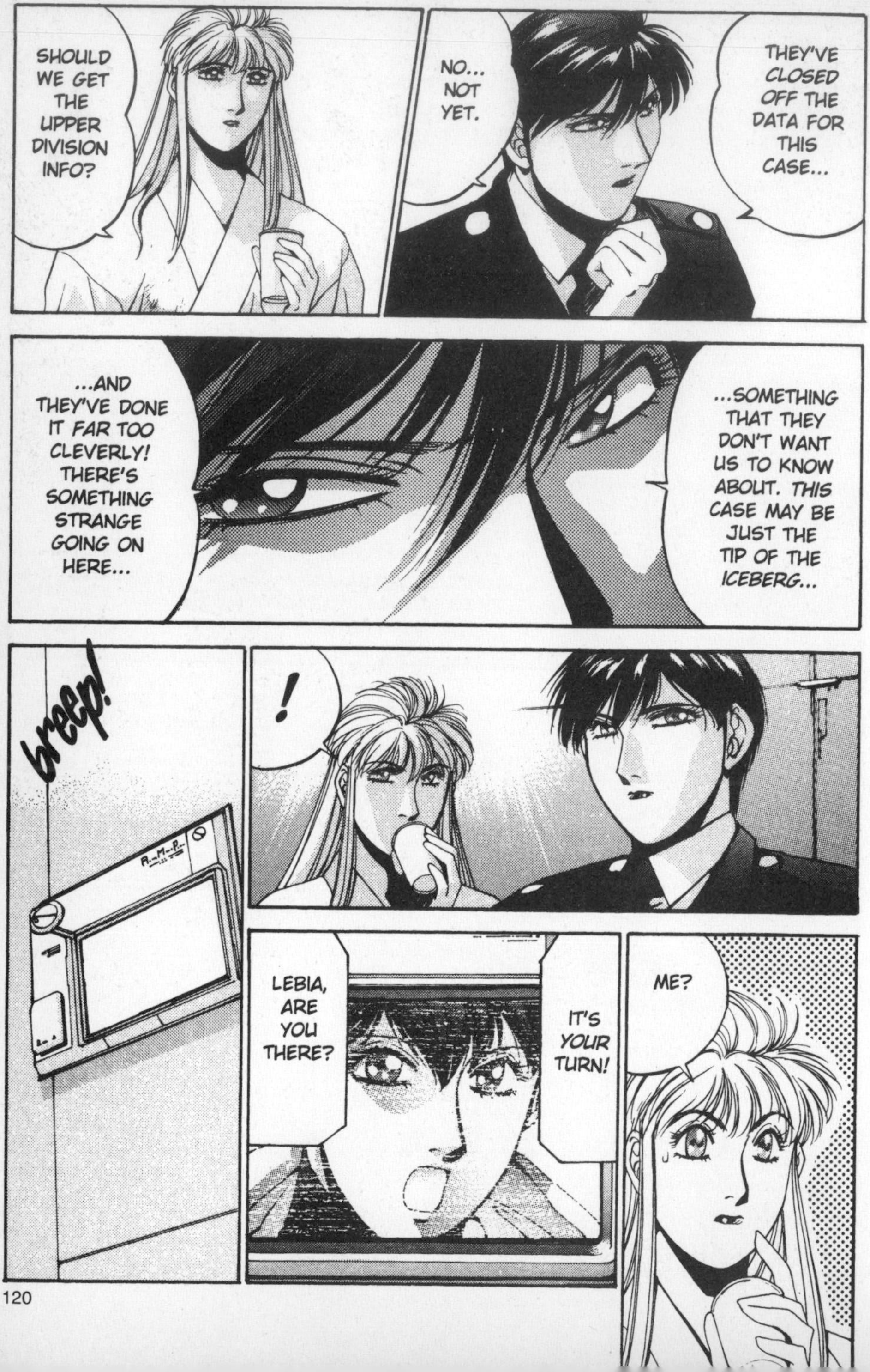
SHOULD WE GET THE UPPER DIVISION INFO?
NO... NOT YET.
THEY'VE CLOSED OFF THE DATA FOR THIS CASE...
...AND THEY'VE DONE IT FAR TOO CLEVERLY! THERE'S SOMETHING STRANGE GOING ON HERE...
...SOMETHING THAT THEY DON'T WANT US TO KNOW ABOUT. THIS CASE MAY BE JUST THE TIP OF THE ICEBERG...
breep!
!
LEBIA, ARE YOU THERE?
IT'S YOUR TURN!
ME?

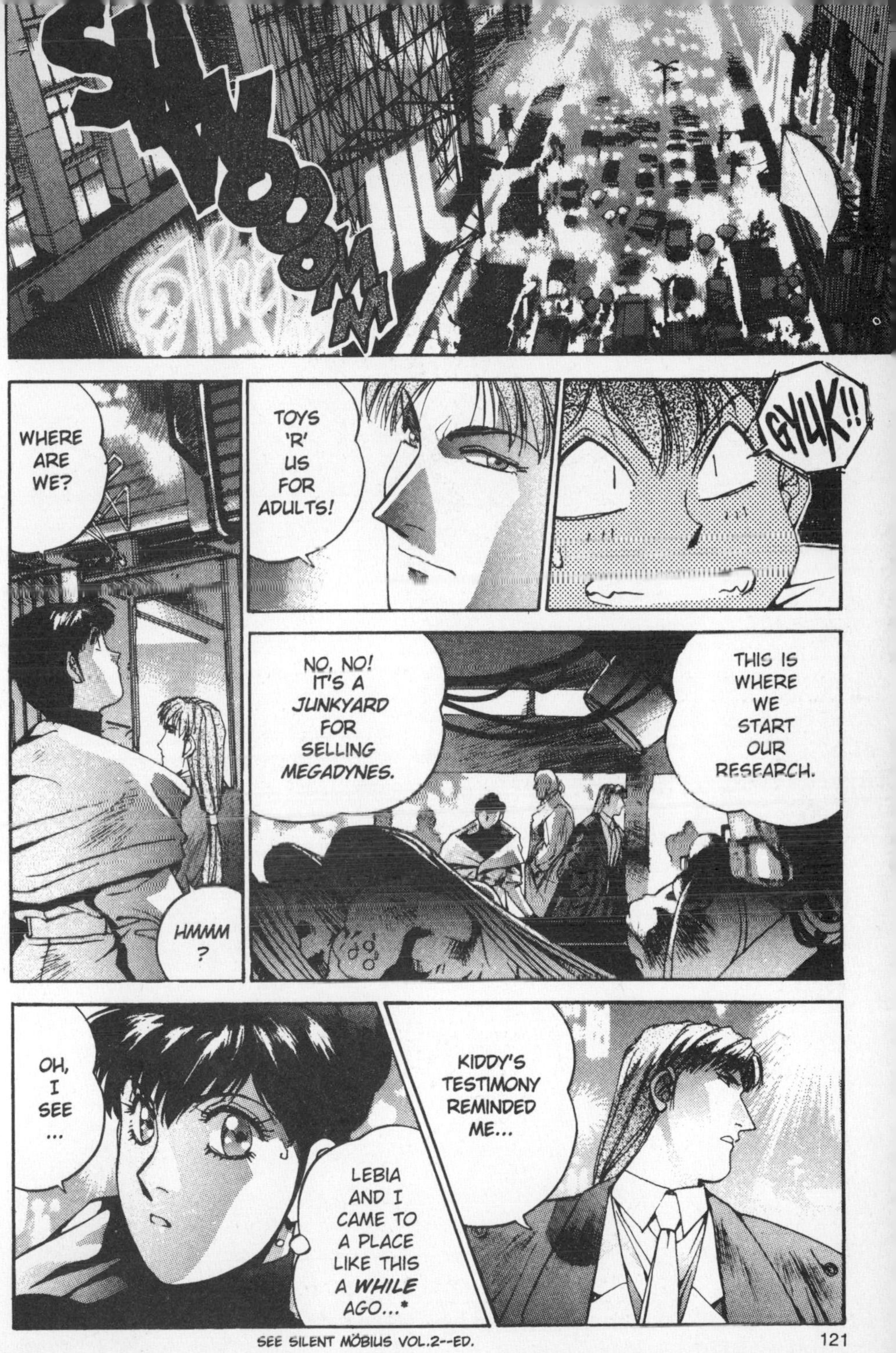
SHWOOOMM
WHERE ARE WE?
TOYS 'R' US FOR ADULTS!
GYUK!!
HMMM?
NO, NO! IT'S A *JUNKYARD* FOR SELLING *MEGADYNES*.
THIS IS WHERE WE START OUR RESEARCH.
OH, I SEE ...
KIDDY'S TESTIMONY REMINDED ME...
LEBIA AND I CAME TO A PLACE LIKE THIS A **WHILE** AGO...*

*SEE SILENT MÖBIUS VOL.2--ED.

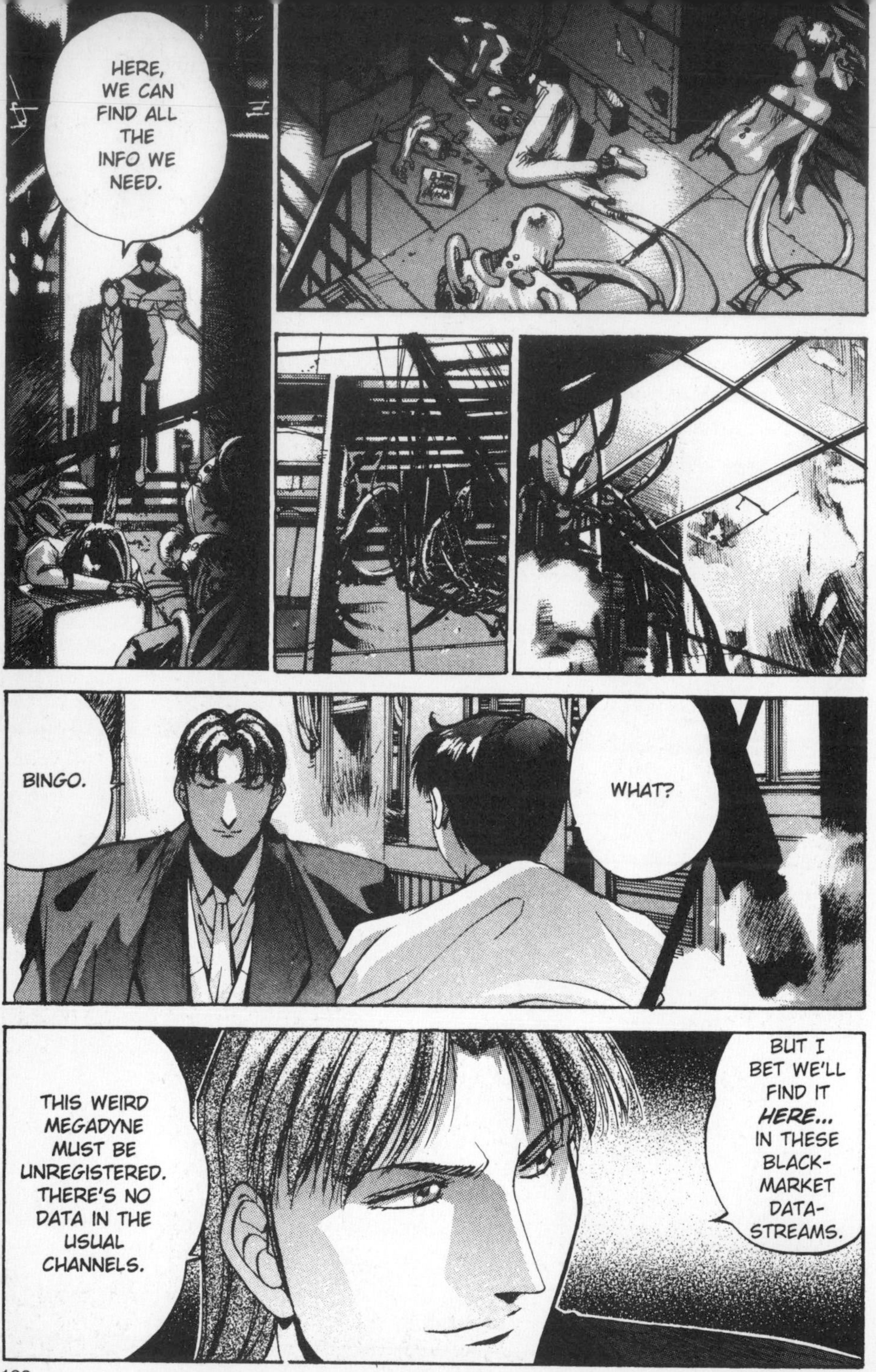
HERE, WE CAN FIND ALL THE INFO WE NEED.
BINGO.
WHAT?
THIS WEIRD MEGADYNE MUST BE UNREGISTERED. THERE'S NO DATA IN THE USUAL CHANNELS.
BUT I BET WE'LL FIND IT ***HERE...*** IN THESE BLACK-MARKET DATA-STREAMS.

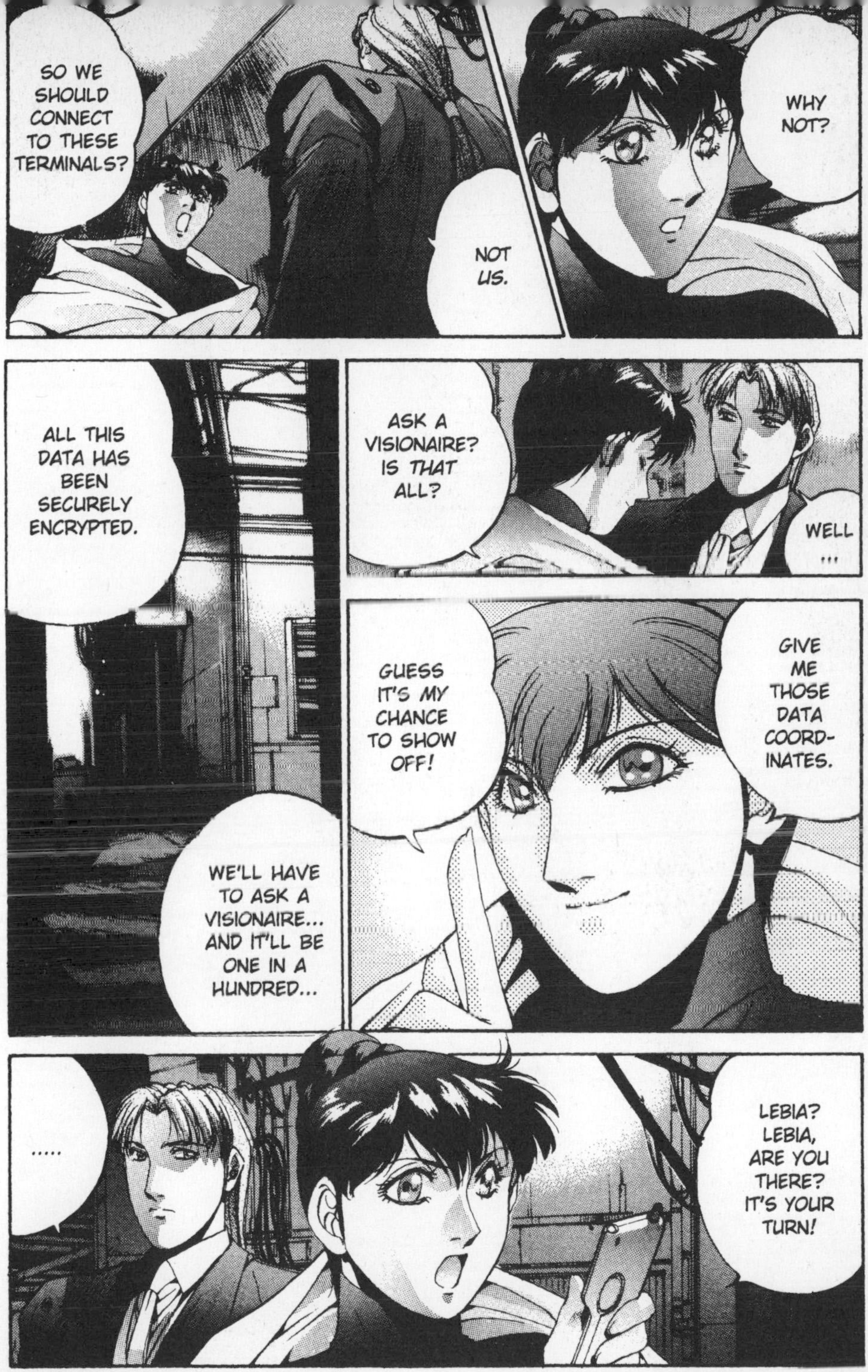
SO WE SHOULD CONNECT TO THESE TERMINALS?
WHY NOT?
NOT US.
ALL THIS DATA HAS BEEN SECURELY ENCRYPTED.
WE'LL HAVE TO ASK A VISIONAIRE... AND IT'LL BE ONE IN A HUNDRED...
ASK A VISIONAIRE? IS *THAT* ALL?
WELL ...
GUESS IT'S MY CHANCE TO SHOW OFF!
GIVE ME THOSE DATA COORD-INATES.
.....
LEBIA? LEBIA, ARE YOU THERE? IT'S YOUR TURN!

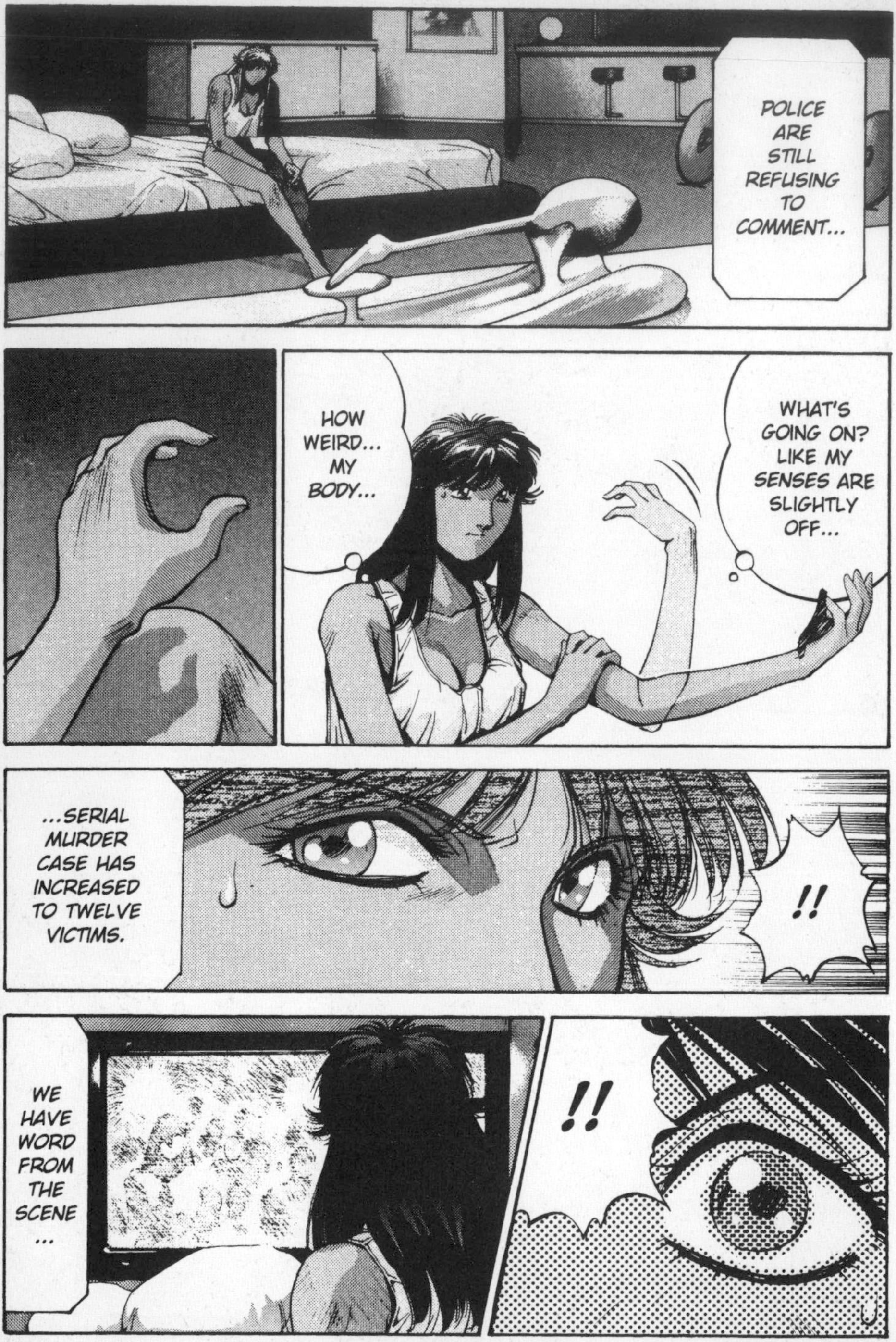
POLICE ARE STILL REFUSING TO COMMENT...
HOW WEIRD... MY BODY...
WHAT'S GOING ON? LIKE MY SENSES ARE SLIGHTLY OFF...
...SERIAL MURDER CASE HAS INCREASED TO TWELVE VICTIMS.
!!
WE HAVE WORD FROM THE SCENE...
!!

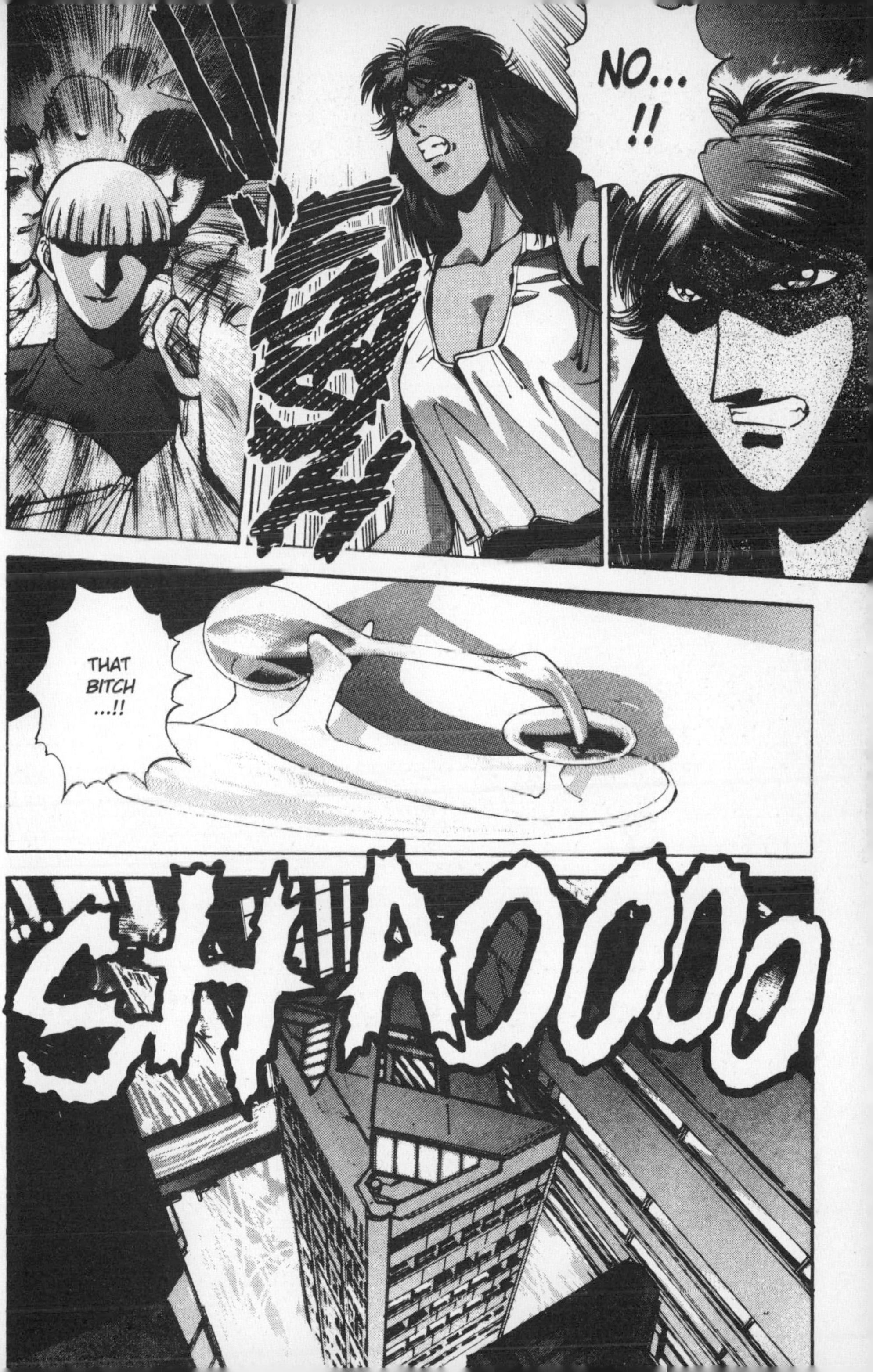
NO... !!
THAT BITCH ...!!
SHAOOOO

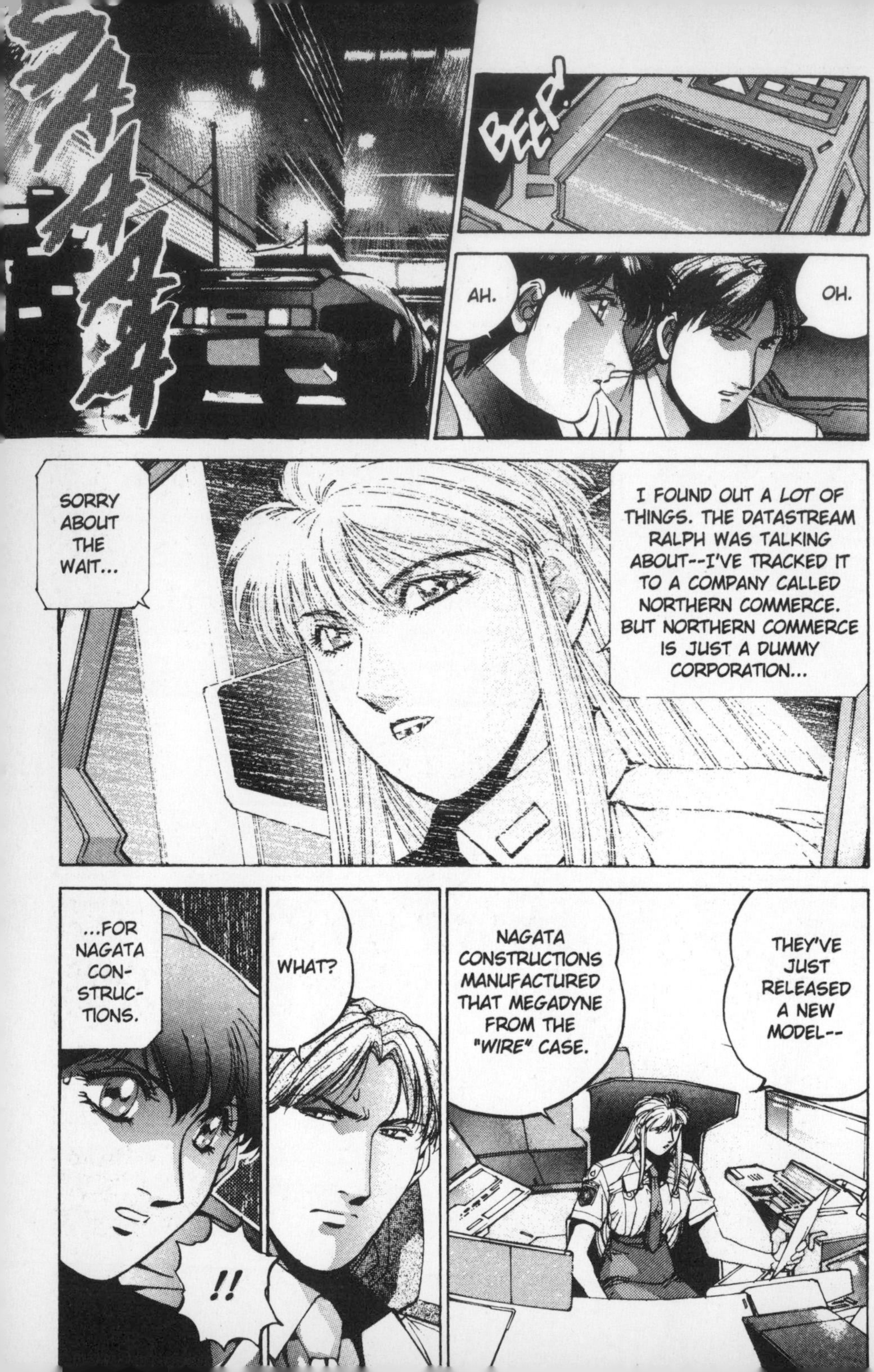
BEEP.
AH.
OH.
SORRY ABOUT THE WAIT...
I FOUND OUT A LOT OF THINGS. THE DATASTREAM RALPH WAS TALKING ABOUT--I'VE TRACKED IT TO A COMPANY CALLED NORTHERN COMMERCE. BUT NORTHERN COMMERCE IS JUST A DUMMY CORPORATION...
...FOR NAGATA CON-STRUC-TIONS.
WHAT?
!!
NAGATA CONSTRUCTIONS MANUFACTURED THAT MEGADYNE FROM THE "WIRE" CASE.
THEY'VE JUST RELEASED A NEW MODEL--

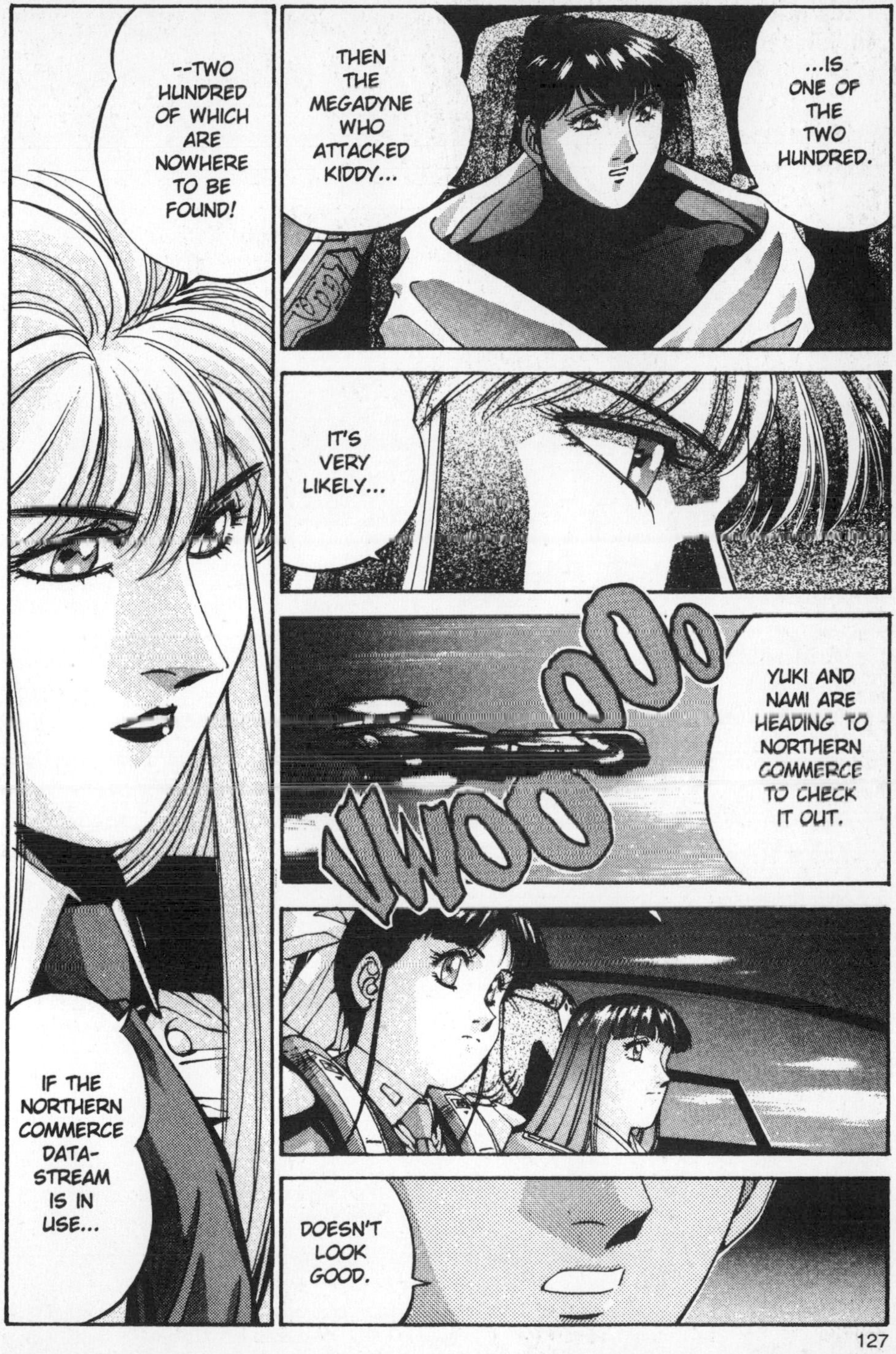
--TWO HUNDRED OF WHICH ARE NOWHERE TO BE FOUND!
IF THE NORTHERN COMMERCE DATA-STREAM IS IN USE...
THEN THE MEGADYNE WHO ATTACKED KIDDY...
...IS ONE OF THE TWO HUNDRED.
IT'S VERY LIKELY...
VWOOOOOO
YUKI AND NAMI ARE HEADING TO NORTHERN COMMERCE TO CHECK IT OUT.
DOESN'T LOOK GOOD.

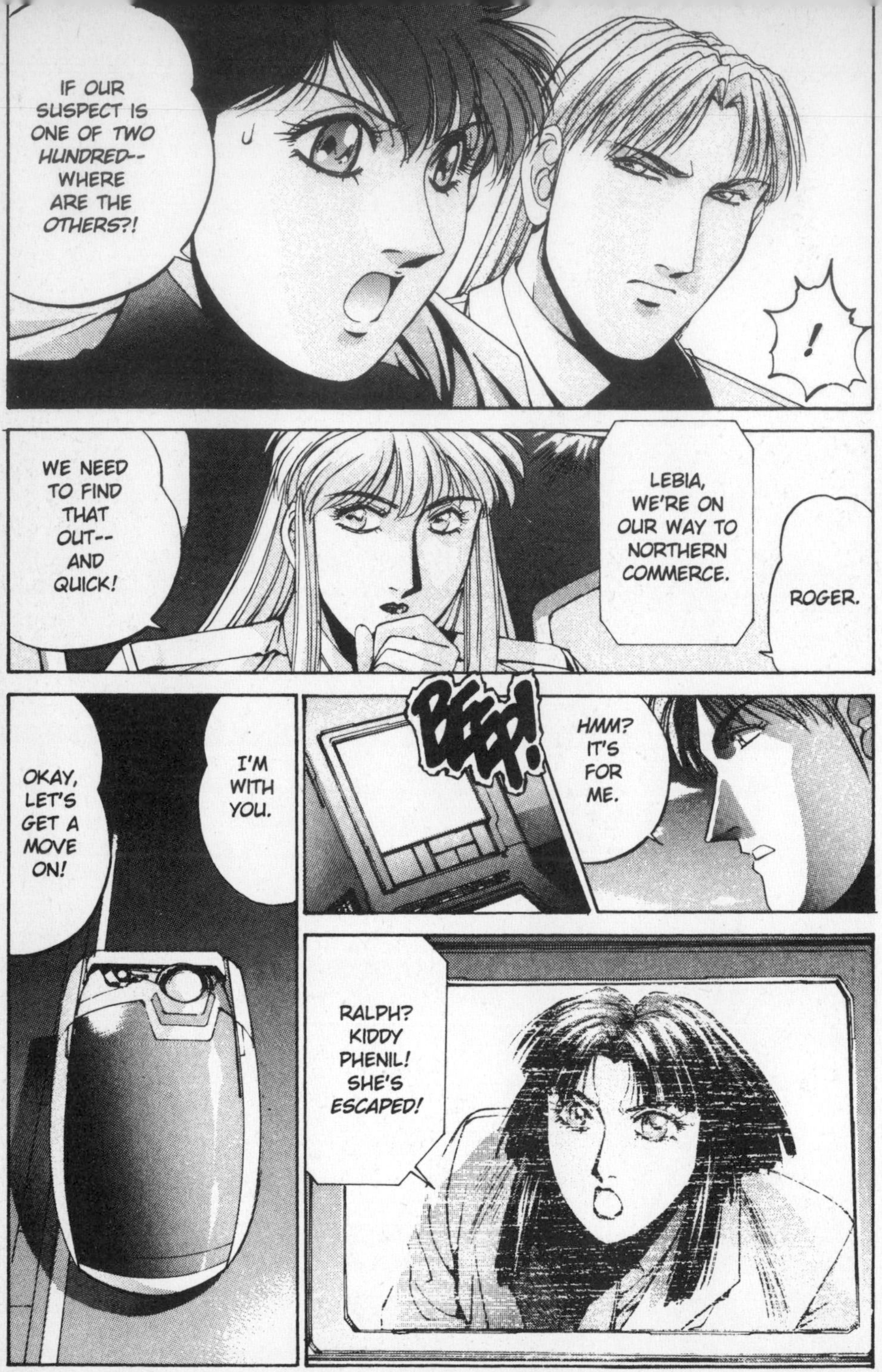
IF OUR SUSPECT IS ONE OF TWO HUNDRED-- WHERE ARE THE OTHERS?!
!
WE NEED TO FIND THAT OUT-- AND QUICK!
LEBIA, WE'RE ON OUR WAY TO NORTHERN COMMERCE.
ROGER.
OKAY, LET'S GET A MOVE ON!
I'M WITH YOU.
BEEP!
HMM? IT'S FOR ME.
RALPH? KIDDY PHENIL! SHE'S ESCAPED!

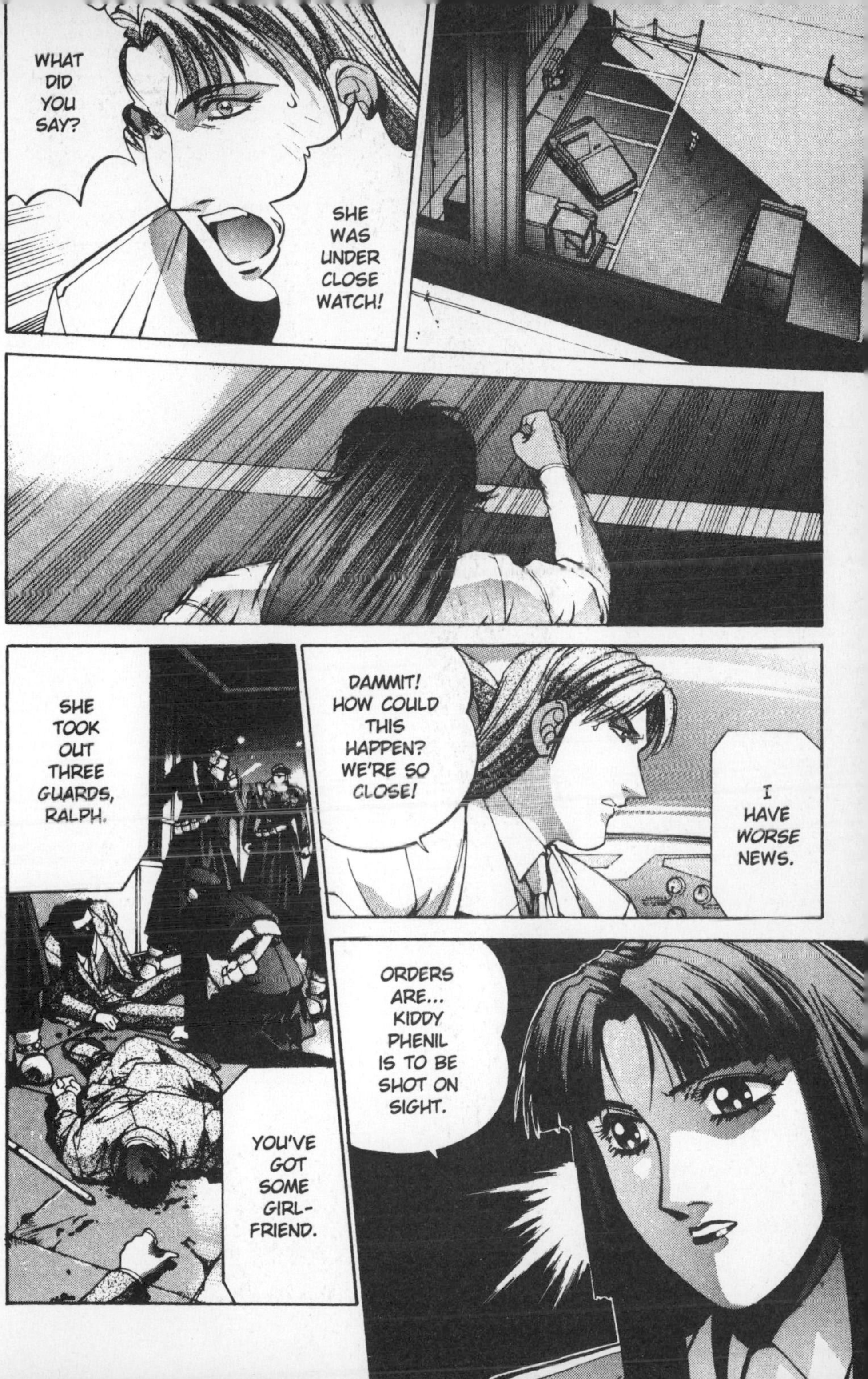

WHAT DID YOU SAY?
SHE WAS UNDER CLOSE WATCH!
SHE TOOK OUT THREE GUARDS, RALPH.
DAMMIT! HOW COULD THIS HAPPEN? WE'RE SO CLOSE!
I HAVE WORSE NEWS.
YOU'VE GOT SOME GIRL-FRIEND.
ORDERS ARE... KIDDY PHENIL IS TO BE SHOT ON SIGHT.

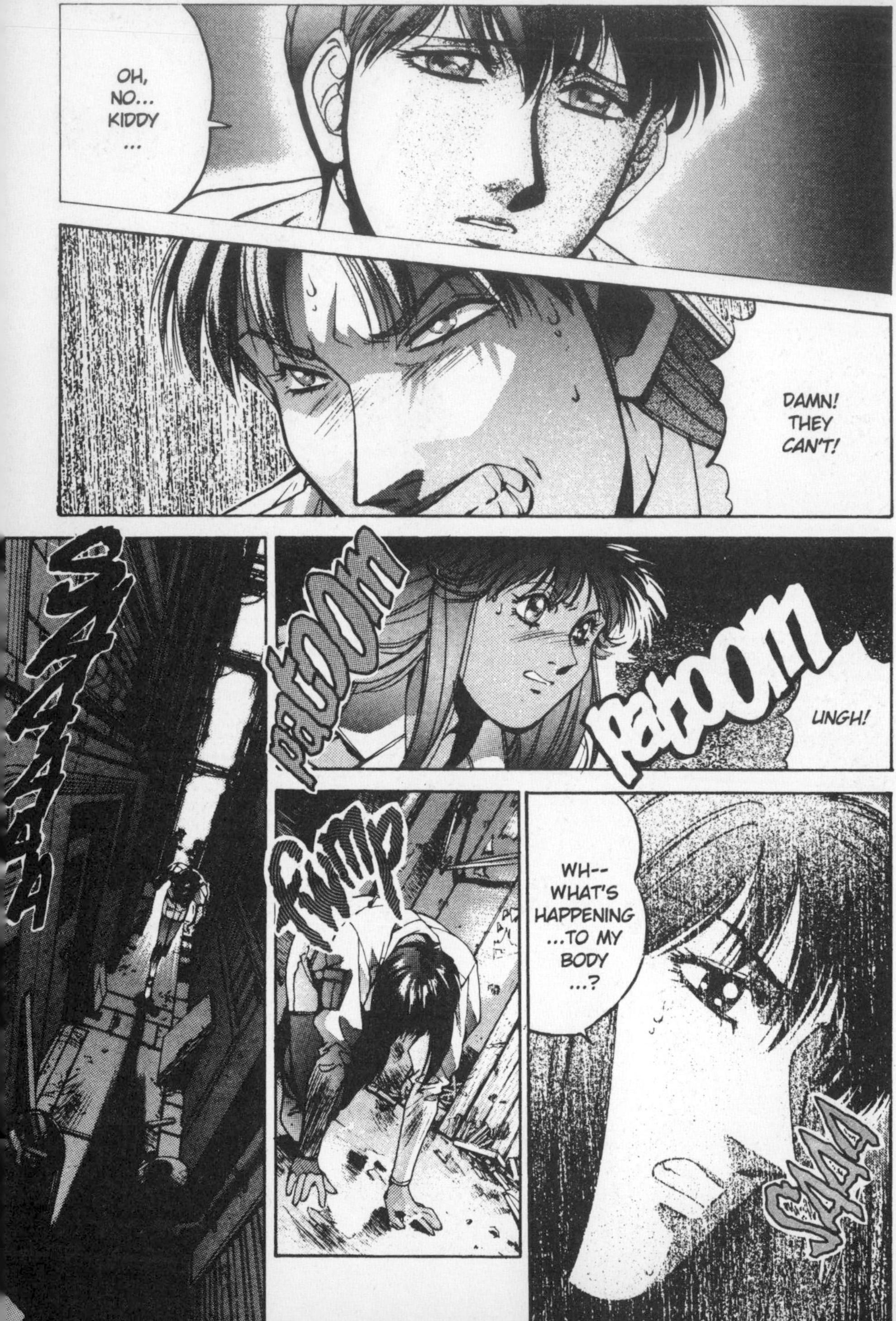
OH, NO... KIDDY ...
DAMN! THEY CAN'T!
PATOOM
PATOOM
UNGH!
WH-- WHAT'S HAPPENING ...TO MY BODY ...?

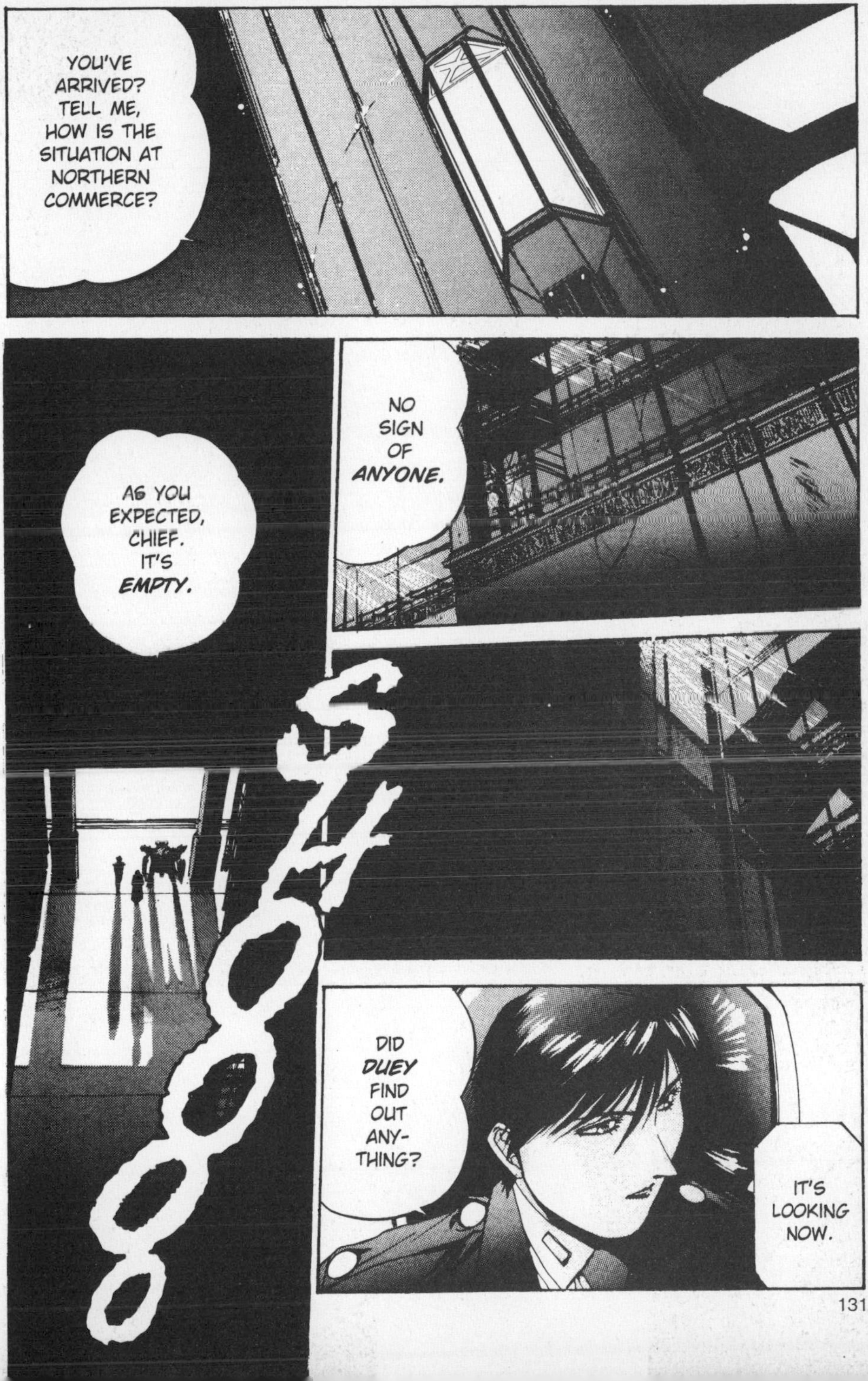
YOU'VE ARRIVED? TELL ME, HOW IS THE SITUATION AT NORTHERN COMMERCE?
AS YOU EXPECTED, CHIEF. IT'S EMPTY.
SHOOOO
NO SIGN OF ANYONE.
DID DUEY FIND OUT ANY-THING?
IT'S LOOKING NOW.

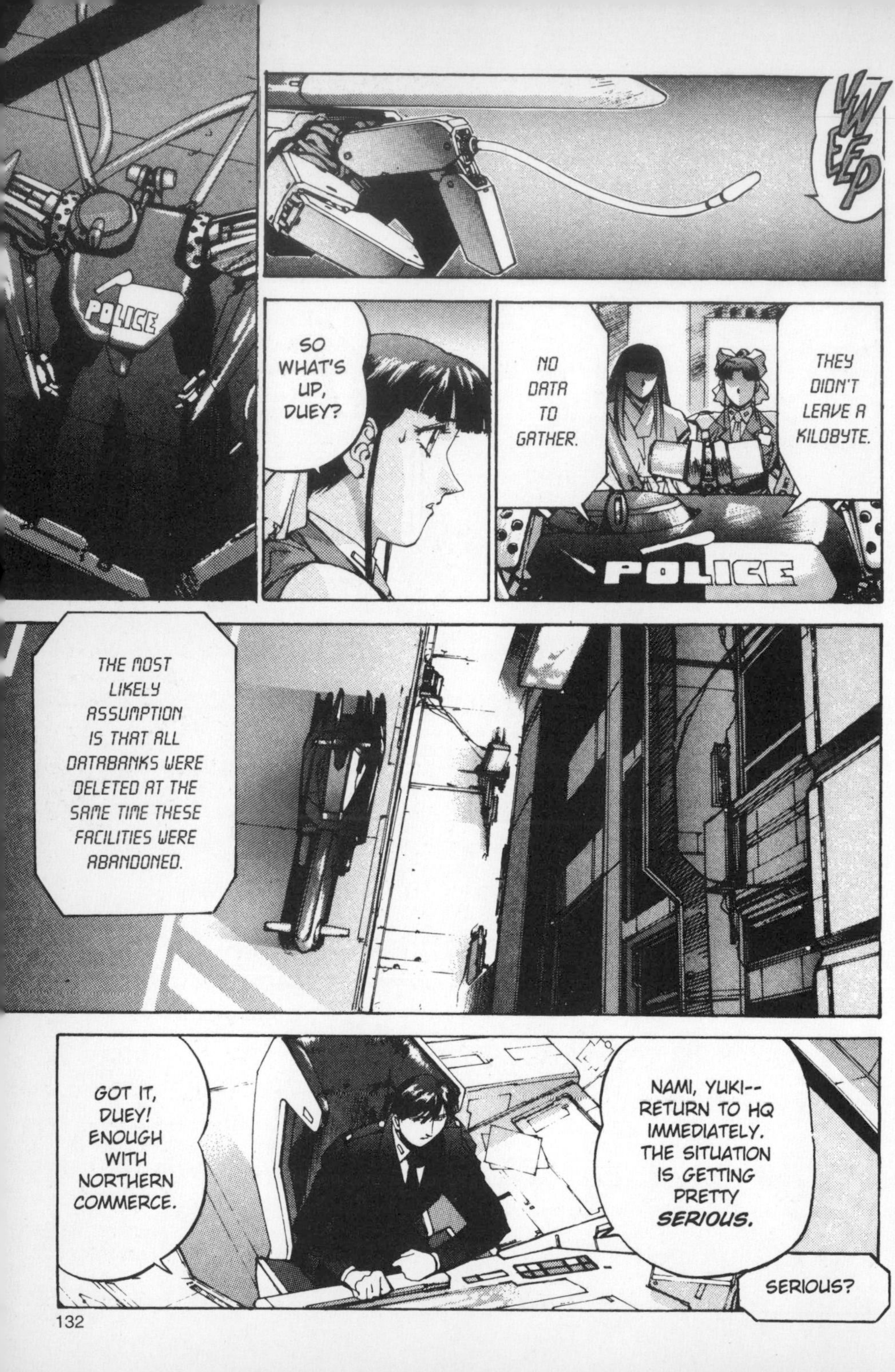
VWEEP
SO WHAT'S UP, DUEY?
NO DATA TO GATHER.
THEY DIDN'T LEAVE A KILOBYTE.
THE MOST LIKELY ASSUMPTION IS THAT ALL DATABANKS WERE DELETED AT THE SAME TIME THESE FACILITIES WERE ABANDONED.
GOT IT, DUEY! ENOUGH WITH NORTHERN COMMERCE.
NAMI, YUKI-- RETURN TO HQ IMMEDIATELY. THE SITUATION IS GETTING PRETTY ***SERIOUS.***
SERIOUS?

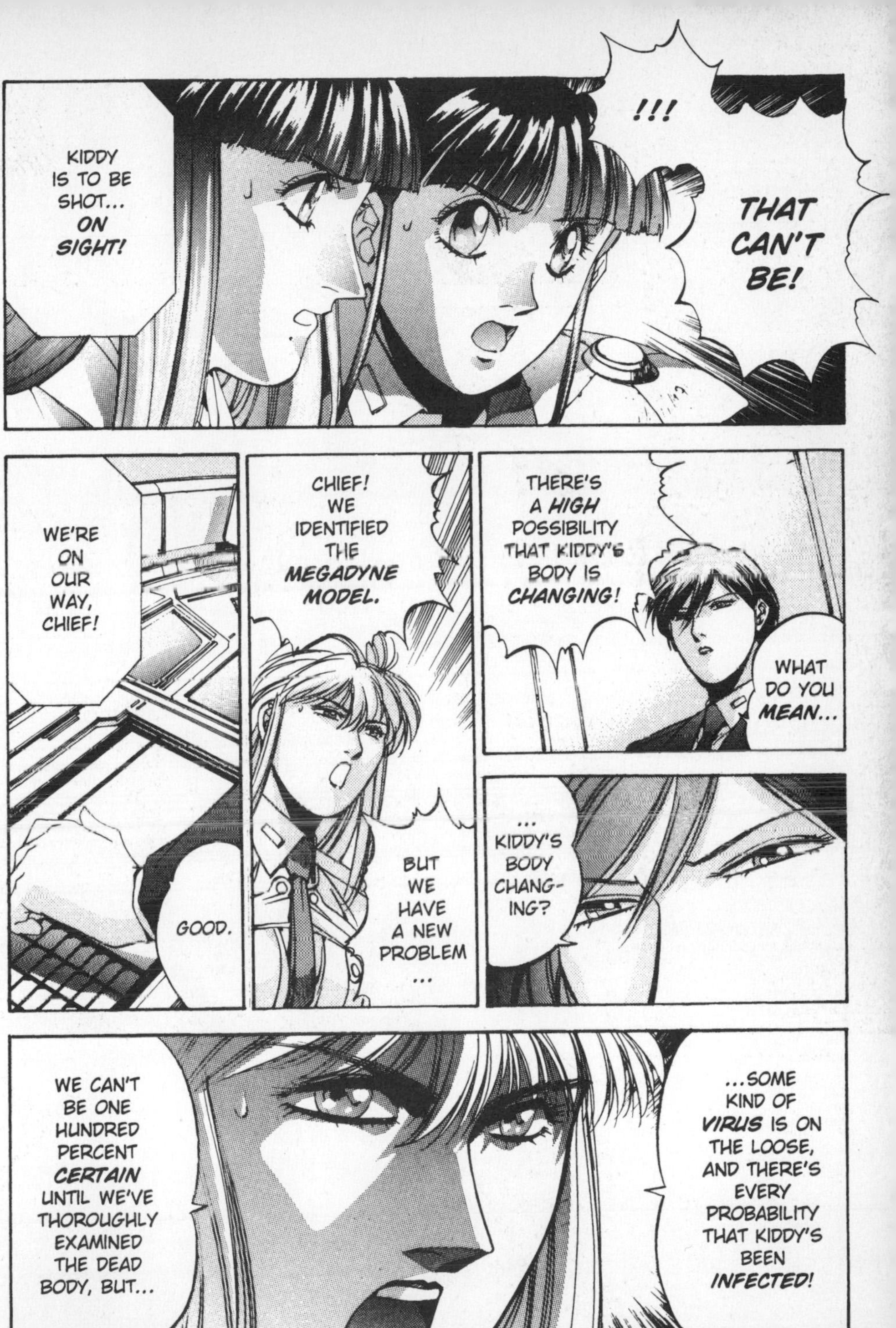

KIDDY IS TO BE SHOT... ON SIGHT!
!!!
THAT CAN'T BE!
WE'RE ON OUR WAY, CHIEF!
GOOD.
CHIEF! WE IDENTIFIED THE MEGADYNE MODEL.
BUT WE HAVE A NEW PROBLEM ...
THERE'S A HIGH POSSIBILITY THAT KIDDY'S BODY IS CHANGING!
WHAT DO YOU MEAN...
... KIDDY'S BODY CHANG-ING?
WE CAN'T BE ONE HUNDRED PERCENT CERTAIN UNTIL WE'VE THOROUGHLY EXAMINED THE DEAD BODY, BUT...
...SOME KIND OF VIRUS IS ON THE LOOSE, AND THERE'S EVERY PROBABILITY THAT KIDDY'S BEEN INFECTED!

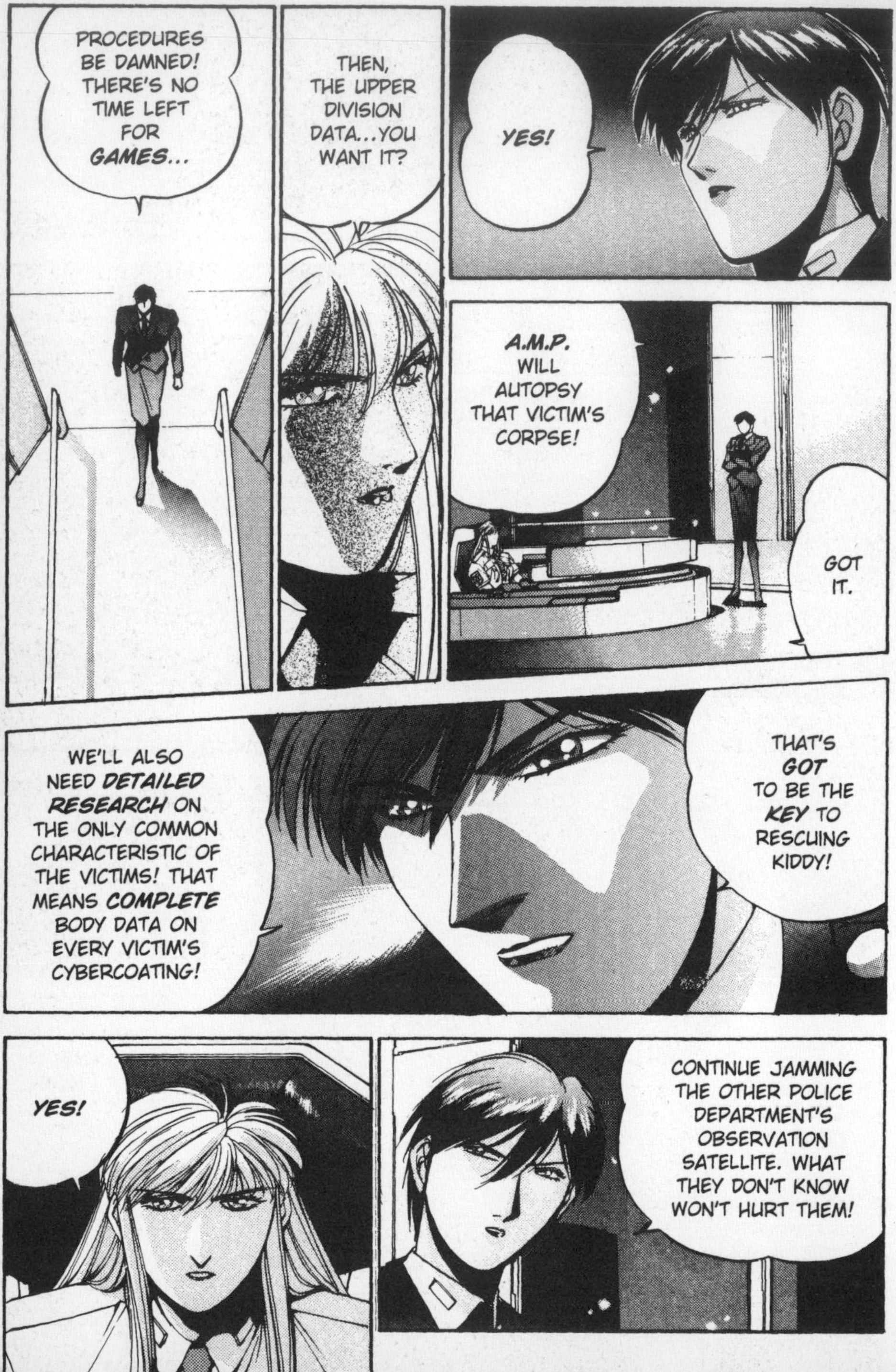
PROCEDURES BE DAMNED! THERE'S NO TIME LEFT FOR **GAMES...**
THEN, THE UPPER DIVISION DATA...YOU WANT IT?
YES!
A.M.P. WILL AUTOPSY THAT VICTIM'S CORPSE!
GOT IT.
WE'LL ALSO NEED **DETAILED RESEARCH** ON THE ONLY COMMON CHARACTERISTIC OF THE VICTIMS! THAT MEANS **COMPLETE** BODY DATA ON EVERY VICTIM'S CYBERCOATING!
THAT'S **GOT** TO BE THE **KEY** TO RESCUING KIDDY!
YES!
CONTINUE JAMMING THE OTHER POLICE DEPARTMENT'S OBSERVATION SATELLITE. WHAT THEY DON'T KNOW WON'T HURT THEM!

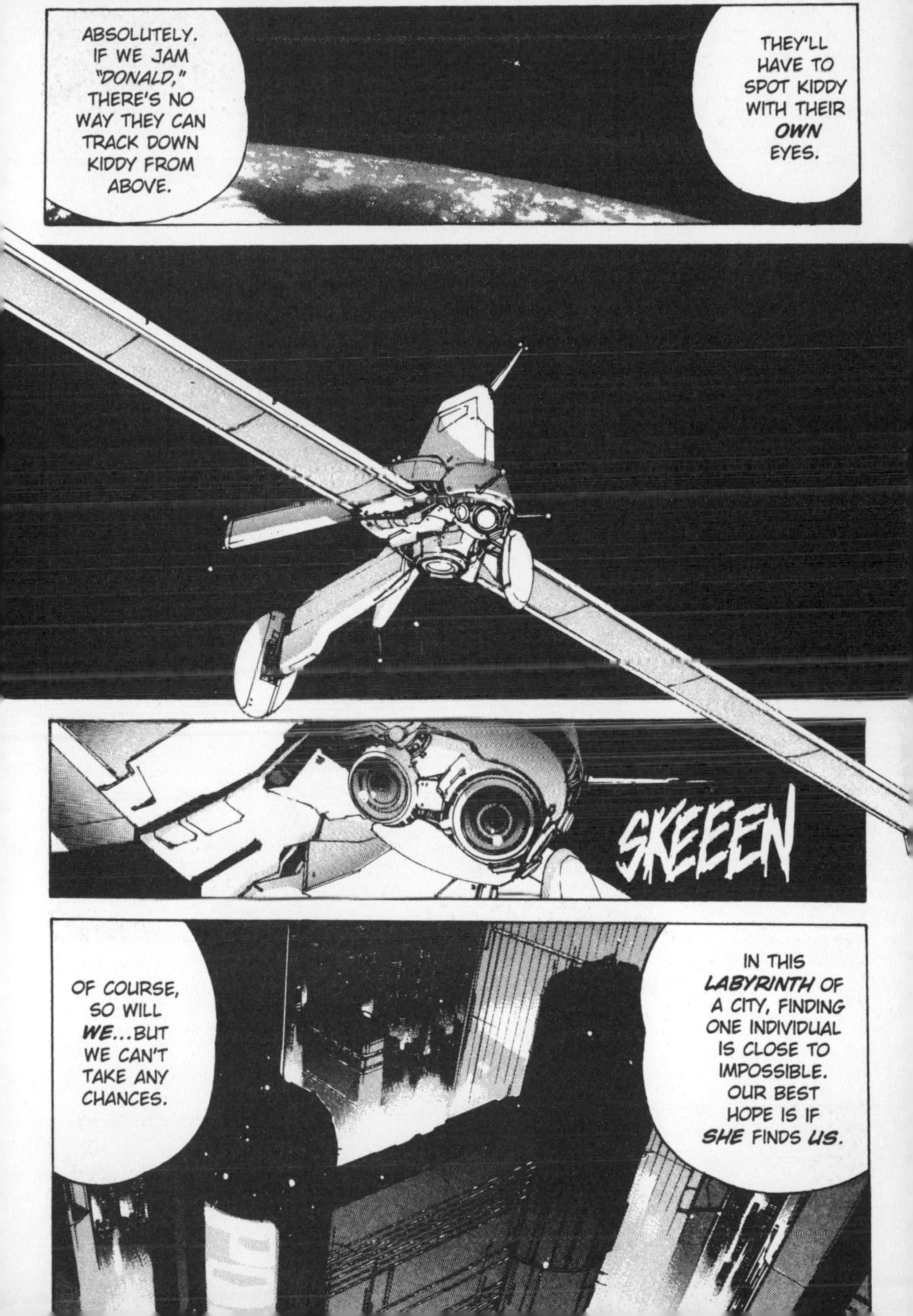
ABSOLUTELY. IF WE JAM "DONALD," THERE'S NO WAY THEY CAN TRACK DOWN KIDDY FROM ABOVE.
THEY'LL HAVE TO SPOT KIDDY WITH THEIR ***OWN*** EYES.
SKEEEN
OF COURSE, SO WILL ***WE***...BUT WE CAN'T TAKE ANY CHANCES.
IN THIS ***LABYRINTH*** OF A CITY, FINDING ONE INDIVIDUAL IS CLOSE TO IMPOSSIBLE. OUR BEST HOPE IS IF ***SHE*** FINDS ***US***.

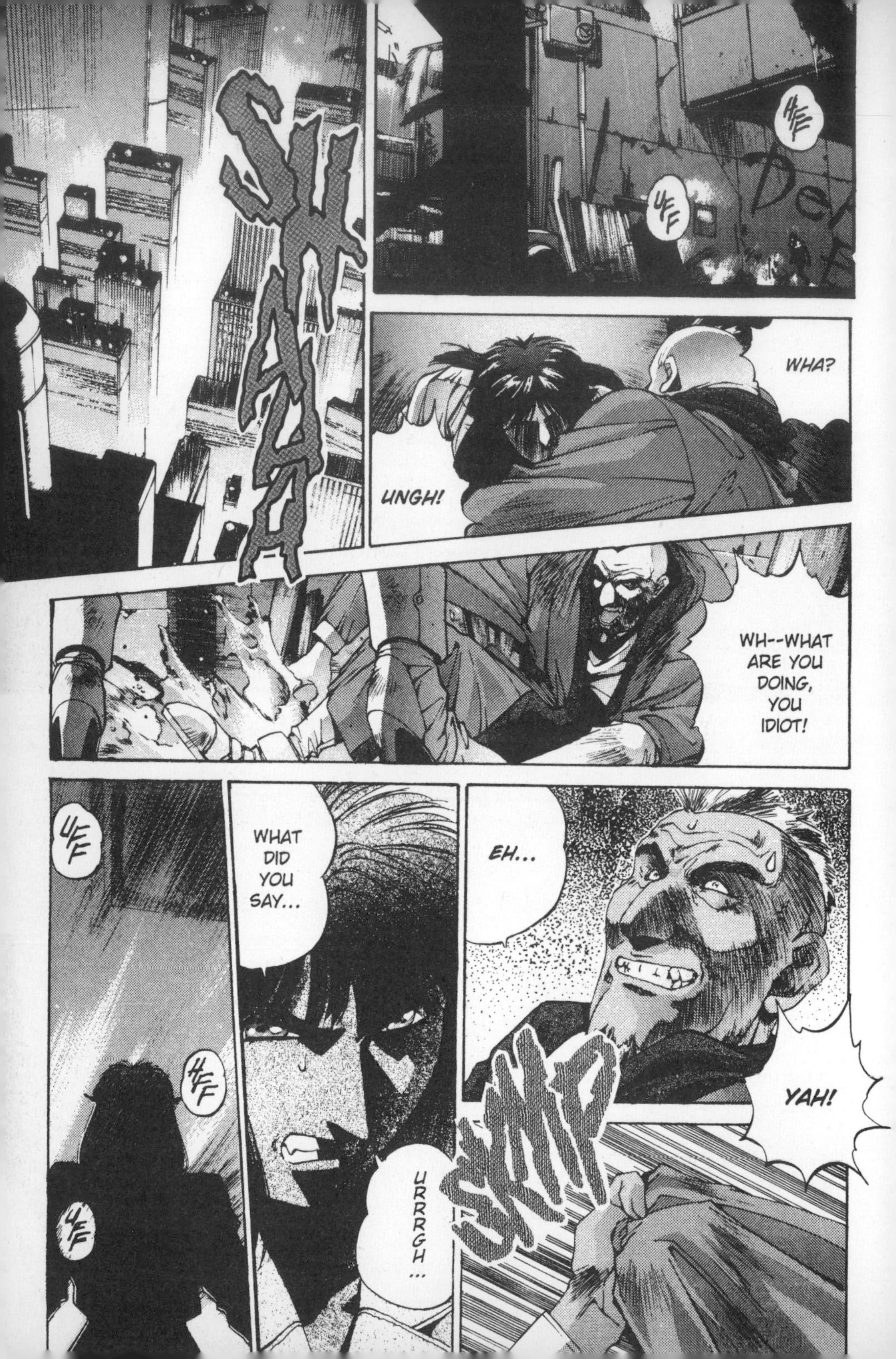
HEFF
UFF
WHA?
UNGH!
WH--WHAT ARE YOU DOING, YOU IDIOT!
UFF
HEFF
UFF
WHAT DID YOU SAY...
URRRGH...
EH...
YAH!

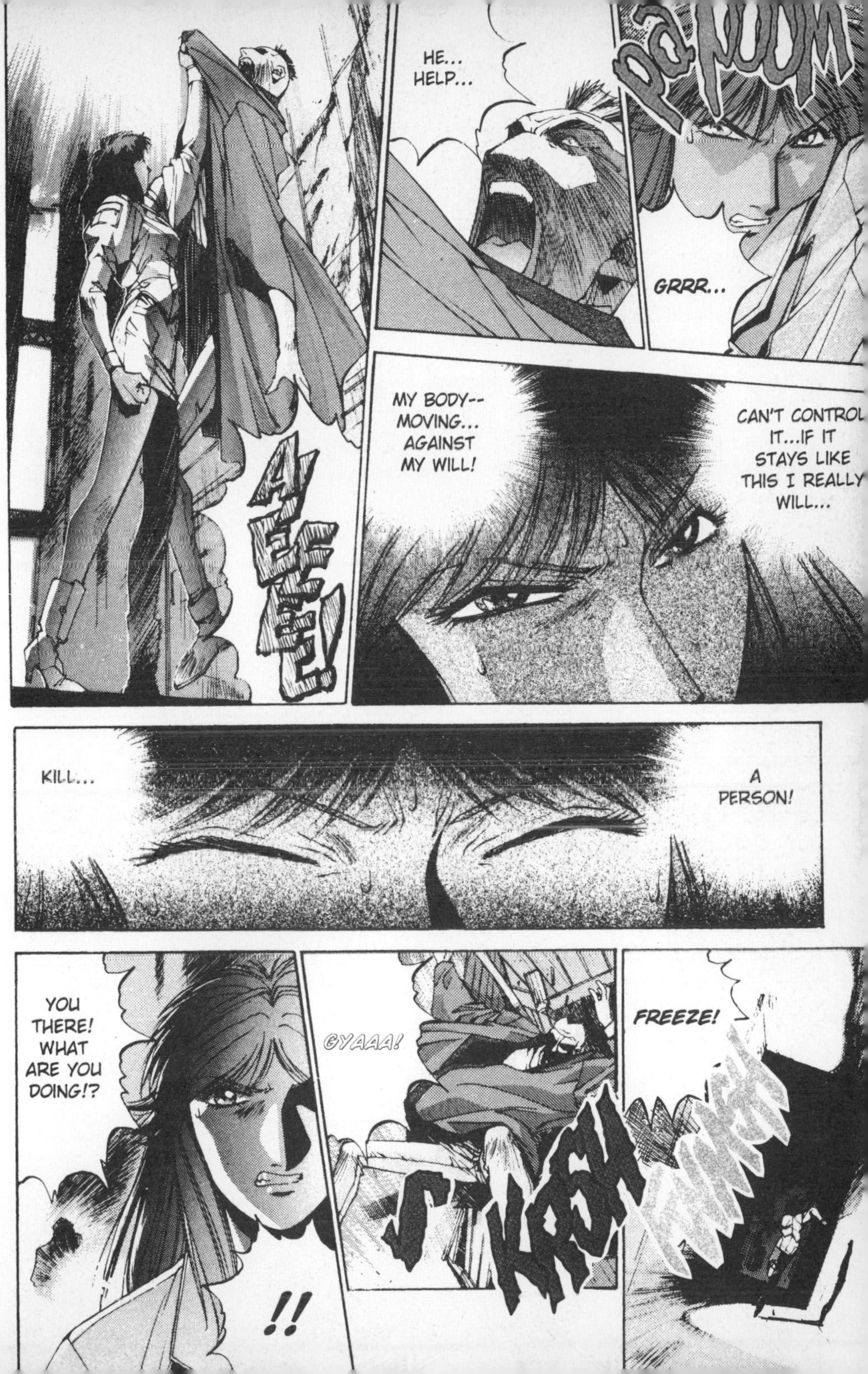

HE... HELP...
GRRR...
MY BODY-- MOVING... AGAINST MY WILL!
CAN'T CONTROL IT...IF IT STAYS LIKE THIS I REALLY WILL...
KILL...
A PERSON!
YOU THERE! WHAT ARE YOU DOING!?
!!
GYAAA!
FREEZE!

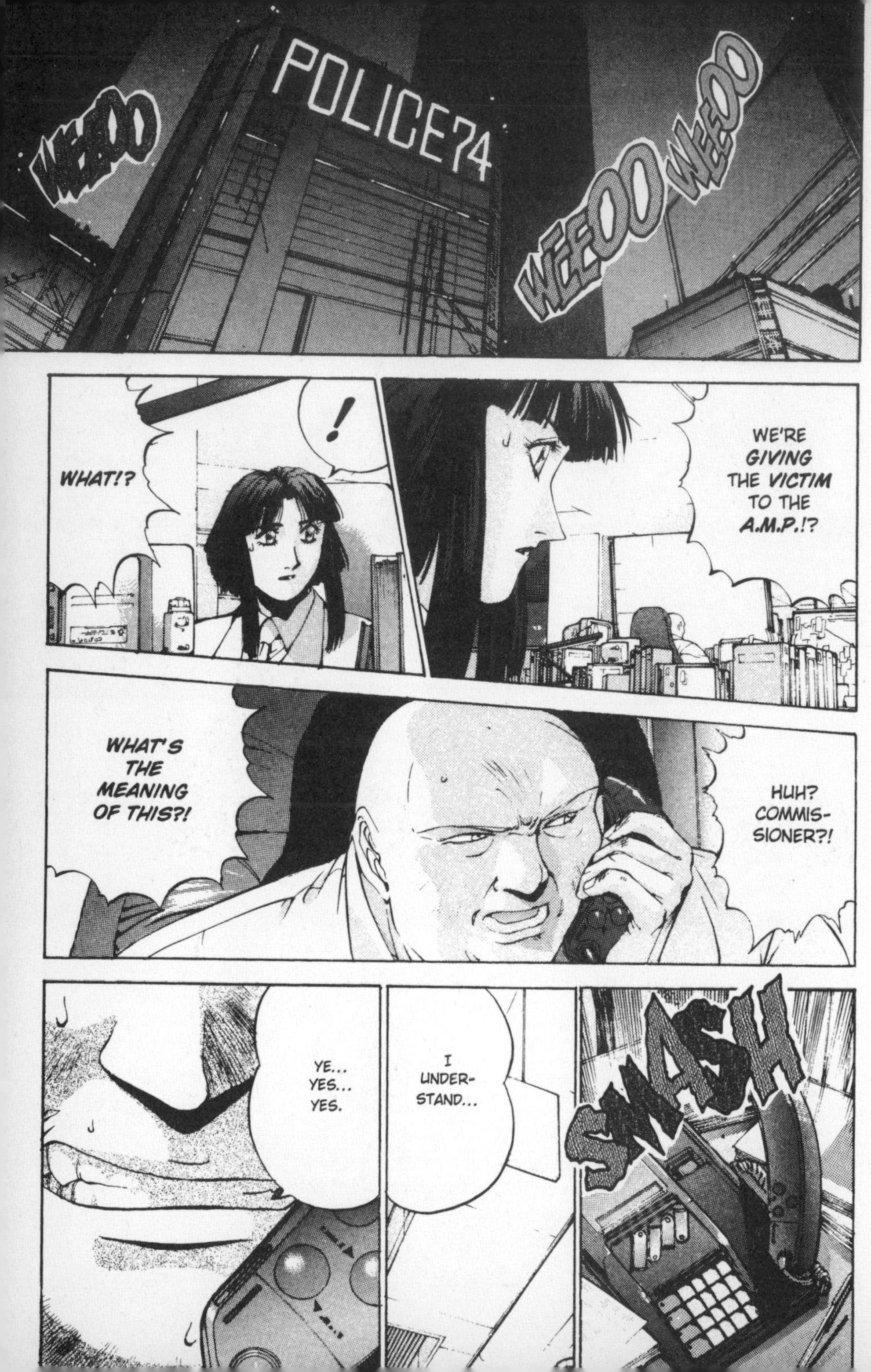
WEEOO
POLICE 74
WEEOO WEEOO
!
WHAT!?
WE'RE GIVING THE VICTIM TO THE A.M.P.!?
WHAT'S THE MEANING OF THIS?!
HUH? COMMIS-SIONER?!
YE... YES... YES.
I UNDER-STAND...
SMASH

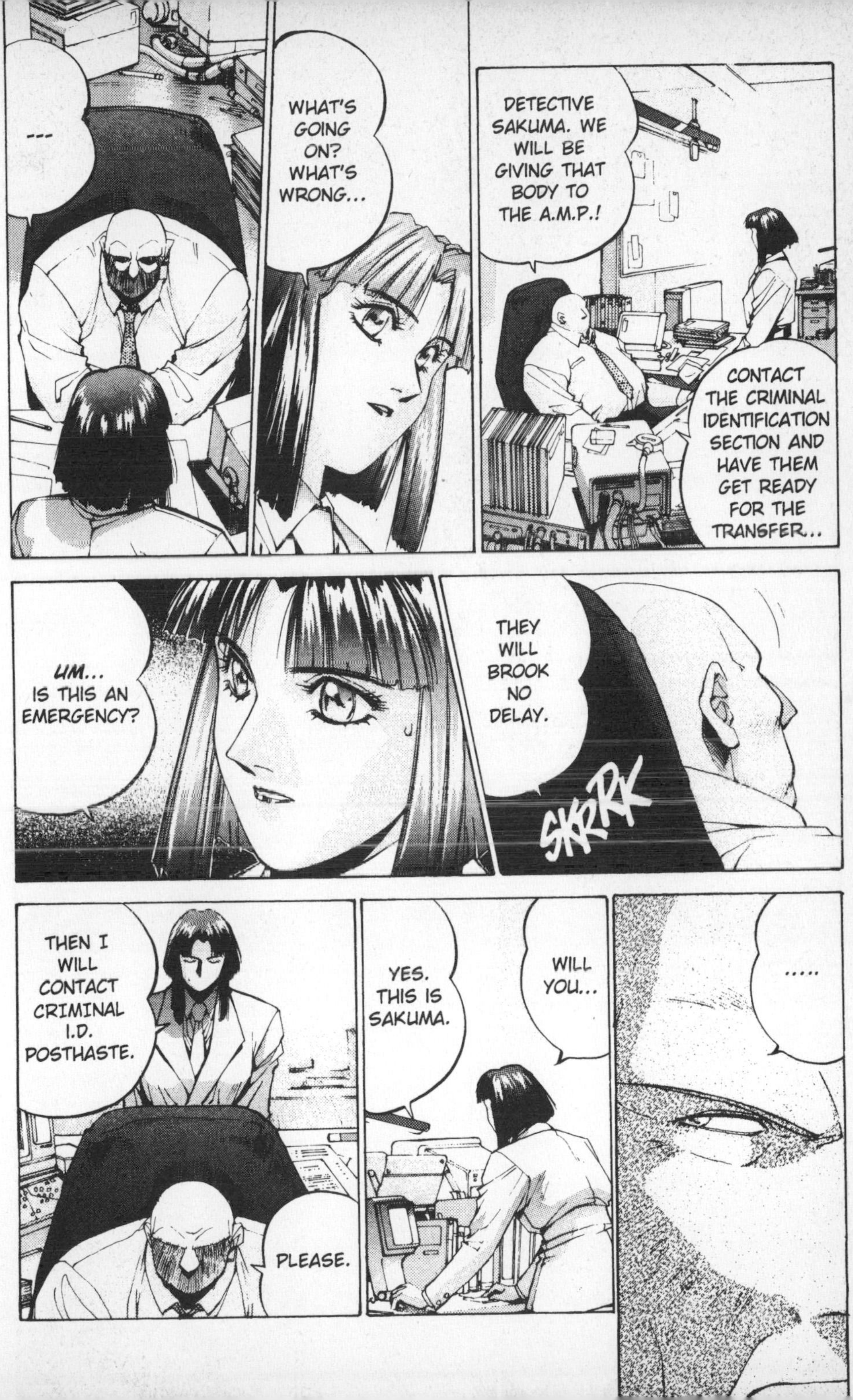

WHAT'S GOING ON? WHAT'S WRONG...
DETECTIVE SAKUMA. WE WILL BE GIVING THAT BODY TO THE A.M.P.!
CONTACT THE CRIMINAL IDENTIFICATION SECTION AND HAVE THEM GET READY FOR THE TRANSFER...
UM... IS THIS AN EMERGENCY?
THEY WILL BROOK NO DELAY.
SKRRK
THEN I WILL CONTACT CRIMINAL I.D. POSTHASTE.
PLEASE.
YES. THIS IS SAKUMA.
WILL YOU...
.....

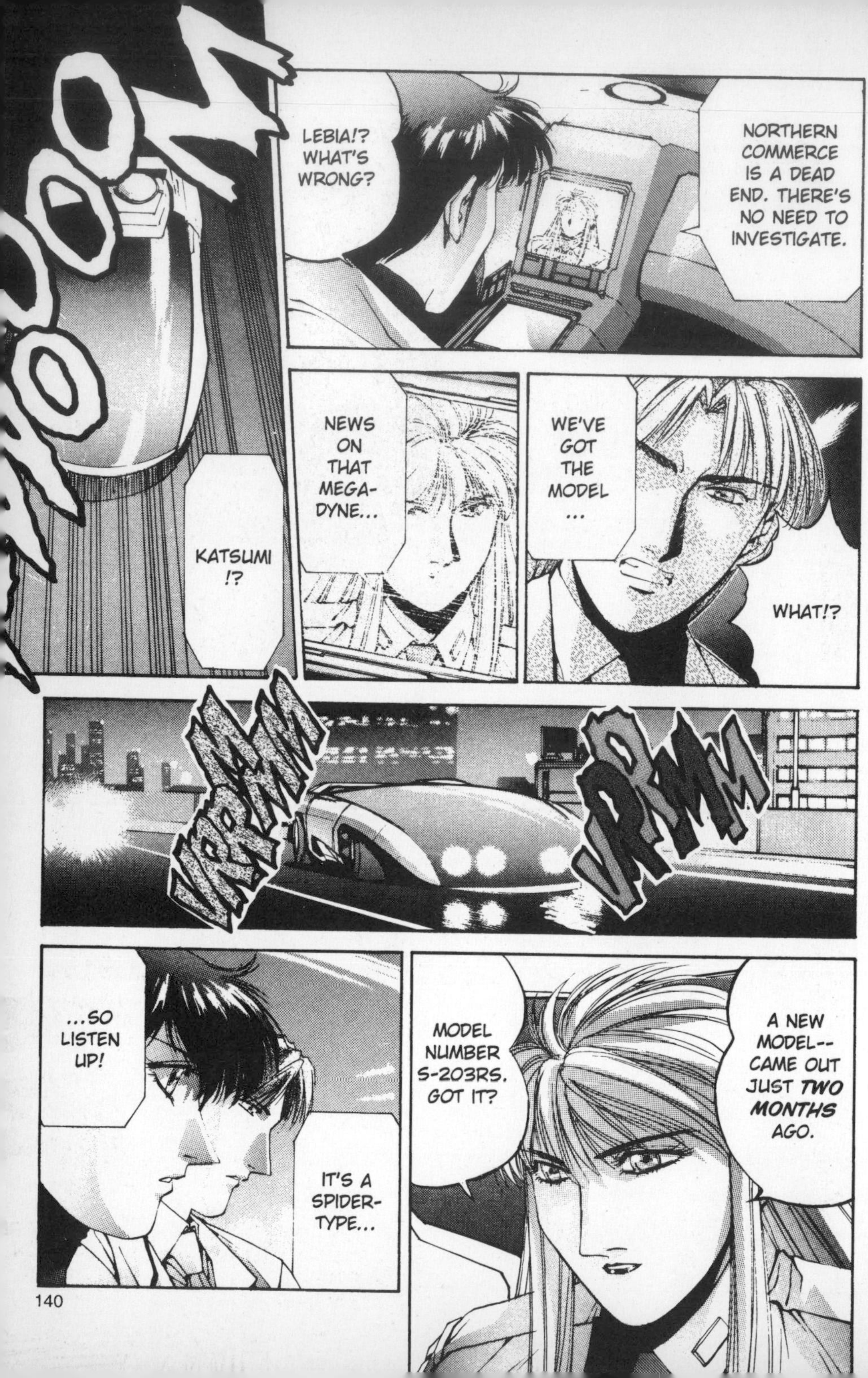
KATSUMI !?
LEBIA!? WHAT'S WRONG?
NORTHERN COMMERCE IS A DEAD END. THERE'S NO NEED TO INVESTIGATE.
NEWS ON THAT MEGA-DYNE...
WE'VE GOT THE MODEL ...
WHAT!?
VRRAMM
VRRMM
...SO LISTEN UP!
IT'S A SPIDER-TYPE...
MODEL NUMBER S-203RS. GOT IT?
A NEW MODEL-- CAME OUT JUST TWO MONTHS AGO.

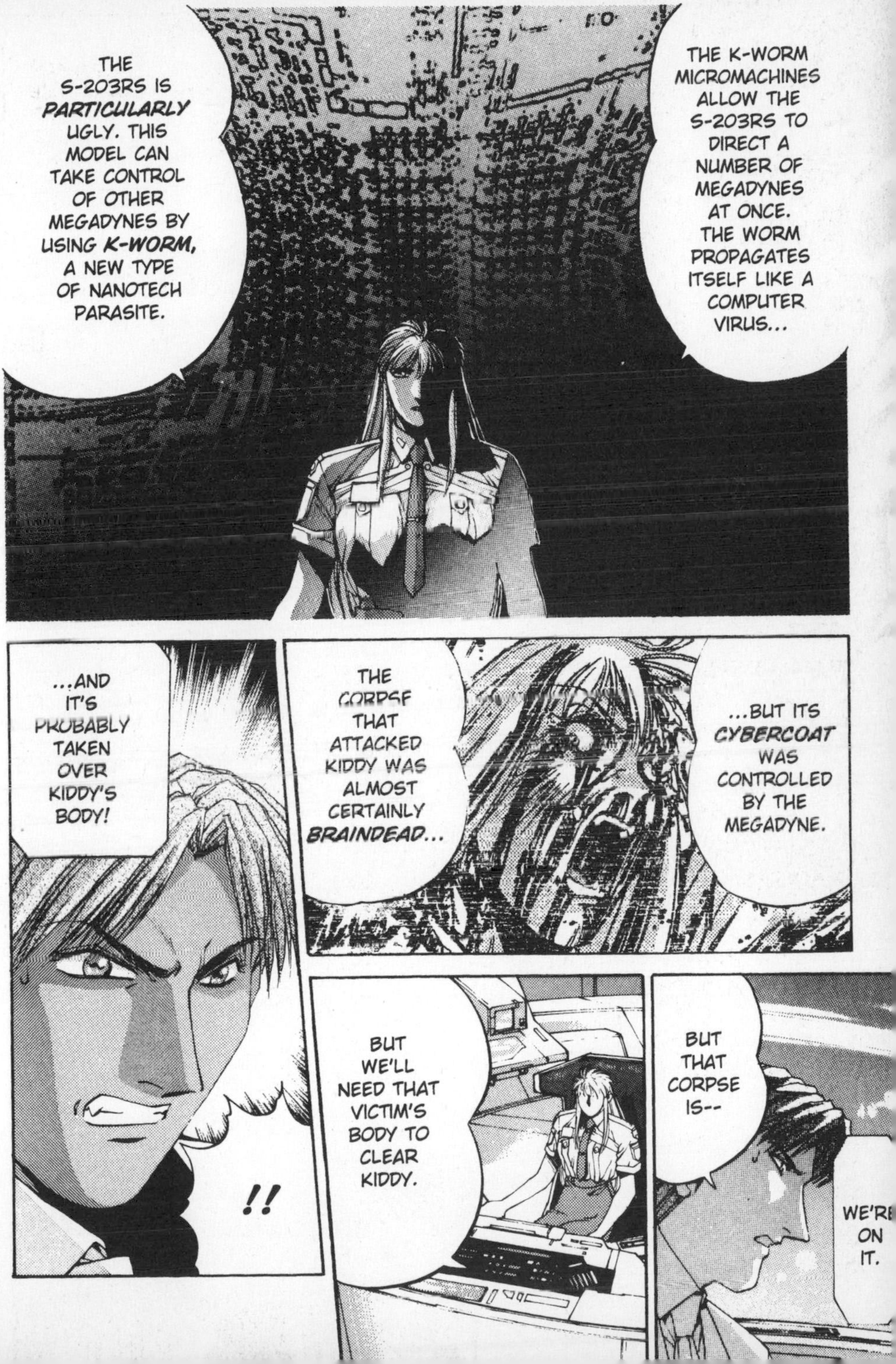
THE S-203RS IS PARTICULARLY UGLY. THIS MODEL CAN TAKE CONTROL OF OTHER MEGADYNES BY USING K-WORM, A NEW TYPE OF NANOTECH PARASITE.
THE K-WORM MICROMACHINES ALLOW THE S-203RS TO DIRECT A NUMBER OF MEGADYNES AT ONCE. THE WORM PROPAGATES ITSELF LIKE A COMPUTER VIRUS...
...AND IT'S PROBABLY TAKEN OVER KIDDY'S BODY!
!!
THE CORPSE THAT ATTACKED KIDDY WAS ALMOST CERTAINLY BRAINDEAD...
...BUT ITS CYBERCOAT WAS CONTROLLED BY THE MEGADYNE.
BUT WE'LL NEED THAT VICTIM'S BODY TO CLEAR KIDDY.
BUT THAT CORPSE IS--
WE'R
ON
IT.

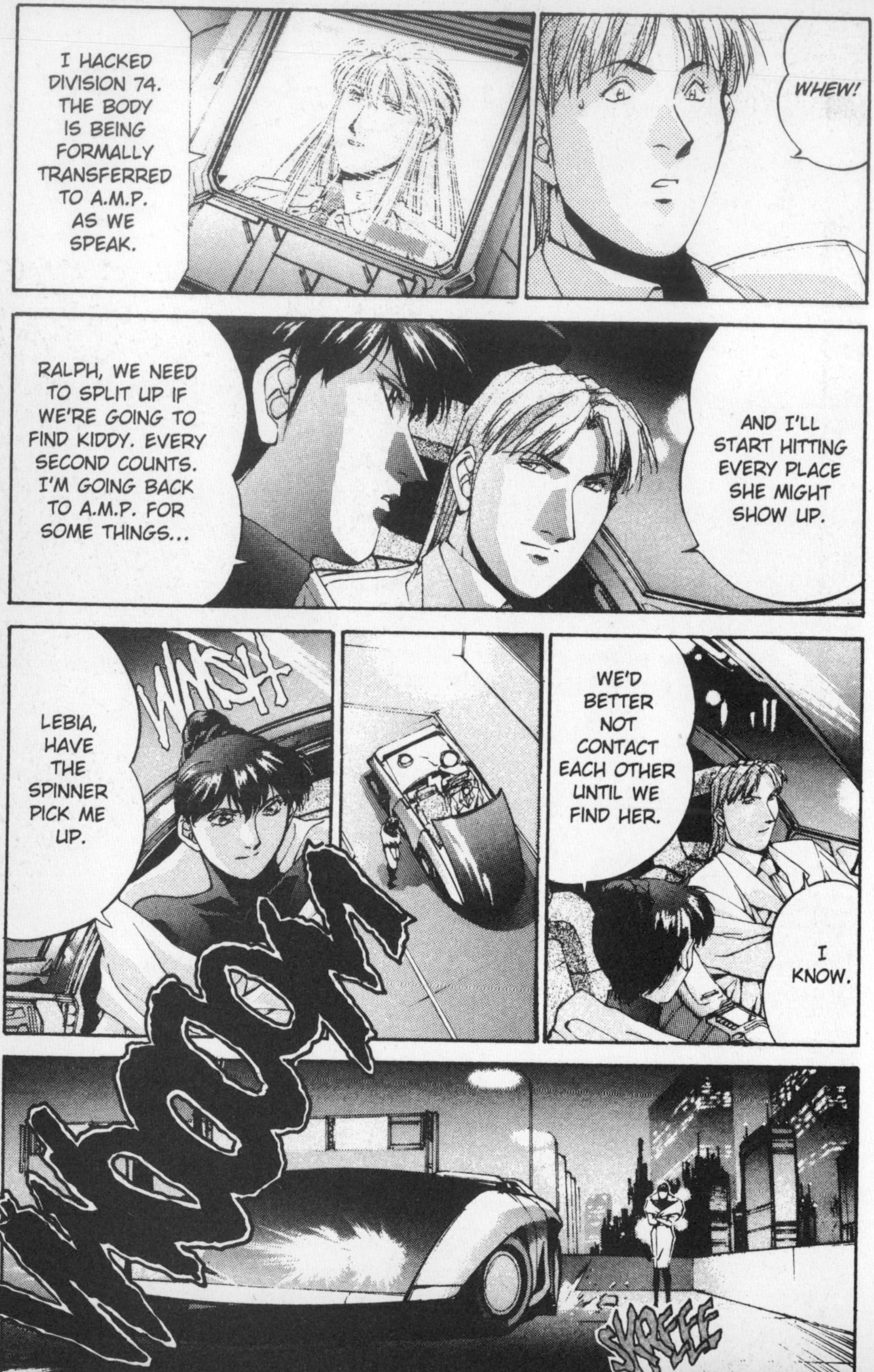
I HACKED DIVISION 74. THE BODY IS BEING FORMALLY TRANSFERRED TO A.M.P. AS WE SPEAK.
WHEW!
RALPH, WE NEED TO SPLIT UP IF WE'RE GOING TO FIND KIDDY. EVERY SECOND COUNTS. I'M GOING BACK TO A.M.P. FOR SOME THINGS...
AND I'LL START HITTING EVERY PLACE SHE MIGHT SHOW UP.
WHSH
LEBIA, HAVE THE SPINNER PICK ME UP.
WE'D BETTER NOT CONTACT EACH OTHER UNTIL WE FIND HER.
I KNOW.
SKREEE

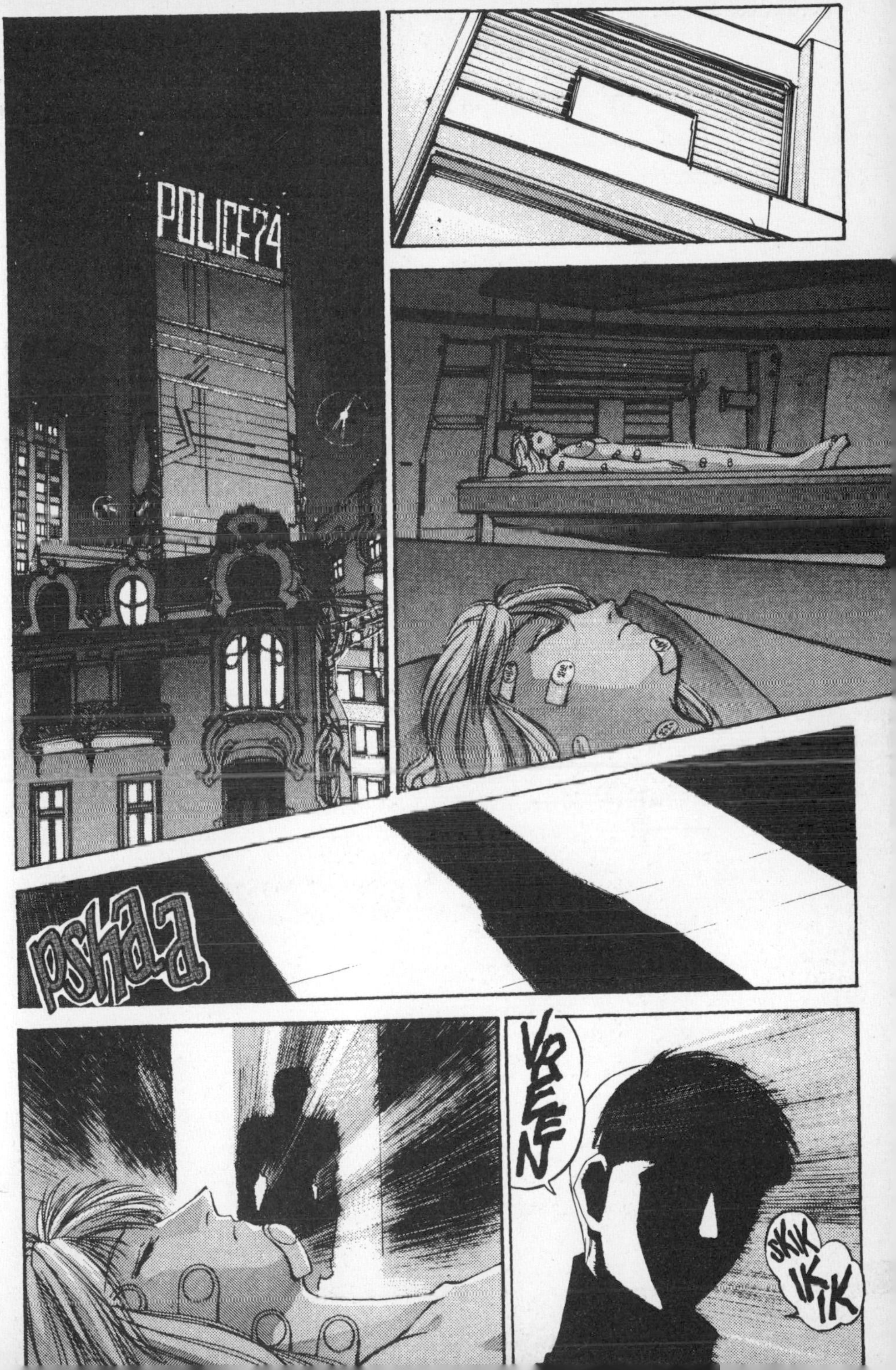
POLICE74
pshaa
VREEN
SKIK IK IK

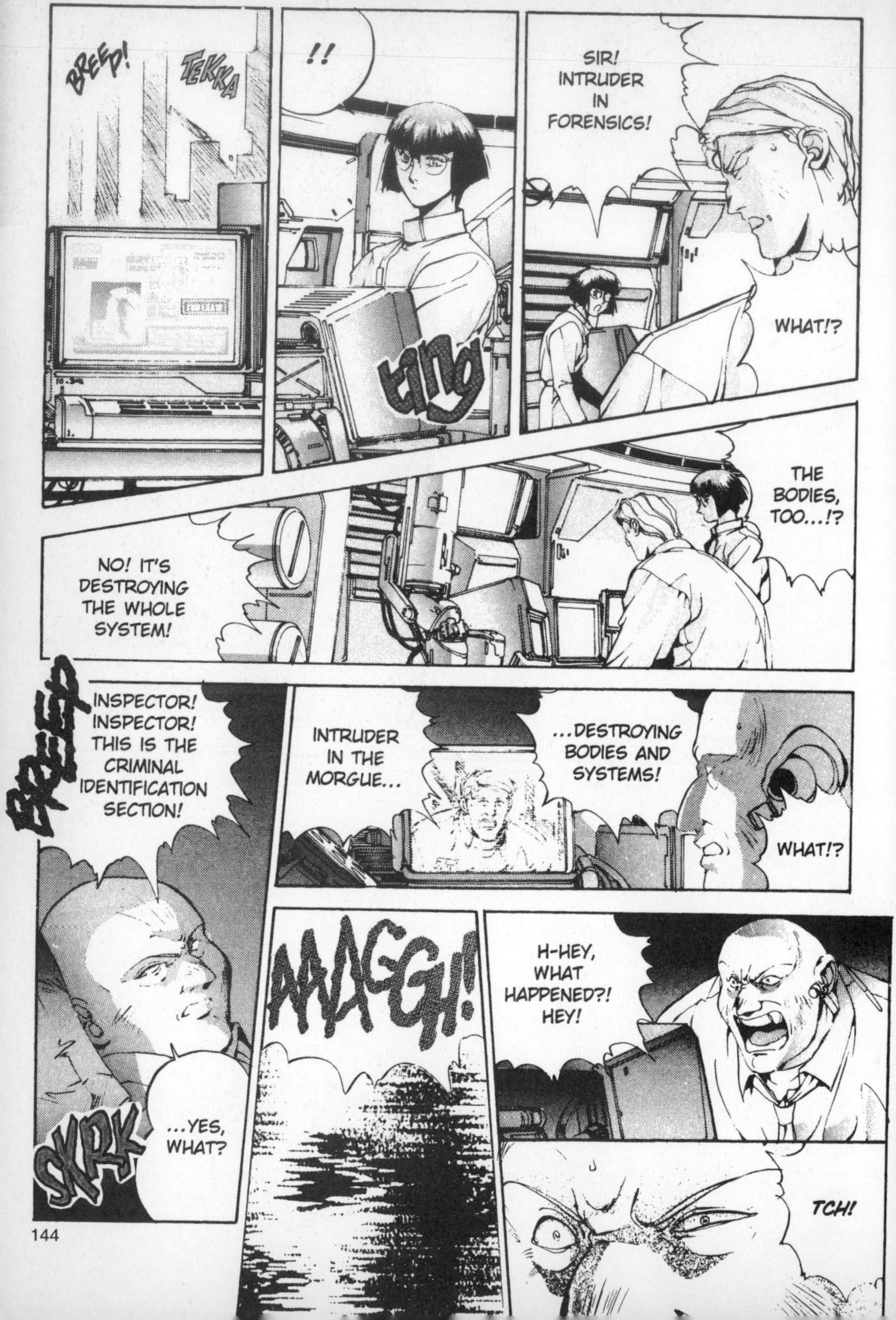

BREEP!
TEKKA
!!
ting
SIR! INTRUDER IN FORENSICS!
WHAT!?
THE BODIES, TOO...!?
NO! IT'S DESTROYING THE WHOLE SYSTEM!
BREEP
INSPECTOR! INSPECTOR! THIS IS THE CRIMINAL IDENTIFICATION SECTION!
INTRUDER IN THE MORGUE...
...DESTROYING BODIES AND SYSTEMS!
WHAT!?
SKRK
...YES, WHAT?
AAAGGH!!
H-HEY, WHAT HAPPENED?! HEY!
TCH!

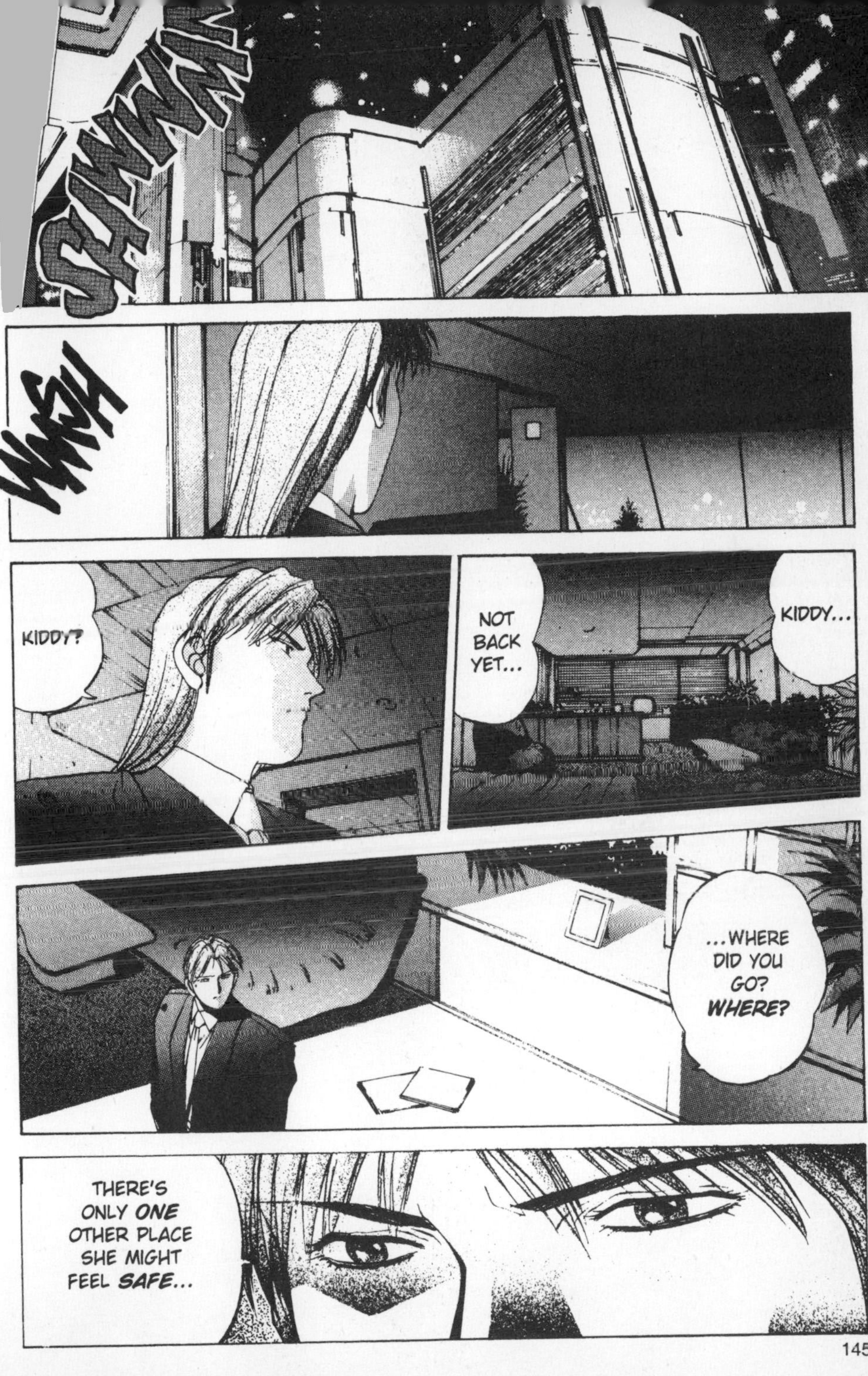
SHWWNN
WHSH
KIDDY?
NOT BACK YET...
KIDDY...
...WHERE DID YOU GO? *WHERE?*
THERE'S ONLY *ONE* OTHER PLACE SHE MIGHT FEEL *SAFE*...

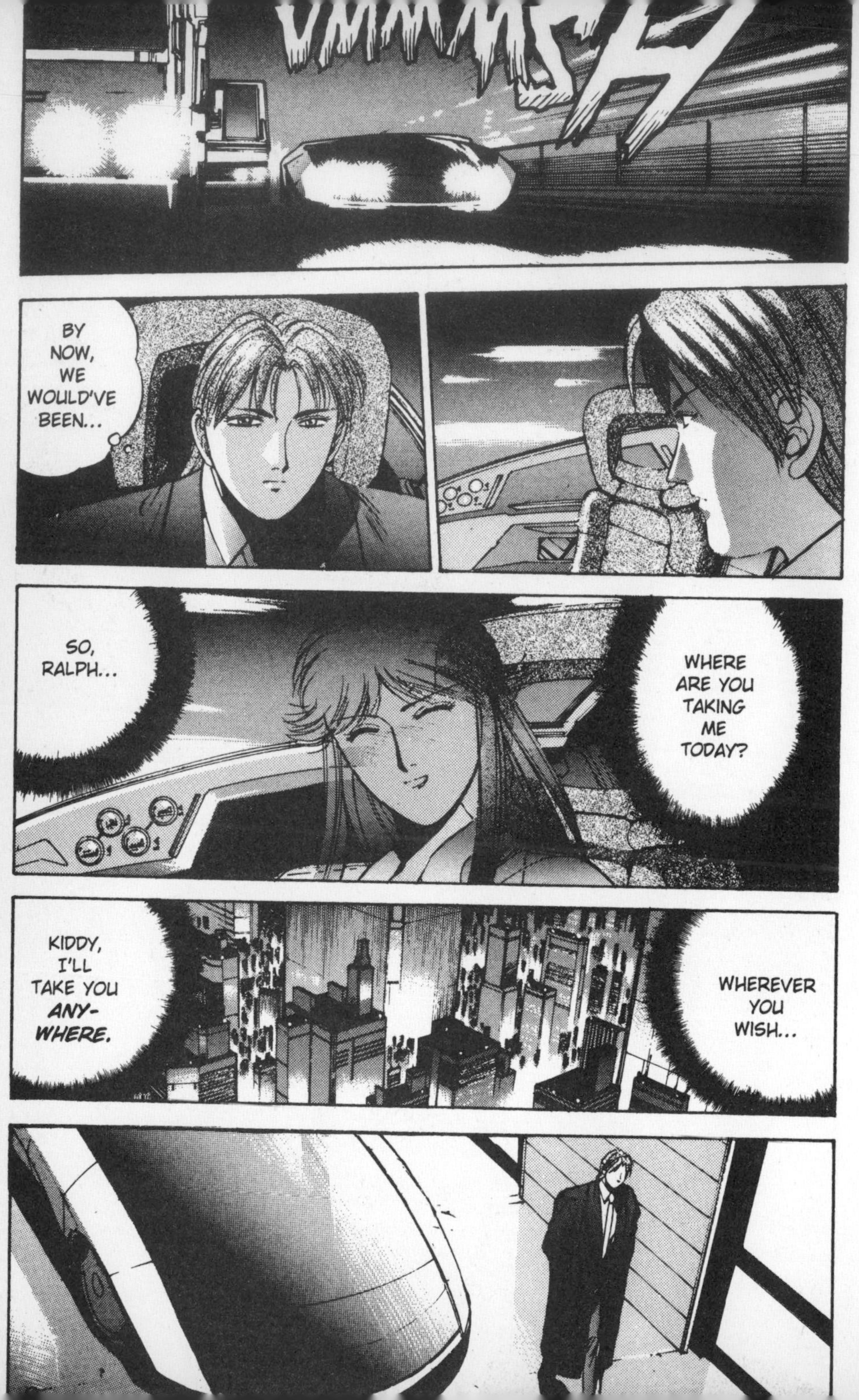
VMMMSH
BY NOW, WE WOULD'VE BEEN...
SO, RALPH...
WHERE ARE YOU TAKING ME TODAY?
KIDDY, I'LL TAKE YOU ANY-WHERE.
WHEREVER YOU WISH...

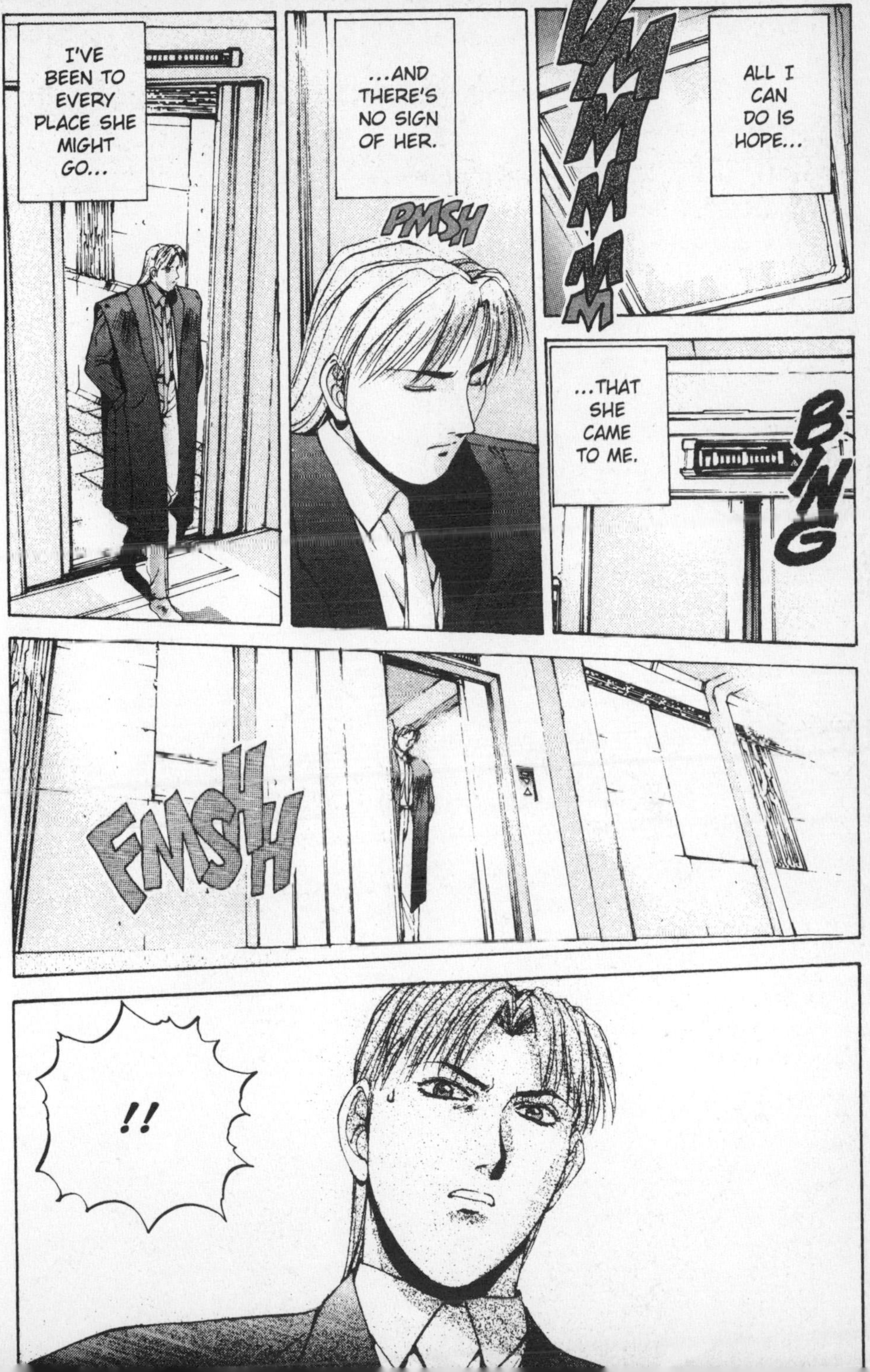
I'VE BEEN TO EVERY PLACE SHE MIGHT GO...
...AND THERE'S NO SIGN OF HER.
PMSH
VMMMMM
ALL I CAN DO IS HOPE...
...THAT SHE CAME TO ME.
BING
FMSHH
!!

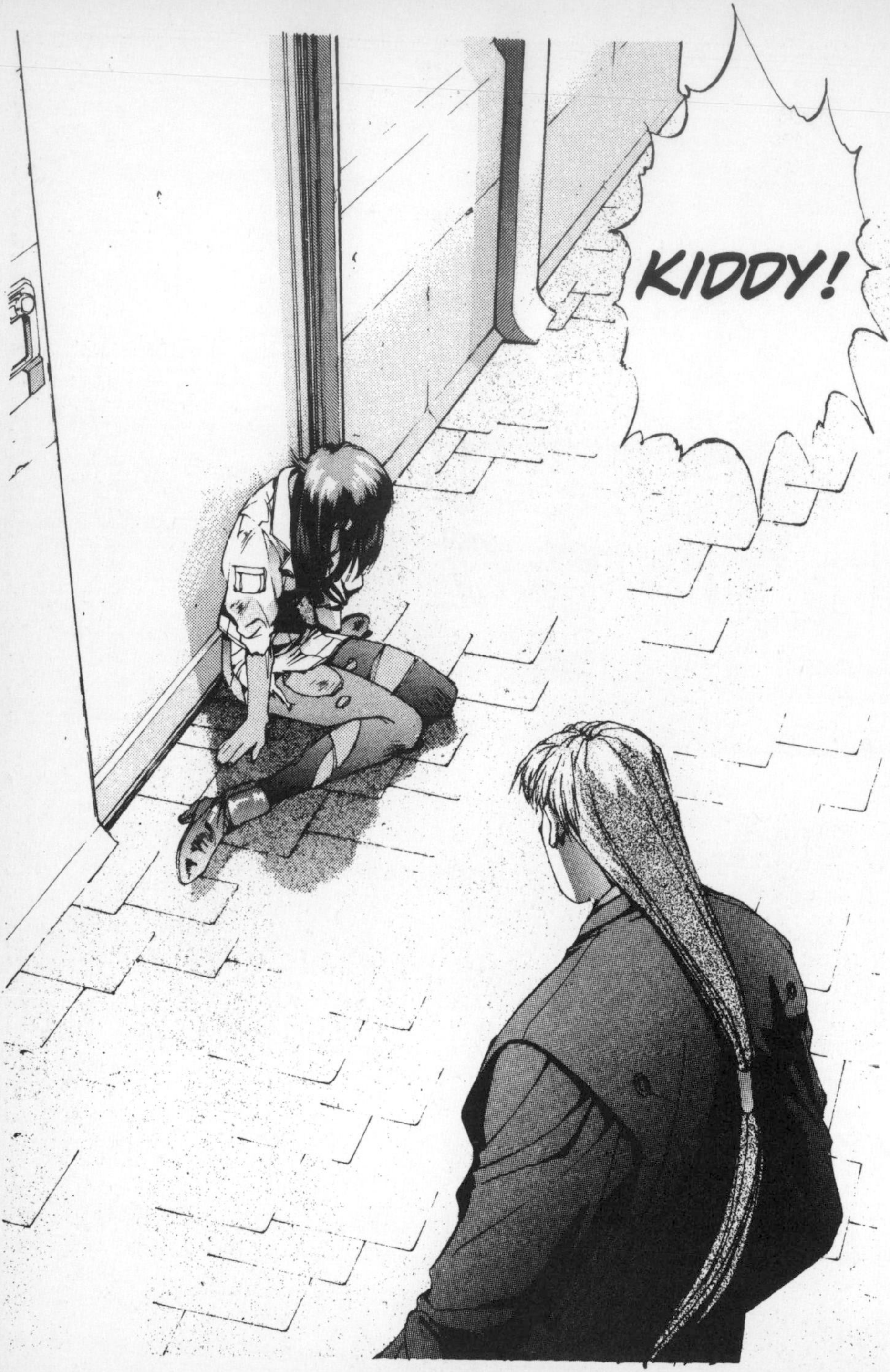
KIDDY!

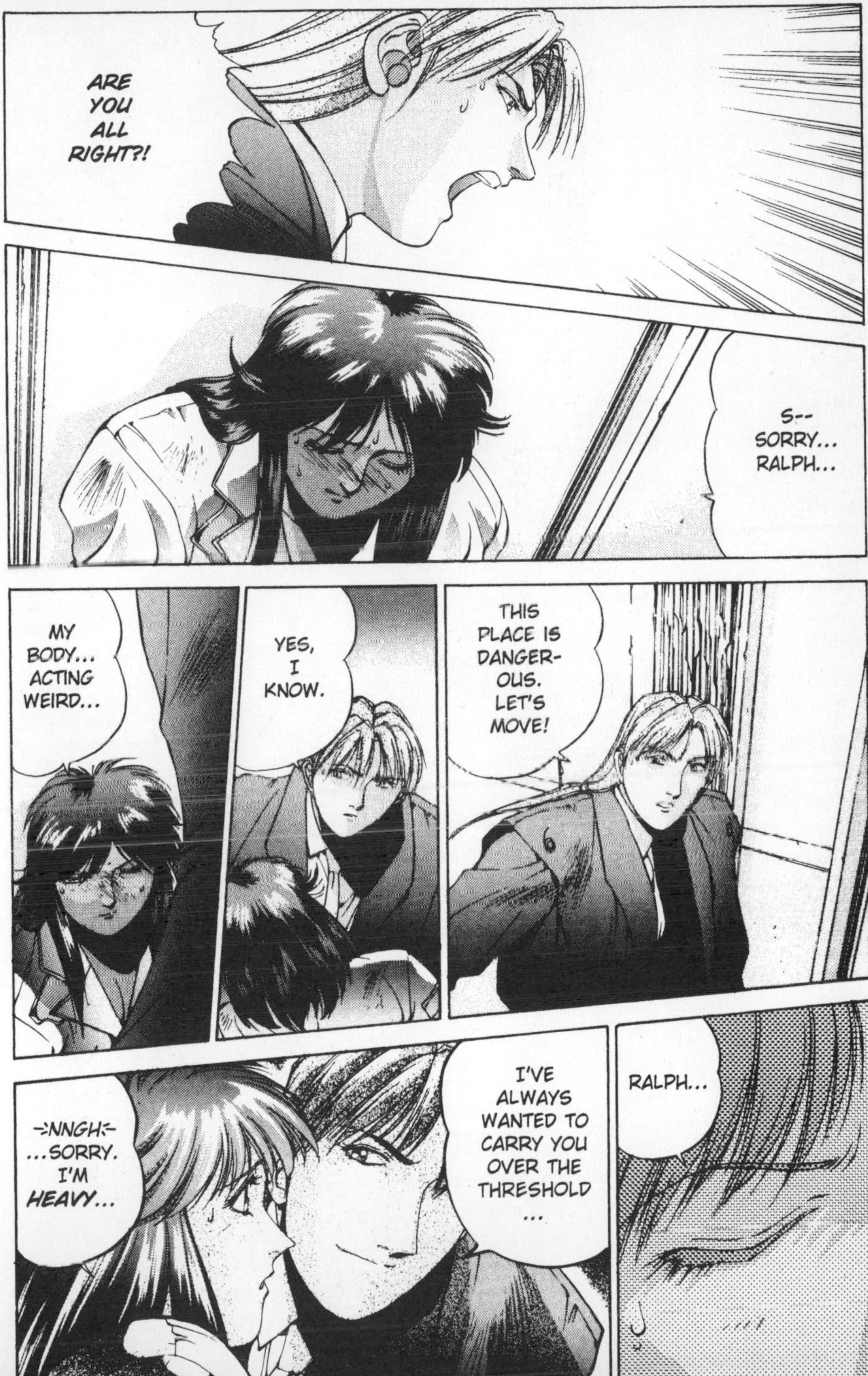
ARE YOU ALL RIGHT?!
S-- SORRY... RALPH...
MY BODY... ACTING WEIRD...
YES, I KNOW.
THIS PLACE IS DANGER-OUS. LET'S MOVE!
-NNGH- ...SORRY. I'M *HEAVY*...
I'VE ALWAYS WANTED TO CARRY YOU OVER THE THRESHOLD ...
RALPH...

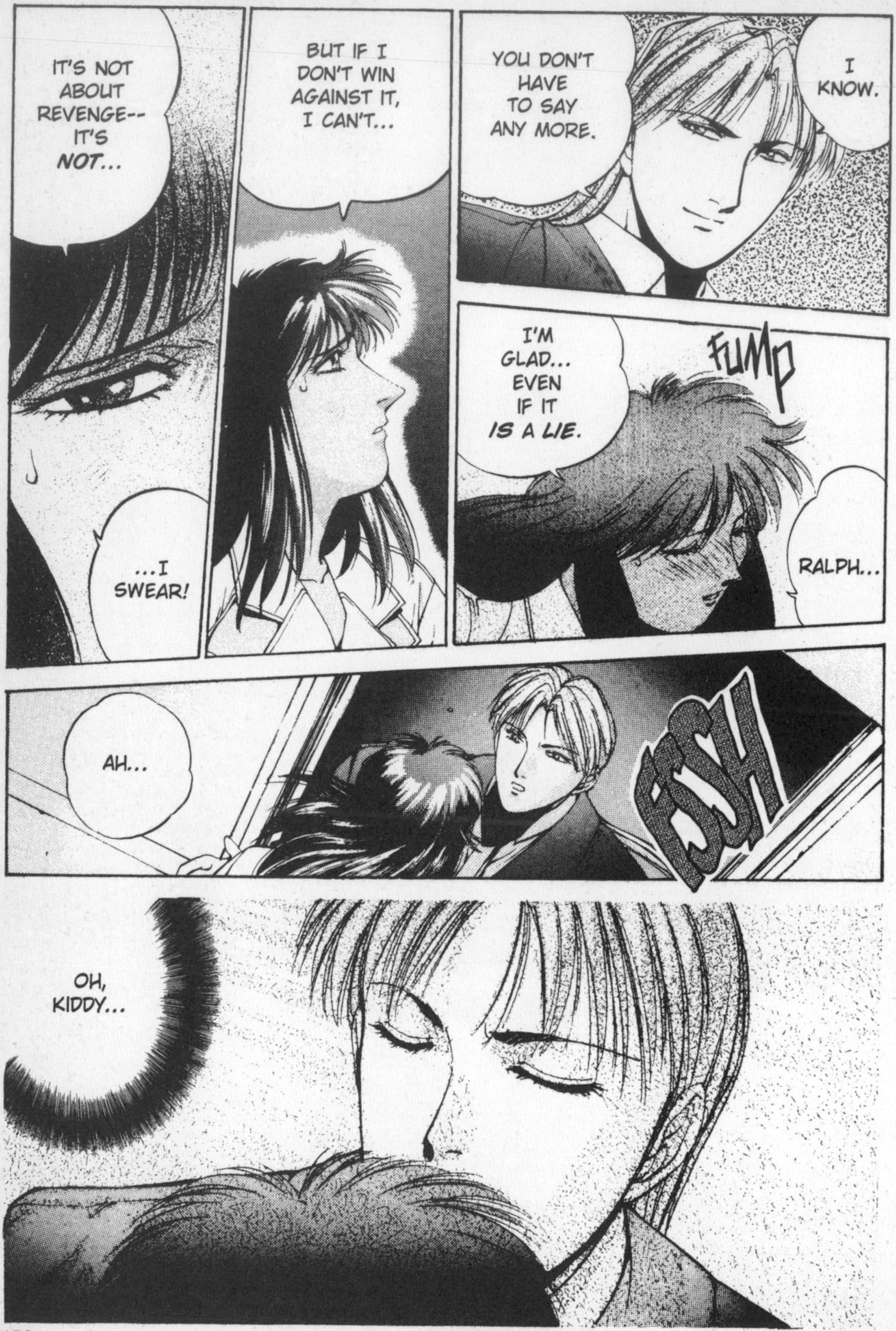

IT'S NOT ABOUT REVENGE-- IT'S *NOT*...
...I SWEAR!
BUT IF I DON'T WIN AGAINST IT, I CAN'T...
YOU DON'T HAVE TO SAY ANY MORE.
I KNOW.
I'M GLAD... EVEN IF IT *IS A LIE*.
FUMP
RALPH...
AH...
FSSH
OH, KIDDY...

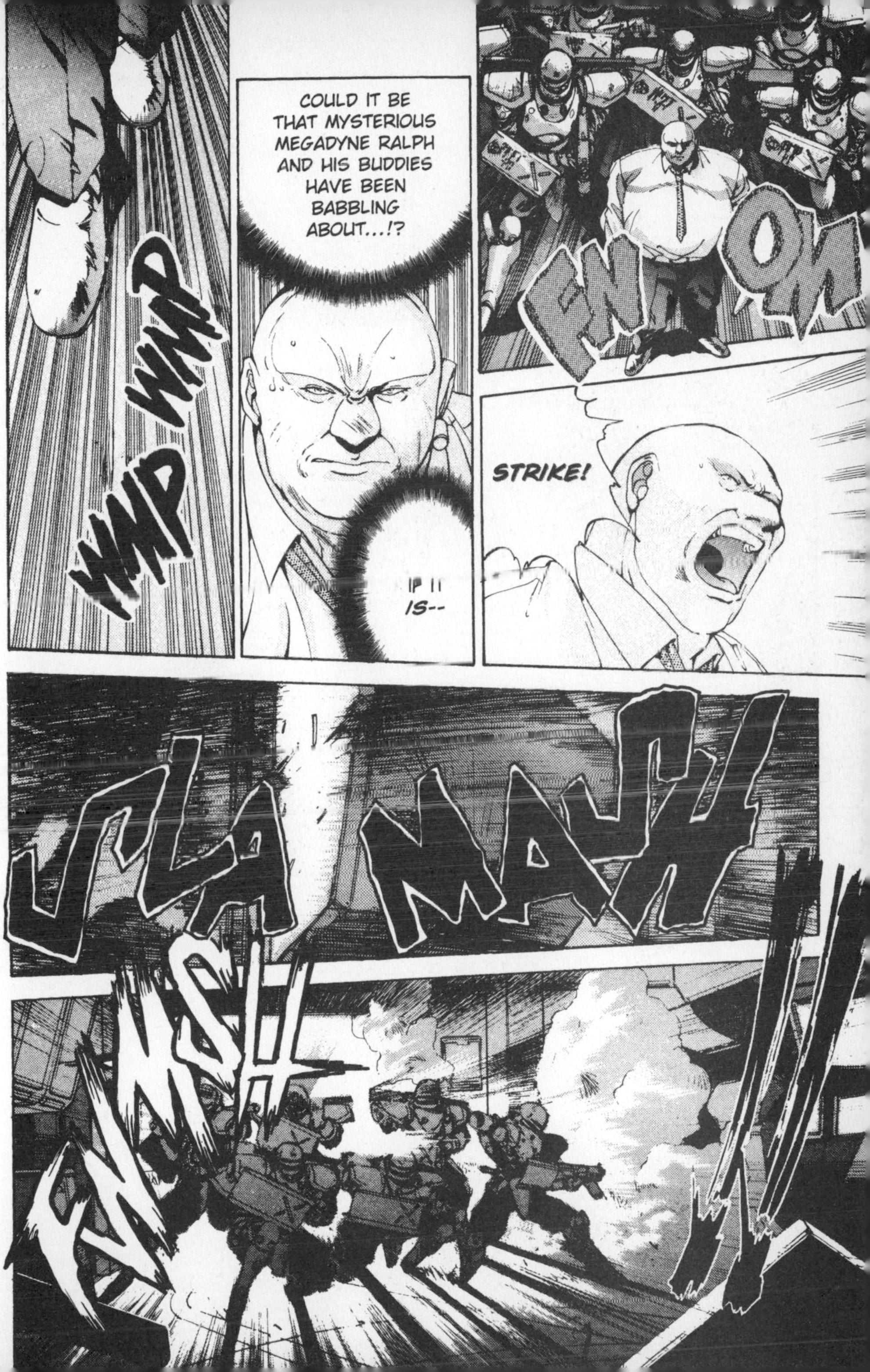
WHMP WHMP
COULD IT BE THAT MYSTERIOUS MEGADYNE RALPH AND HIS BUDDIES HAVE BEEN BABBLING ABOUT...!?
IF IT IS--
STRIKE!

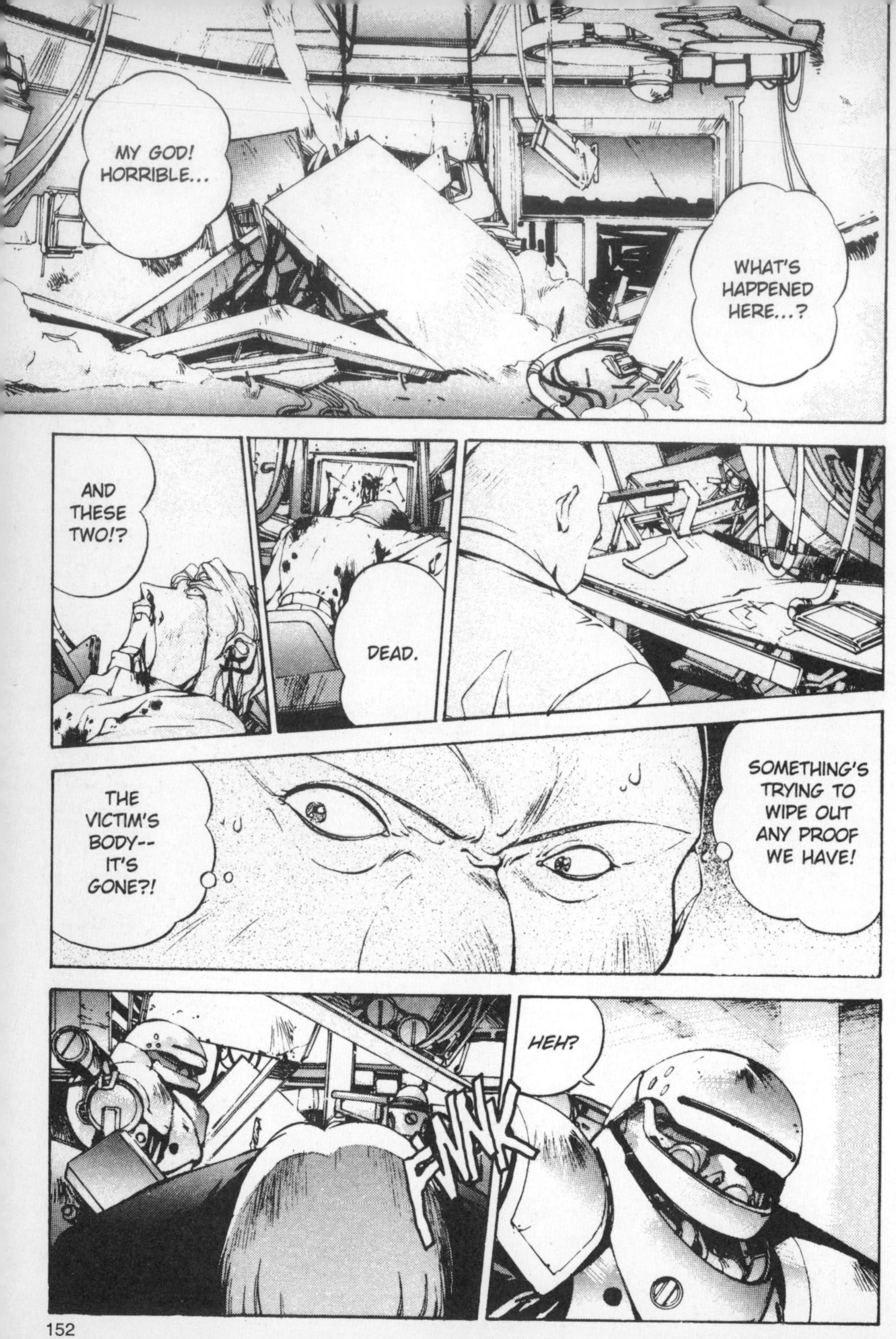
MY GOD! HORRIBLE...
WHAT'S HAPPENED HERE...?
AND THESE TWO!?
DEAD.
THE VICTIM'S BODY-- IT'S GONE?!
SOMETHING'S TRYING TO WIPE OUT ANY PROOF WE HAVE!
HEH?
FNNK

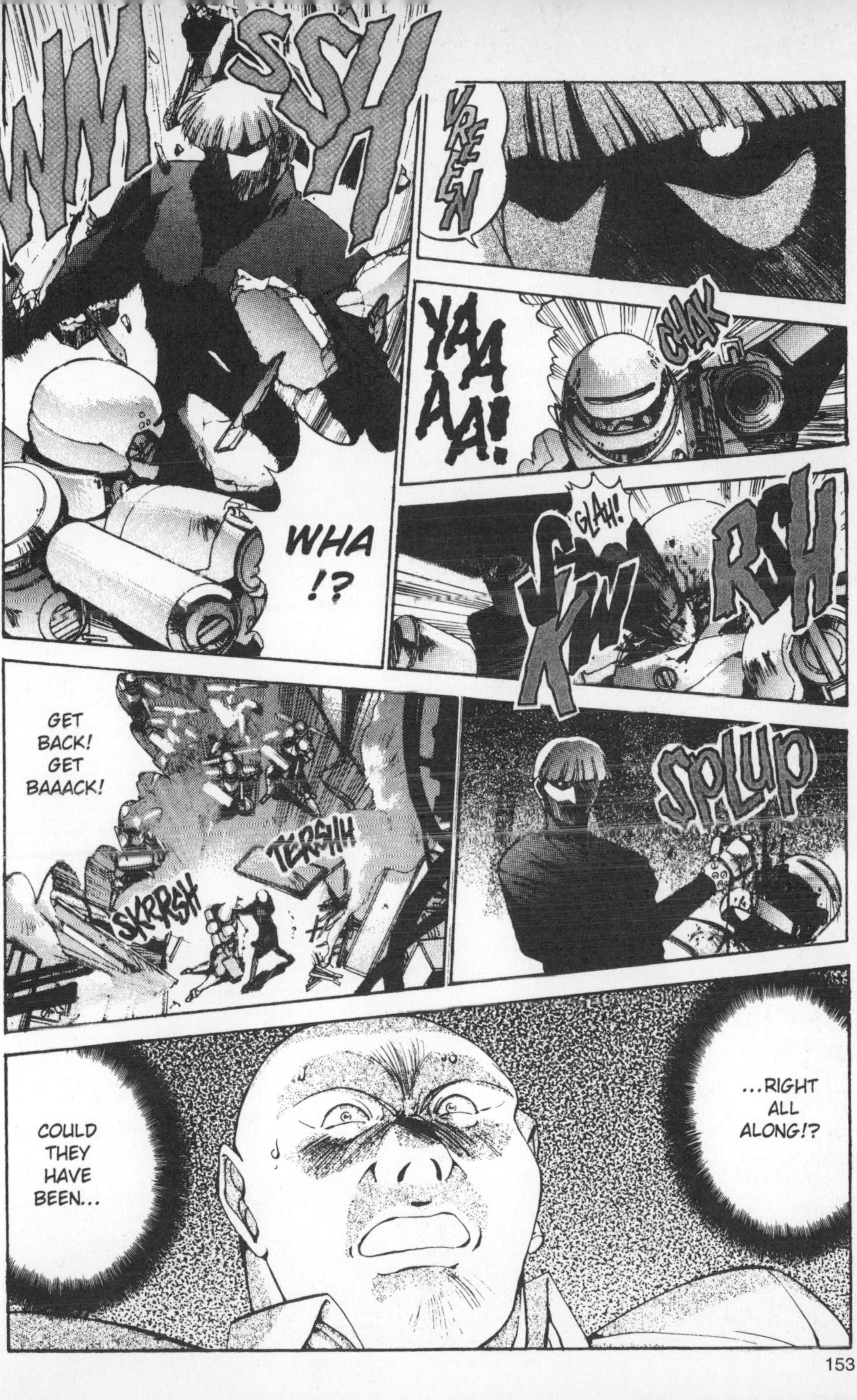
WMSSH
WHA !?
VREEN
YAAAAA!
CHAK
GLAH!
RSH
GET BACK! GET BAAACK!
TERSHH
SKRRSH
SPLUP
COULD THEY HAVE BEEN...
...RIGHT ALL ALONG!?

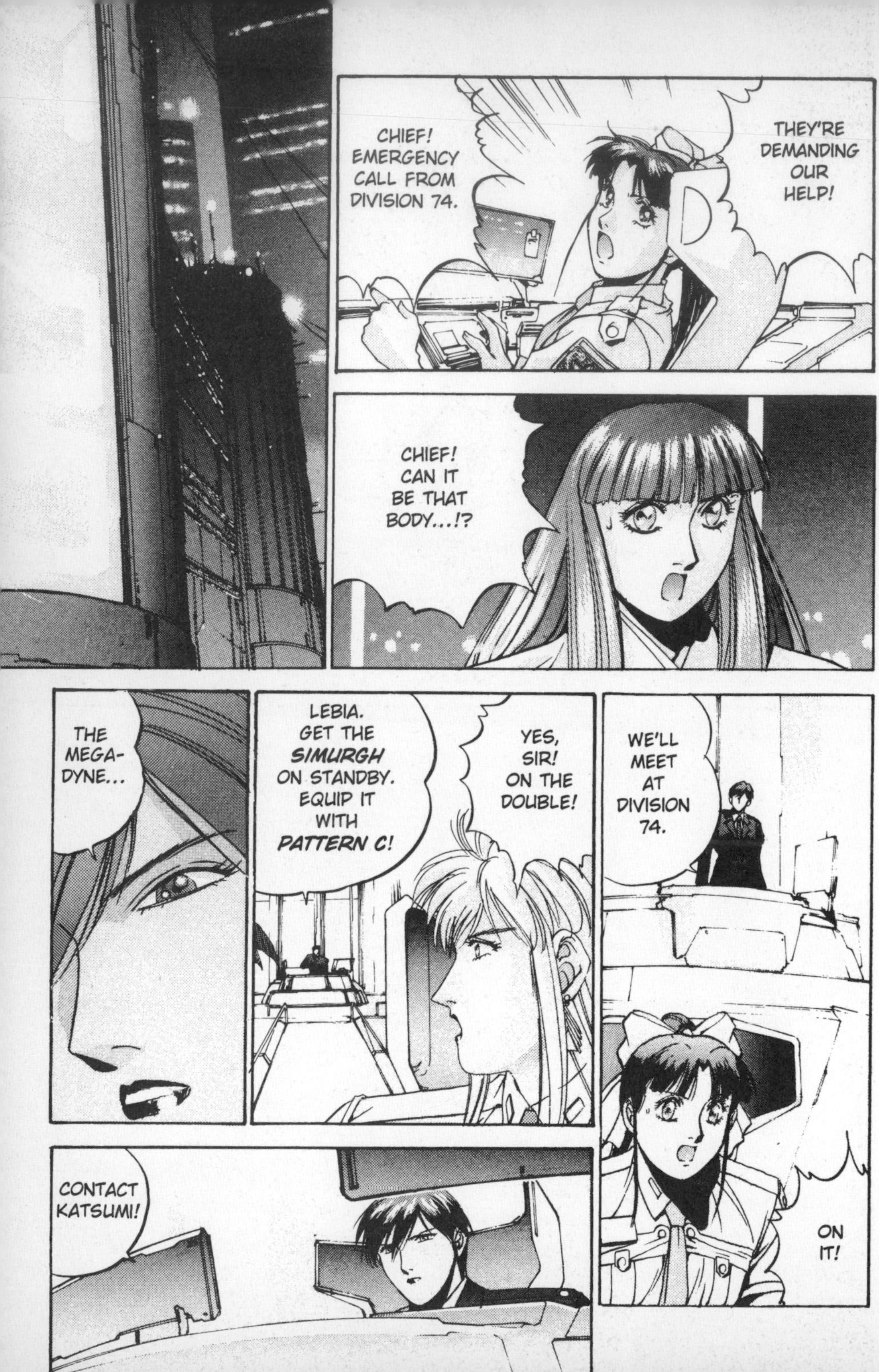
CHIEF! EMERGENCY CALL FROM DIVISION 74.
THEY'RE DEMANDING OUR HELP!
CHIEF! CAN IT BE THAT BODY...!?
THE MEGA-DYNE...
LEBIA. GET THE ***SIMURGH*** ON STANDBY. EQUIP IT WITH ***PATTERN C!***
YES, SIR! ON THE DOUBLE!
CONTACT KATSUMI!
WE'LL MEET AT DIVISION 74.
ON IT!

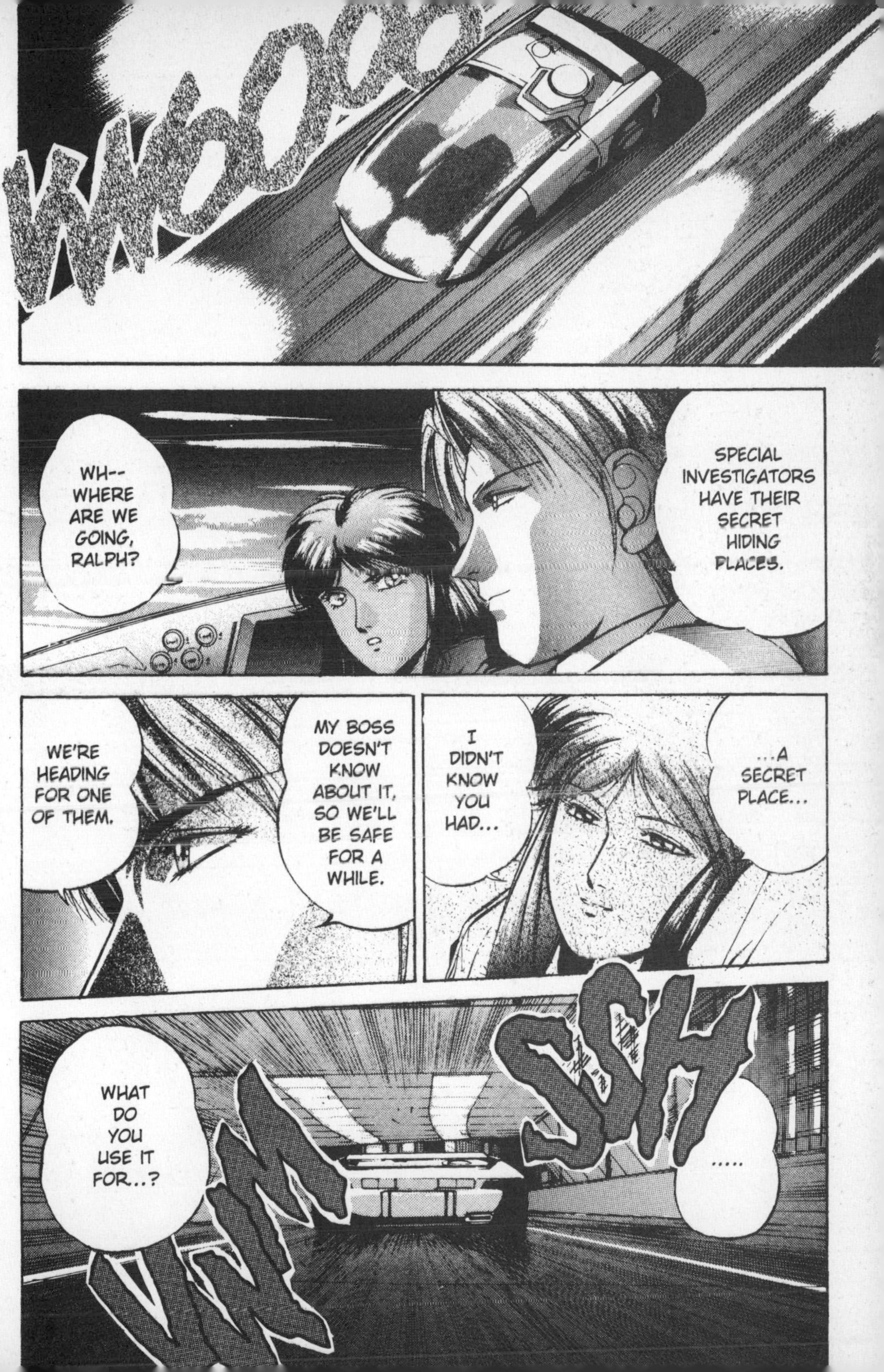
WHOOOOO
WH-- WHERE ARE WE GOING, RALPH?
SPECIAL INVESTIGATORS HAVE THEIR SECRET HIDING PLACES.
WE'RE HEADING FOR ONE OF THEM.
MY BOSS DOESN'T KNOW ABOUT IT, SO WE'LL BE SAFE FOR A WHILE.
I DIDN'T KNOW YOU HAD...
...A SECRET PLACE...
WHAT DO YOU USE IT FOR...?
.....
VWOOSH

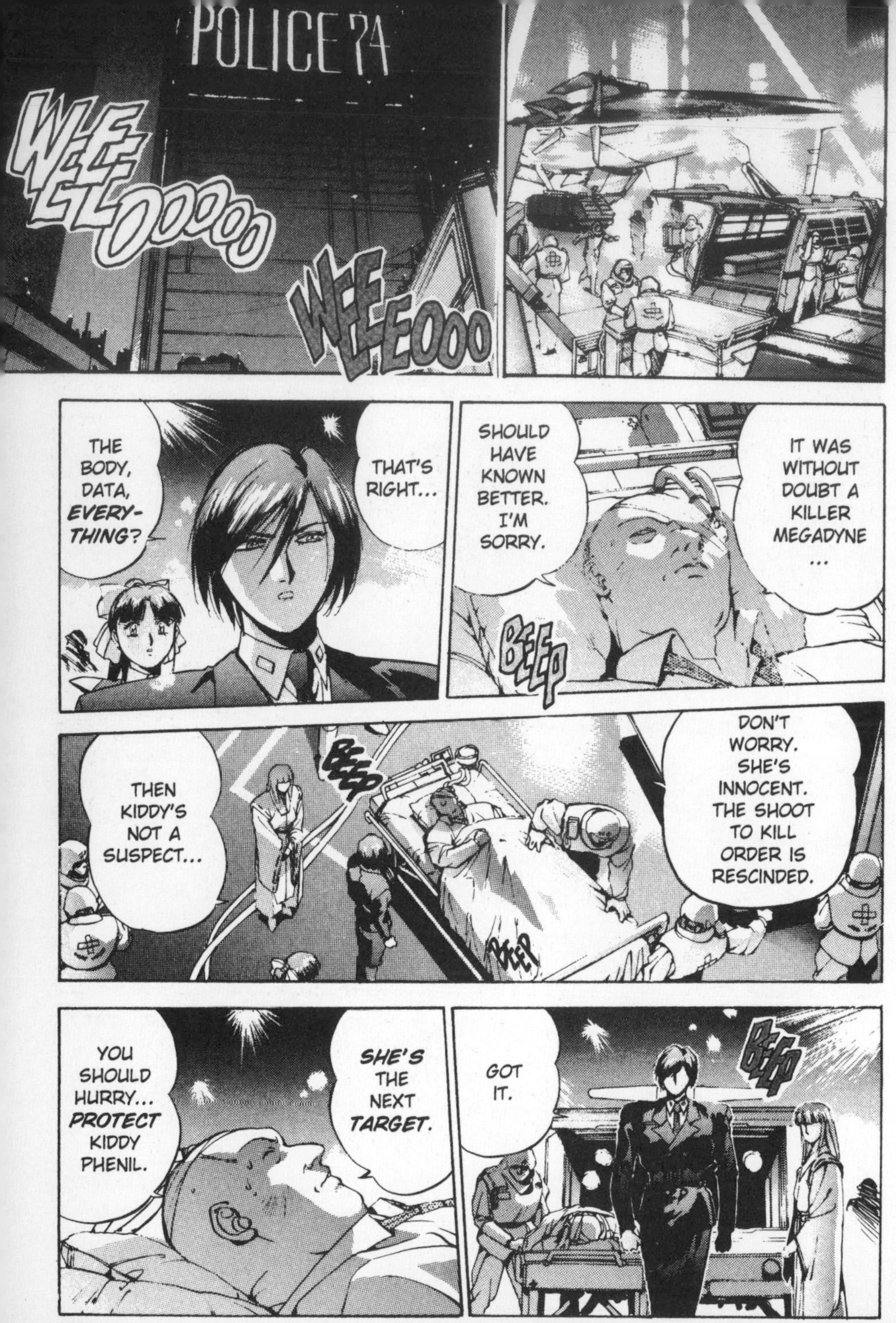
POLICE 74
WEEELLOOOOOO
WEEEEOOO
THE BODY, DATA, *EVERYTHING?*
THAT'S RIGHT...
SHOULD HAVE KNOWN BETTER. I'M SORRY.
IT WAS WITHOUT DOUBT A KILLER MEGADYNE...
BEEP
THEN KIDDY'S NOT A SUSPECT...
BEEP
DON'T WORRY. SHE'S INNOCENT. THE SHOOT TO KILL ORDER IS RESCINDED.
BEEP
YOU SHOULD HURRY... *PROTECT* KIDDY PHENIL.
SHE'S THE NEXT *TARGET.*
GOT IT.
BEEP

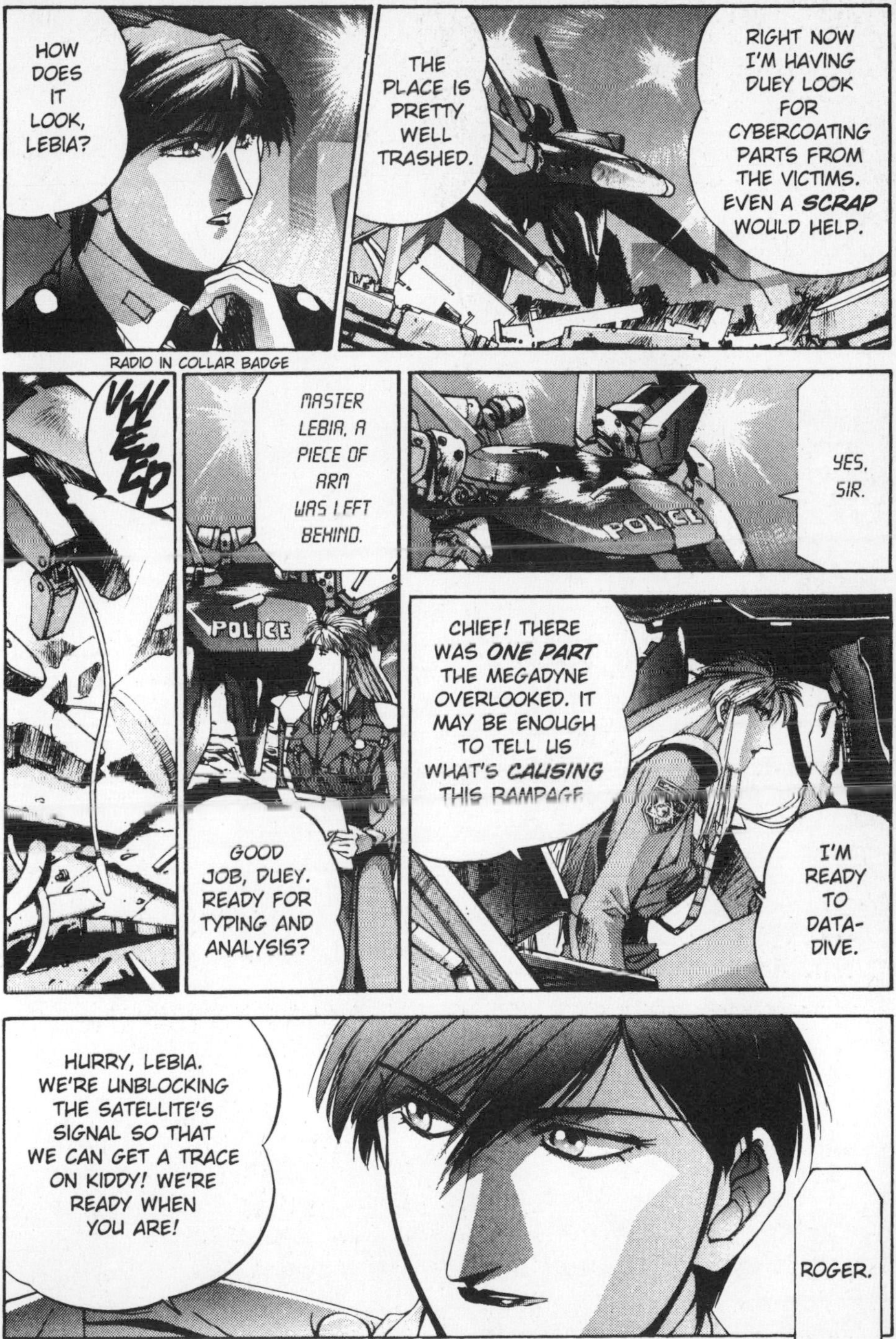
HOW DOES IT LOOK, LEBIA?
THE PLACE IS PRETTY WELL TRASHED.
RIGHT NOW I'M HAVING DUEY LOOK FOR CYBERCOATING PARTS FROM THE VICTIMS. EVEN A SCRAP WOULD HELP.
RADIO IN COLLAR BADGE
VWEEP
MASTER LEBIA, A PIECE OF ARM WAS LEFT BEHIND.
GOOD JOB, DUEY. READY FOR TYPING AND ANALYSIS?
YES, SIR.
CHIEF! THERE WAS ONE PART THE MEGADYNE OVERLOOKED. IT MAY BE ENOUGH TO TELL US WHAT'S CAUSING THIS RAMPAGE
I'M READY TO DATA-DIVE.
HURRY, LEBIA. WE'RE UNBLOCKING THE SATELLITE'S SIGNAL SO THAT WE CAN GET A TRACE ON KIDDY! WE'RE READY WHEN YOU ARE!
ROGER.

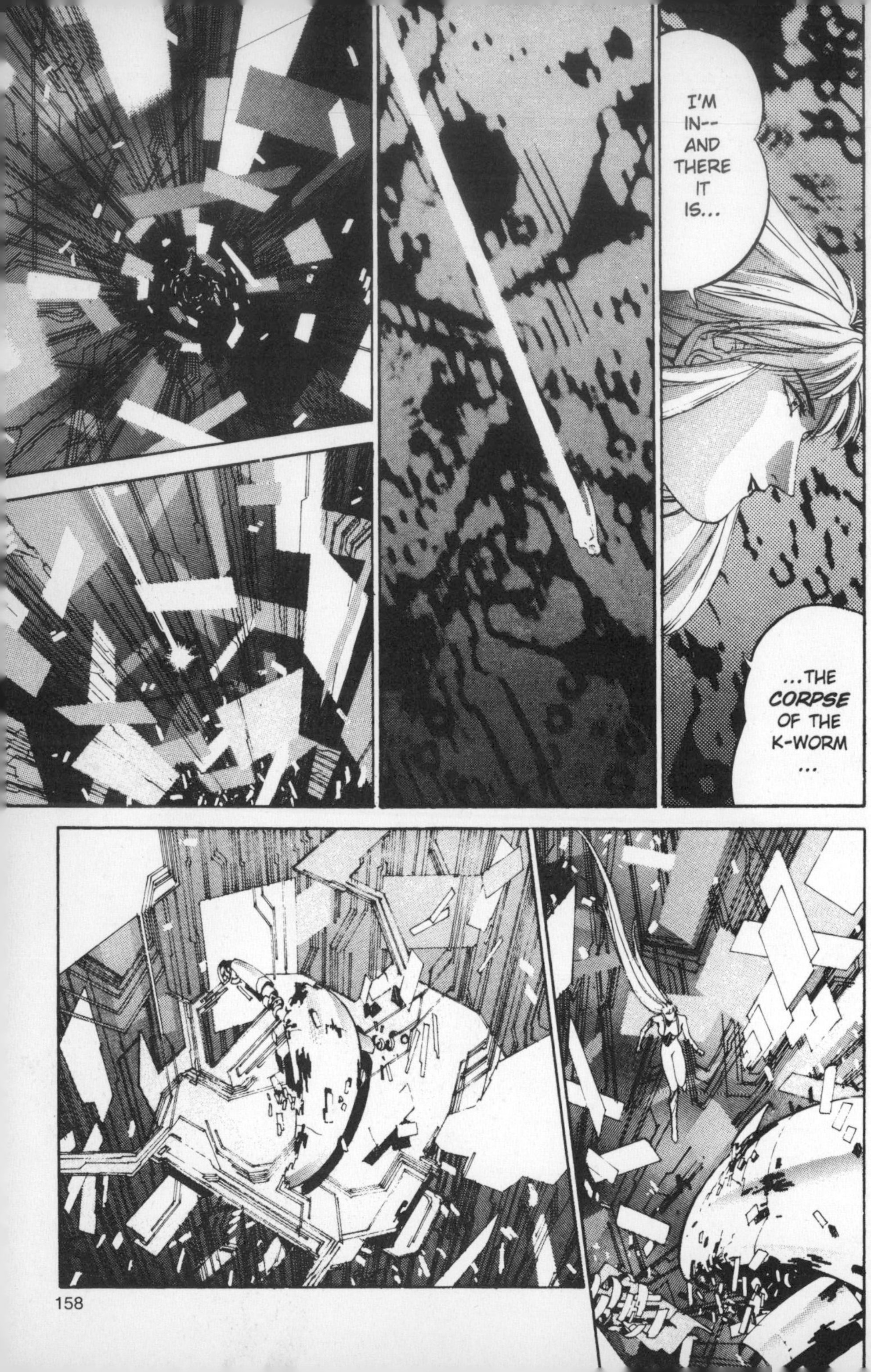
I'M IN-- AND THERE IT IS...
...THE *CORPSE* OF THE K-WORM ...

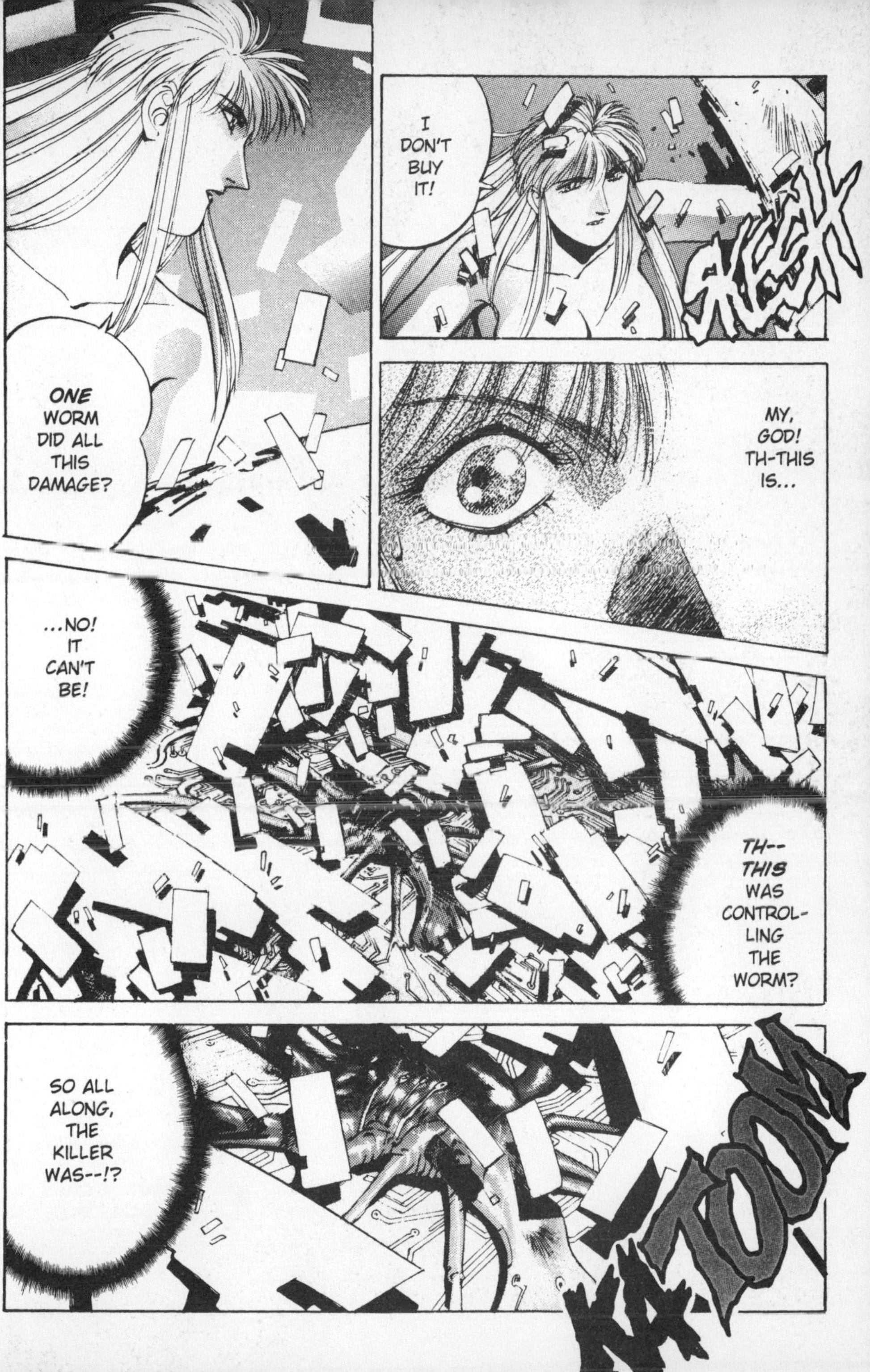
ONE WORM DID ALL THIS DAMAGE?
I DON'T BUY IT!
SKEEK
MY, GOD! TH-THIS IS...
...NO! IT CAN'T BE!
TH--THIS WAS CONTROL-LING THE WORM?
SO ALL ALONG, THE KILLER WAS--!?
KA-TOOM

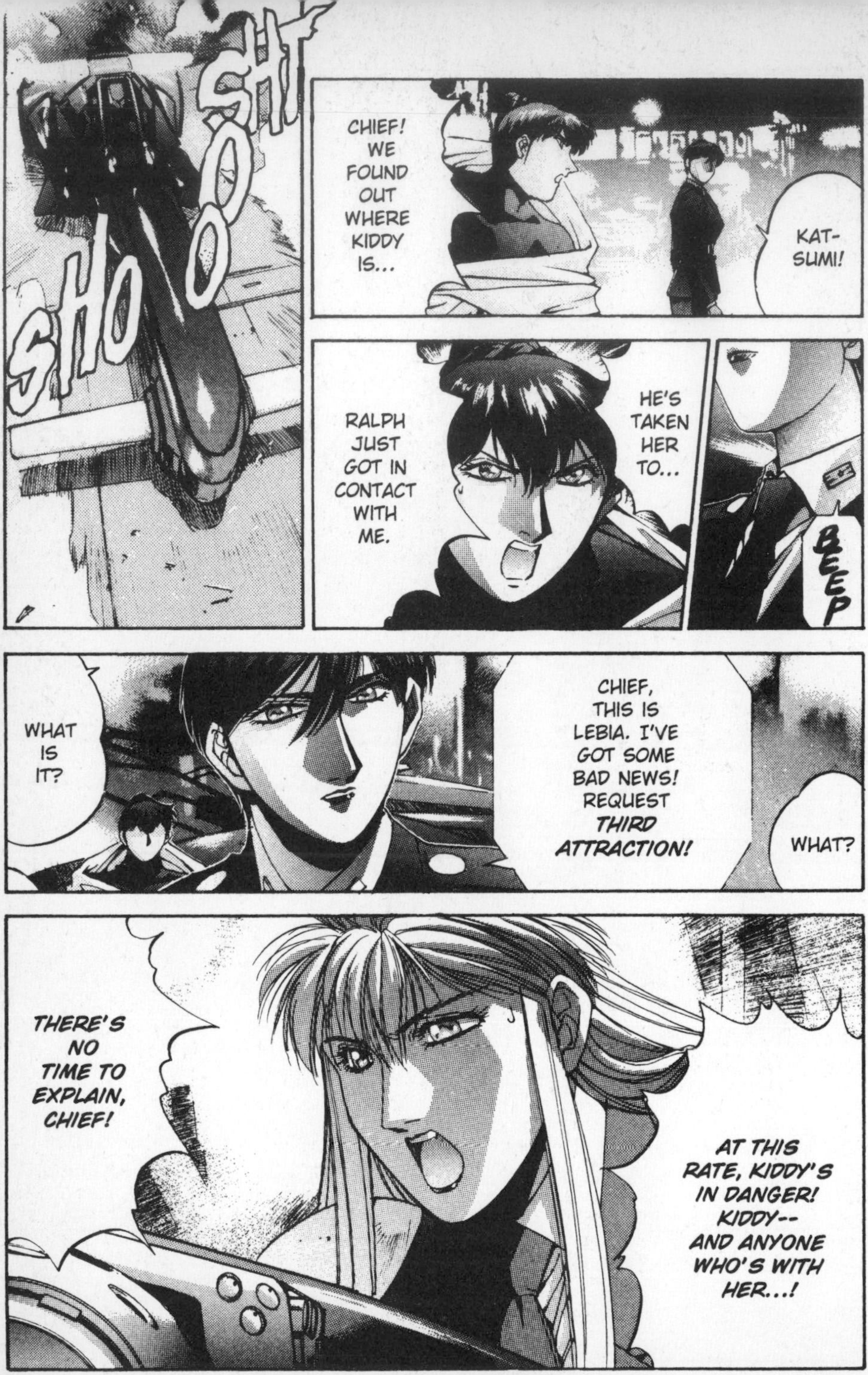
SHOOOT
CHIEF! WE FOUND OUT WHERE KIDDY IS...
KAT-SUMI!
RALPH JUST GOT IN CONTACT WITH ME.
HE'S TAKEN HER TO...
BEEP
WHAT IS IT?
CHIEF, THIS IS LEBIA. I'VE GOT SOME BAD NEWS! REQUEST *THIRD ATTRACTION!*
WHAT?
THERE'S NO TIME TO EXPLAIN, CHIEF!
AT THIS RATE, KIDDY'S IN DANGER! KIDDY-- AND ANYONE WHO'S WITH HER...!

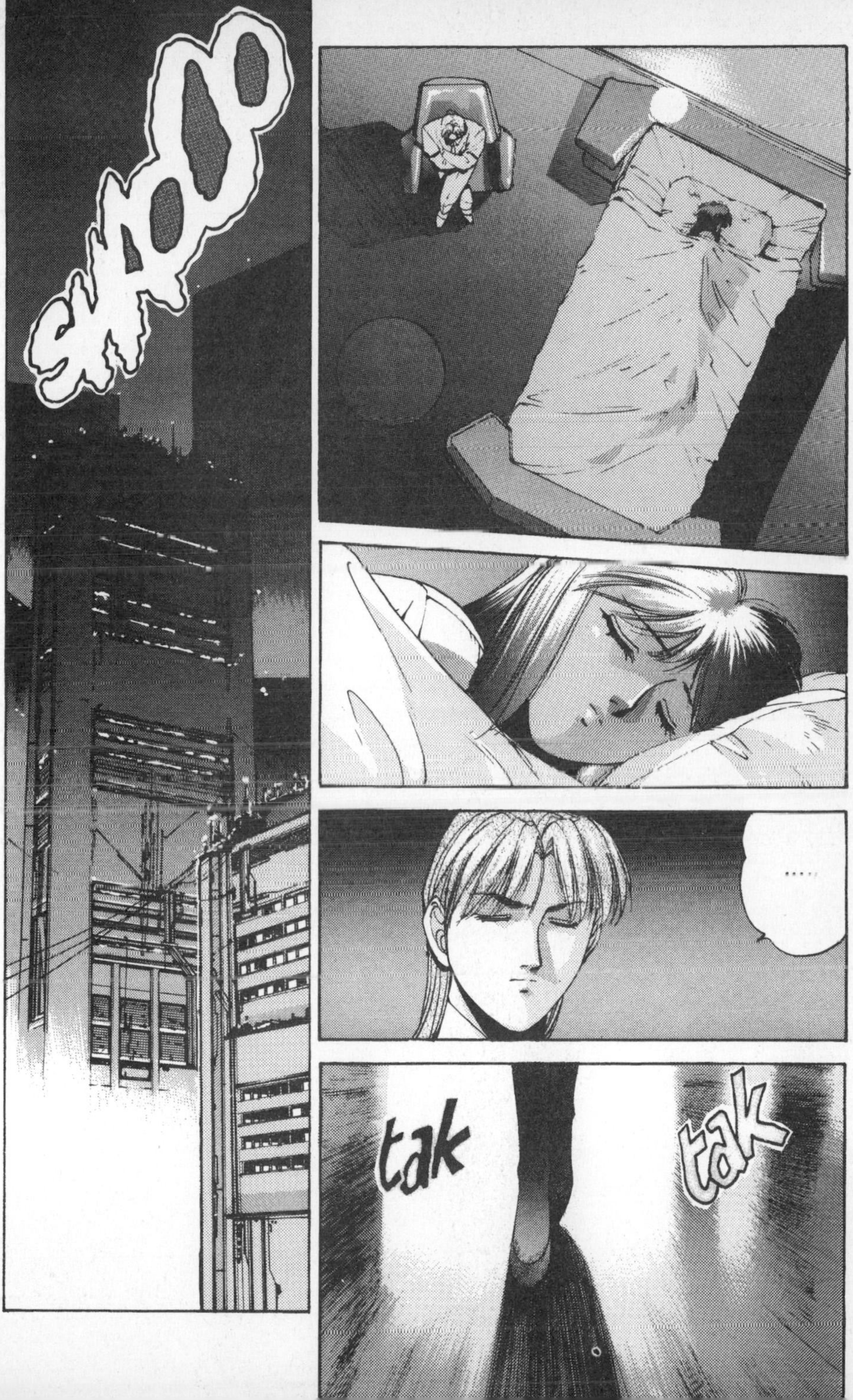
SKOOO
....!
tak
tak

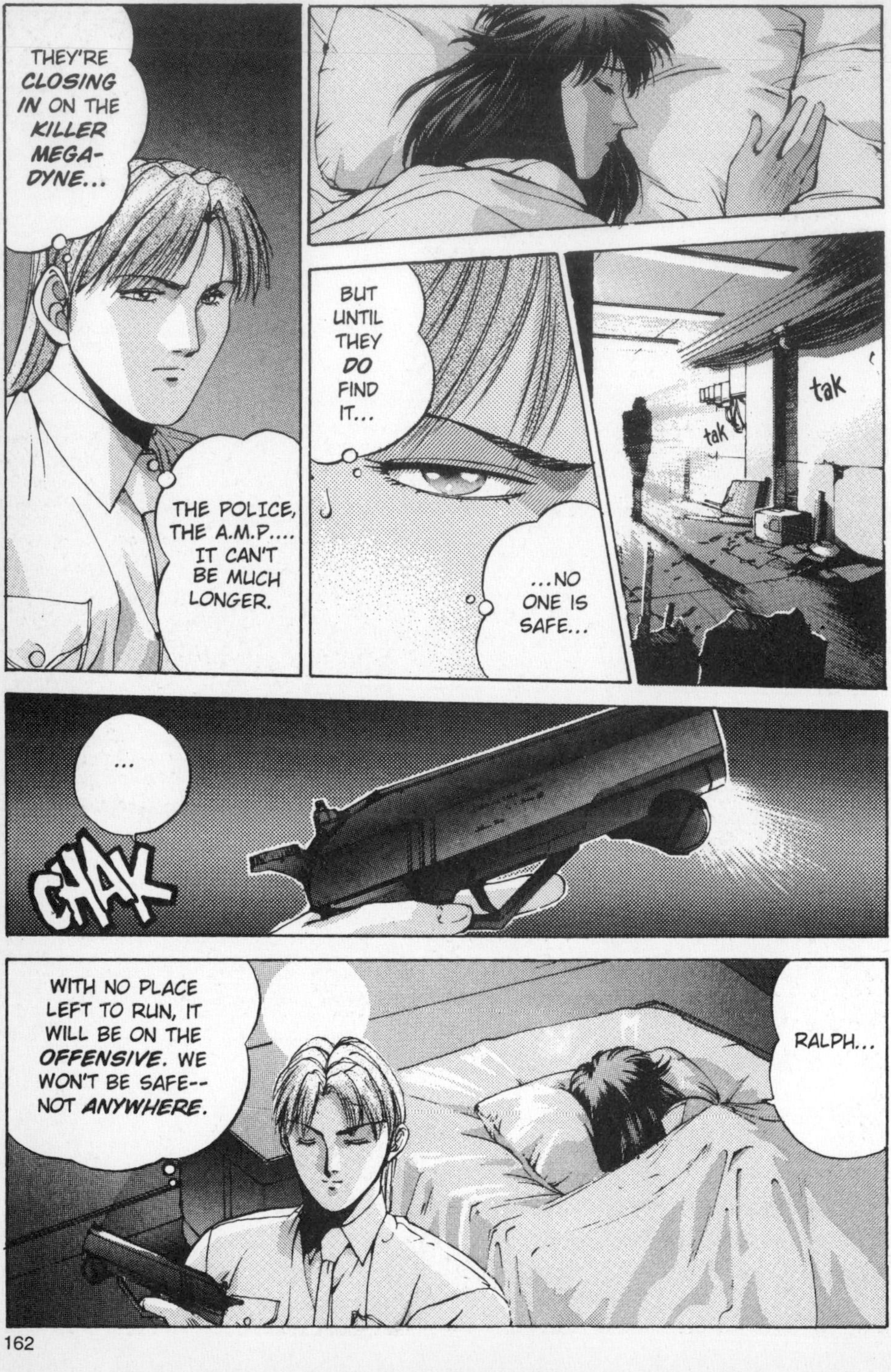
THEY'RE CLOSING IN ON THE KILLER MEGA-DYNE...
THE POLICE, THE A.M.P.... IT CAN'T BE MUCH LONGER.
BUT UNTIL THEY DO FIND IT...
...NO ONE IS SAFE...
tak
tak
...
CHAK
WITH NO PLACE LEFT TO RUN, IT WILL BE ON THE OFFENSIVE. WE WON'T BE SAFE-- NOT ANYWHERE.
RALPH...

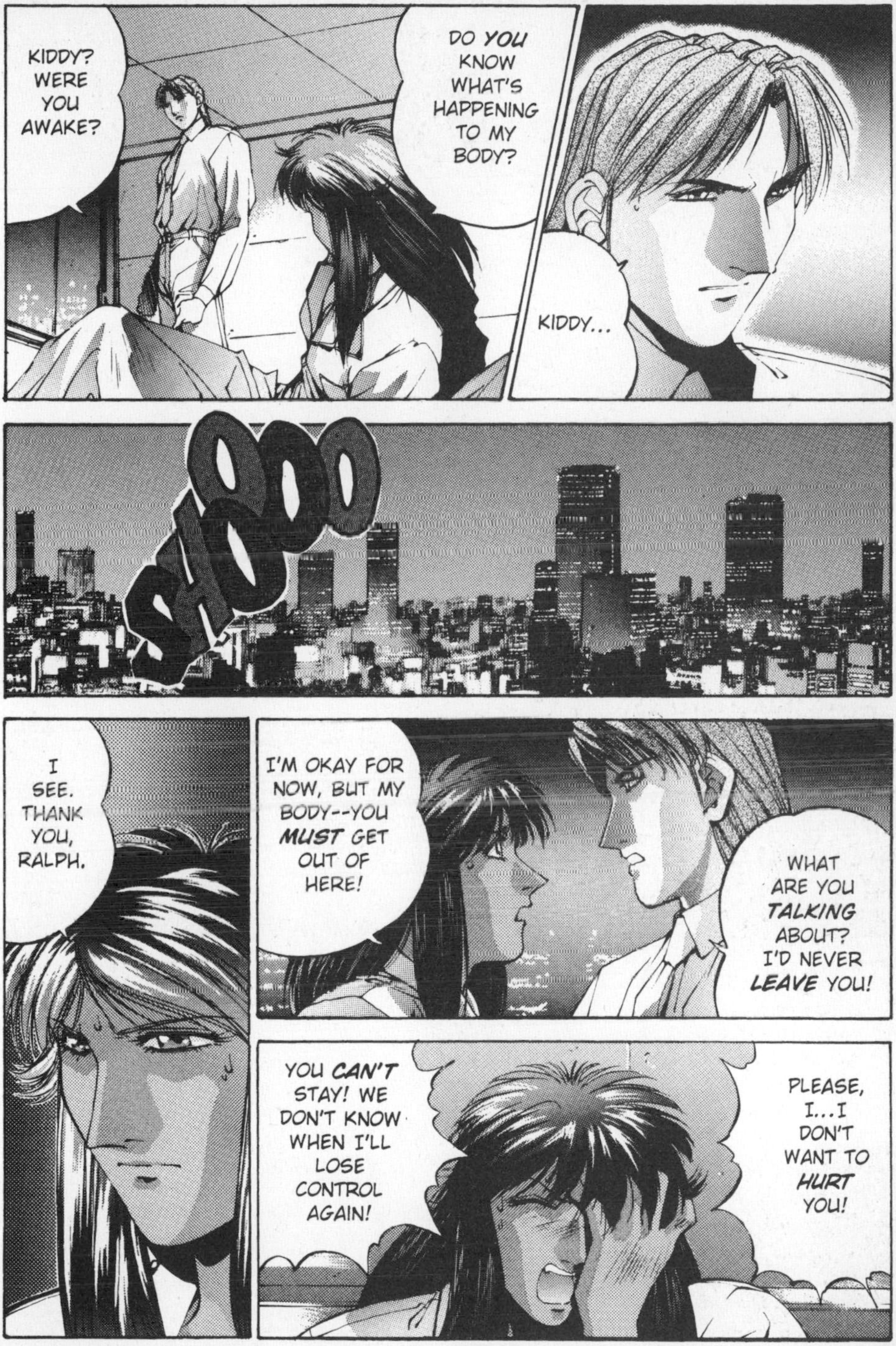
KIDDY? WERE YOU AWAKE?
DO *YOU* KNOW WHAT'S HAPPENING TO MY BODY?
KIDDY...
SHOOOO
I SEE. THANK YOU, RALPH.
I'M OKAY FOR NOW, BUT MY BODY--YOU *MUST* GET OUT OF HERE!
WHAT ARE YOU *TALKING* ABOUT? I'D NEVER *LEAVE* YOU!
YOU *CAN'T* STAY! WE DON'T KNOW WHEN I'LL LOSE CONTROL AGAIN!
PLEASE, I...I DON'T WANT TO *HURT* YOU!

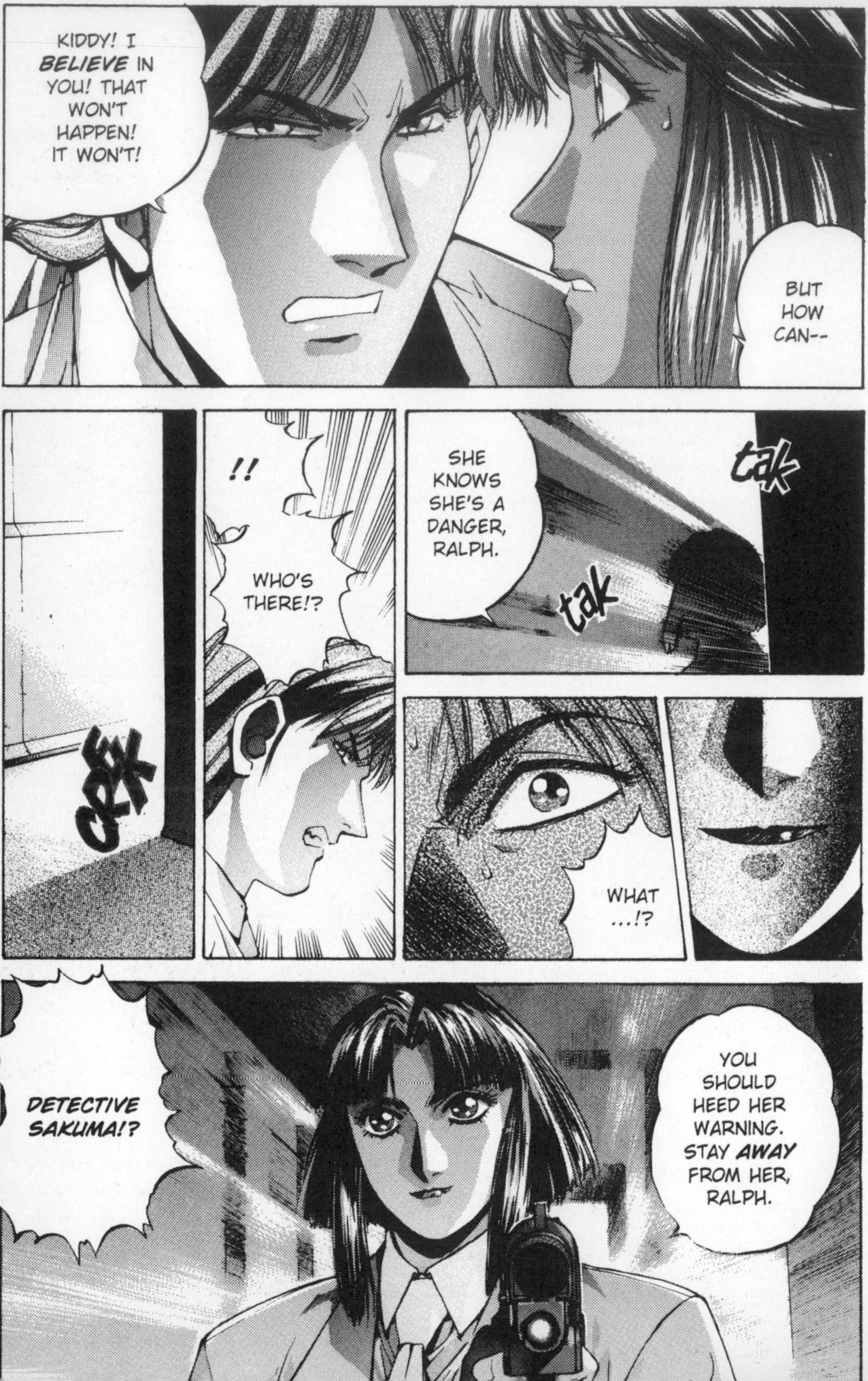
KIDDY! I *BELIEVE* IN YOU! THAT WON'T HAPPEN! IT WON'T!
BUT HOW CAN--
CREAK
!!
WHO'S THERE!?
SHE KNOWS SHE'S A DANGER, RALPH.
tak
tak
WHAT ...!?
DETECTIVE SAKUMA!?
YOU SHOULD HEED HER WARNING. STAY *AWAY* FROM HER, RALPH.

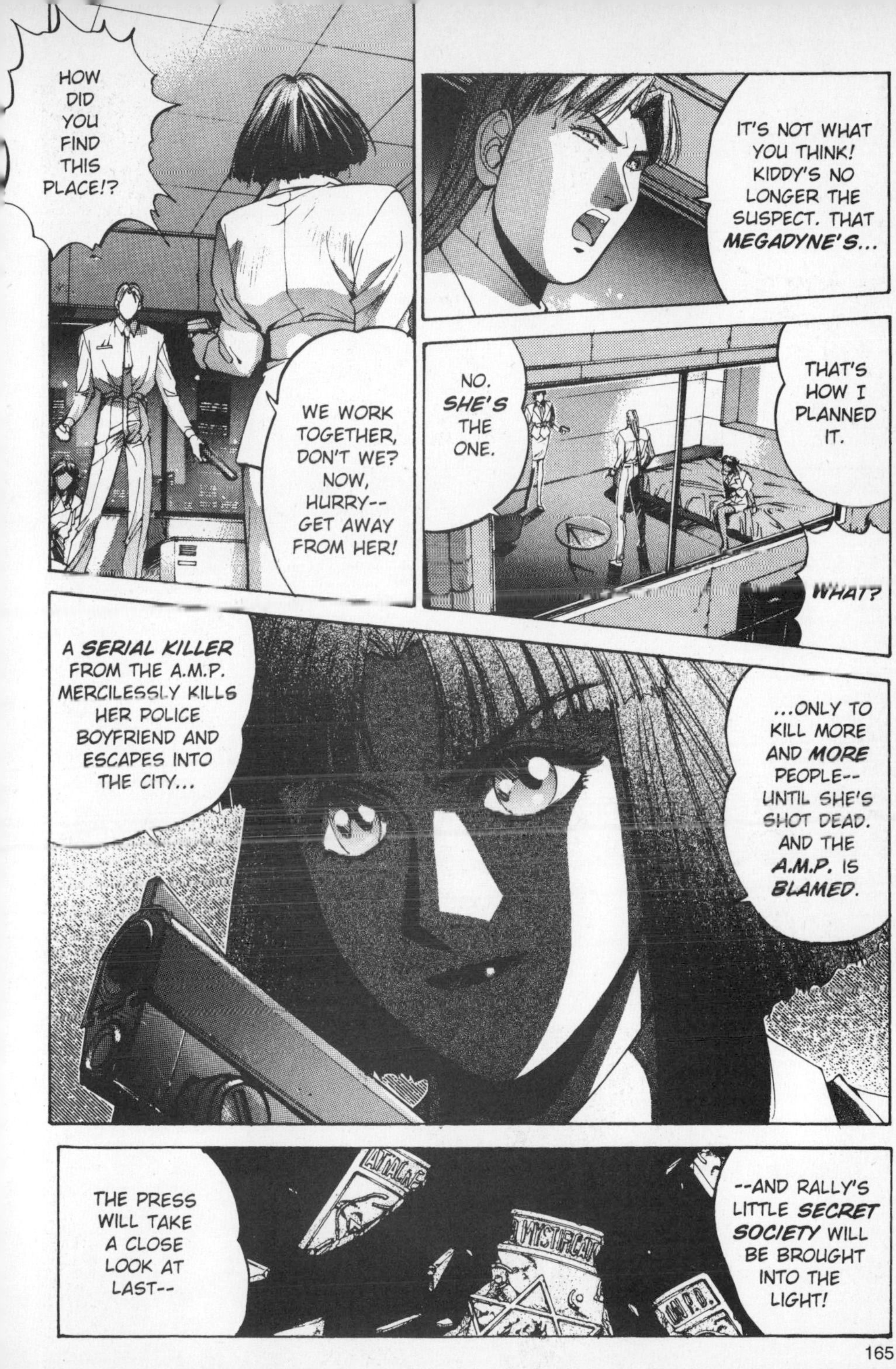
HOW DID YOU FIND THIS PLACE!?
IT'S NOT WHAT YOU THINK! KIDDY'S NO LONGER THE SUSPECT. THAT MEGADYNE'S...
WE WORK TOGETHER, DON'T WE? NOW, HURRY-- GET AWAY FROM HER!
NO. SHE'S THE ONE.
THAT'S HOW I PLANNED IT.
WHAT?
A SERIAL KILLER FROM THE A.M.P. MERCILESSLY KILLS HER POLICE BOYFRIEND AND ESCAPES INTO THE CITY...
...ONLY TO KILL MORE AND MORE PEOPLE-- UNTIL SHE'S SHOT DEAD. AND THE A.M.P. IS BLAMED.
THE PRESS WILL TAKE A CLOSE LOOK AT LAST--
--AND RALLY'S LITTLE SECRET SOCIETY WILL BE BROUGHT INTO THE LIGHT!

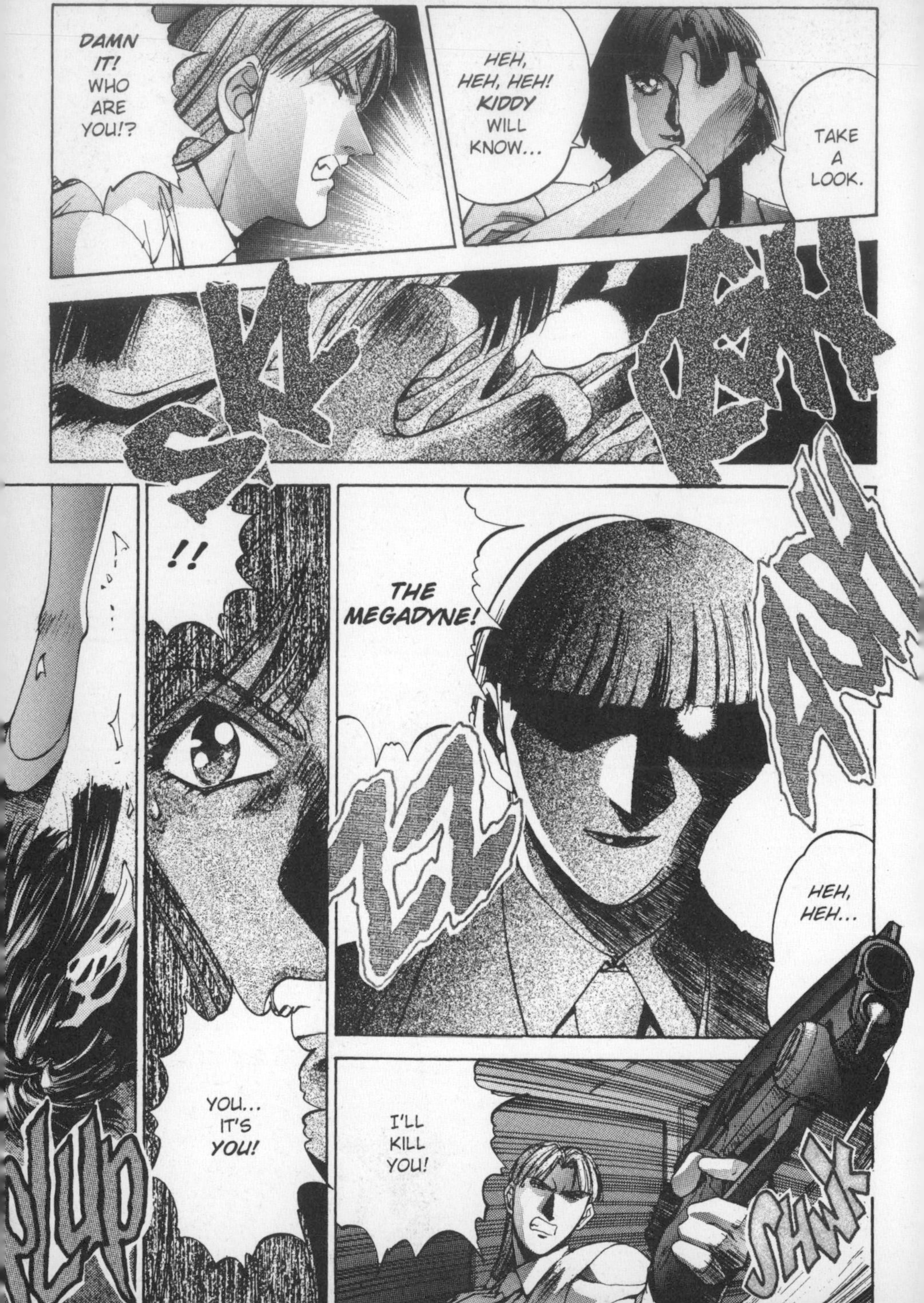
DAMN IT! WHO ARE YOU!?
HEH, HEH, HEH! KIDDY WILL KNOW...
TAKE A LOOK.
PLUP
!!
YOU... IT'S YOU!
THE MEGADYNE!
HEH, HEH...
I'LL KILL YOU!
SHWK

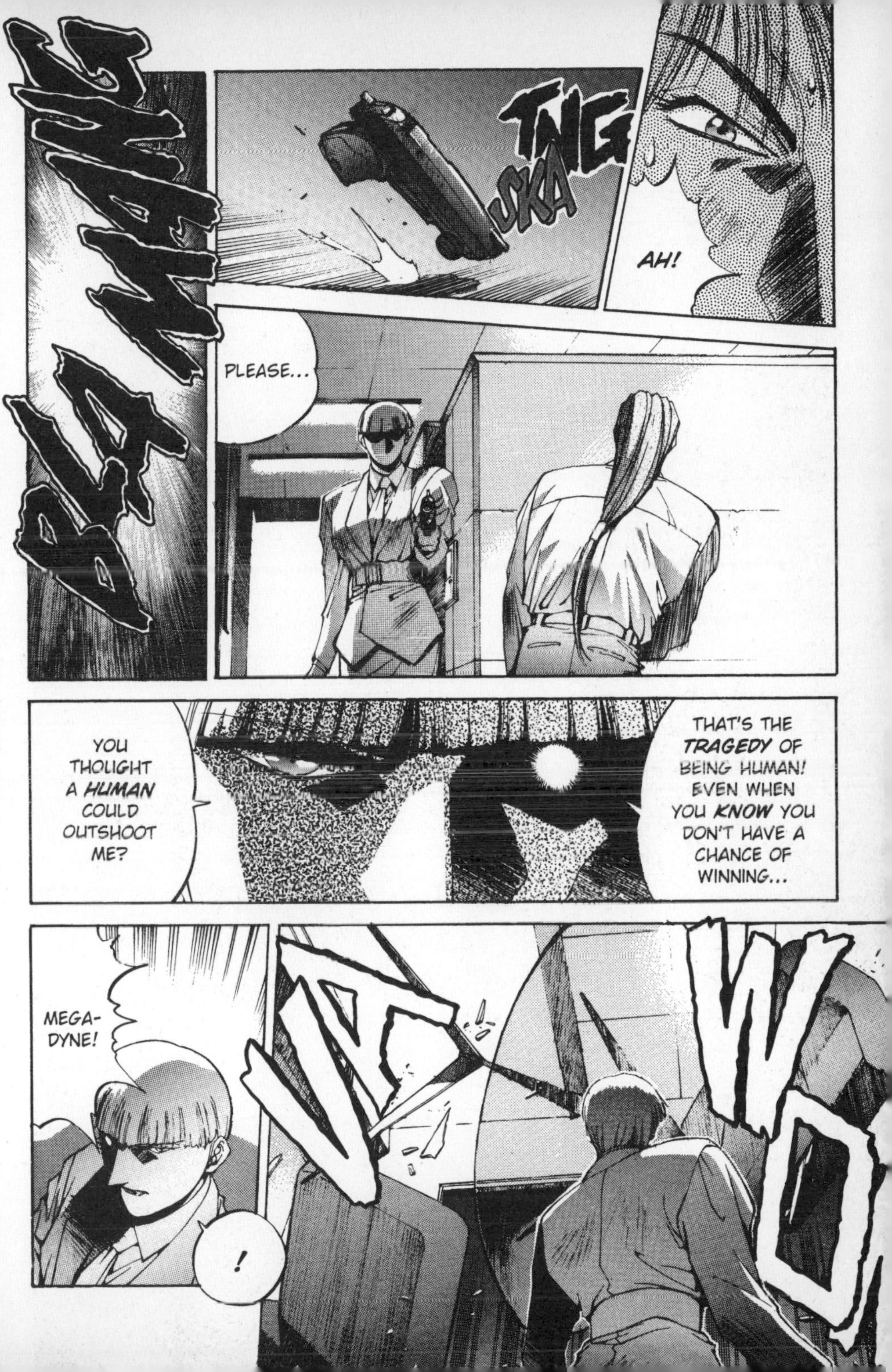
TNG
SKA
AH!
PLEASE...
YOU THOUGHT A *HUMAN* COULD OUTSHOOT ME?
THAT'S THE *TRAGEDY* OF BEING HUMAN! EVEN WHEN YOU *KNOW* YOU DON'T HAVE A CHANCE OF WINNING...
MEGA-DYNE!
!

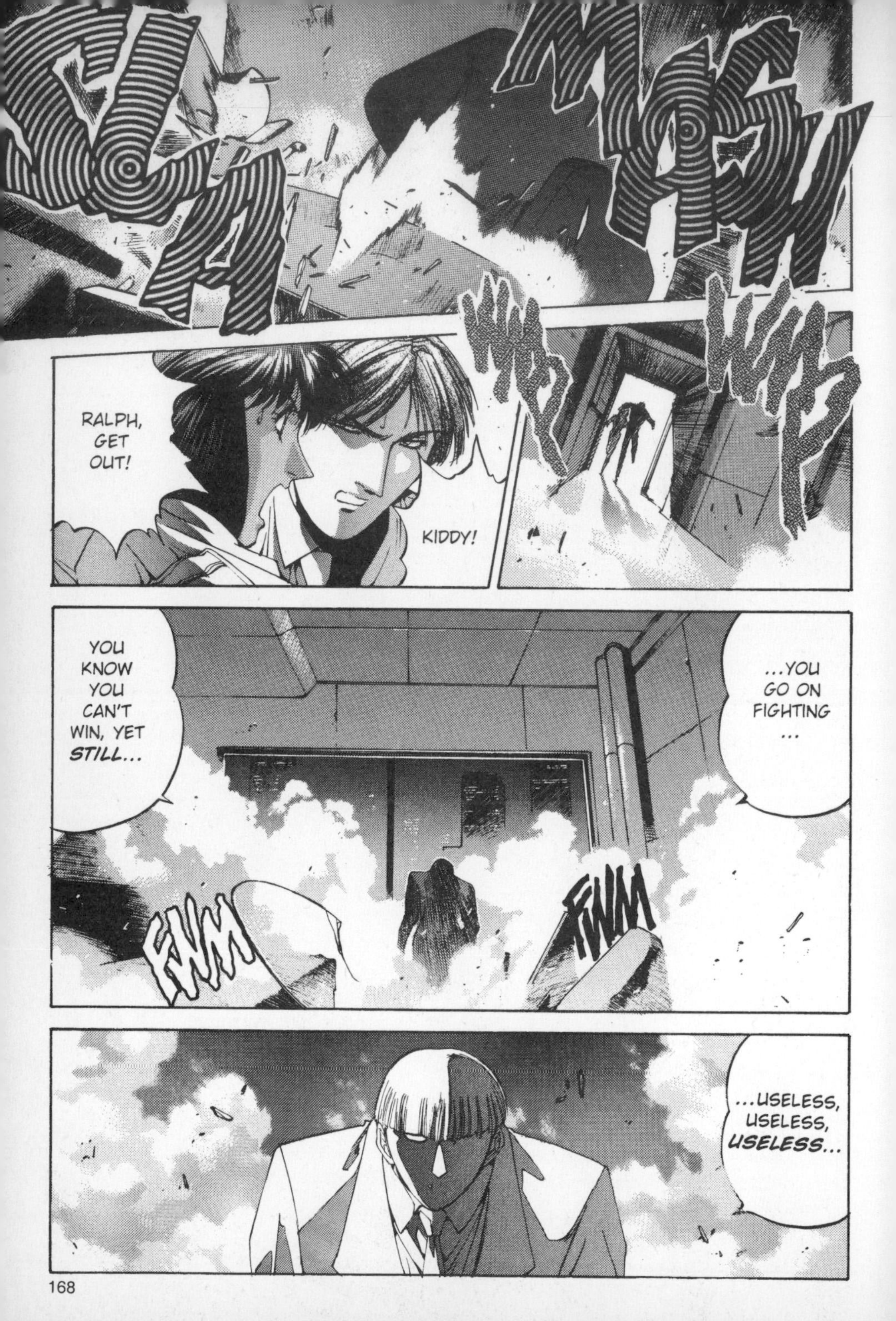
RALPH, GET OUT!
KIDDY!
YOU KNOW YOU CAN'T WIN, YET *STILL*...
...YOU GO ON FIGHTING...
FWM
FWM
...USELESS, USELESS, *USELESS*...

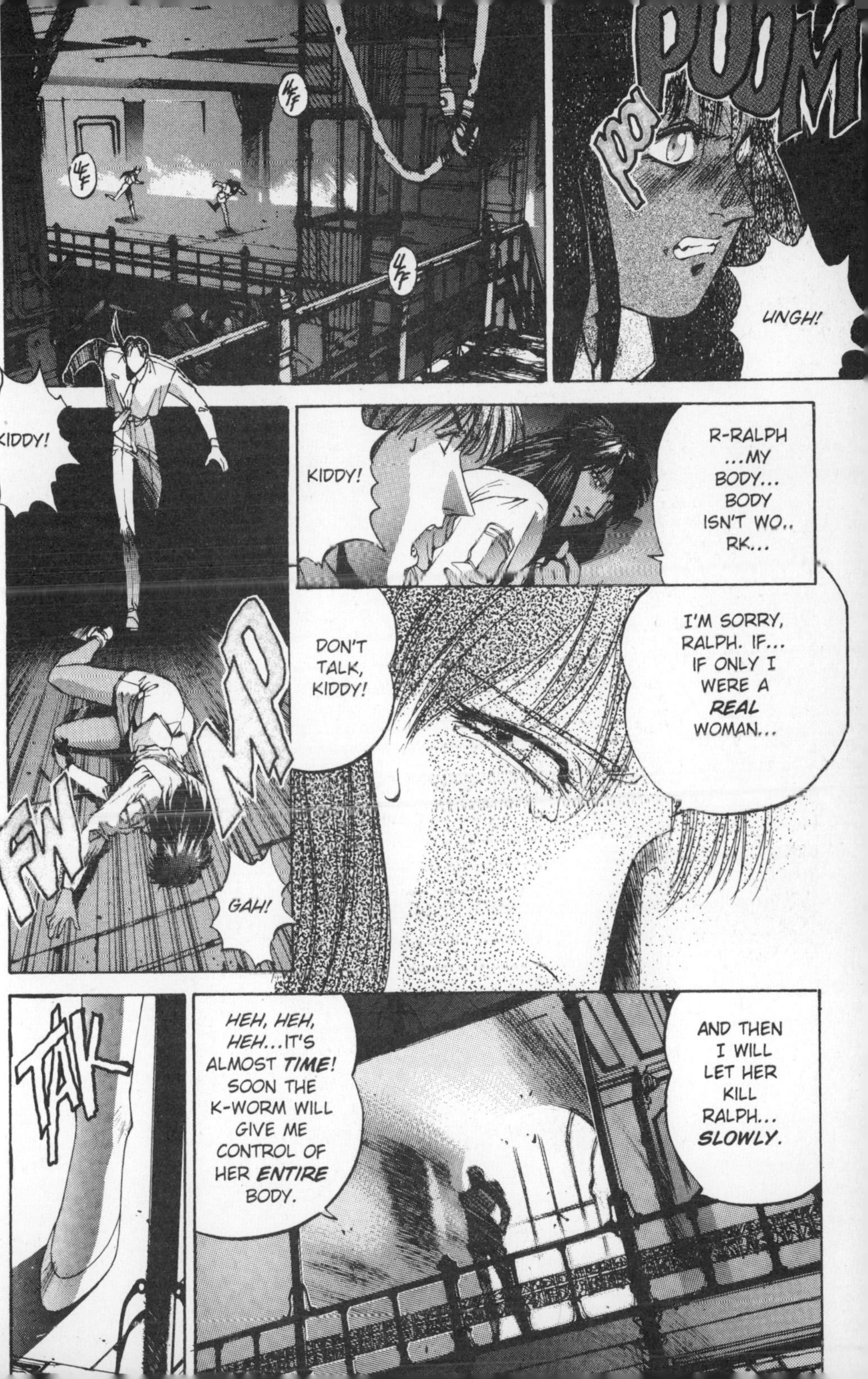
UFF
UFF
UFF
POOM
UNGH!
KIDDY!
FWMP
GAH!
KIDDY!
R-RALPH ...MY BODY... BODY ISN'T WO.. RK...
DON'T TALK, KIDDY!
I'M SORRY, RALPH. IF... IF ONLY I WERE A ***REAL*** WOMAN...
TAK
HEH, HEH, HEH...IT'S ALMOST ***TIME!*** SOON THE K-WORM WILL GIVE ME CONTROL OF HER ***ENTIRE*** BODY.
AND THEN I WILL LET HER KILL RALPH... ***SLOWLY***.

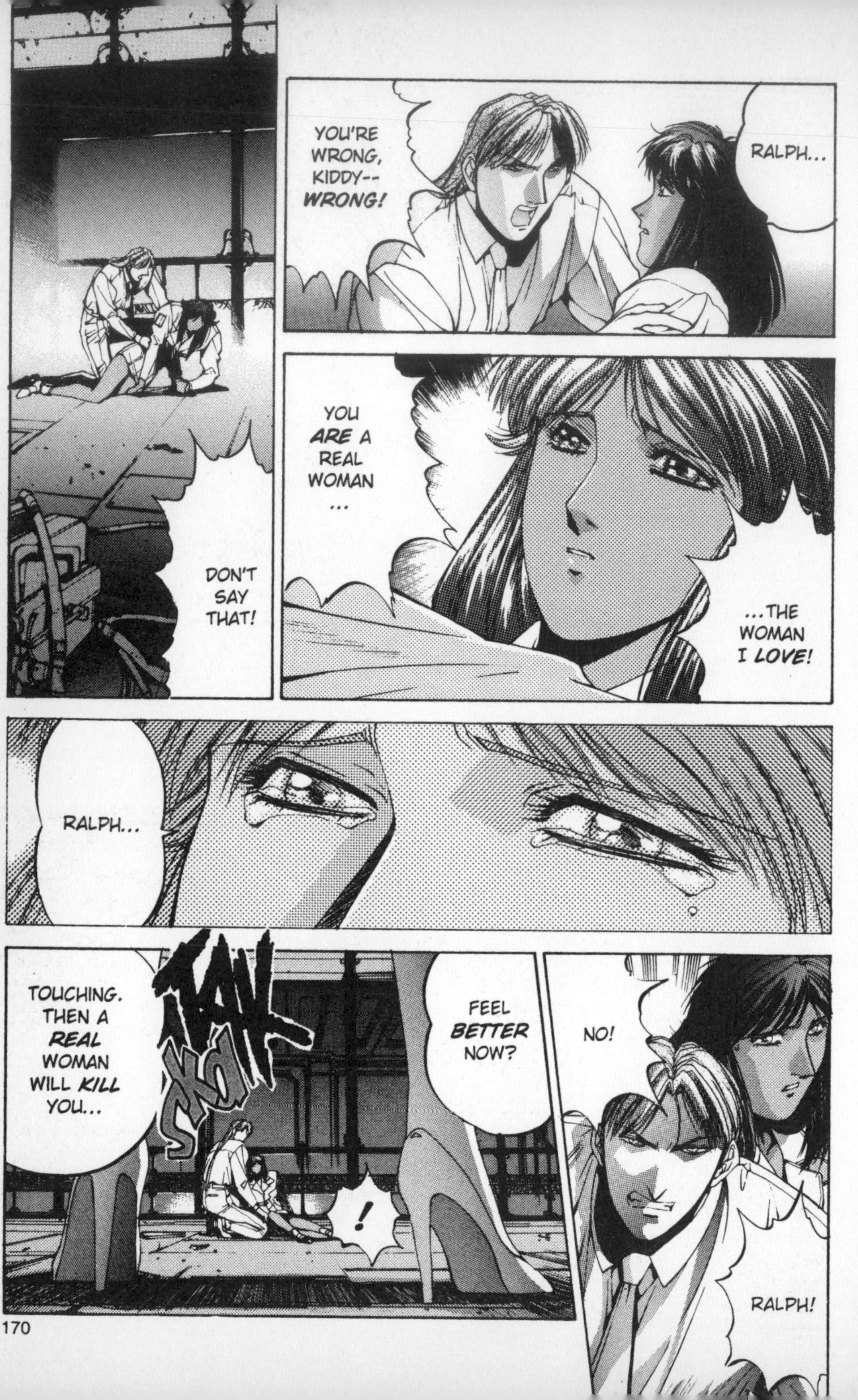
DON'T SAY THAT!
YOU'RE WRONG, KIDDY-- WRONG!
RALPH...
YOU ARE A REAL WOMAN ...
...THE WOMAN I LOVE!
RALPH...
TOUCHING. THEN A REAL WOMAN WILL KILL YOU...
TAK
!
FEEL BETTER NOW?
NO!
RALPH!

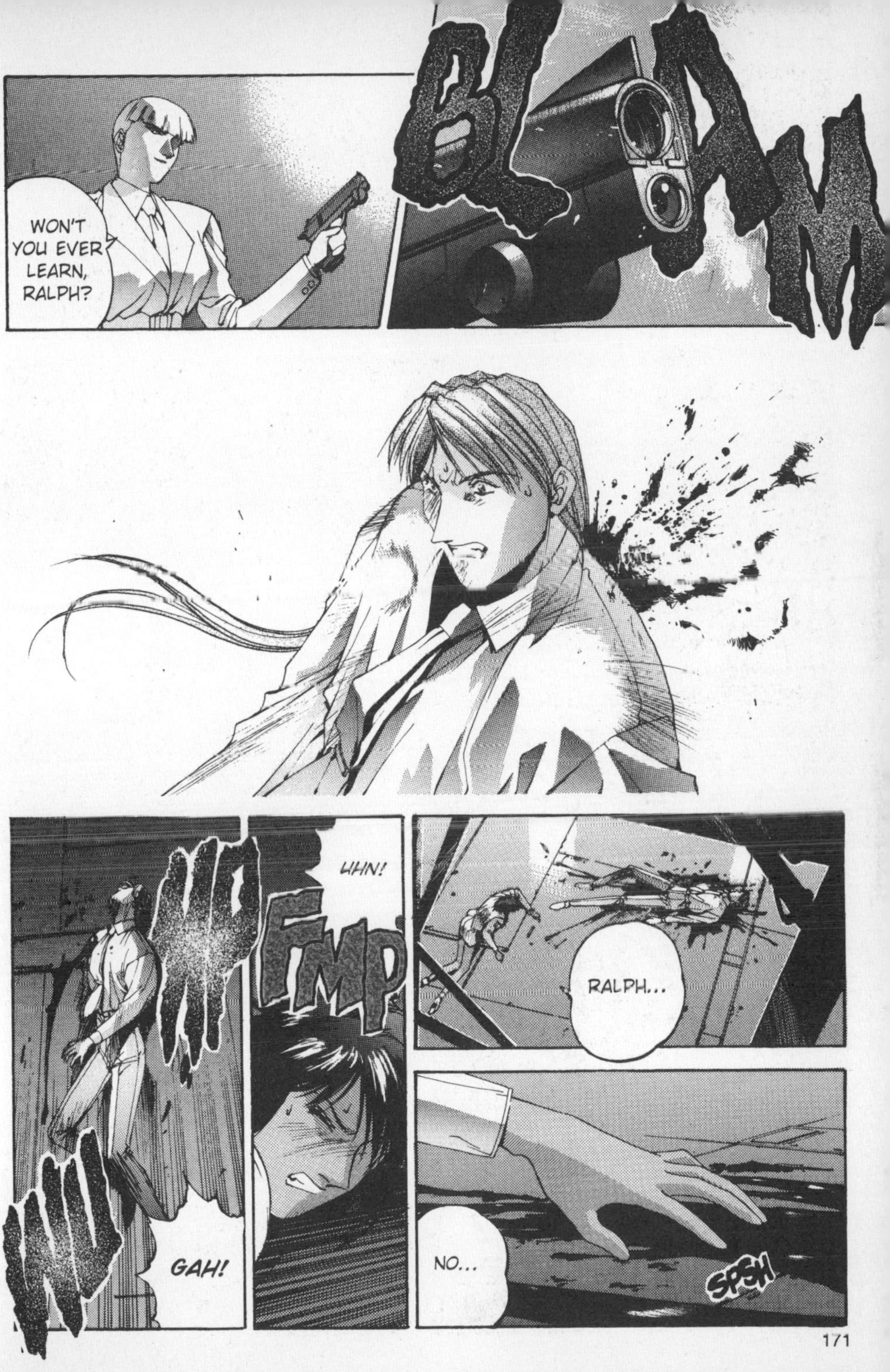
WON'T YOU EVER LEARN, RALPH?
BLAM
GAH!
UHN!
FMP
RALPH...
NO...
SPSH

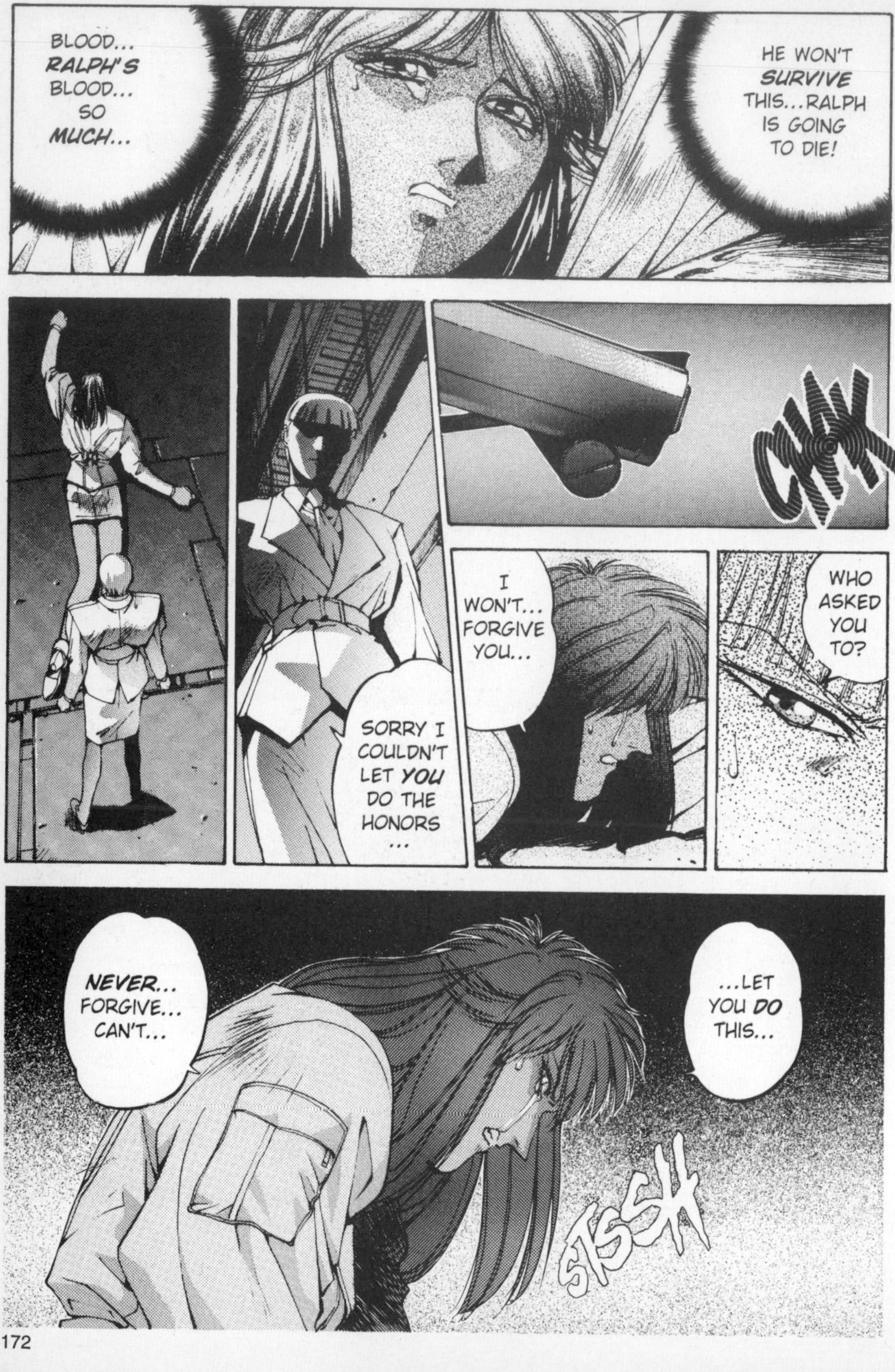
BLOOD... **RALPH'S** BLOOD... SO **MUCH**...
HE WON'T **SURVIVE** THIS...RALPH IS GOING TO DIE!
SORRY I COULDN'T LET **YOU** DO THE HONORS ...
CHAK
I WON'T... FORGIVE YOU...
WHO ASKED YOU TO?
NEVER... FORGIVE... CAN'T...
...LET YOU **DO** THIS...
STSSH

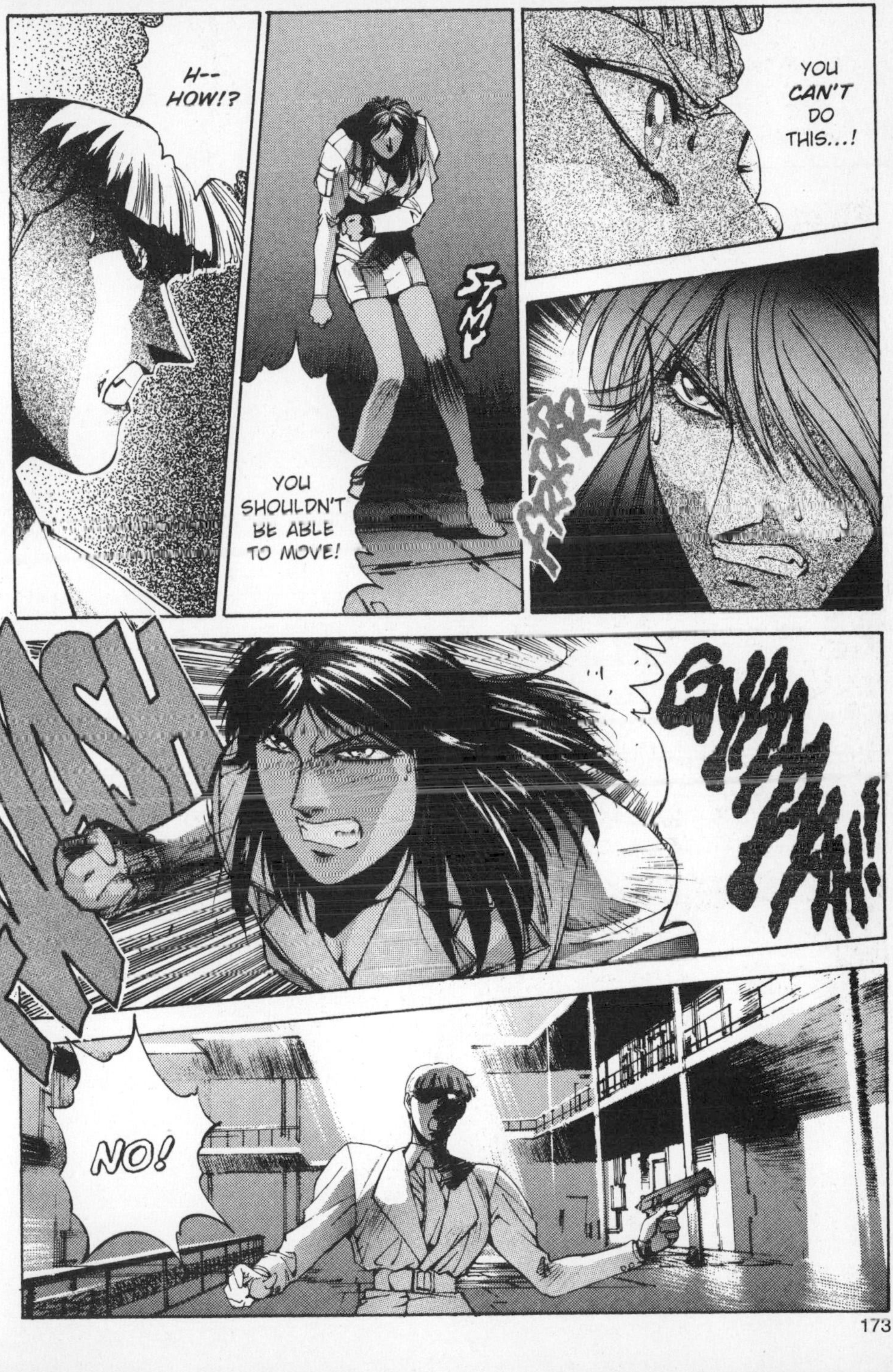
H-- HOW!?
STMP
YOU SHOULDN'T BE ABLE TO MOVE!
YOU CAN'T DO THIS...!
NO!

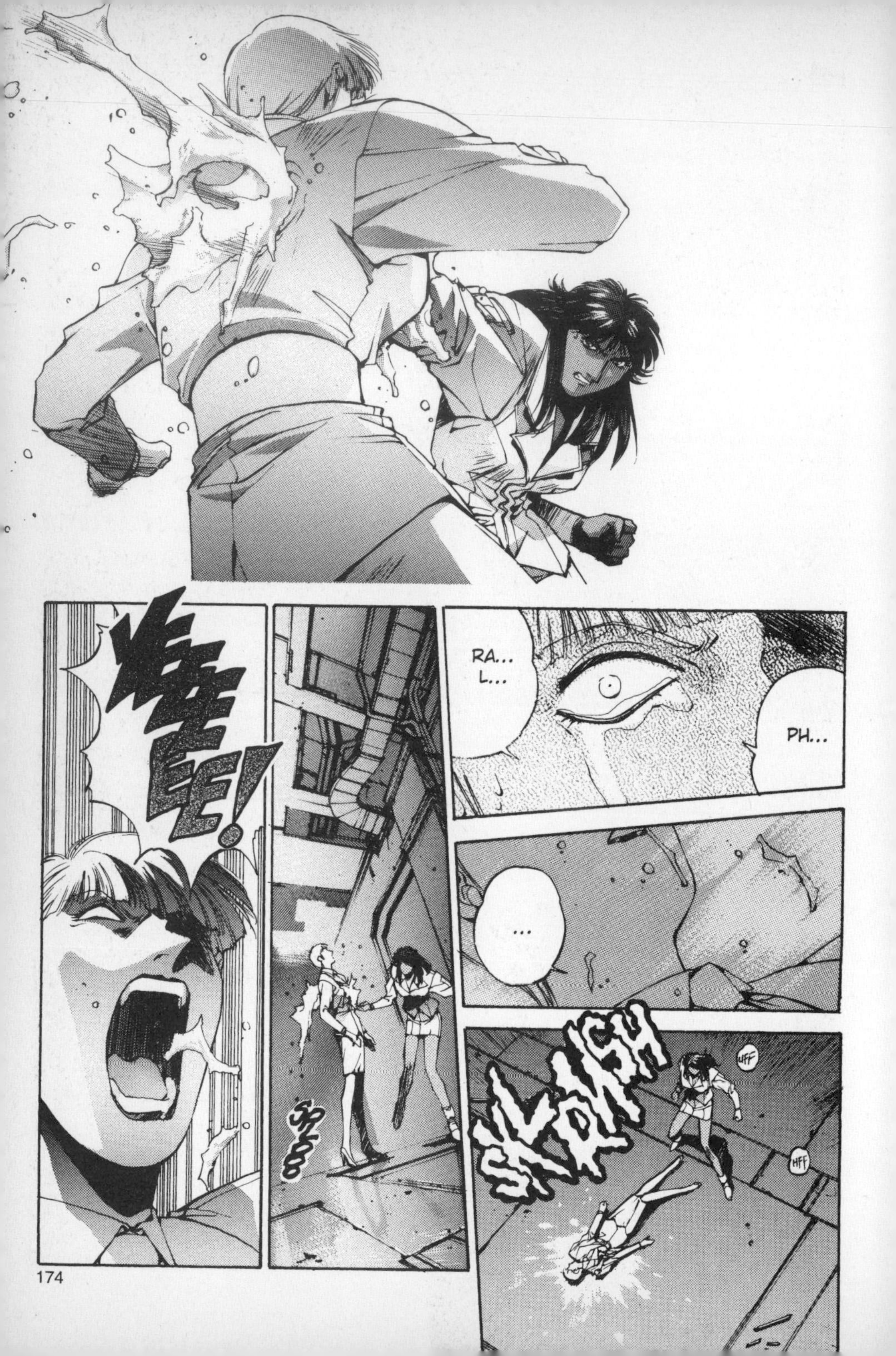
RA... L...
PH...
...
UFF
HFF

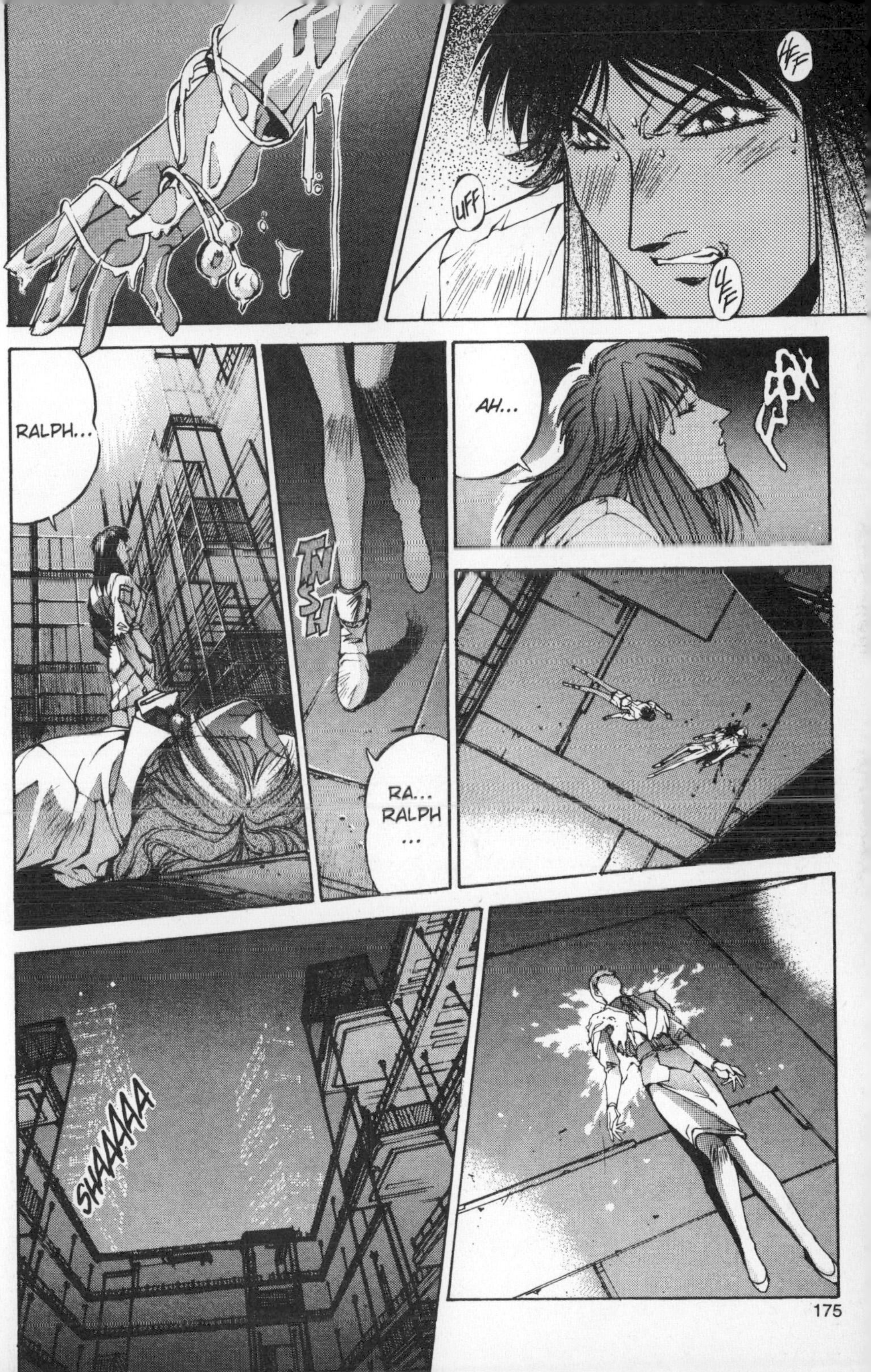
HFF
UFF
UFF
RALPH...
TNSH
RA... RALPH ...
AH...
SHAAAAA

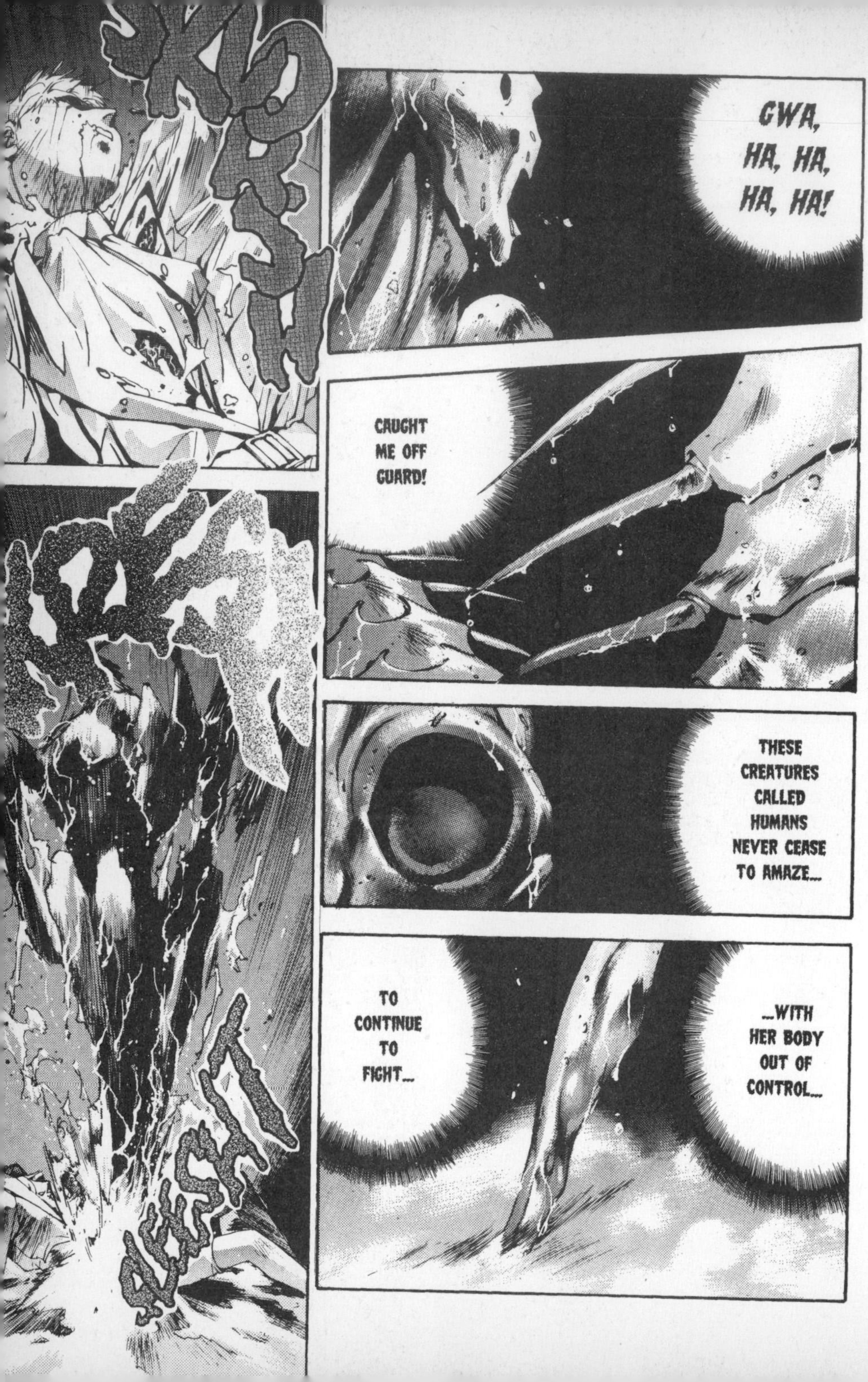
GWA, HA, HA, HA, HA!
CAUGHT ME OFF GUARD!
THESE CREATURES CALLED HUMANS NEVER CEASE TO AMAZE...
TO CONTINUE TO FIGHT...
...WITH HER BODY OUT OF CONTROL...

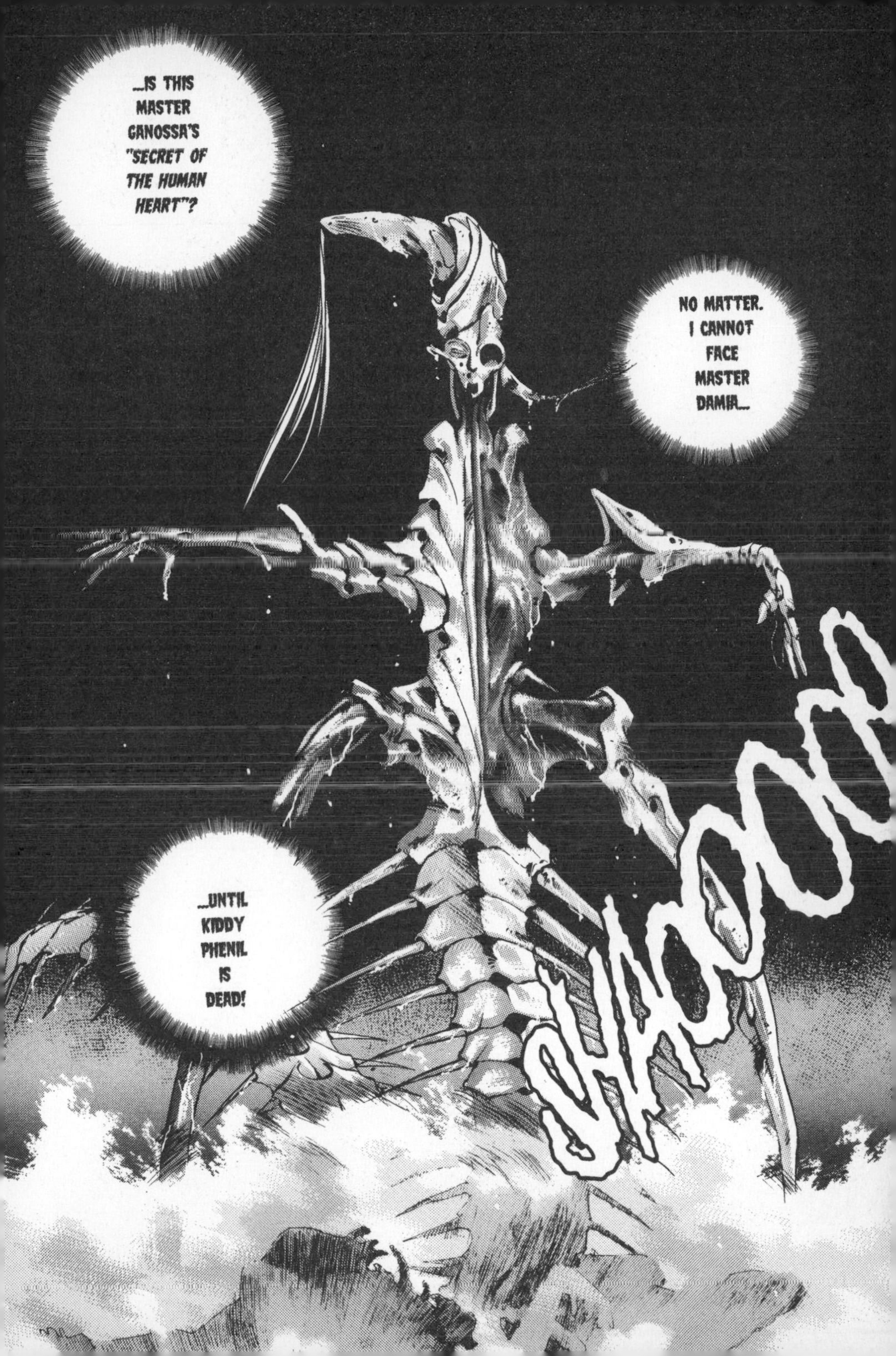
...IS THIS MASTER GANOSSA'S "SECRET OF THE HUMAN HEART"?
NO MATTER. I CANNOT FACE MASTER DAMIA...
...UNTIL KIDDY PHENIL IS DEAD!

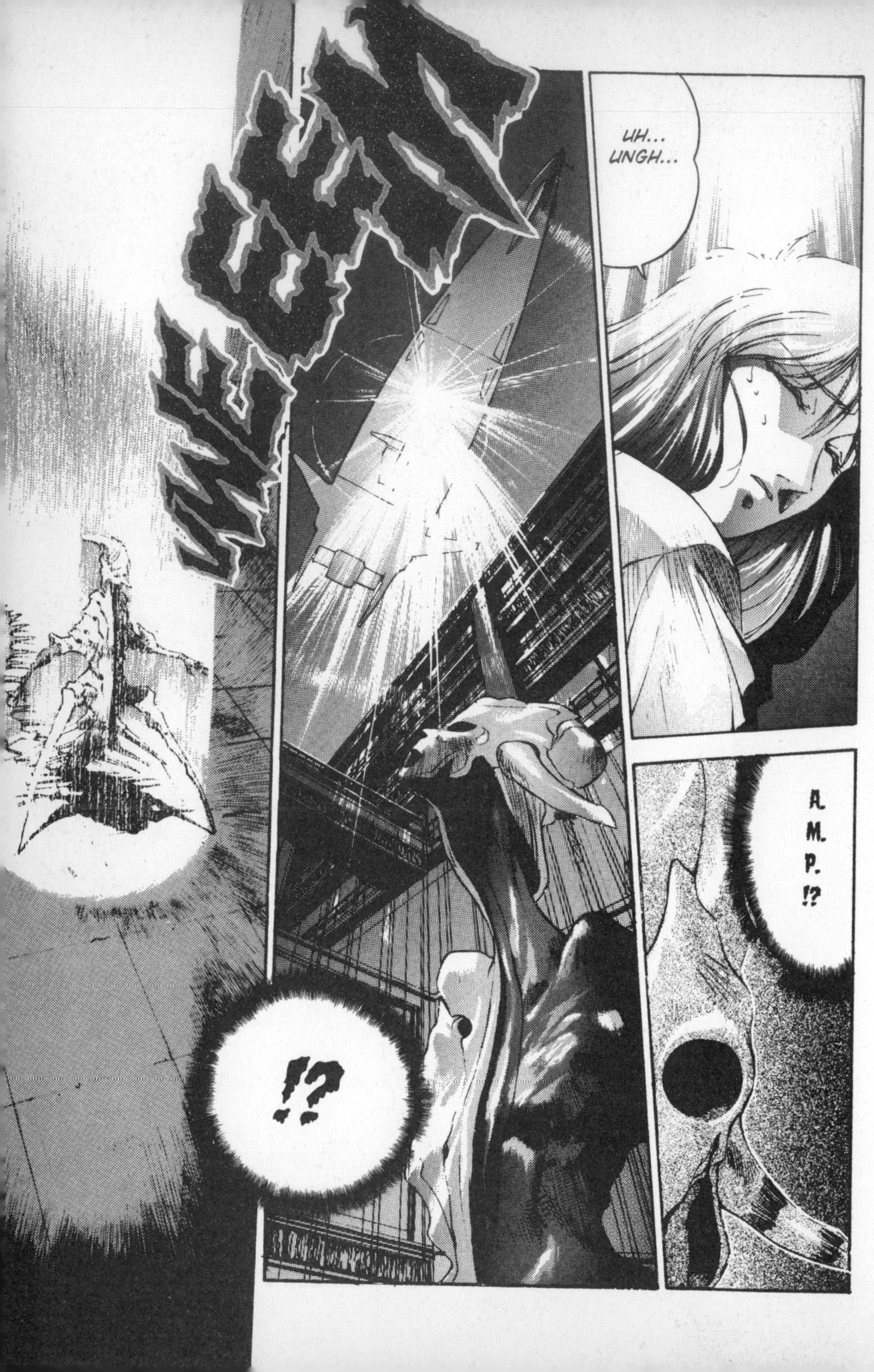
!?
UH... UNGH...
A. M. P. !?

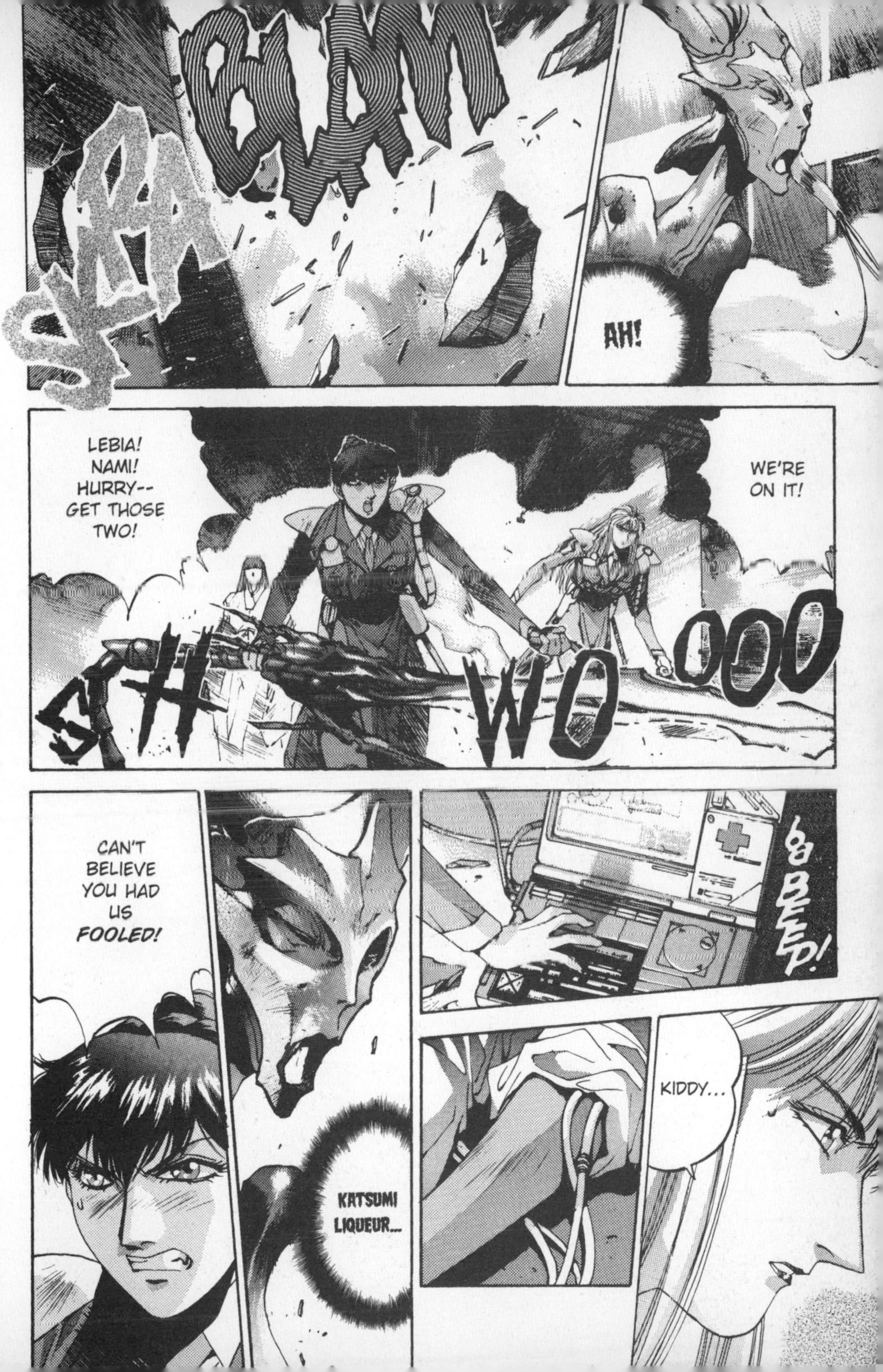

SKRA
BLAM
AH!
LEBIA! NAMI! HURRY-- GET THOSE TWO!
WE'RE ON IT!
SHWOOOO
CAN'T BELIEVE YOU HAD US FOOLED!
KATSUMI LIQUEUR...
BEEP!
KIDDY...

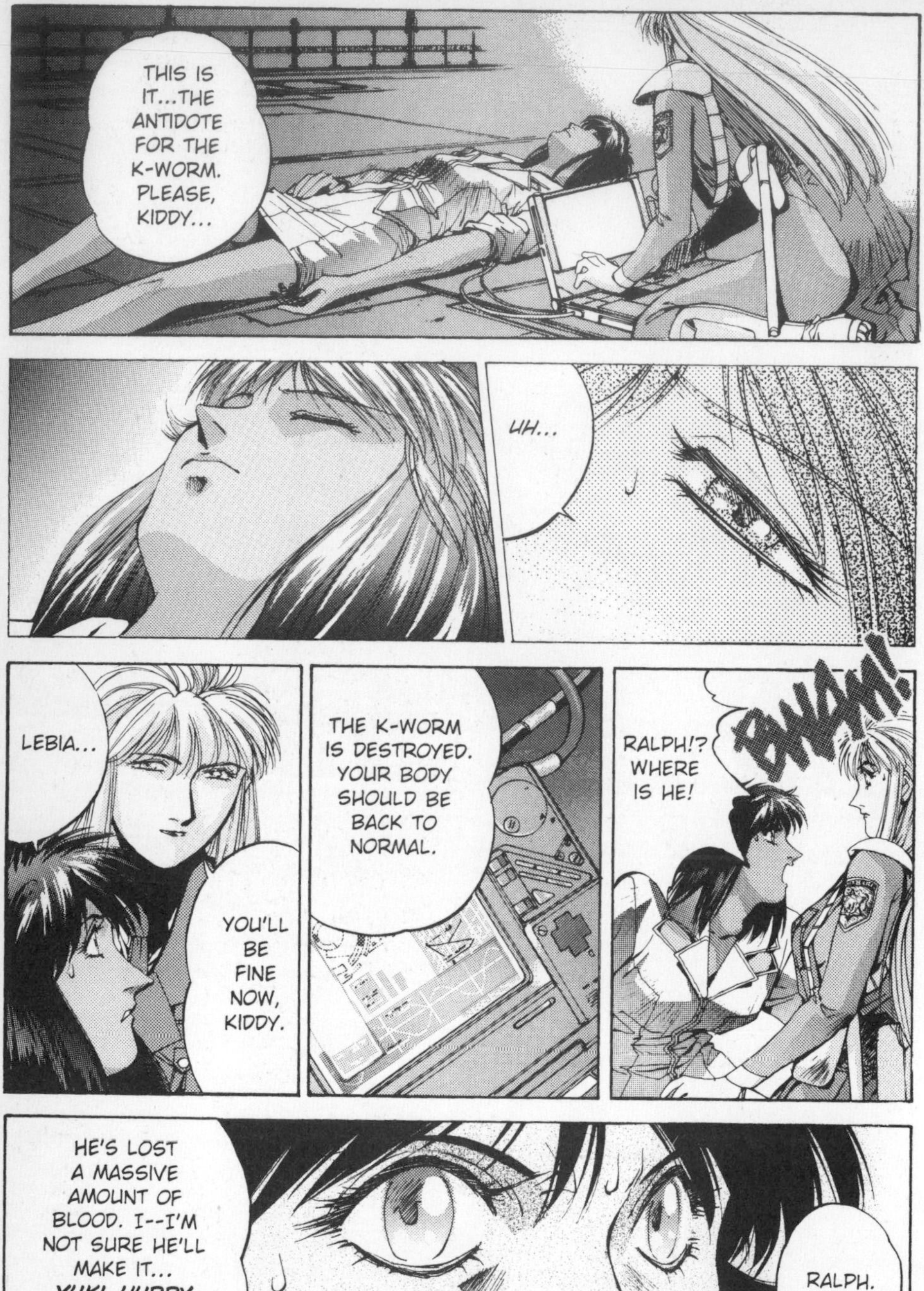
THIS IS IT...THE ANTIDOTE FOR THE K-WORM. PLEASE, KIDDY...
UH...
LEBIA...
YOU'LL BE FINE NOW, KIDDY.
THE K-WORM IS DESTROYED. YOUR BODY SHOULD BE BACK TO NORMAL.
BWAM!
RALPH!? WHERE IS HE!
HE'S LOST A MASSIVE AMOUNT OF BLOOD. I--I'M NOT SURE HE'LL MAKE IT... YUKI, HURRY WITH THE AMBULANCE!
RALPH.

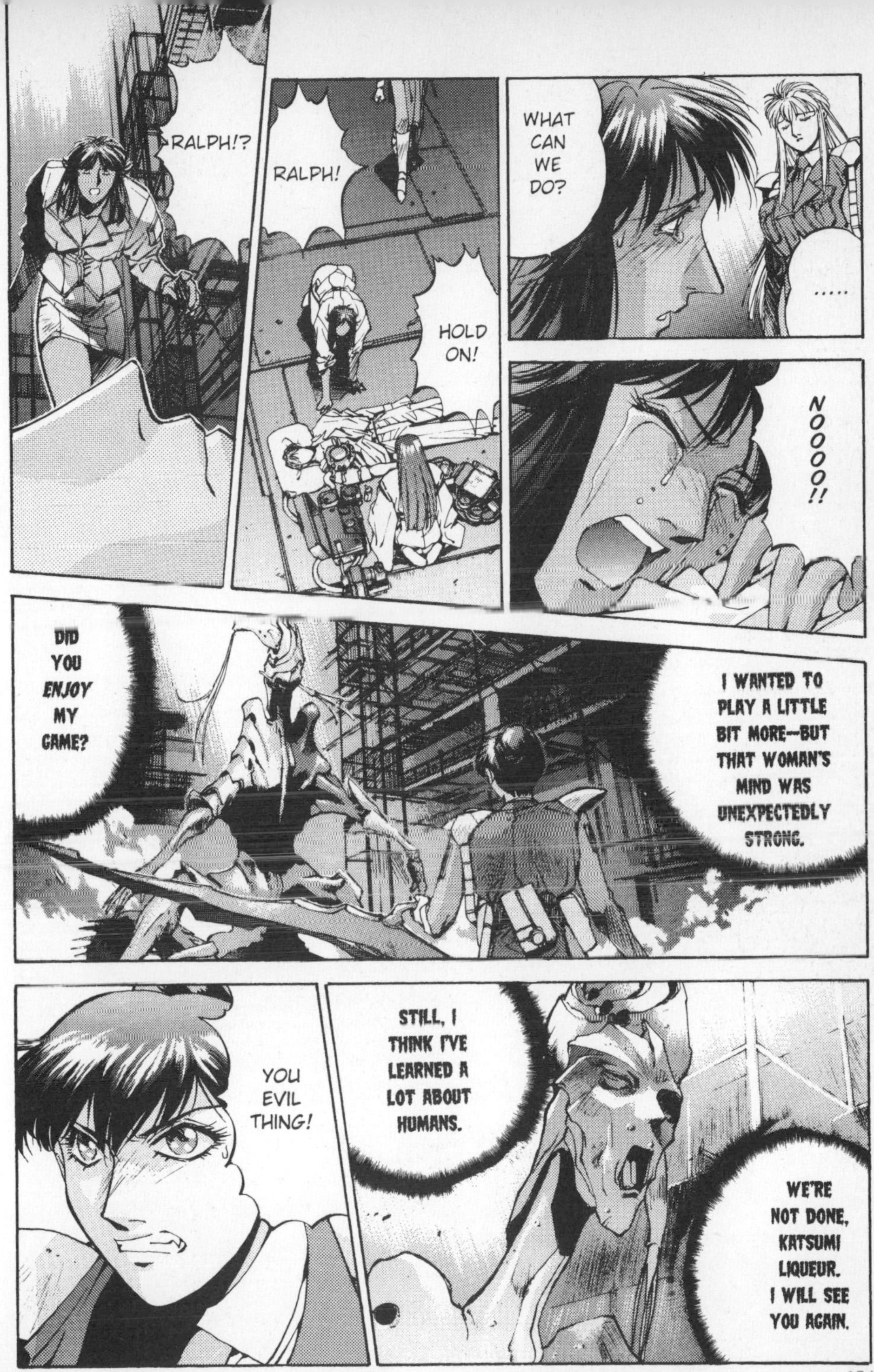
RALPH!?
RALPH!
HOLD ON!
WHAT CAN WE DO?
.....
NOOOOO!!
DID YOU *ENJOY* MY GAME?
I WANTED TO PLAY A LITTLE BIT MORE--BUT THAT WOMAN'S MIND WAS UNEXPECTEDLY STRONG.
YOU EVIL THING!
STILL, I THINK I'VE LEARNED A LOT ABOUT HUMANS.
WE'RE NOT DONE, KATSUMI LIQUEUR. I WILL SEE YOU AGAIN.

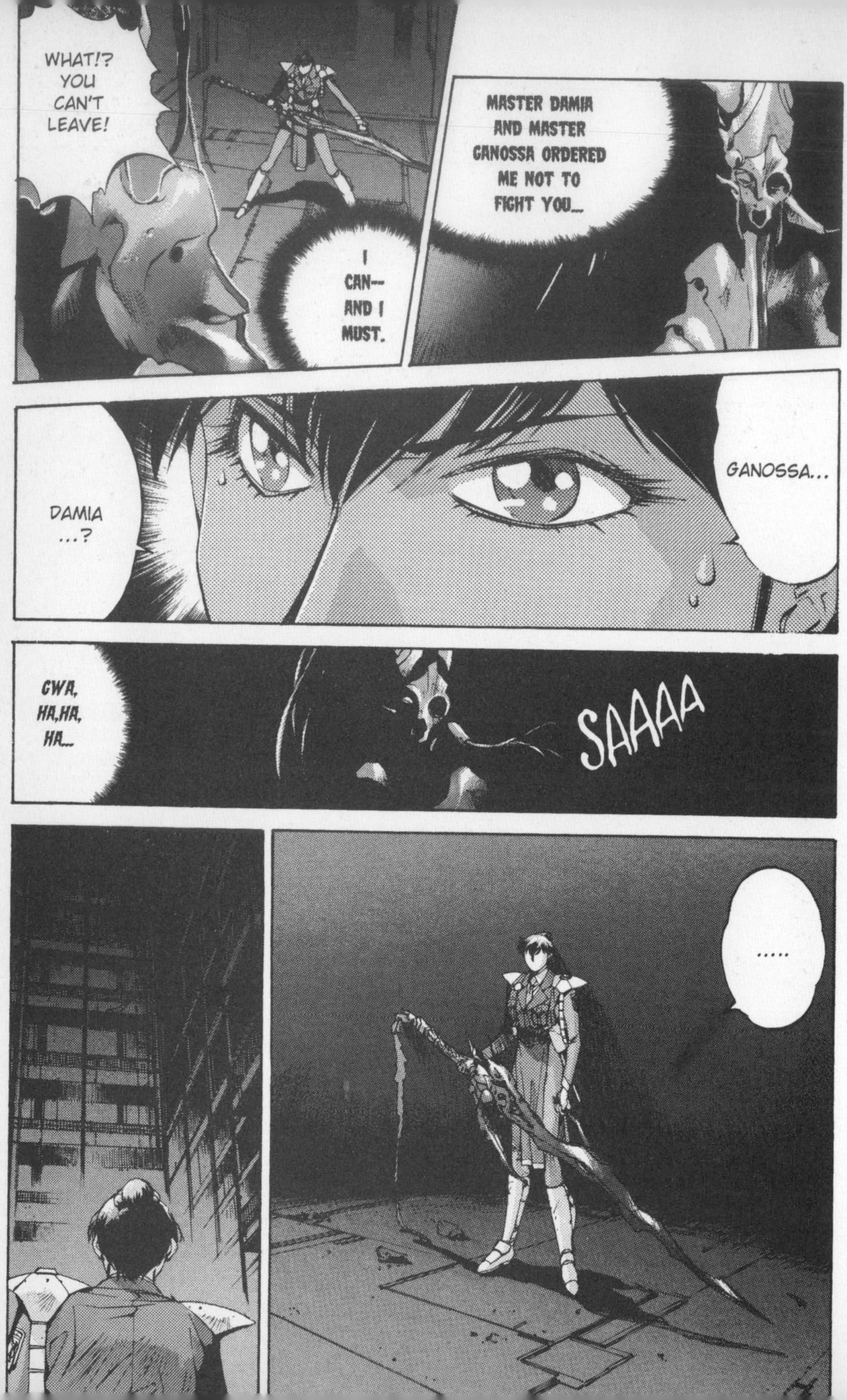
WHAT!? YOU CAN'T LEAVE!
I CAN-- AND I MUST.
MASTER DAMIA AND MASTER GANOSSA ORDERED ME NOT TO FIGHT YOU...
DAMIA ...?
GANOSSA...
GWA, HA,HA, HA...
SAAAA
.....

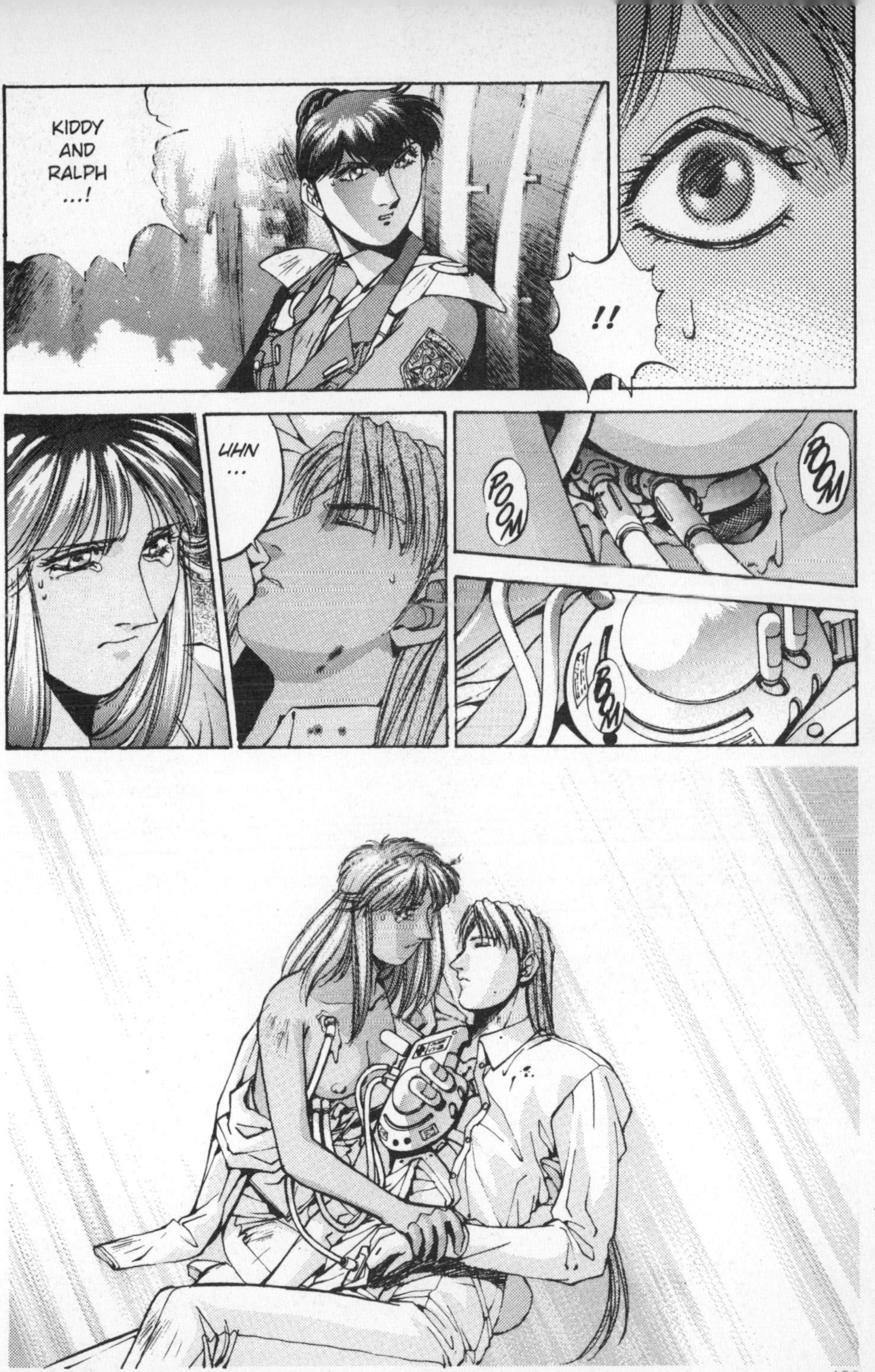
KIDDY AND RALPH ...!
!!
UHN ...
ROOM
ROOM
ROOM

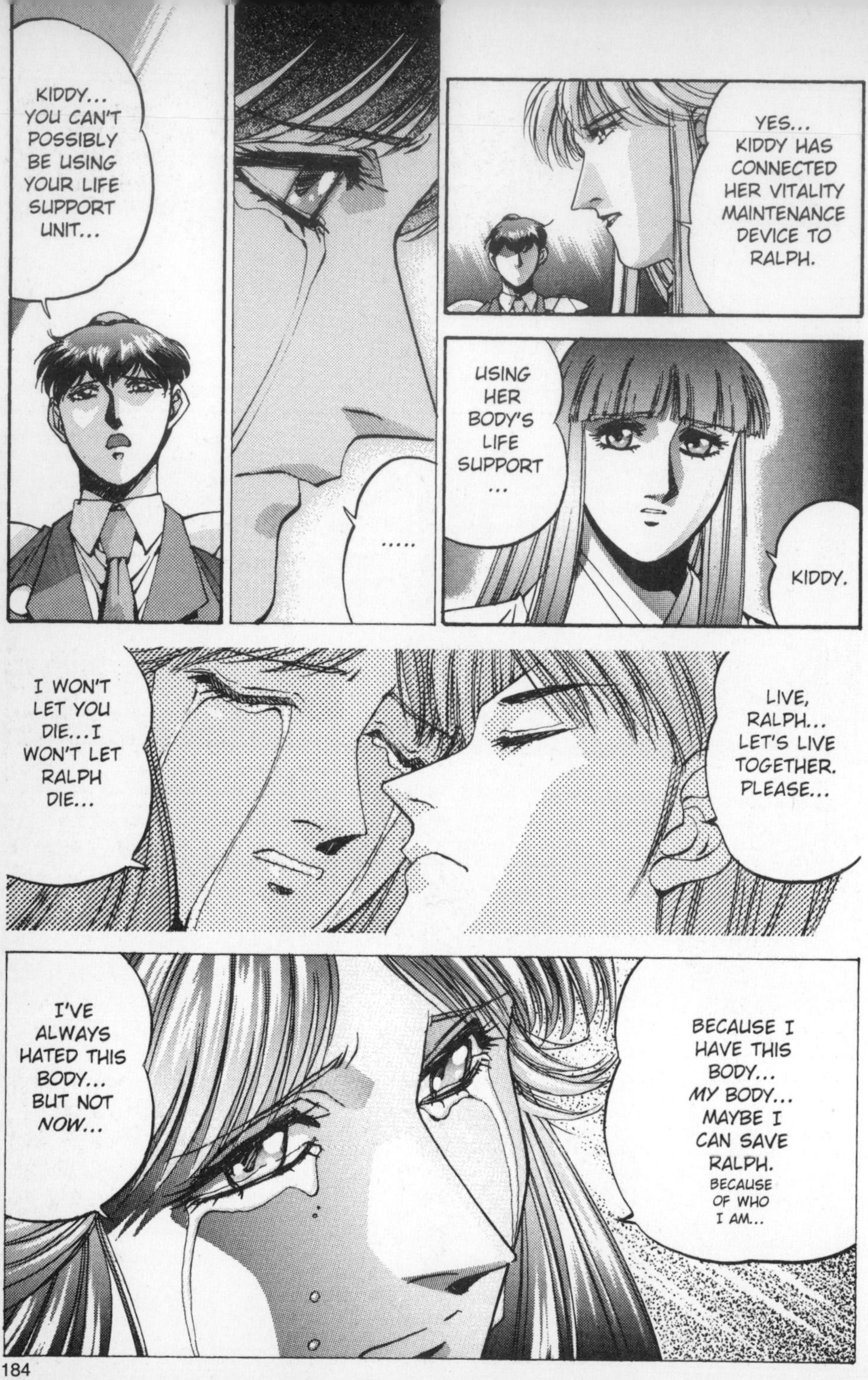
KIDDY... YOU CAN'T POSSIBLY BE USING YOUR LIFE SUPPORT UNIT...
.....
YES... KIDDY HAS CONNECTED HER VITALITY MAINTENANCE DEVICE TO RALPH.
USING HER BODY'S LIFE SUPPORT ...
KIDDY.
I WON'T LET YOU DIE...I WON'T LET RALPH DIE...
LIVE, RALPH... LET'S LIVE TOGETHER. PLEASE...
I'VE ALWAYS HATED THIS BODY... BUT NOT *NOW*...
BECAUSE I HAVE THIS BODY... *MY* BODY... MAYBE I CAN SAVE RALPH.
BECAUSE OF WHO I AM...

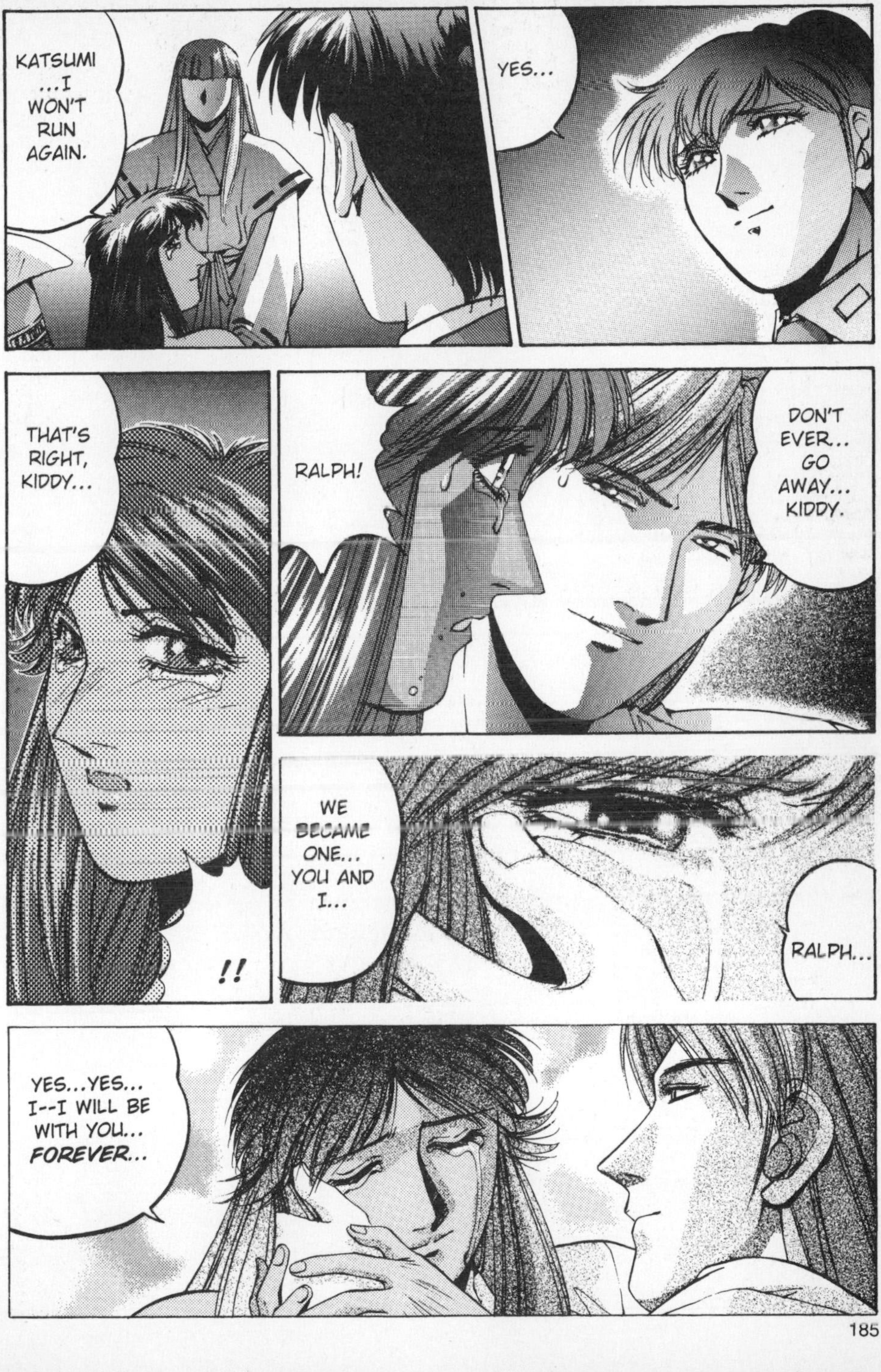
KATSUMI ...I WON'T RUN AGAIN.
YES...
THAT'S RIGHT, KIDDY...
!!
RALPH!
DON'T EVER... GO AWAY... KIDDY.
WE BECAME ONE... YOU AND I...
RALPH...
YES...YES... I--I WILL BE WITH YOU... *FOREVER*...

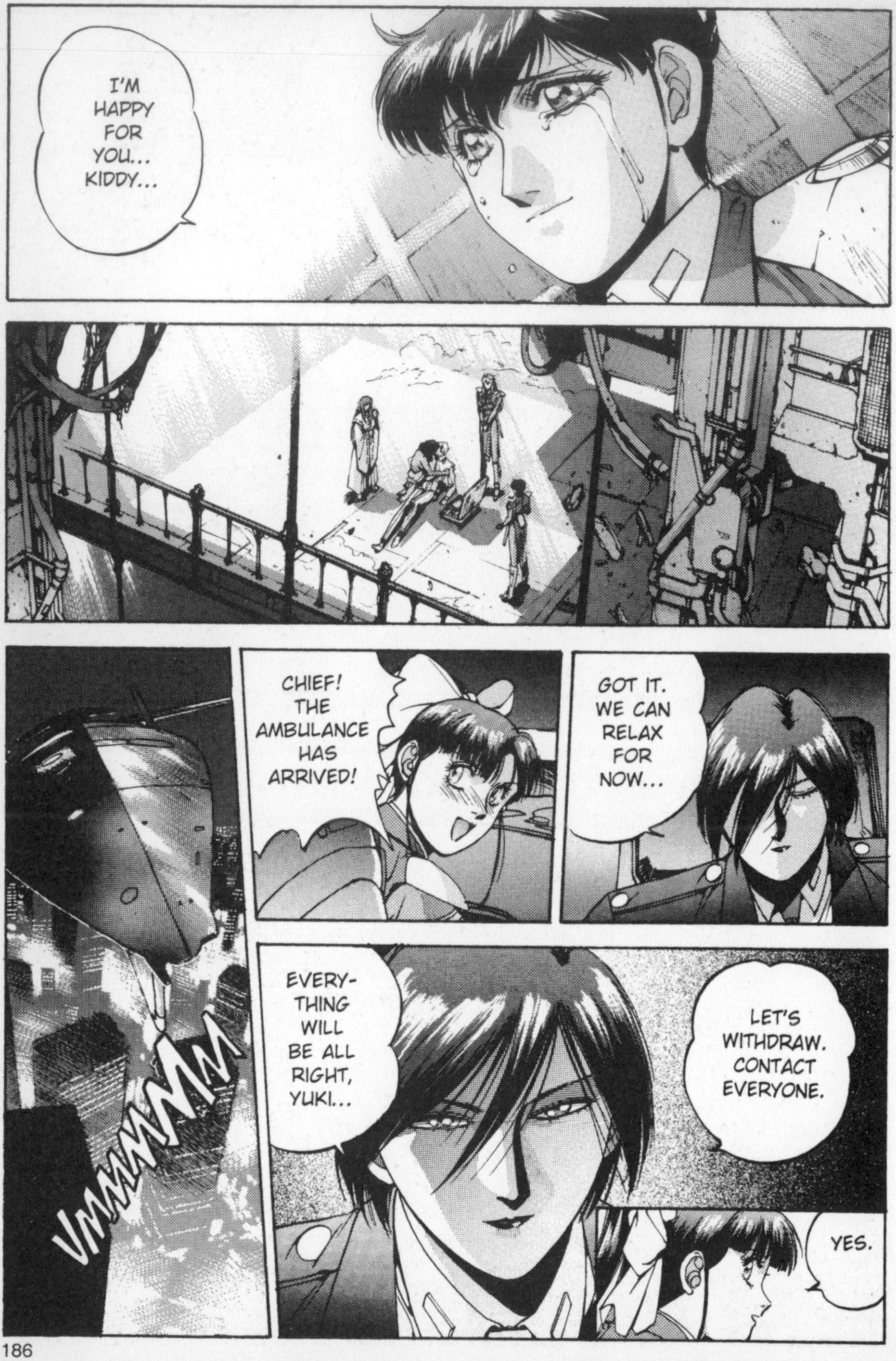
I'M HAPPY FOR YOU... KIDDY...
CHIEF! THE AMBULANCE HAS ARRIVED!
GOT IT. WE CAN RELAX FOR NOW...
EVERY-THING WILL BE ALL RIGHT, YUKI...
LET'S WITHDRAW. CONTACT EVERYONE.
YES.

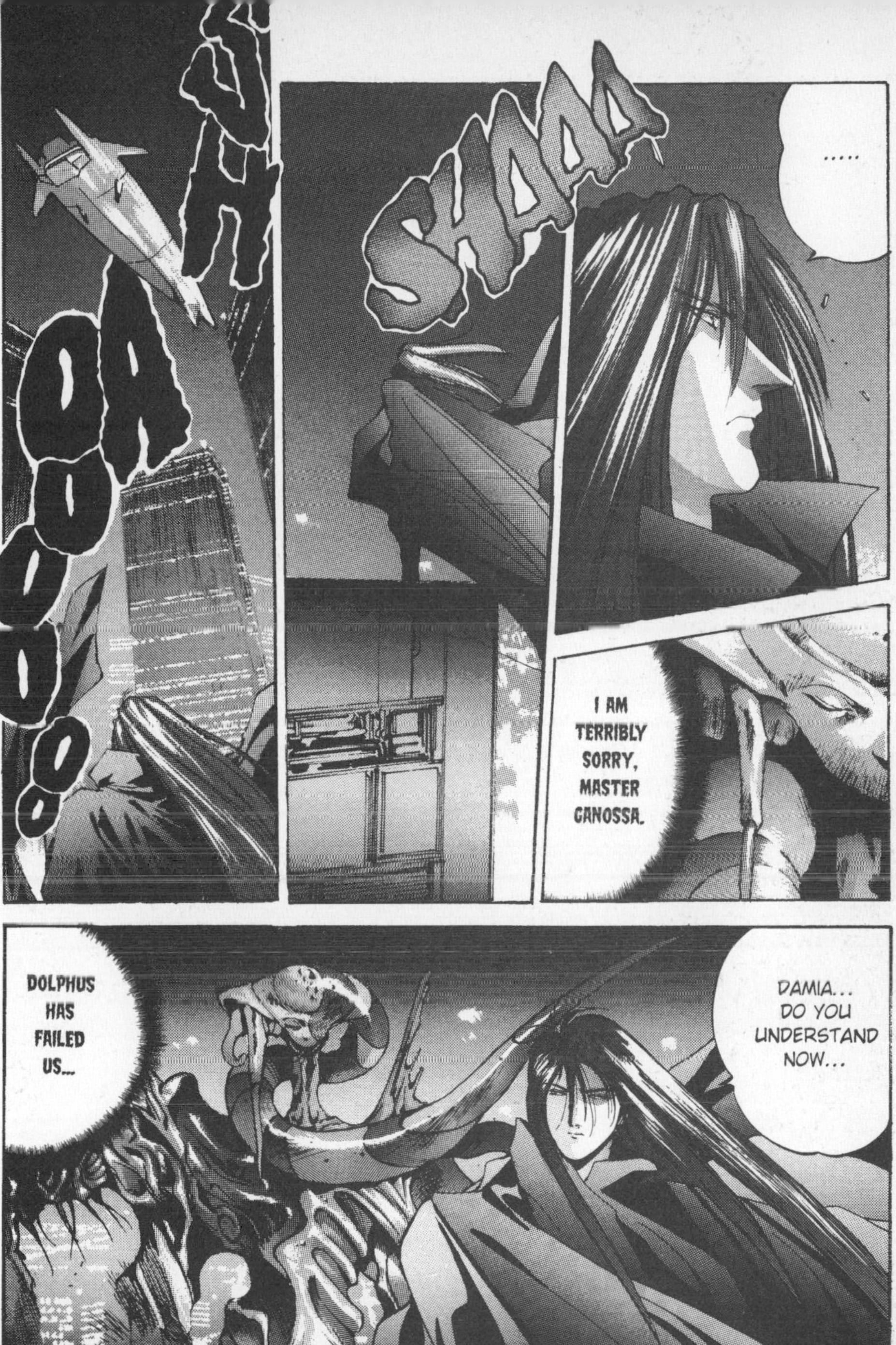
.....
I AM TERRIBLY SORRY, MASTER GANOSSA.
DOLPHUS HAS FAILED US...
DAMIA... DO YOU UNDERSTAND NOW...

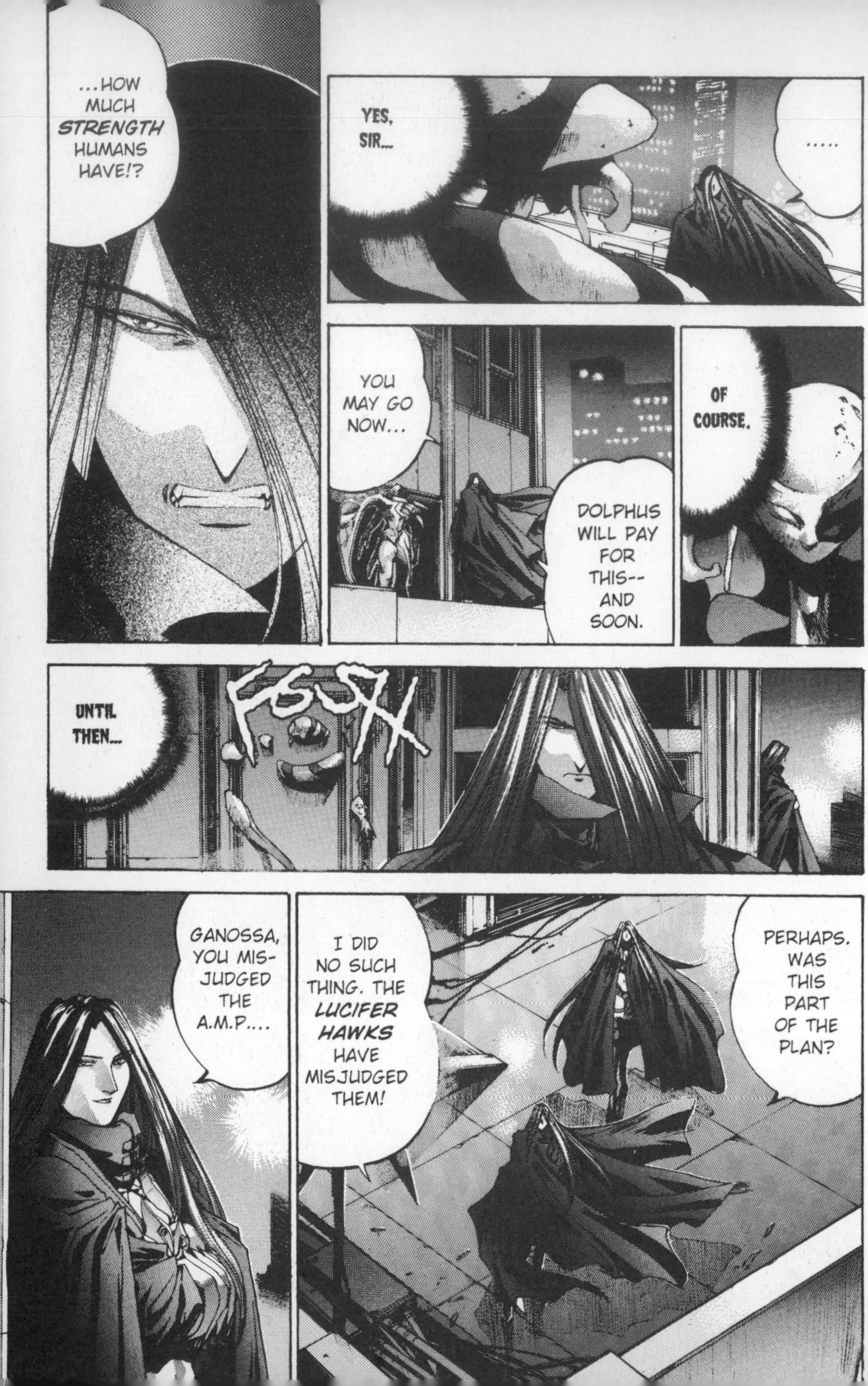
...HOW MUCH STRENGTH HUMANS HAVE!?
YES, SIR...
.....
YOU MAY GO NOW...
DOLPHUS WILL PAY FOR THIS-- AND SOON.
OF COURSE.
UNTIL THEN...
GANOSSA, YOU MIS-JUDGED THE A.M.P....
I DID NO SUCH THING. THE LUCIFER HAWKS HAVE MISJUDGED THEM!
PERHAPS. WAS THIS PART OF THE PLAN?

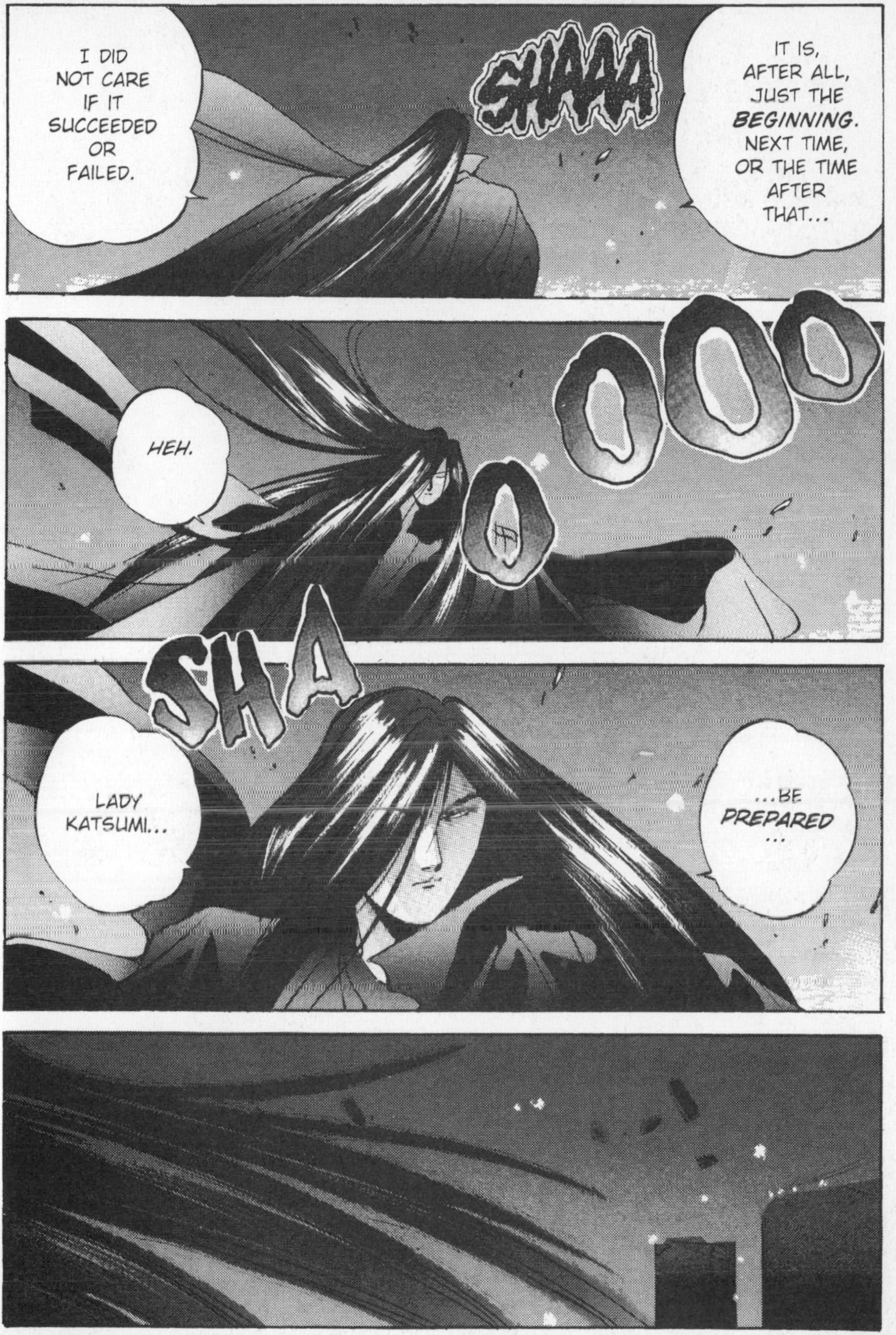
I DID NOT CARE IF IT SUCCEEDED OR FAILED.
SHAAA
IT IS, AFTER ALL, JUST THE *BEGINNING*. NEXT TIME, OR THE TIME AFTER THAT...
HEH.
OOOOO
SHA
LADY KATSUMI...
...BE *PREPARED* ...

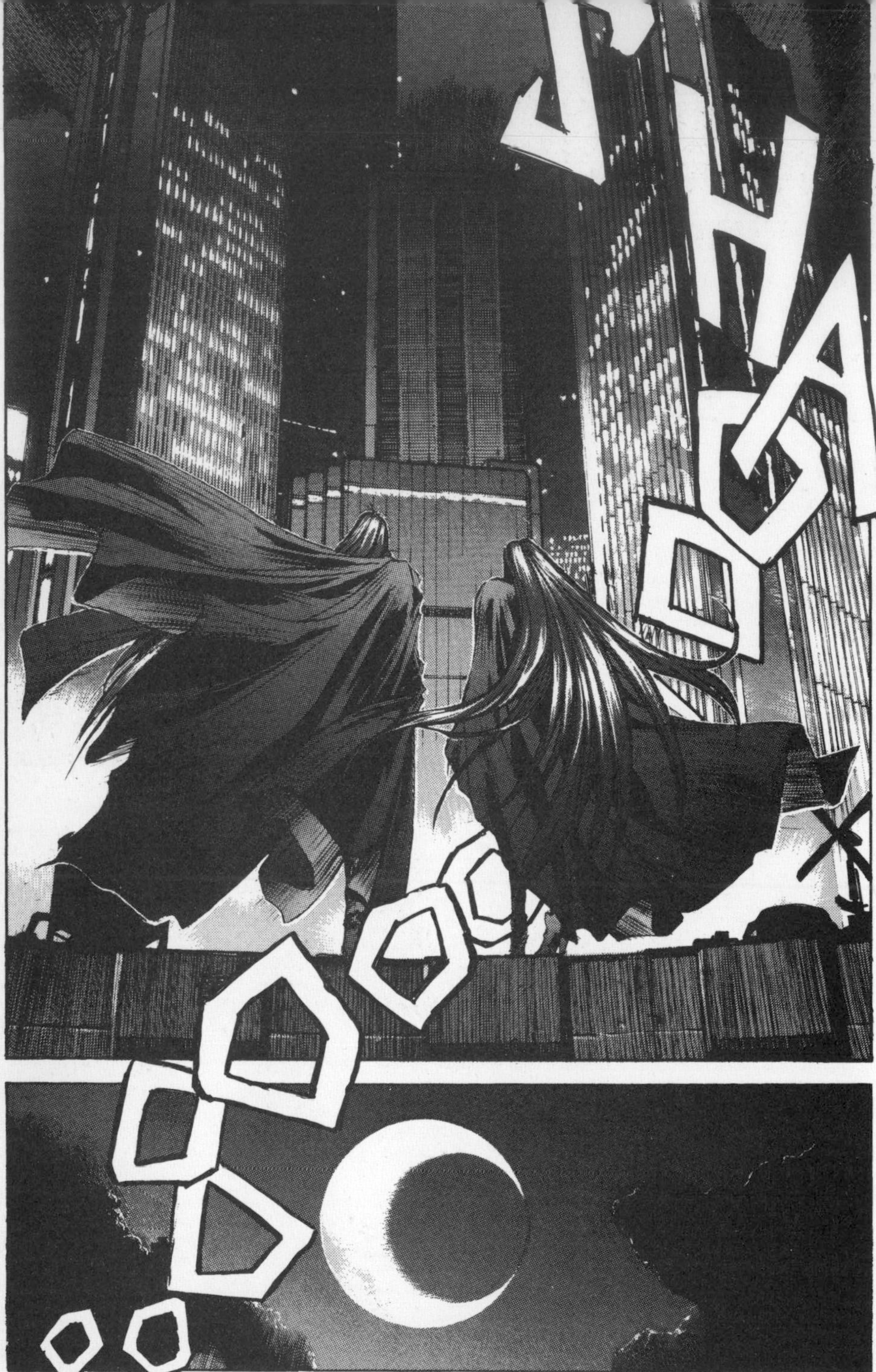

TO BE CONTINUED IN SILENT MÖBIUS VOL. 7!

CHAPTER : 15

INTERMISSION: DINNER WITH THE A.M.P.

MANGA'S FIRST VIRTUAL DINING EXPERIENCE!

(NOTE: FOR FULL ENJOYMENT, IMAGINE THE SOUNDS AND SMELLS OF A KOREAN *YAKINIKU-YA* BARBEQUE RESTAURANT!)

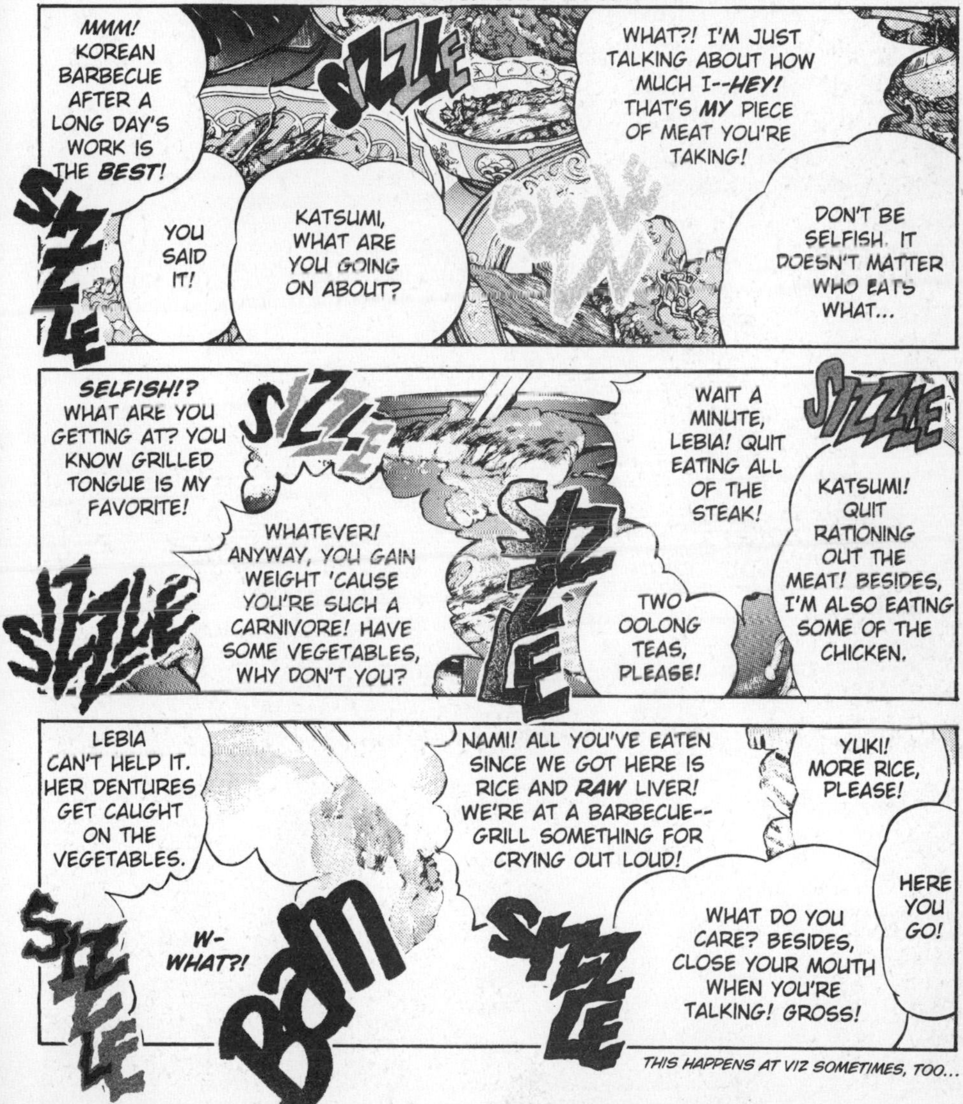
MMM! KOREAN BARBECUE AFTER A LONG DAY'S WORK IS THE *BEST*!
SIZZLE
SIZZLE
YOU SAID IT!
KATSUMI, WHAT ARE YOU GOING ON ABOUT?
WHAT?! I'M JUST TALKING ABOUT HOW MUCH I--*HEY!* THAT'S *MY* PIECE OF MEAT YOU'RE TAKING!
DON'T BE SELFISH. IT DOESN'T MATTER WHO EATS WHAT...
SELFISH!? WHAT ARE YOU GETTING AT? YOU KNOW GRILLED TONGUE IS MY FAVORITE!
SIZZLE
SIZZLE
WHATEVER! ANYWAY, YOU GAIN WEIGHT 'CAUSE YOU'RE SUCH A CARNIVORE! HAVE SOME VEGETABLES, WHY DON'T YOU?
SIZZLE
WAIT A MINUTE, LEBIA! QUIT EATING ALL OF THE STEAK!
TWO OOLONG TEAS, PLEASE!
SIZZLE
KATSUMI! QUIT RATIONING OUT THE MEAT! BESIDES, I'M ALSO EATING SOME OF THE CHICKEN.
LEBIA CAN'T HELP IT. HER DENTURES GET CAUGHT ON THE VEGETABLES.
SIZZLE
W-WHAT?!
Bam
NAMI! ALL YOU'VE EATEN SINCE WE GOT HERE IS RICE AND *RAW* LIVER! WE'RE AT A BARBECUE--GRILL SOMETHING FOR CRYING OUT LOUD!
SIZZLE
WHAT DO YOU CARE? BESIDES, CLOSE YOUR MOUTH WHEN YOU'RE TALKING! GROSS!
YUKI! MORE RICE, PLEASE!
HERE YOU GO!

THIS HAPPENS AT VIZ SOMETIMES, TOO...

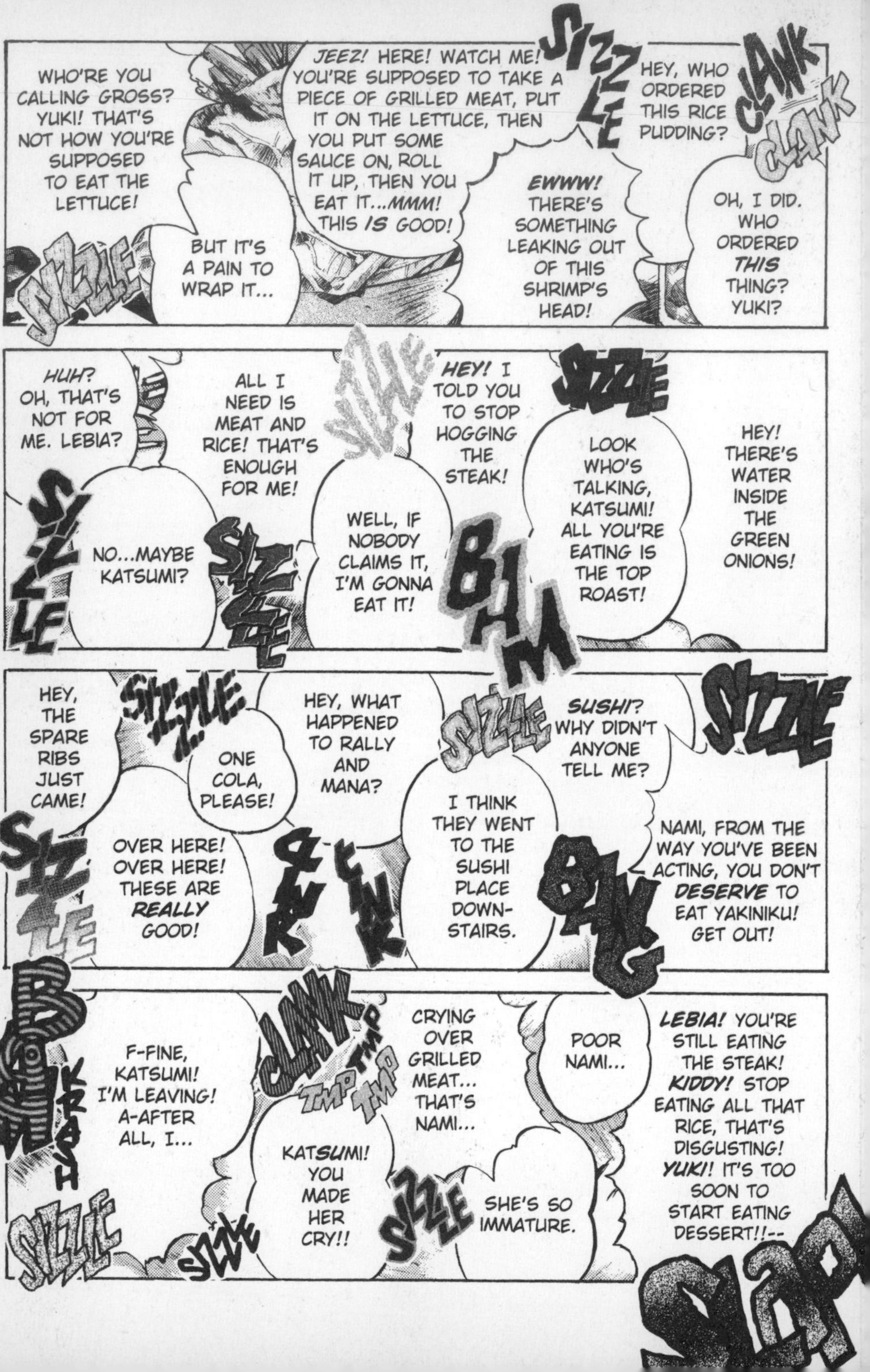
WHO'RE YOU CALLING GROSS? YUKI! THAT'S NOT HOW YOU'RE SUPPOSED TO EAT THE LETTUCE!
SIZZLE
BUT IT'S A PAIN TO WRAP IT...
JEEZ! HERE! WATCH ME! YOU'RE SUPPOSED TO TAKE A PIECE OF GRILLED MEAT, PUT IT ON THE LETTUCE, THEN YOU PUT SOME SAUCE ON, ROLL IT UP, THEN YOU EAT IT...MMM! THIS IS GOOD!
SIZZLE
EWWW! THERE'S SOMETHING LEAKING OUT OF THIS SHRIMP'S HEAD!
HEY, WHO ORDERED THIS RICE PUDDING?
CLANK CLANK
OH, I DID. WHO ORDERED THIS THING? YUKI?
HUH? OH, THAT'S NOT FOR ME. LEBIA?
SIZZLE
NO...MAYBE KATSUMI?
ALL I NEED IS MEAT AND RICE! THAT'S ENOUGH FOR ME!
SIZZLE
SIZZLE
WELL, IF NOBODY CLAIMS IT, I'M GONNA EAT IT!
HEY! I TOLD YOU TO STOP HOGGING THE STEAK!
BAM
SIZZLE
LOOK WHO'S TALKING, KATSUMI! ALL YOU'RE EATING IS THE TOP ROAST!
HEY! THERE'S WATER INSIDE THE GREEN ONIONS!
HEY, THE SPARE RIBS JUST CAME!
SIZZLE
SIZZLE
OVER HERE! OVER HERE! THESE ARE REALLY GOOD!
ONE COLA, PLEASE!
HEY, WHAT HAPPENED TO RALLY AND MANA?
CLINK CLINK
SIZZLE
I THINK THEY WENT TO THE SUSHI PLACE DOWN-STAIRS.
SUSHI? WHY DIDN'T ANYONE TELL ME?
SIZZLE
BANG
NAMI, FROM THE WAY YOU'VE BEEN ACTING, YOU DON'T DESERVE TO EAT YAKINIKU! GET OUT!
BAM
KRASH
F-FINE, KATSUMI! I'M LEAVING! A-AFTER ALL, I...
SIZZLE
CLANK
TMP TMP TMP
SIZZLE
KATSUMI! YOU MADE HER CRY!!
CRYING OVER GRILLED MEAT... THAT'S NAMI...
SIZZLE
POOR NAMI...
SHE'S SO IMMATURE.
LEBIA! YOU'RE STILL EATING THE STEAK! KIDDY! STOP EATING ALL THAT RICE, THAT'S DISGUSTING! YUKI! IT'S TOO SOON TO START EATING DESSERT!!--
SLAP!